TRAVELER'S NEW ENGLAND COMPANION

The Traveler's Companions

ARGENTINA • AUSTRALIA • BALI • CALIFORNIA • CANADA • CHINA • COSTA RICA • CUBA • EASTERN CANADA • ECUADOR • FLORIDA • HAWAII • HONG KONG • INDIA • INDONESIA • JAPAN • KENYA • MALAYSIA & SINGAPORE • MEDITERRANEAN FRANCE • MEXICO • NEPAL • NEW ENGLAND • NEW ZEALAND • PERU • PHILIPPINES • PORTUGAL • RUSSIA • SOUTH AFRICA • SOUTHERN ENGLAND • SPAIN • THAILAND • TURKEY • VENEZUELA • VIETNAM, LAOS AND CAMBODIA • WESTERN CANADA

Traveler's New England Companion

First published 1998
Third Edition 2002
The Globe Pequot Press
246 Goose Lane, PO Box 480
Guilford, CT 06437 USA
www.globe-pequot.com

ISBN: 0-7627-2523-0

Created, edited and produced by
Allan Amsel Publishing, 53, rue Beaudouin
27700 Les Andelys, France.
E-mail: AAmsel@aol.com

Editor in Chief: Allan Amsel
Editor: Anne Trager
Picture editor and book designer: Roberto Rossi

Updated by: Patricia Harris and David Lyon

Printed by Samwha Printing Co. Ltd., Seoul, South Korea

TRAVELER'S NEW ENGLAND COMPANION

by Laura Purdom

photographs by Robert Holmes

Third Edition

Contents

Restaurant

Maple Syrup

TRAVELER'S NEW ENGLAND COMPANION

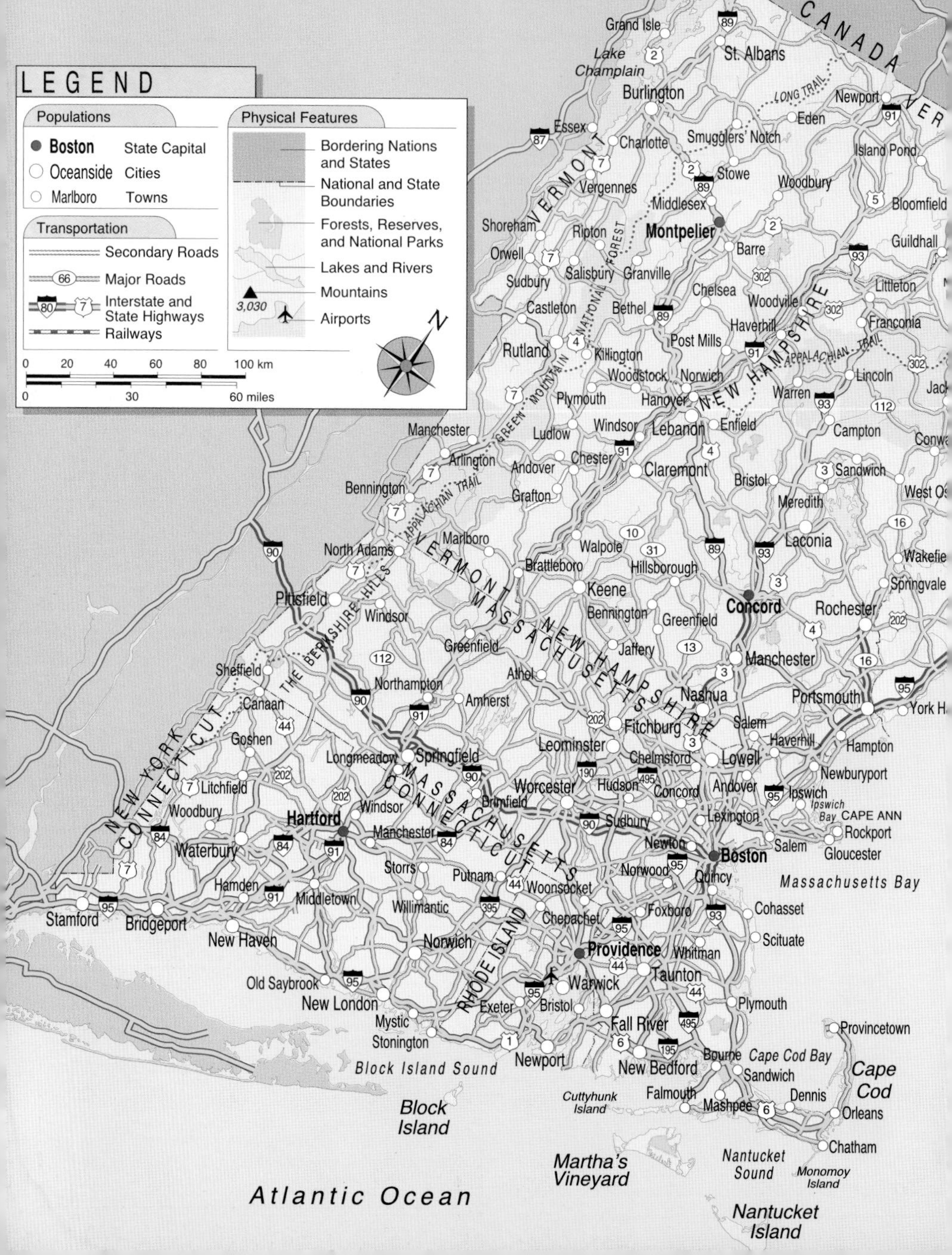

LEGEND

Populations

- Boston — State Capital
- Oceanside — Cities
- Marlboro — Towns

Transportation

- Secondary Roads
- 66 Major Roads
- 80 7 Interstate and State Highways
- Railways

Physical Features

- Bordering Nations and States
- National and State Boundaries
- Forests, Reserves, and National Parks
- Lakes and Rivers
- 3,030 Mountains
- Airports

0 20 40 60 80 100 km

0 30 60 miles

Atlantic Ocean

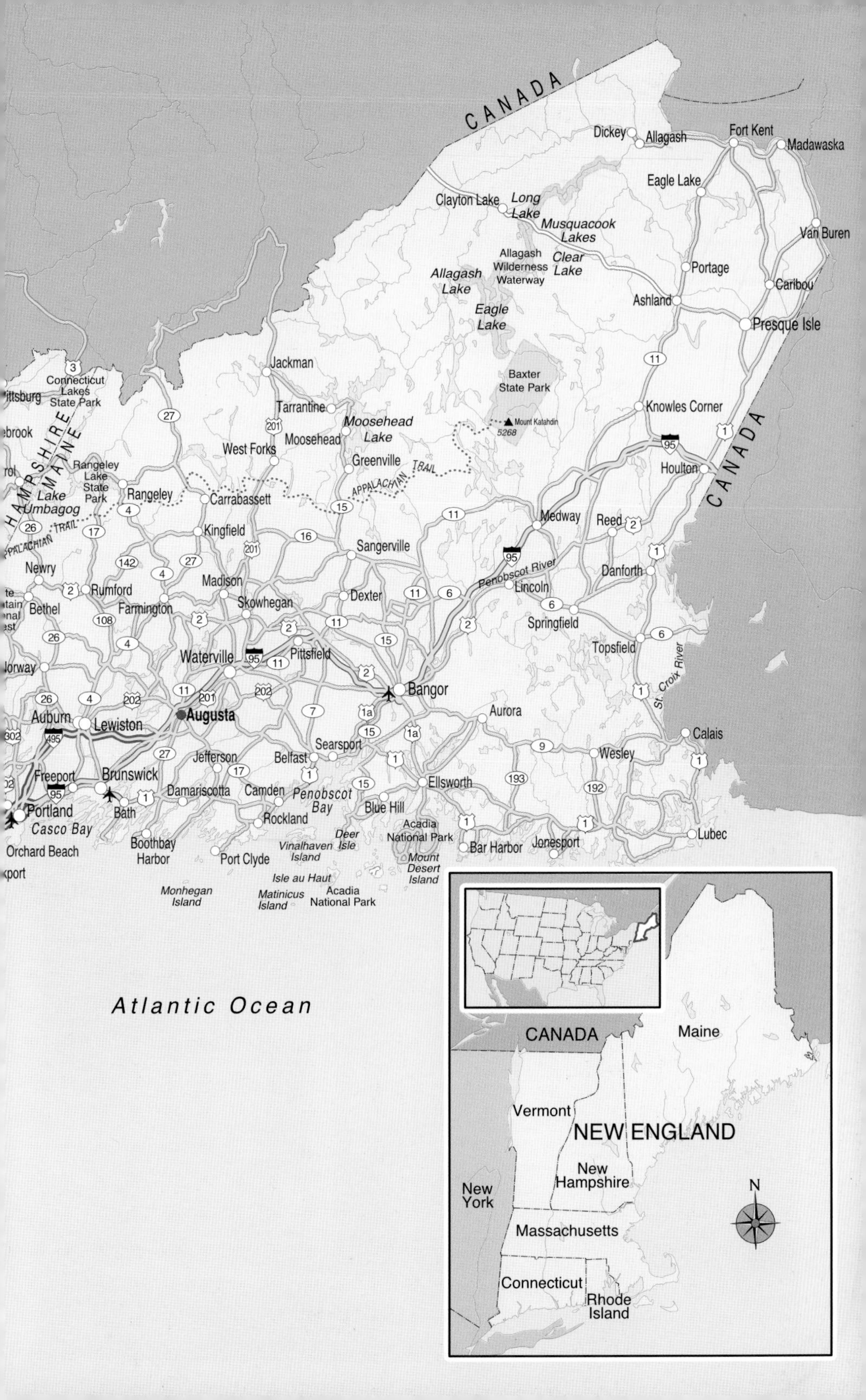

CANADA
Dickey
Allagash
Fort Kent
Madawaska
Eagle Lake
Clayton Lake
Long Lake
Musquacook Lakes
Van Buren
Allagash Wilderness Waterway
Clear Lake
Allagash Lake
Portage
Caribou
Ashland
Eagle Lake
Presque Isle
Baxter State Park
Mount Katahdin
5268
Jackman
Connecticut Lakes State Park
Tarrantine
Knowles Corner
Moosehead Lake
Moosehead
West Forks
Greenville
APPALACHIAN TRAIL
Houlton
NEW HAMPSHIRE
MAINE
Rangeley Lake State Park
Lake Umbagog
Rangeley
Carrabassett
Kingfield
Medway
Reed
Sangerville
Newry
Rumford
Madison
Penobscot River
Lincoln
Danforth
Bethel
Farmington
Skowhegan
Dexter
Springfield
Waterville
Pittsfield
Topsfield
St. Croix River
Bangor
Auburn
Lewiston
Augusta
Aurora
Calais
Searsport
Belfast
Jefferson
Wesley
Freeport
Brunswick
Damariscotta
Camden
Penobscot Bay
Ellsworth
Portland
Bath
Rockland
Blue Hill
Casco Bay
Orchard Beach
Boothbay Harbor
Port Clyde
Vinalhaven Island
Deer Isle
Acadia National Park
Bar Harbor
Jonesport
Lubec
Mount Desert Island
Isle au Haut
Monhegan Island
Matinicus Island
Acadia National Park
Atlantic Ocean
CANADA
Maine
Vermont
NEW ENGLAND
New Hampshire
New York
Massachusetts
Connecticut
Rhode Island
N

TOP SPOTS

Fall for New England

Autumn in New England is an exultation of color. Each day's drop in temperature inches a plaid coverlet farther south, blanketing the hills in a riot of pumpkin, cranberry, saffron, crimson and ruby. The northern hardwoods — beech, birch and sugar maple — turn golden-yellow and orange. The famous swamp maple becomes yellow and deep red. Ash produces a reddish-purple against which the light yellow of aspen glows.

Leaf-peepers mark their forays along country roads with stops at farm stands overflowing with harvests of squash, pumpkins, pears and sparkling apple cider. Hikers cap a day of rambling in the resplendent forests with a mug of local mulled wine sipped before a fire at a neighborly tavern or inn, while children devour dozens of cinnamon-covered cider donuts. Summer corn has come and gone, but New Englanders hang bunches of tricolor Indian corn on front doors of city apartments and country cottages.

In woodsy Vermont, fall foliage attracts spectators from around the world. This least-populated portion of New England has sweeping, panoramic views. The state's compactness (180 miles or 290 km long and about 60 miles or 97 km at its widest point) makes it easy to traverse. Get off the main highways, and you'll find back roads lined with old stone walls or set off against fading green pastures of rolling countryside. Scores of small Vermont towns celebrate the season with festivals that might include guided tours, bazaars, live entertainment, and homemade New England foods.

The leaves begin to change in early September at higher elevations in northern Vermont, New Hampshire, Maine and along the Canadian border. From here, the color season moves southward, ending in the final weeks of October. Columbus Day weekend marks the peak of the leaf-peeping season. Oktoberfest celebrations abound throughout the towns of Massachusetts, New Hampshire and Vermont. Local harvest festivals, countryside hayrides, and theater performances round out the calendar of events.

From northern Maine to southern Connecticut, autumn paints the New England countryside in brilliant hues. OPPOSITE: Litchfield, Connecticut, ablaze with fall colors. ABOVE: Fallen leaves in Shelburne Falls, Massachusetts.

Throughout New England, volunteers track and report on their community's color quotient — furnishing state tourism offices with biweekly reports. Call the following numbers for fall foliage hot spots: Maine TOLL-FREE (800) 777-0317; New Hampshire TOLL-FREE (800) 258-3608; Massachusetts TOLL-FREE (800) 227-6277; Rhode Island TOLL-FREE (800) 556-2484; Connecticut TOLL-FREE (800) 282-6863; Vermont ☎ (802) 828-3239 TOLL-FREE (800) 837-6668; or the United States Forest Service foliage hotline TOLL-FREE (800) 354-4595.

Reserve well in advance for overnight lodging along popular fall-color routes.

Explore Acadia

Sand Beach: a humble name for what must be the most splendid sweep of seashore in all of New England. Situated on Mount Desert Island, Maine, Sand Beach embodies the spirit of this northern island, home to Acadia National Park.

Acadia is one of the nation's most distinctive national parks. Small by comparison with the likes of Yellowstone or Yosemite (40,000 acres or 16,200 hectares), it has nonetheless a grand diversity of landscapes, colors, flora and fauna. It is home to some 250 different bird species and over 500 varieties of wildflowers. In ecological zones, it varies from sandy and rock-strewn beaches to coastal coniferous forests to mountain rock and lichen.

The view from Sand Beach says it all, coupling the salty crash of the ocean with the damp hush of the boreal forest. Cradled by two rocky headlands and backed by dunes and marshy flats, the beach marks the starting point for rambling walks that lead up onto promontories for an eyeful of bay, forest and sea.

Dozens of such laid-back walks lace Acadia, while more strenuous trails, such as the Beehive — a steep scramble up a ragged precipice — challenge the nimble. From the roadway below the Beehive you can make out the forms of climbers on their way to the summit along a series of iron ladders. In Acadia's forested interior, gentle carriage roads, perfect for walkers and bikers, meander over a series of stone bridges. Along Acadia's Park Loop Road, motorists potter along, gaping in awe at the splendid sights. The Ocean Drive section of the loop runs one-way for 11 miles (18 km) along the park's eastern perimeter with the pink cliffs of the Champlain Mountain ahead. On the loop's southeastern section, Otter Cliffs loom more than 100 ft (30 m) above the ocean.

Seasonal changes add yet another dimension to Acadia's kaleidoscopic personality. Fall's explosion of color comes and goes quickly as deciduous trees flame into muted hues. Once the last leaves have fallen in October, the "afterglow" begins when the low-lying blueberry bushes turn ruby red. Winter is milder here on the coast than in the interior, and rain is not uncommon. But in the deep of winter, cross-country skiers enjoy trackless powder along the carriage roads. Spring, though chilly, riots with flowers. They bloom in mid-May before the trees have budded, offering early-bird visitors unhampered visions of forest floors carpeted in wildflowers. In summer, Maine's mild weather draws hoards of travelers escaping sultry days in southern states. Plan ahead if you want to visit in the summer high season. This pocket-sized national park packs in the tourists during July and August.

Linger with Literary Lights

In terms of literary output, few places in America can match Concord, Massachusetts. Henry David Thoreau (1817–62), Nathaniel Hawthorne (1804–64), Ralph Waldo Emerson (1803–82), and Louisa May Alcott (1832–88) called it home — what's more, all lived here at the same time.

The rugged shores of Acadia National Park on Mount Desert Island, Maine.

Walk along the banks of the Concord River to the site of Thoreau's cabin, now within a state reservation. Thoreau lived in these woods from 1845 to 1847. Seven years later, he wrote of his experiences here in his classic work, *Walden*, in which he advocated a life lived in harmony with nature. In *Walden*, Thoreau wrote, "I went to the woods because I wished to live deliberately, to front only the essential facts of life, and to see if I could not learn what it had to teach and not, when I came to die, discover that I had not lived."

Near Thoreau's cabin, you'll see a spring-fed pond where contemporary Concordians sun and swim. Rent a canoe at the South Bridge Boathouse ☎ (978) 369-9438, west of the town center, and paddle the river any time from April until the first snowfall. A round-trip float of about two hours will take you to the famous wooden span of the North Bridge, site of the firing of "the shot heard 'round the world," that sparked America's Revolutionary War. All along the river, fine homes line the banks.

Thoreau was a friend of fellow Concordian, Ralph Waldo Emerson, best known as a major figure in the Transcendentalist movement. Emerson's *Nature*, published in 1836, became the authoritative statement of the Transcendentalist philosophy, whose credo professed a belief in the divinity and unity of man and nature. After its publication, the essayist, poet and philosopher gained renown as a public speaker. Ralph Waldo Emerson House ☎ (978) 369-2236, 28 Cambridge Turnpike at Lexington Road, was Emerson's home from 1835 to 1889. The house is open from mid-April through October, Thursdays through Sundays. An admission fee is charged.

Next to the North Bridge stands the Old Manse ☎ (978) 369-3909, on Monument Street, where Nathaniel Hawthorne, author of *The Scarlet Letter* and *The House of the Seven Gables*, lived for three years. His friends, the Emersons, and their descendants owned the house for centuries until

it was deeded to the National Park Service. It's now a museum displaying mementos of the Emersons and of the early years of Nathaniel and Sophia Hawthorne's marriage.

The Alcott family moved to Concord in 1858 when Louisa May, author of *Little Women*, was in her mid-20s. Her father, Bronson, was a great friend of Emerson's and a committed Transcendentalist. Although poor, the Alcotts hosted weekly social gatherings at Orchard House ☎ (978) 369-4118, 399 Lexington Road, where they lived for 19 years. The house became the setting for *Little Women*, published in 1868, one of the most widely distributed children's books ever written. A third Hollywood movie of the semi-

autobiographical novel appeared in 1994 (filmed elsewhere). Almost all of the structure and furnishings of Orchard House remain. You'll see the original soapstone sink that Louisa bought for her mother with her first royalty check. Upstairs, several of her sister Mary's sketches, some drawn on the walls, are on display, along with costumes used by the girls when they gave their famous plays. Descendants of the Alcott family (or one of their notable neighbors) lead monthly tours. Open daily; an admission fee is charged.

To end your Concord visit, stroll through the hillside hush of Sleepy Hollow Cemetery, near the center of town, to Author's Ridge, the burial place of many of the local literary figures. Ralph Waldo Emerson's tombstone rests here, marked by a simple rough-hewn rock of native marble.

Kiss on a Covered Bridge

Covered wooden bridges once proliferated in New Hampshire and Vermont. Built from the 1830s onward, the bridges were covered to protect floorboards from the decaying effects of snow, ice and rain. Some say the

Immortalized in Ralph Waldo Emerson's "Concord Hymn," the North Bridge was the sight of "the shot heard 'round the world," which signaled the beginning of the American Revolution.

barn-like walls kept skittish horses from taking fright. In those days, travelers who waited out a storm under a bridge's cover could pass the time reading posted handbills touting circus dates, religious revivals, job openings in lumber factories, and cure-all potions. Covered bridges even hosted church suppers and militia meetings.

In New Hampshire, the Cornish–Windsor Bridge, the nation's longest covered bridge, with a 460-ft (140-m) span, crosses the Connecticut River in Cornish. The state also lays claim to the shortest of such bridges — a 12-ft (three-and-a-half-meter) expanse on a private estate in Alstead — and to more than half the covered bridges in New England.

A testament to their craftsmanship, more than 100 covered bridges still stand in Vermont. The Bennington region in the southwestern corner of Vermont abounds in these architectural artifacts. Across from a covered bridge that spans the Battenkill River in West Arlington, The Inn at Covered Bridge Green was the 10-year home of artist Norman Rockwell. Contact The Inn at Covered Bridge Green ☎ (802) 375-9489 TOLL-FREE (800) 726-9480, RD 1, PO Box 3550, Arlington, VT 05250 (mid-range), for reservations.

Vermont's largest concentration of covered bridges links riverbanks north of the resort town of Stowe. Outside Waterville, in tiny Belvedere, are the Morgan and the Mill covered bridges. From the neat little village of Waterville, Route 109 twists back and forth along the North Branch of the Lamoille River. Rocky ledges and strong currents make this an exuberant river, and a slew of covered bridges afford fine lookouts. One of them, Waterville's Codding Bridge, bears a sign tacked onto it in the 1950s that started a local tradition: "The Kissin' Bridge." Give it a whirl.

Cruise on a Windjammer

A flotilla of two- and three-masted working ships once hauled granite, lumber, fish and lime to ports up and down the Eastern Seaboard. Retired from service when rail and road shipping became cheap, these sleek and graceful wooden ships were saved from extinction in the 1930s by Maine artist Frank Swift, who began refitting them to carry passengers and gave them the tempestuous name they bear today — windjammers.

More than a dozen schooners still sail out of Camden, Rockport, and Rockland, plying Maine's jagged coast as far north as Bar Harbor. Captain Kip Files of Maine's *Victory Chimes* windjammer says his state's mid-coast offers the second finest cruising grounds in the world. When asked for the whereabouts of the first, he says, "I don't know. I'm still looking for it."

Master carpenters have restored these sturdy, 100-year-old vessels, endowing them with modern comforts. Ships vary in length from 64 to 132 ft (20 to 40 m). Depending on its size, each ship sleeps 20 to 44 guests in single, double and triple cabins. Huge gaff-rigged sails, in keeping with nineteenth-century style, festoon the masts.

With a shout of "Haul away!" the captain orders the crew to hoist the sheets and set sail. Once at sea, wind and tides determine the ship's direction, and

ABOVE: Union Church and covered bridge in Stark, NewHampshire. RIGHT: Tallships ply coastal waters from Connecticut to Maine.

novice sailors drink in the sounds and scenery. The sea froths against a backdrop of granite mountains. Gulls wail overhead. Sure, no swaying palm trees line the harbors of distant isles, but they beckon just the same.

The ship weighs anchor each evening near a different coastal hamlet — perhaps a fishing village that looks much as it did at the turn of the last century when these schooners first sailed. Other anchorages lead to busy resort towns humming with holiday shoppers in search of local crafts and antiques.

Back on board and eager for exercise, passengers practice "schoonerobics" by hoisting and lowering the sails or taking a turn at the wheel. To hone navigational skills, they plot a course with the compass and charts that the captain provides. Before or after the day's sail, they swim, go for a run, borrow the ship's rowboat or explore the local islands on foot. Once under sail, passengers stretch out on deck with a good book, or bask in the salt air and sunshine under the hypnotic influence of the schooner's billowing sails.

All that activity builds up a sailor's appetite. Schooners offer hearty home-cooked meals, prepared in the below-deck galley. With fresh-baked muffins and blueberry pancakes for breakfast, no one leaves the table hungry. Creamy fish chowder and turkey roast with all the fixings round out the staples of schooner fare. All hands look forward to the traditional island lobster bake, with fresh lobster and corn in the husk steamed in seaweed over a driftwood fire.

Most of the two- and three-masted schooners are based in Rockland and Camden, Maine, "The Windjammer Capital of the World." Choose one of the reproduction ships or an authentic old schooner, such as the *Victory Chimes*, sailing out of Rockland Harbor. The Maine Windjammer Association TOLL-FREE (800) 807-9463 WEB SITE www.sailmainecoast.com, PO Box 317P, Augusta, ME 04332, provides complete information on voyaging with the windjammer fleet.

Go for the Snow

A group of ice climbers file past the lodge at Pinkham Notch in the January pre-dawn darkness. They look like seven dwarves heading off to the diamond mines: picks in hand, crampons clinking, headlamp beams sparkling on the crusty snow. "Hi ho," says a bystander. One of the climbers nods with a flicker of a smile as the group disappears up Tuckerman Ravine Trail — on their way no doubt to greet the dawn on the summit of 6,288-ft (1,916-m) Mount Washington.

Scenes such as this unfold in New England's winter landscape each year as thousands travel north to Vermont, New Hampshire and Maine to revel in one of the region's most precious natural resources: snow. While skiing remains the most popular winter sport (see SPORTING SPREE, page 32 in YOUR CHOICE), a diamond mine of other winter adventures awaits the intrepid.

Strap a fiberglass plank to your feet and plunge down an icy slope: that just about sums up snowboarding. Owing much to the sport of skateboarding (including terminology like "half pipe" and "shredding"), some people claim snowboarding was invented in Vermont. It has skyrocketed in popularity over the last decade, and today anywhere skiers ski, riders ride; and as with skiing, instruction is often available. It's reputedly easier to master than skiing.

Speed! Noise! Gas fumes! Ah, the great outdoors. Snowmobiling is not a sport for the faint of heart. This flannel-shirted recreation rules in the macho northern forests of New England. Vermont and New Hampshire have extensive snowmobiling trails, but Maine has the highest vroom-vroom quotient. Rangeley, Jackman, Rockwood, Greenville, Millinocket, Houlton, Presque Isle and Caribou are the state's major snowmobiling centers. Local outfitters (see under RANGELEY LAKES REGION, page 332) rent Ski-Doos and Arctic Cats (those are brand names for you rookies). After a day of careening down trails at breakneck speed, relax at an inn that caters to snowmobilers, such as the Rangeley Inn, where the day winds down with a fireside cocktail and a gourmet dinner (see under RANGELEY LAKES REGION, page 332). Guided tours are available in some communities. In Vermont, northern Maine and New Hampshire local chambers of commerce are the best sources of information on the sport. Each state tourism bureau also has information on snowmobiling hot spots and tour guides.

Snowmobiling, of course, descended from the age-old art of dog sledding, or mushing. Though not much practiced in New England, in recent years there has been a resurgence of interest in the sport in northern Maine. Teams of huskies compete in races, working on their "off days" in the tourism business. Sign up

Early morning groomers have sculpted a fresh layer of corduroy on the slopes at Stowe, Vermont.

for a multi-day trip and learn to handle the dogs yourself, camping in the rough and living the life of the backwoods Mainer. Or opt for a short sample of the sport in Carrabassett Valley, Maine, with Tim Diehl and his team of exuberant white Samoyeds.

Tim has been running sled dogs for around 20 years, his operation is small, and the dogs are friendly. They gather around the sled, roll in the snow, and greet sled riders who've been tucked into thick lap robes. The 30-minute ride whirls through one and a half miles (two and a half kilometers) of wooded terrain glittering with frost. For information and reservations contact Tim Diehl, T.A.D. Dog Sled Services ☎ (207) 246-4461 (evenings only), PO Box 147, Stratton, ME 04982. The base is located on Route 27 in the Carrabassett Valley, 500 ft (150m) north of the Sugarloaf/USA access road. Other dog sledding outfits include: Mahoosuc Guide Service ☎ (207) 824-2073, Bear River Road, Newry, ME 04261; and Winter Journeys ☎ (207) 928-2026, RR 2, PO Box 1105, Lovell, ME 04051, with excursions running from a few hours to several days.

Can't get enough of winter fun? Try ice fishing on Lake Champlain, tobogganing in Boston's Arnold Arboretum, ice climbing at Smugglers' Notch, a sleigh ride at Fair Winds Farm in Brattleboro, snowshoeing at Great Glen Trails in New Hampshire. Make a snow angel, build a snow fort.... When it comes to winter in New England, you'll never run out of ideas; and New England will never run out of snow.

Meander through Mansions

Newport's opulent mansions were born in those heady "pre-income tax" days when every cent of a dollar went into a man's pocket, and the *nouveau riche* yearned to duplicate the palaces and châteaux that had so inspired them on their grand tours of Europe. So it was during Newport's heyday that families such as the Astors, Vanderbilts and Morgans created a summer society resort unmatched for glitter and opulence.

Although hundreds of these "cottages" existed during Newport's Gilded Age, only a handful remain. Eight of these cottages are owned by the Preservation Society of Newport ☎ (401) 847-1000, which, true to its name, has preserved these palaces of pomp, opening them to public inspection for the price of an admission fee. America's largest collection of what Europeans might call castles can keep you enthralled, if not appalled by their ostentation, for days.

Most visitors are content, however, to visit one or two of these bungalows. Aficionados consider Cornelius Vanderbilt's The Breakers to be the most grandiloquent of the Newport mansions.

This Italian Renaissance-style palace was completed in 1892 with 70 rooms awash in marble, alabaster, gilt, crystal and stained glass. Its Grand Salon was constructed in France and shipped to Newport. Bathtubs have a choice of fresh or salt water.

The romantically inclined fall limply in love with Rosecliff, the setting for the wooing of Mia Farrow in *The Great Gatsby*. The heiress Mrs. J. Hermann Oelrichs commissioned Stanford White to design Rosecliff in the image of the Grand Trianon of Louis XIV in Versailles. The 80-ft (24-m) by 40-ft (12-m) living room doubled as a ballroom and Mrs. Oelrichs is reputed to have spent $25,000 each summer for perfume to rub on the light fixtures. Note the grand staircase built in the shape of a heart. Appropriate, *n'est-ce pas?*

When your head begins to reel with visions of crystal chandeliers and marble banisters, step out for a coastal promenade on the Cliff Walk, a three-and-a-half-mile (five-and-a half-kilometer) path that overlooks Rhode Island Sound and borders the gardens of several of the mansions. The views, both seaward and inland, are fabulous. Walk the walk, ogle the mansions and yachts — and revel in all that is — and was — Newport.

OPPOSITE, TOP and BOTTOM: Snowshoeing and its aftermath in Manchester, Vermont. ABOVE: The gold ballroom still glitters at Newport's marvelous Marble House.

Stay the Night at a Light

Set on steep, rocky promontories surrounded by crashing surf, New England lighthouses shine out over splendid, rugged landscapes. Built from the eighteenth century onward to warn mariners away from rocky shoals, hundreds of these coastal beauties still perform their appointed duty up and down the serrated New England coast. And while these beacons flash out their message of warning for sailors to steer clear, they also exert a strong magnetism on another sort of traveler — those who come to admire, to photograph, to gaze on lighthouse artifacts and to learn some lighthouse lore. Some voyagers even come to stay the night.

Toward the end of the nineteenth century, while tramping on Cape Cod, Henry David Thoreau had the privilege of spending the night in the keeper's house at the Highland Light at North Truro, which was built in 1797. Just as fascinated with coastal beacons as travelers are today, the naturalist wrote from his lighthouse chamber:

"I thought as I lay there half awake and half asleep looking upward through the window to the lights above my head, how many sleepless eyes from far out on the ocean stream... were directed toward my couch."

More than 100 years after Thoreau's sojourn, there are a handful of lighthouses in Maine, Massachusetts and Rhode Island where visitors can stay the night in a lighthouse chamber. The most famous New England lighthouse lodging is the Keeper's House, located on Isle au Haut Acadia National Park's outermost island. Could there be a more idyllic setting in all of New England? Guests, who arrive on the mail boat from the fishing village of Stonington (see page 323), find a working lighthouse station that remains just about as it was when it was built in 1907. There are no telephones at the Keeper's House, and only limited electricity. Candles, kerosene lanterns, a few dim bulbs and the occasional moonbeam provide lighting. Rooms are large and furnished with painted antiques, and meals feature local seafood, served family-style in the dining room facing the beacon tower. For information, contact Jeff and Judi Burke ☎ (207) 367-2261, Robinson Point Lighthouse, Isle Au Haut, Maine 04645. Expect to pay $294 to $335 per night for double occupancy; the rate includes meals and the use of bicycles (minimum two-night stay in July and August).

Moving south to "the graveyard of the Atlantic," Cape Cod bristles with coastal beacons. The Cape Cod Museum of Natural History's "Staying Overnight at a Lighthouse" program combines a day of wildlife watching with lodging Spartan enough to have pleased Thoreau. The museum sponsors overnights at the South Monomoy Lighthouse, which stands sentry off the coast of Chatham on one of the two islands that make up the Monomoy National Wildlife Refuge. Formerly a fishing village, the island now harbors hundreds of species of birds, deer, fox, coyote and seals. South Monomoy is a famous flyway for migratory birds, and though the island's low terrain might look unpromising, the island is populated year-round by a variety of small hawks and songbirds. Provided in the $200 per-person cost is transportation to South Monomoy by boat, along with nature tours, dinner and breakfast; minimum age 12.

Finally there is the Rose Island Lighthouse in Newport Harbor, Rhode Island. A museum by day, the lighthouse looks just as it did at the turn of the last century. After hours, the two restored keeper's bedrooms are made available for overnight guests, who can pack a cooler with food or order a clam boil dinner for their sleepover. There is no running water; you pump the rainwater you need from the cistern and wash up with the bowl and pitcher in your room. For information, contact the Rose Island Lighthouse Foundation ((401) 847-4242, PO Box 1419, Newport, RI 02840-0997; $180 to $220, available only in summer.

The Keeper's House, South Monomoy, Rose Island: even the names speak of safe harbors, places where, as Thoreau once did, guests settle down for a night's slumbering voyage "in no danger of being wrecked."

Watch Whales at Stellwagen Bank

Twenty-five nautical miles off the Massachusetts coast, a roughly rectangular boundary demarcates Stellwagen Bank, one of the richest marine environments in the United States. A combination of physical, oceanographic, and meteorological circumstances in this 640-sq-mile (2,180-sq-km) area produces a mother lode of plankton that lures a veritable stampede of hungry pelagic fish, sea birds, turtles and marine mammals for their yearly summer feeding frenzy. This Noah's arc of marine life attracts yet another species to Stellwagen Bank — sightseers — millions of whom board whale-

Working lighthouses dot the coast of New England. These are in Maine, at Isleboro OPPOSITE, and Pemaquid Point RIGHT.

watching boats each year to visit this national marine sanctuary. With this increased pressure on the fragile marine environment, further regulation of whale watching is likely. Sensitive visitors will want to select an excursion company with strong ties to the marine-mammal research community, such as those listed below.

The sightseers are rarely disappointed. One of the most important areas in the North Atlantic for whales, Stellwagen Bank is both the principal feeding ground and nursery for large and small whale species including minke, fin, northern right, pilot and orca. Also sometimes spotted are white-sided and bottlenose dolphin, leatherback turtle, harbor seals and porpoises, and sea birds from the common gull to the endangered roseate tern.

It is, however, the humpback whale that provides the most awesome sight. Though the days of whaling are over, the mighty mammals still exert the same fascination they did in Melville's day when he called the humpback "the most gamesome and lighthearted of all the whales, making more gay foam and white water generally than any other of them…." Scientists don't know why humpbacks frolic they way they do. To the layman, it sure looks as if they're playing when these behemoths slap the surface with their flippers, roll belly up out of the water, or even nudge the boat. Their impressive feeding habits are no mystery: They lunge from the depths, jaws agape and working like sieves, to capture a ton of plankton at a gulp.

Getting on board for this adventure couldn't be easier. Cruises depart April to October from Gloucester, Newburyport, Salem, Boston, Plymouth, Barnstable Harbor and Provincetown. All whale-watching outfits are not alike, however. Some boats are little more than floating fast-food and souvenir stands that happen to ply the waters the whales frequent. Others offer expert narration, video replays of the day's sightings, and decent food. A few enterprising cruise operators "guarantee" whale sightings, claiming a 95 percent success rate; if you fail to spot any whales, the company offers a free trip to try again.

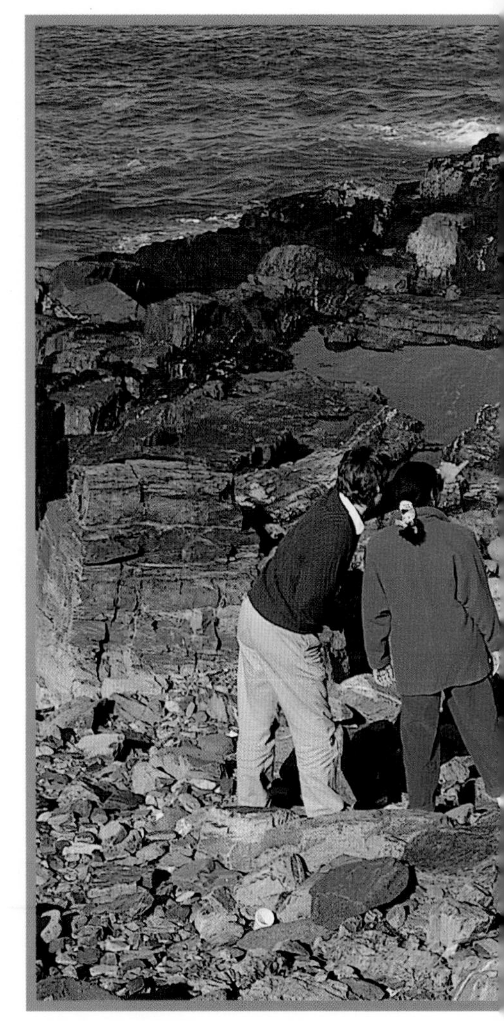

The Dolphin Fleet of Provincetown (see below) originated whale watching on the East Coast and is the largest and most experienced of all the operations, having made more than 8,000 trips since 1975. Their boats, built for whale watching, are stable and are never allowed to fill to capacity. Cruises are led by scientists from the Center for Coastal Studies, one of the world's leading whale research and conservation organizations and an acknowledged authority on the humpback whales. Through years of research, Coastal Studies scientists have identified several

hundred individual humpbacks and will offer you their individual histories. A portion of each ticket sale is donated to conservation efforts.

Below is a partial list of whale-watching outfits in Massachusetts. Be sure to inquire in advance about what each one offers before making your reservation.

Barnstable (Cape Cod): Hyannis Whale Watcher ☎ (508) 362-6088 TOLL-FREE IN EASTERN MASSACHUSETTS (800) 287-0374.

Boston: A.C. Cruise Lines ☎ (617) 261-6633, Boston Harbor Cruises ☎ (617) 227-4321 TOLL-FREE (877) 733-9425, New England Aquarium Whale Watch ☎ (617) 973-5227 or for recorded information ☎ (617) 973-5277.

Newburyport (North Shore): Newburyport Whale Watch ☎ (978) 499-0832 TOLL-FREE IN NEW ENGLAND (800) 848-1111.

Plymouth (South Shore): Andy-Lynn Whale Watch ☎ (508) 746-7776, Captain John Boats ☎ (508) 746-2643 TOLL-FREE (800) 242-2469.

Salem (North Shore): East India Cruise Co. ☎ (508) 741-0434 TOLL-FREE (800) 745-9594.

Provincetown (Cape Cod): Dolphin Fleet of Provincetown ☎ (508) 349-1900 TOLL-FREE (800) 826-9300, *Portuguese Princess* Whale Watch ☎ (508) 487-2651 TOLL-FREE (800) 442-3188.

York, Maine: Vigilant coastal walkers can sometimes spot humpback whales frolicking at sea. Bring binoculars!

YOUR CHOICE

The Great Outdoors

What is it about the New England landscape? There is no Grand Canyon to stun the senses, no Niagara Falls to gape at in awe. The region's tallest mountains, while they present a challenge to the climber, are mere bumps when compared with mountain ranges in the West. Yet anyone who visits New England falls instantly in love with it. Stalwart lighthouses watch over rocky islands, and harbors brim with tall-masted ships. Trim villages, their church steeples pointing heavenward, dot hills and valleys. Here and there a weathered dairy barn tacks down the corner of a neat patchwork of fields. In silvery groves of birch, tumbledown stone fences crisscross the land — remnants of a time when a checkerboard of small farms framed much of the countryside.

Of all the cherished aspects of the New England landscape, it is the mountains that hikers and ramblers most dote upon. The Appalachians, embracing much of western New England, run south from Mount Katahdin in northern Maine through the White Mountains of New Hampshire. In Vermont the peaks mellow, becoming the lower, forested Green Mountains, which stretch the length of the state, continuing into Massachusetts as the Berkshire Hills moving on across Connecticut to join the Taconic Mountains of New York.

Spanning this range of rolling hills and ragged mountains, the northeast section of the **Appalachian Trail** stretches south from Mount Katahdin in Baxter State Park and exits the region near Kent in Connecticut's Litchfield Hills. In all, more than 654 miles (1,046 km) of the 2,000-mile (3,220-km) trail wind through New England. Maintained throughout its length by teams of volunteers, the trail is accessible to all types of adventurers, from "through-hikers" (those trekking from Georgia to Maine) to day-hikers.

Start your trekking plans by contacting the Appalachian Mountain Club (AMC) ☎ (603) 466-2727 FAX (603) 466-3871

OPPOSITE: The White Mountains of New Hampshire are one of New England's prime vacation lands. ABOVE: The Woodstock Ski Touring Center in Vermont.

(reservations for huts and workshops), Route 16, PO Box 298, Gorham, NH 03581. The AMC offers guided adventures from their Pinkham Notch Visitor Center ☎ (603) 466-2721 in the **White Mountain National Forest**, including hut-to-hut trips following the trail as it links a series of high-mountain rustic lodges, each less than a day's hike from the next. AMC guidebooks are essential for independent hikers. To order, call TOLL-FREE (800) 262-4455. Books describe the long-distance hiking trails of the six New England states, with detailed topographical maps and symbols for shelters, water sources, ranger stations, emergency telephones, and lookout points along the way. You can also use the huts as an independent hiker, but you must make reservations in advance.

In Vermont, the easygoing **Green Mountains** are irresistible to hikers, skiers and naturalists. The mountains' diverse terrain ranges from pastoral foothills to summits with panoramic views. Some trails make a perfect afternoon climb, others demand a multi-day commitment. Running the length of the Green Mountains from Massachusetts to Canada, the **Long Trail**, a 265-mile (424-km) footpath, merges with the Appalachian Trail for 104 miles (167 km) of its length. In north-central Vermont, the trail traverses **Mount Mansfield State Forest and Park** as it climbs over 4,393 ft (1,339 m) Mount Mansfield through breathtaking Smugglers' Notch. This area has some of the best hiking in the state. The Green Mountain Club ☎ (802) 244-7037 WEB SITE www.greenmountainclub.org, GMC Headquarters, 4711 Waterbury-Stowe Road, Waterbury Center, VT 05677, publishes guides to the Long Trail and offers year-round outings and programs throughout Vermont.

Outside of the region's two long-distance trails and their tributaries, footpaths radiate through parks, over mountains and along river, sea and bog in just about every county in New England. In this embarrassment of riches, two places deserve special mention: the **Cape Cod National Seashore** and **Acadia National Park**.

Hiking trails delve into the various habitats of the Cape Cod National Seashore. The **Nauset Marsh Trail** glides along salt ponds and marshes; the **Atlantic White Cedar Swamp Trail** skirts a white cedar swamp, beginning near Marconi Station; the **Beech Forest Trail**, near Provincetown, crosses sand dunes and beech forests; and the **Cranberry Bog Trail**, east of Truro, leads through a wild cranberry patch. Trail pamphlets are available from the visitor centers in Provincetown and Eastham, or at trailheads for these 30- to 40-minute walks.

The exposed pink granite peaks of Mount Desert Island tower over Maine's Down East town of Bar Harbor. Forty thousand acres (16,200 hectares) of the island belong to Acadia National Park, a forested enchantment of mountains, footpaths, hiking trails and carriage roads. A climb or drive to the 1,530-ft (466-m) peak of **Cadillac Mountain** will put you at the highest point on the eastern seaboard. Make the trek before dawn and you'll be among the first in the nation to greet the new day. A shorter trail up **Acadia Mountain** on the island's western side affords stupendous views of Somes Sound, the only fjord on the east coast. Climbers delight in the park's steep cliffs as well as its 150 miles (240 km) of

OPPOSITE: Pemaquid Point Lighthouse on Maine's central coast. ABOVE: Marginal Way in Ogunquit, Maine.

hiking trails. A free newspaper, *The Acadia Beaver Log*, lists tours, guided walks, events and cruises between June and October (see also EXPLORE ACADIA, page 15 in TOP SPOTS).

Sporting Spree

Sports in New England are omnipresent. Everywhere you go you're likely to see amateurs doing their thing: ultimate Frisbee players on Boston Common, in-line skaters on a Vermont recreation path, wet-suited surfers on Maine coastal crests, hoop shooters in a "pickup" game of basketball on a New Haven lot, a skateboarder delivering pizza in Providence… and don't think that winter puts a damper on the fun. A change of season merely means trading in-line skates for skis and skateboards for snowboards, while basketball players pick up ice hockey sticks and surfers hop on the luge. In short, New England sports are ready and waiting for you to jump in and play.

BICYCLING

Mountain biking happens anywhere there is challenging terrain. Many of the large ski resorts turn their attention to alpine biking once the snow melts in May (see SPORTS AND OUTDOOR ACTIVITIES under individual destinations). From spring melt to mid-October, Maine's Sugarloaf/USA becomes the East's most challenging mountain biking turf, with 50 miles (80 km) of trails for intermediate and advanced riders. Rental bikes are available and a shuttle bus takes daredevils to the top of the mountain.

Vermont has been rated as the top roadway bicycling state in America: Its rolling hills, low mountain passes, country back roads, outstanding state parks and light traffic make it a cyclist's paradise. On Cape Cod, bicyclists will find miles and miles of dedicated trails, many of them paralleling the seashore. Visitors to New Hampshire's Lakes Region get away from the summer crush by biking around beautiful Lake Winnipesaukee along a series of back roads and wide-open highways. Island bikeways abound all along the coast from "Little Rhody's" Block Island to Martha's Vineyard and Nantucket to Maine's Calendar Islands to Mount Desert's wildly scenic carriage roads.

PADDLING

Whitewater rafting and **canoeing** begin in earnest in spring when seasonal rains swell rivers. Maine's Kennebec River thrills rafters as it courses through an eye-popping 12-mile (19-km) gorge. Many rafting companies along the Kennebec, Penobscot and Dead Rivers supply instruction and all equipment, including boxed lunches. Children eight years or older, accompanied by adults, are welcome on some river rides. Professional River Runners ☎ (207) 663-2229 TOLL-FREE (800) 325-3911 WEB SITE www.proriverrunners.com, PO Box 92, Route 201, West Forks, ME 04985, is one of Maine's respected outfitters and guide services.

Maine paddlers get away from it all on the 98-mile (158-km) Allagash Wilderness Waterway. Accessible only by canoe, this superlative, forest-lined chain of lakes, ponds, streams and rivers flows from the northern edge of Baxter State Park to the

town of Allagash, a few miles south of the Canadian border. Contact the Bureau of Parks and Lands ☎ (207) 287-3821, 22 State House Station, Augusta, ME 04333, for maps, regulations and up-to-date reports on conditions. Greenville outfitters rent canoes. Contact the Moosehead Lake Region Chamber of Commerce ☎ (207) 695-2702 TOLL-FREE (888) 876-2778 WEB SITE www.mooseheadlake.org, PO Box 581, Main Street, Greenville, ME 04441, for recommendations.

In New Hampshire, the gentle Saco River winds through the splendid wilderness scenery of the Mount Washington Valley; it's a good choice for families and novices. Saco Bound & Maine Whitewater ☎ (603) 447-2177 WEB SITE www.sacobound.com, PO Box 119, Center Conway, NH 03813, two miles (three kilometers) east of Conway Center on Route 302, offers guided canoe trips. They also have rafting trips on the Swift, Rapid, Kennebec, Dead and Penobscot Rivers.

SKIING

When urban New Englanders feel the first cold winds of winter they sigh, envisioning another season of shoveling. But winter-sports enthusiasts see quite a different picture. When the first flakes fall sometime in November (or October!) thousands of snow buffs head for New England's slopes and trails. Even if it's not a banner year for snowfall, snowmaking machines at larger resorts stretch the season from November through May.

Ski fever began in New Hampshire's logging camps in the 1870s when Scandinavian immigrants brought their native sport to the new land. It spread to the college community in 1914 when Dartmouth University librarian Nathaniel Goodrich descended Vermont's highest peak, Mount Mansfield, in Stowe. Skiing flourished in those days, without the benefit of gondolas or aerial trams, much less rope tows. Woodstock, Vermont is credited with the invention, in 1934, of the rope tow. Powered by a Model T Ford engine, it pulled skiers up Mount Tom, revolutionizing the ski industry. Today skiing is a multimillion-dollar enterprise and one of the region's major allures.

OPPOSITE: Trout fishing in New Hampshire's White Mountains. ABOVE: Wishing for a pony ride at Scott's Orchard, Deep River, Connecticut.

As a rule, the smaller resorts of New Hampshire, Maine and Vermont offer tranquillity and fine cuisine; the bigger resorts offer more activities and conveniences. In the latter camp, Killington, in Shelburne Center, Vermont, spans seven peaks and is New England's largest ski resort. Further north, Stowe, Vermont, named by *Mountain Sports & Living* magazine as one of the "10 best ski towns" in the United States, exudes European-style hospitality in a sparkling alpine setting. Sugarloaf/USA in Maine's Carrabassett Valley is that state's top ski resort. For sheer height, Sugarloaf Mountain is hard to beat, with a summit of 4,237 ft (1,291 m), and an annual snowfall of 14 ft (over four meters). Challenging terrain abounds, and the base lodge village has a back-to-nature 1960s ambiance. At Bretton Woods Mountain Resort in New Hampshire's White Mountains, snow squalls known as "Bretton Woods flurries" blanket a landscape that offers some of the best views in the east. This ski area is strong on beginner to intermediate slopes and has an excellent ski school with private as well as group instruction.

If you're thinking of a weekend on the slopes, call ahead for recorded information on **skiing conditions** at most resorts; or use these 24-hour "snow phone" numbers in Maine TOLL-FREE (888) 624-6345, Vermont TOLL-FREE (800) 837-6668 and New Hampshire TOLL-FREE (800) 258-3608.

Most ski resorts cater to **Nordic-style skiers** (or cross-country skiers) as fully as they do alpine skiers. There are also wonderful places dedicated to the sport. Grafton Ponds Nordic Ski and Mountain Bike Center in Grafton, Vermont, has 37 miles (60 km) of trails through pastoral countryside and an amazing three miles (five kilometers) of snowmaking capability. Great Glen Trails in Pinkham Notch, New Hampshire has 40 miles (64 km) of trails and a warm ambiance. The base lodge offers all sorts of services, unusual for a Nordic lodge, including childcare, a deli serving breakfast and lunch, and a retail shop. Nearby, in the Victorian village of Jackson, the Jackson Ski Touring Center has been called "the finest cross-country skiing network in the East." A downhill Mecca, Bethel, Maine also teems with cross-country skiers. The Bethel Inn & Country Club, Carter's X-C Ski Center and the Telemark Inn Wilderness Ski Lodge all have excellent facilities with miles of forest and meadow

trails… and lots of snow. To prove it, Bethel climbed into the annals of the *Guinness Book of World Records* by building the "world's tallest snowman." For more on winter sports, see GO FOR THE SNOW, page 20 in TOP SPOTS.

The Open Road

"Concentrate on Your Driving!" admonishes a signpost along the Maine Turnpike as the road drones across the land. Boredom is the danger, as along its superhighways, Maine could be Anywhere, USA. But abandon the expressways, and reminders to "concentrate on your driving" take on new meaning: The back roads of New England are bewitching, and impossible to mistake for anywhere else in the world. It's here, too, that rubbernecking drivers must take heed. My advice: keep at least one eye on the road and allow plenty of time for exploring.

LITCHFIELD HILLS LOOP

In a northwest corner of the state, a 60-mile (96-km) circuit tours the highlands of Connecticut. Detour into any town along the route and you're likely to find a venerable inn, an art gallery and an antique shop or two.

North of **Candlewood Lake**, drive north along Route 7 from the town of **New Milford**. Cross the old, covered **Bulls Bridge**, one of only two passable covered bridges left in the state. You'll traverse the bucolic **Housatonic Valley** through natural unspoiled terrain of pine and hardwood, on to the town of **Kent**, an antique shopper's delight. Follow the flow of the Housatonic River north along Route 7 to **Kent Falls State Park**, a 275-acre (111-hectare) preserve and a perfect spot for a picnic. In warm weather, cool off in one of the refreshing swimming pools created by water cascading down a natural staircase.

North of Kent, still on Route 7, the photogenic **Cornwall covered bridge** spans the river, providing another opportunity to cross a covered bridge. Follow signs to the storybook town of **Litchfield** via Route 63, where a classic white-steepled Congregational Church

OPPOSITE: The Ridgeview Trail, Stowe Mountain Resort, Vermont. ABOVE: A horse farm in Connecticut's Litchfield Hills.

dominates the village green. Regal white, clapboard houses flank both sides of the village's elm-lined North and South Streets in this state-designated historical district. One of the world's largest collections of works by Ralph Earl, a famous eighteenth-century portrait painter, hangs at the Litchfield Historical Society. America's first law school, a small structure, stands on the grounds of the Tapping Reeve House. The birthplaces of three illustrious Americans — Harriet Beecher Stowe, Ethan Allen and Henry Ward Beecher — cluster on North Street.

West from Litchfield, Route 202 passes **Mount Tom State Park**, where a mile-long trail leads to the 1,325-ft (404-m) summit and surrounding views. Tucked beneath

the hills, **Lake Waramaug**, near the junction of Route 45, has a crescent beach with boating, swimming, and campsites. Crown the day by raising a glass in the **Hopkins Vineyard** tasting room.

Once back on Route 202, consider a side trip via Route 47 to the **Institute for American Indian Studies** ✆ (860) 868-0518, 38 Curtis Road (off Route 199), a research center and educational museum in the village of Washington. You'll walk through a seventeenth-century Native American village with a Paleo-Indian campsite and a life-size longhouse. Some of the Algonquian artifacts are more than 10,000 years old. The museum is open daily April to December, closed Monday and Tuesday January to March. The circuit of the Indian village is less than a mile (one and a half kilometers) long.

CRUISING THE CHAMPLAIN VALLEY

Home to the Holstein and the haystack, the open lands of Vermont's Champlain Valley stretch west to **Lake Champlain** from **Middlebury** and the town of **Brandon** to the south. Vistas of cornfields and apple orchards bear testimony to the region's agricultural focus. You may want to linger a day or more in Middlebury with its fine restaurants and cafés, especially after you review the campus cultural schedule, usually packed with plays, dance performances, musical events, films and art exhibitions. This is also a prime area for touring dairies, tapping into the maple sugar scene and visiting apple orchards, as well as for tasting and buying Vermont cheddar and honey.

Begin your tour by driving west out of Middlebury via Route 125, and turning right at a rotary onto Route 23. You'll see signs for the **University of Vermont (UVM) Morgan Horse Farm** in Weybridge. These handsome steeds are

TOP: A store in Waitsfield, Vermont, advertises its teddy wares. BOTTOM: Plymouth, Vermont, birthplace of President Calvin Coolidge. RIGHT: Lake Champlain sunset, Charlotte, Vermont.

the descendants of the bay stallion Justin Morgan. Tour the stables, housed in a late-1800s slate-roofed barn, and observe the Morgans at work as you wander the grounds.

From Middlebury, follow Route 125 west past farmlands and pastoral views free of billboards and roadside commerce. Head south on Route 22A, passing through the tiny village of Bridgeport en route to **Shoreham**, where you'll find an antique shop, country store, crafts and the **Shoreham Inn**, built in 1799. It's said that, back in 1840, packs of wolves prowled the outskirts of town, where more than 40,000 sheep grazed. Threatened townspeople formed wolf-hunting posses to protect the herds. No such threat exists today in this region where acres of orchards nurture apples galore.

Wind east on Route 73 to a turnoff just before the upcoming town of Orwell. Signs direct you, via a fork in the road, to the ruins of a **Revolutionary War fort**, built in 1776. In and around the ruins, several miles of narrow, marked trails offer scenic outlooks. Carrying on to Orwell via Route 73, park downtown and take another step back in time at **The First National Bank**. Vermont's smallest bank is an ornate Victorian Gothic building where tellers still transact business from behind brass wire cages.

From Orwell, Route 73 travels east, climbing a major ridge, one of the last before the Taconic Mountain Range melts into the Champlain Valley. As you drive through the village of **Sudbury**, notice the Gothic tower looking down on the village from atop the white town hall. Outside Sudbury, the road crests several ridges as it continues east, each ridge affording open vistas of fields dotted with silos and barns. Route 73 eventually hugs **Otter Creek**, following its banks before bending away to enter **Brandon**.

In the center of town stands the childhood home of Stephen A. Douglas. As a young man, Douglas earned his living as a cabinetmaker before moving west to gain fame as an orator, a congressman and a presidential candidate who opposed Abraham

Lincoln. Near the Douglas house, on Pearl Street, stands a landmark of Vermont's antislavery movement, the home of abolitionist state senator R.V. Marsh. Before the Civil War, Senator Marsh and members of Brandon's Baptist community banded together to harbor runaway slaves in their homes. Marsh's home, a red-brick mansion, was a stop on this "underground railroad," with a tunnel, dozens of hiding closets, and eight secret stairways. For more information, contact **Brandon Area Chamber of Commerce** ☎ (802) 247-6401, PO Box 267, Brandon, VT 05733.

ROAD-O-RAMA

Beyond the two classic trips we've detailed above, there are many more great New England road journeys. Carved out of the green western Massachusetts hills, the **Mohawk Trail** breezes over a succession of WPA-era bridges. On Cape Cod, the **Old King's Highway** runs from Sandwich to Orleans, passing through compact villages with a bonanza of antique shops and galleries. Another Depression-era project, the **Merritt Parkway**, a National Scenic Byway, crosses Connecticut's southeast corner. A network of slow-paced back roads meanders through **New Hampshire's Lakes Region**, and in Maine some people call Route 17 **"Moose Alley"** after the moose-spotting opportunities it offers. You're sure to discover your own favorite New England drives. Just remember: "Concentrate!"

Backpacking

New England's gift to cost-conscious travelers is its compactness. This cuts down on transportation costs and means that — should you be confined to public transportation — you can still see a great deal in a short amount of time. "College towns" are another boon to penny-pinching travelers. Metropolitan areas with large student populations such as Boston, New Haven, Burlington and Providence, have cheap eats and free street-side entertainment. Most of these cities also have youth hostels. All of them are connected by frequent bus service.

In New Hampshire's White Mountain National Forest, the Appalachian Mountain Club (AMC) offers low budget lodging at Pinkham Notch and Crawford Notch, and their hiker's shuttle links the notches and most of the major trailheads. Concord Trailways runs from Boston's South Station to the AMC headquarters at Pinkham Notch Lodge.

Despite the region's compact nature, **transportation** will probably take a generous slice out of your budget. Short of hitchhiking (not recommended, but common enough in rural areas), the bus is usually the least expensive way to go. Greyhound and the other bus lines (see TRAVELERS' TIPS, page 344) ply nearly every route in the region. Greyhound offers a North American Discovery Pass for 4 to 60 days, as well as advance purchase discounts, two-for-one offers and discounts to children. Couples or groups of travelers can usually save money and time by renting a car.

For solo travelers, New England's **hostels** are the least expensive places to bed down — costing from around $10

to $25 per night, per person. They also provide a refreshing change from the isolation of hotels. Many of them include cooking facilities, offering additional savings on food cost.

Those who plan to do a fair amount of hostelling will benefit by joining **Hostelling International–American Youth Hostels** ☎ (202) 783-6161 TOLL-FREE (800) 909-4776 WEB SITE www.hiayh.org, 733 Fifteenth Street NW, Washington, DC 20005. A membership not only reduces your nightly fees, but also gets you some business discounts. Write to obtain the *Official Guide to Hostels in Canada and the United States of America.*

There are dozens of **campgrounds** in New England. Each state's tourism office publishes its guide to state parks and campgrounds. In warmer months, the high demand for campsites means you'll have to arrive early to secure one. In fact, for the weekend, plan to reserve your site by Thursday, if possible. The most popular campgrounds, such as those in

LEFT: In Vermont's Green Mountains, Moss Glenn Falls tumble through Granville Gulf State Park. ABOVE: Dogs know their place in Chester, Connecticut.

Baxter State Park (Maine) and Roland C. Nickerson State Park (Cape Cod), take reservations and get booked up months in advance.

Living It Up

One of the curious ironies of wealth in America is the enthusiasm of the rich to pay dearly to live simply. This philosophy produces meals of French peasant food with tabs of $100 per person and up, or multi-thousand-dollar price tags for a week of backwoods rustication. The *ne plus ultra* experience in this category is an extended stay at a Maine fishing camp, ideally one that has been in business more than a century and is accessible only by float plane or canoe. The most luxurious (i.e., with flush toilets and electric lights) is **Libby Camps** ((207) 435-8274 FAX (207) 435-3230 WEB SITE www.libbycamps.com, Drawer 10, Ashland, ME 04732, on Millinocket Lake, about 100 air miles (161 km) north of Bangor. Equally inaccessible and entirely primitive (hence more chic), **Nugent's Chamberlain Lake Camps** ((207) 944-5991 WEB SITE www.nugent-mcnallycamps.com, HCR 76, Box 632, Greenville, ME 04441, sits directly on the Allagash Wilderness Waterway. The location precludes such amenities as running water. Star athletes, politicians and captains of industry flock to wet their lines for trout and salmon.

Maine, in particular, is a getaway haven for high-powered business people, many of whom choose to decompress in the simple woodsy atmosphere of **Quisisana Resort** ((914) 833-0293 September through May or (207) 925-3500

June through August FAX (914) 833-4140 WEB SITE www.quisisanaresort.com, Box 142, Larchmont, NY 10538, or (summer) Center Lovell, ME 04016. At this magical retreat on Lake Kezar in the western Maine mountains, the waiters, waitresses, chambermaids and lifeguards seem always ready to burst into song — those who don't play the flute, cello or violin, that is. Think of it as summer with a sound track.

Of course, New England has its share of places that cater to people who prefer more hands-on pampering. **Canyon Ranch in the Berkshires** ☎ (413) 637-4100 TOLL-FREE (800) 326-7080 FAX (413) 637-0057 in western Massachusetts is reputed to have some of the most talented masseurs and masseuses in North America, and its spa cuisine is the hit of the Manhattan penthouse crowd. The **Spa at Norwich** ☎ (860) 886-2401 TOLL-FREE (800) 275-4772 is always up to date on the latest muds, potions, lotions and ways to rub them in to forestall the telltale signs of aging. In Ogunquit, Maine, the posh **Cliff House** ☎ (207) 361-1000 FAX (207) 361-2122 opened a new spa building with 32 oversized guest rooms in May 2002. At present it is the only oceanfront spa in New England. Guest and treatment rooms have exquisite views of the sea.

Several of America's oldest yacht clubs are found in New England. The waters of Long Island Sound are particularly suited for skippering a sail or motor yacht. Visitors who have not arrived on their own marine transport can rent a yacht at the **Coastline Yacht Club** TOLL-FREE (800) 749-7245 FAX (860) 572-7796, 44 Water Street, Mystic, CT 06355. Located in downtown Mystic at Fort Rachel Marine, Coastline arranges both skippered and, for appropriately licensed operators, bare-boat charters of sailcraft up to 50 ft (15 m), as well as classic motor yachts.

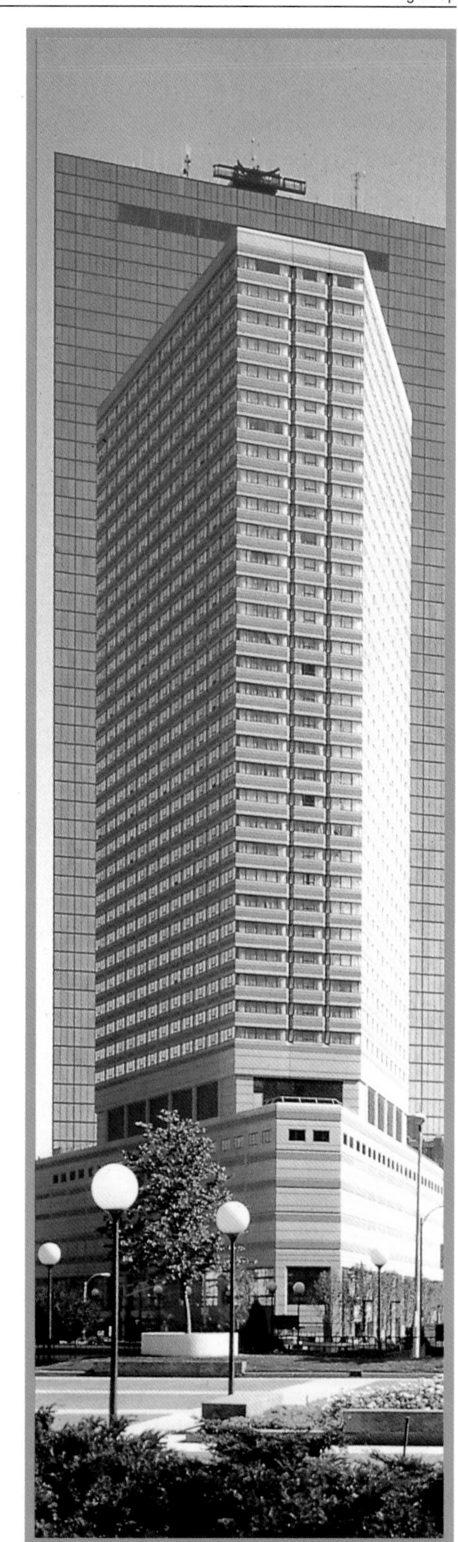

OPPOSITE: The Balsams Grand Resort Hotel TOP offers four seasons of pampering in New Hampshire's North Woods. White-linen ambiance BOTTOM at Maine's York Harbor Inn. RIGHT: Guestrooms at the Westin Hotel in Boston's Copley Place afford city and river views.

Family Fun

What better place than New England to learn about the history of the nation? History-book stories come alive at the Boston Tea Party Ship, Plimoth Plantation, and the Mystic Seaport. Cobblestone streets in Salem and Portland lead back in time to the sights and sounds of another era. And museums chock-full of artifacts cater to kids' penchants to see, hear, touch, smell and taste it all.

But remember, while New England is educational, it's also just plain fun.

BEST BEACHES

Cape Cod's shoreline possesses miles of gorgeous white-sand beaches where children can sun, swim and sail. Toddlers have given their stamp of approval to Falmouth's **Old Silver Beach**, an extended crescent where a sandbar at one end keeps the water shallow. The beach has lifeguards, showers and a snack bar. Also attractive for families, Cape Cod's **Sandy Neck**, off Route 6A in West Barnstable, is a natural playground where children romp over the sand dunes, splash in the small pools that form at low tide or observe marine life in the tidal zone. When the sun gets too hot, families find cool amusement on hiking and biking trails, and in museums.

Families searching for an old-fashioned beach resort will find it at **Block Island**, 13 miles (eight kilometers) off the Rhode Island coast. Bring the bare essentials: bathing suits, bikes if you have them, windbreakers for cool nights and a fishing rod. Though the island measures only three miles (five kilometers) wide and seven miles (11 km) long, it wraps 200-ft-high (60-m) bluffs, creamy sand beaches, gentle dunes and rolling surf into a kid-sized package. Local children play summer baseball games two nights a week, and visitors aged six to 12 are welcome to join.

"KIDS LOVE BOSTON"

And Boston loves kids! Plan a family picnic on Boston's beautiful Esplanade along the Charles River, where, at dusk, a giant screen at the Hatch Shell displays full-length G- or PG-rated feature films. The **Friday Flicks** series runs from Memorial Day through the end of September. The **Scooper Bowl Festival**, another summer tradition, brings hundreds of families to Boston Common in the first week of June for a lip-smacking salute to ice cream.

Boston's oldest walking tour company offers a child's-eye view of the Freedom Trail's architecture and history, every Saturday, Sunday and Monday, with their **Boston by Little Feet Walking Tours** for children age 6 to 12. Contact Boston By Foot ☎ (617) 367-2345, 77 North Washington Street, Boston, MA 02114. Families with tiny tots mustn't miss the "Make Way for Ducklings" sculpture, based on Robert McCloskey's children's classic of the same name. The eight ducklings — Jack, Kack, Lack, Mack, Nack, Ouack, Pack and Quack — and the mother duck have been polished to a golden sheen by hundreds of toddlers' bottoms.

These and scores of other sights and activities are detailed in the *Kids Love Boston* annual guidebook, part of the

Boston Family Visitor Kit, which also includes a list of hotel packages and special discounts tailored to families planning a stay in Boston. To order the kit, or for information on the events listed above, contact the Greater Boston Convention and Visitors Bureau ☎ (617) 536-4100 TOLL-FREE (800) 888-5515, 2 Copley Place, Boston, MA 02116.

ANIMAL CRACKERS

New England's most impressive zoo is the **Roger Williams Park Zoo** in Providence (Rhode Island), a 430-acre (174-hectare) Victorian park with formal gardens, paddleboats, and animals from six continents residing in simulations of their natural habitats. Boston's Franklin Park Zoo has the popular **African Tropical Forest** ☎ (617) 541-5466, 10–12 Blue Hill Avenue. A meandering jungle path takes visitors through a lush three-acre (one-and-a-quarter-hectare) domed habitat where more than 100 birds fly through the trees. Lowland gorillas, pygmy hippos, baboons and spotted leopards inhabit the forest.

On Boston's waterfront, the **New England Aquarium** has a spectacular four-story Giant Ocean Tank, populated by hammerhead sharks, huge sea turtles, and hundreds of varieties of fish. Two species of penguins live in the ground-level pools. The rockhopper penguin's head feathers resemble a punk hairdo, while the jackass penguin acquired its name because it brays like a donkey. Sea lion and dolphin shows take place aboard a floating pavilion. The museum also conducts whale-watching excursions.

Giving the venerable New England Aquarium a run for its money, the renovated **Mystic Aquarium** in Connecticut is a grand space for watching marine life, from the rock lobster in her quiet tidal pool to immense beluga whales in their new outdoor tank. (These arctic mammals love the cold Connecticut winters.) At the new tidal pool, gaze down into the colorful habitat of hermit crabs, anemones and sea cucumbers. Surrounding the pool are tanks swarming with Day-Glo tropical fish as well as the somber estuarine varieties of the Mystic region.

OPPOSITE: A large-scale model at Boston's Museum of Science demonstrates the habits of one of New England's most annoying denizens.
ABOVE: A rocky secluded beach at Ogunquit, Maine.

The Eastern Seaboard is a prime area for whale watching. Typical sighting cruises last from four to six hours. Several companies offer **whale-watching** cruises from downtown Boston, where you can visit the New England Aquarium, before or after a cruise. See the TOURS AND EXCURSIONS sections in the Bar Harbor, Boston, Cape Ann, The Kennebunks, Hyannis, Plymouth, Portsmouth and Provincetown listings; see also WATCH WHALES AT STELLWAGEN BANK, page 25 in TOP SPOTS. Whale-watching season begins in spring and extends through October.

"PICK-YOUR-OWN" APPLES

On October weekends, hoards of families descend on burgeoning orchards throughout New England in a "Pick-Your-Own" free-for-all, filling bushels with crisp ripe apples for pie-baking and lunch boxes. A short drive from Boston, **Honey Pot Orchards** ☎ (978) 562-5666, 144 Sudbury Road, Stowe, Massachusetts, has acres of apples as well as pumpkins for sale, along with caramel apples, cider and delicious "cider donuts" on which to feast. Hayrides to and from the orchards, a petting farm, and other sideshows keep everyone cheerful.

North of Worcester, off Interstates 495 and 190, several more orchards are ripe with opportunities for pick-your-own buffs. **Nashoba Valley Winery and Orchard** ☎ (508) 779-5521, 100 Wattaquadoc Road, Bolton, pleases adults and children with fruit-picking, winery tours and a good restaurant on its 55 acres (22 hectares). There are peaches, blackberries and 100 varieties of apples to pick in season, and visitors can set up a picnic on the grounds. It's open weekdays from 11 AM to 4:30 PM, and on weekends from 10 AM to 5 PM. The **Clearview Farm** ☎ (978) 422-6442, 4 Kendall Hill Road, Sterling, also offers pick-your-own apples on weekends in September and October. You can also pick apples at the **Berlin Orchards** ☎ (978) 838-0463, 200 Central Street, Berlin, MA 01503, where hayrides take you out to the choicest spots.

Cultural Kicks

New England's cultural riches are plentiful and pervasive. Each new season heralds annual events and openings at concert halls and theaters in all six states, from homegrown theatrics such as Vermont's famous Bread and Puppet Theater ☎ (802) 525-3031, PO Box 153, Glover, VT 05839, to timeless traditions such as the Boston Symphony Orchestra's summer season at the Berkshire Hills' Tanglewood.

You could spend days enjoying **Boston**'s Museum of Fine Arts' (MFA) vast collections, gallery talks, and special lectures and films. Not far from the MFA is the elegant Isabella Stewart Gardner Museum, where architecture, art and formal gardens combine in an impressive aesthetic. The Huntington Theater Company and the American Repertory Theater present first-rate drama. Boston's Wang Center for the Performing Arts, in a building restored to its original Roaring Twenties luster, hosts the Boston Ballet Company. Each year more than a million people attend some 250 concerts

performed by the Boston Symphony Orchestra (BSO) at Symphony Hall. The Boston Pops puts on a series of concerts at the Hatch Shell on the Esplanade along the Charles River each summer, where thousands converge every Fourth of July — blankets and picnic baskets in tow — for the annual Independence Day Concert, culminating in an explosion of fireworks over the water.

During the summer season, the **Berkshire Hills** resonate with music, theater and dance, and BSO moves its headquarters to Tanglewood. Musicians playing on original instruments perform at the Aston Magna Festival in Great Barrington. Arias ring out from the stage of the Berkshire Opera House in Great Barrington. The town of Becket celebrates the return of the Jacob's Pillow Dance Festival, a 10-week season. You could indulge yourself every night of the week in July and August and still not see it all. For a calendar of events, contact the Berkshire Visitors Bureau ☎ (413) 443-9186 TOLL-FREE (800) 237-5747 FAX (413) 443-1970, Berkshire Common, Plaza Level, Pittsfield, MA 01201. Along with their events calendar, they put out *Culture in the Country*, a brochure in five languages listing cultural happenings. Each Thursday, the Calendar Section of the *Boston Globe* lists cultural events throughout Massachusetts.

Newport, Rhode Island, fills its summer music schedule to the brim with afternoon and evening concerts in the restored mansions along Bellevue Avenue. There are changing exhibits at the Newport Art Association on Bellevue Avenue, and the Newport Historical Society displays collections of Colonial art and early American glass and furniture. You may want to visit the Redwood Library on Bellevue Avenue; among its patrons were writers William and Henry James and Edith Wharton. Obtain an events schedule from the Newport County Convention and Visitors Bureau (see NEWPORT, page 222 in RHODE ISLAND.)

From Benefit Street's "Mile of History" on the east side to festive Federal Hill, Rhode Island's "Little Italy," the capital city of **Providence** is prized for its abundance of historic and cultural

Boston's Museum of Fine Arts.

attractions. Streets are lined with immaculately preserved Colonial, Federal, Greek revival and Victorian houses representing four centuries of history. The Tony Award-winning Trinity Repertory Company, the Rhode Island Philharmonic and the Museum of Art/ Rhode Island School of Design offer acclaimed theater, fine arts and orchestral music. The seasonal "Broadway" series at the Providence Performing Arts Center and the alternative theater and dance productions at AS220 round out the city's cultural calendar.

New Haven, Connecticut, home to Yale University, has earned a reputation as a proving ground for Broadway-bound plays. The university contributes mightily to the city's vibrant arts scene by staging major productions all year at the Yale Repertory Theater. Also known for a consistent menu of well-reviewed plays, the Long Wharf Theater rounds out the city's theater scene. Reminders of the state's contribution to American Impressionism spatter the Connecticut countryside. The "**Connecticut Impressionist Trail**" self-guided tour visits art colonies and museums that supported this movement. Send a self-addressed, stamped envelope to Connecticut Impressionist Art Trail, PO Box 793, Old Lyme, CT 06371, for a brochure or see WEB SITE www.arttrail.org.

The **New England coast**, from Rhode Island to Maine, has inspired artists for centuries. Three of New England's most prolific artists, N.C., Andrew and Jamie Wyeth, drew and continue to draw inspiration from the drama of the northeastern landscape. Cushing, Maine is the subject of many of Andrew Wyeth's paintings, including the iconic *Christina's World*. In Rockland, Maine, the Farnsworth Art Museum exhibits paintings by all three generations of Wyeths. Also on exhibit here are works by artists who summered and studied on the coast. The New York Ash Can School is well represented, as are the works of many Maine artists, including sculptor Louise Nevelson, a Maine native (see ROCKLAND, page 317 in MAINE).

Shop till You Drop

ANTIQUES

Hot spots for antique hunting in New England run from Newbury Street in Boston to the lakes and mountains region of western Maine. Three times a year — in mid-May, July and September — more than 2,000 dealers set up shop at the **Brimfield Antique Fair** in central Massachusetts. If you love antiques you won't want to miss one of these events.

In central Massachusetts, the **Berkshire County Antique Dealers Association** lists more than 60 members, most of them concentrated along and near Route 7. For a brochure, write to BCADA, PO Box 95, Sheffield, MA 01257. Other resources for antique dealers' listings are the **New Hampshire Antique Dealers Association**, PO Box 904, Wolfeboro, NH 03894, and the **National Art and Antique Dealers Association of America**

OPPOSITE: Courtyard of the Isabella Stewart Gardner Museum, Boston. ABOVE: A psychedelic sign announces the "Dollar-a-Pound" department at the Garment District vintage clothing store in Cambridge, Massachusetts.

((212) 826-9707 FAX (212) 319-0471 E-MAIL AADAA @dir-dd.com WEB SITE www.dir-dd.com/naadaa.html, 12 East 56th Street, New York, NY 10022.

ART AND CRAFTS

Shops throughout New England specialize in locally crafted merchandise. You can find durable and attractive children's pull toys and puzzles. Handmade cotton clothing, stuffed animals and kitchen items are also plentiful. Many are products of cottage industries that play an important role in the economies of small New England towns.

Vermont, especially, is noted for its high quality crafts: look for handmade quilts, beeswax candles, handcrafted furniture and blown glass. The **Vermont State Craft Center at the Equinox** ((802) 362-3321, Historic Route 7A, in Manchester, displays and sells the best works of the state's many artisans. The center also has galleries in Middlebury and Burlington (see under MIDDLEBURY, page 251, and BURLINGTON, page 259).

Information on craft fairs and galleries is available from the **League of New Hampshire Craftsmen** ((603) 224-3375, 205 North Main Street, Concord, NH 03302; the **Maine Crafts Association** ((207) 780-1807 WEB SITE www.mainecrafts.org, 15 Walton Street, Portland, ME 04103; and the **Vermont Crafts Council** ((802) 223-3380 WEB SITE www.vermontcrafts.org, PO Box 938, Montpelier, VT 05601.

BOSTON CITY SHOPPING

For a true study in contrasts, balance antique and crafts shopping with a day spent in the aisles of **Filene's Basement Store** on Washington Street (Downtown Crossing), a Boston institution for decades, known to locals as "the basement." Many a Brahmin elite and blue-collar worker have clothed their families well and thriftily from the goods offered by this original mother of all markdown emporiums. Along with fashions, the giftware, lingerie and luggage departments offer whopping bargains. Filene's has several satellite stores in suburban towns, but the Boston basement remains the best.

In the same neighborhood, the restored **Faneuil Hall Marketplace** jingles with commercial activity — though you'll see more tourists here than locals. The marketplace is lined with food shops selling bagels fresh from the oven, gargantuan fresh deli sandwiches, homemade pizza, steamed lobster, and cuisine from every corner of the world. Fortify yourself here before taking on the marketplace's upscale retail boutiques.

In the city's Back Bay, **Newbury Street** rivals New York City's Fifth Avenue with its fashionable couture salons, designer hair stylists, antique stores and world-class art galleries. At the upper end of Newbury Street, **Virgin Records** ranks among the largest record stores in the world. Late evenings, the atmosphere grows social here, with a midnight closing hour and dozens of listening-stations. For used books, browse the crammed shelves at **Avenue Victor Hugo Bookshop** ☎ (617) 266-7746, 339 Newbury, where you can pick up a disposable 25¢ romance novel along with a treasured limited edition. It's the best secondhand-book store in town. Another Newbury Street landmark store, **Louis of Boston** (men's clothing), resides in the former Museum of Natural History building, along with a chic café.

OUTLETS

Until a quarter of a century ago, all the New England factory towns had stores that sold their "accidented" products. A family could be dressed and shod for a fraction of the retail cost. Now most of these factories are closed, but outlet stores remain. They are not the great sources of bargains they once were, but the discounts are still sizeable, sometimes as much as 50 to 60 percent off regular prices. Products include seconds, remaindered stock, samples, and overruns of almost every name brand sold in the United States.

The most famous of the outlet towns is Freeport, Maine. Promoted to notoriety in 1912 when Leon L. Bean starting selling shilling boots to Maine hunters, the store reached legendary status in the 1980s when yuppie styles turned to down vests, plaid shirts and "Maine hunters." For 365 days a year, 24 hours a day, L.L. Bean parking lots are crammed with the cars of shoppers who are confronted inside the building with camping gear, hunting and fishing goods, wilderness and outdoor clothing and accessories. **L.L. Bean** ☎ (207) 865-4761 TOLL-FREE (800) 341-4341 is in plain view on Main Street, at No. 95, while the **Outlet** is craftily hidden one block off the main drag. Next door to the retail store you'll find **L.L. Kids**.

L.L. Bean has drawn a mob of other outlets and retailers to Freeport, transforming what was once a pretty, colonial town into a shopping mall. Still it's one of the more pleasant malls you'll find anywhere, with rows of neat, restored clapboard houses bearing famous brand names from Burberry's to Timberland. It's important to realize that not every store in Freeport is an outlet. So note carefully, or you'll end up spending more than you bargained for.

SOUVENIRS

You've got to bring something back for the folks at home, but what to buy? To help you decide, I've compiled my official "top-ten list of best New England souvenirs." Ready?

10. A chocolate "cow pie" from Tom and Sally's Handmade Chocolates in Brattleboro;

9. A used lobster trap from the Maine coast (makes a nice coffee table);

8. A dozen pints of Ben & Jerry's Cherry Garcia ice cream (named in honor of the Grateful Dead's Jerry Garcia), packed in dry ice;

7. A couple of live lobsters;

6. A gallon of Vermont maple syrup;

5. Boxer shorts emblazoned with the Harvard or Yale logo;

4. Silver or pewter ware wrought in designs originated by patriot Paul Revere;

3. A Red Sox baseball autographed by Pedro Martinez;

2. A wheel of Vermont cheddar;

and **1.** A couple of antique wooden duck decoys (they make good bookends).

Crafts demonstrations and galleries displaying locally made items are abundant in New Hampshire and Vermont.

Short Breaks

Because it's so packed with pleasures, New England excels in long weekends and quickie vacations. How about celebrating spring break on the island of **Nantucket** when millions of daffodils burst into bloom? With its antique houses, cobblestone streets, working windmill and old lighthouse, Nantucket harks back to its seventeenth-century whaling days. The Nantucket Steamship Authority runs Ferries to Nantucket year-round from Hyannis on Cape Cod.

From Hyannis on Cape Cod a 45-minute ferry ride brings you to **Martha's Vineyard**. Architecture buffs, especially, have a field day on the Vineyard. Handsome ship captains' houses line the streets of Edgartown and a community of several hundred Carpenter Gothic Victorian cottages graces Oak Bluffs. This island is only 20 miles (32 km) long and 10 miles (16 km) wide, so you can acquaint yourself with its rolling moors, colored cliffs, cove and salt marshes in short order. Explore the island by car or by bike (bring one along on the ferry or rent in Vineyard Haven). Sloops, schooners and dinghies, some available for day hire, beckon in the harbor.

North of Boston, **Cape Ann** makes a fine day trip any time of the year. But the best time is spring when migrating humpback whales arrive from their southern sojourn, breaching the waters within view of the whale-watching boats. **Marblehead** and **Salem**, the historic towns of Massachusetts' North Shore, are also within easy striking distance from Boston.

New Yorkers have been escaping for quick getaways into southern Connecticut and the Berkshires since the invention of the weekend. Connecticut's unspoiled upper shoreline draws weekenders who enjoy its three-century history of seafaring lore, beginning with its days of rigged schooners and clipper ships. When Mamie Eisenhower swung a bottle of champagne over the bow of the USS *Nautilus* in 1954

it was the first nuclear-powered ship in the world. Now the submarine is dry-docked in **Groton**, next to the Submarine Force Library and Museum. Both are open to the public. Recapture the days of America's shipbuilding industry at nearby **Mystic Seaport**, where the fastest clipper ships in the world were built. You'll want to spend a full day at the Seaport, starting with a tour of one of the more than 50 antique fishing vessels and yachts that fill its waterfront. On the *Charles W. Morgan*, a nineteenth-century wooden whaler, you can climb all over the ship, dive into the cramped crew's quarters, and join an impromptu round of shanty singing (see MYSTIC, page 188, and GROTON, page 194 in CONNECTICUT)

Maine's coastal villages and countless islands are just a few hours by bus or car from Boston. The state's mid-coast port towns of **Camden**, **Rockport** and **Rockland** offer superb cuisine, fine art at Rockland's Farnsworth Museum and day-cruising on windjammers. Stay at one of the many comfortable bed-and-breakfast inns in Camden within walking distance of shops and restaurants, or opt for the luxury of Samoset Resort on the ocean, in Rockport. Although the weather is best in Maine in the summer and fall, don't let the off-season keep you from exploring. Each season has its special virtues.

New Hampshire's southwestern **Mount Monadnock** is an easy drive from Boston. On arrival, a two-hour hike takes you to the top of the 3,165-ft (965-m) pinnacle, a fine spot to enjoy lunch while taking in the five-state view. In winter, you can enjoy the area's network of cross-country ski trails.

The capital city of **Providence**, Rhode Island, renowned for its magnificent architecture and historic landmarks, makes an enticing short break for walkers and garden lovers. The new Waterplace, a two-mile (just over three-kilometer) riverfront walkway interspersed with park benches and Venice-inspired footbridges, winds its way through the

Idyllic Isleboro lies three miles (five kilometers) off the Maine coast in Penobscot Bay.

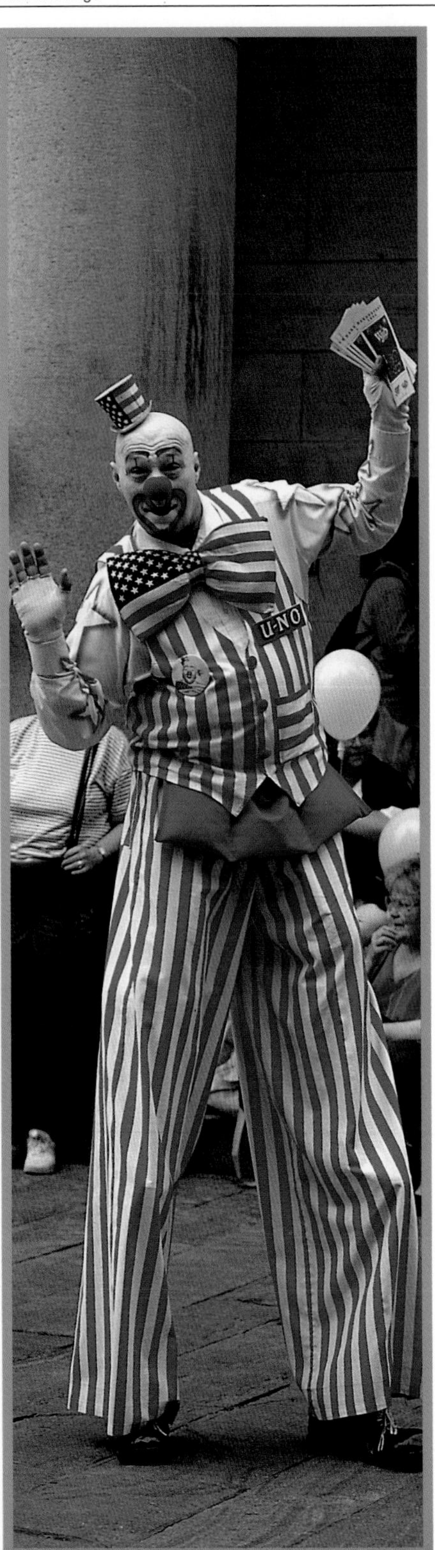

heart of the city to Narragansett Bay. An outdoor amphitheater on the grounds presents live shows. Guided walking tours of the city's historic East Side take place year round. Providence's Tony Award-winning Trinity Repertory Company, one of the top five repertory companies in the country, offers comedies and classics in two theaters.

Festive Flings

All year long, celebrations — many commemorating historical events or the changing of seasons — enliven New England's streets and fields. Spring bursts forth with flower shows, maple syrup harvesting and lobster bakes. Summer and fall bring country fairs selling handicrafts and local produce. In winter, snow sports, caroling and tree-lighting ceremonies bring warmth to chilly days and nights. Contact each state's tourism bureau for dates and details (see TOURIST INFORMATION, page 343 in TRAVELERS' TIPS).

SPRING

The **New England Spring Flower Show**, one of the nation's oldest and biggest, draws enthusiasts to Boston over a nine-day period in March. Beer tasting takes on a new dimension on March 17, when Irish-Americans celebrate **Saint Patrick's Day** by tipping green food coloring into their mugs. Boston's Saint Patrick's Day Parade is the nation's most festive… when it happens (it was interrupted for several years when parade organizers refused to allow a gay community group to participate). Nantucket celebrates its **Daffodil Festival** in April with a parade of antique autos upholstered with blossoms, as well as decorated shop windows and a flower show. Throughout March and into April, **maple-tree tapping** sweetens the states of Massachusetts, Maine, New Hampshire, and Vermont. On **Patriot's Day** in April, the **Boston Marathon** begins in Hopkinton and ends with lots of partying in Boston.

On the same day in Lexington and Concord the opening battles of the American Revolution are recreated as crowds of onlookers cheer.

Memorial Day weekend signals the official start of the summer season. The holiday commemorates the country's veterans with parades and celebrations over the three-day weekend. On this holiday Connecticut kicks off its **Lobster Weekend**, an old-fashioned lobster bake accompanied by live entertainment. In early June, Burlington, Vermont's **Discover Jazz Festival** takes to the streets.

SUMMER

Music festivals hit a high note in summer. Berkshire County in Massachusetts hosts two summer-long happenings. At Tanglewood, in Lenox, the **Boston Symphony Orchestra** performs. **Jacob's Pillow Dance Festival** in Becket, the oldest dance festival in the nation, presents the best in contemporary dance. There's the week-long **Vermont Mozart Festival** in Burlington. Newport, Rhode Island, buzzes with music in August, starting with the annual **Newport Folk Festival**, which is followed by the **Newport Jazz Festival**.

Parties, parades and fireworks throughout New England mark America's birthday, **Independence Day** (July 4). The legendary Boston Pops Fourth of July concert on the Charles River Esplanade culminates in a magnificent fireworks display. At the **Mashpee Powwow** — held in July in Mashpee, Massachusetts — Native Americans come together for three days to honor their heritage with dance competitions, drumming circles and athletic meets. In Maine, the **Bar Harbor Festival** serves up jazz and classical concerts for two weeks from late July into August. The world-famous **Newport Jazz Festival** returns each August with the likes of Aretha Franklin, Chic Corea and Dave Brubeck. The last month of summer brings a round of celebrations to Maine: In Rockland, the annual **Lobster Festival** takes place at the beginning of August, and many towns hold **blueberry festivals**, celebrating Maine's juicy role as the principal producer of blueberries in the nation.

OPPOSITE: A long-legged clown celebrates Independence Day in Boston. ABOVE: Plimoth Plantation recreates the lives of the Pilgrim settlers and their native helpers, complete with a yearly Thanksgiving feast.

The last hurrah, the **Vermont State Fair**, in Rutland, marks the close of the summer season.

AUTUMN

September heralds the start of the fall foliage season, with cooler nights and mild days. Food festivals happen every weekend with the arrival of harvest time. Vermont holds bushels of apple festivals throughout the state. The **Woodstock Apples and Crafts Fair** in early October is one of the best. The month-long **Stratton Arts Festival**, near Manchester, Vermont features the work of more than 200 artisans. **Columbus Day**, celebrated the second Monday in October, brings leaf-peepers out in droves. It's a good time to listen to folk music at one of the country concerts held this time of year. The **National Traditional Old-Time Fiddler's Contest** in Barre, Vermont, the **Cajun and Bluegrass Music, Dance, and Food Festival** at Stepping Stone Ranch, Escoheag, Rhode Island, and the **Rockport Folk Festival** in Rockport, Maine are the top choices for foot stomping and hand clapping. In Massachusetts, Labor Day weekend is celebrated with old-time fervor in Lawrence, famous for the history-making **Bread and Roses Strike** of 1912, which it commemorates with an annual festival. In October, South Carver, Massachusetts celebrates its cranberry crop with a **Cranberry Festival**; it's worth going just to watch the growers wading up to their chests through millions of flame-red floating berries.

WINTER

Celebrate **Thanksgiving**, the fourth Thursday in November, in Plymouth, Massachusetts where you can partake in a **Pilgrims' procession**, a traditional dinner and a Thanksgiving service. Once Thanksgiving is over, Plimoth Plantation preparations for **Christmas Day** begin in earnest with tree lighting, caroling and candlelight strolls. Boston has two **Christmas tree-lighting ceremonies** in December, one on Boston Common and another at the Prudential Center — accomplished with the merry accompaniment of a shiny brass ensemble.

Several mansions in Newport, Rhode Island open for the holidays, and for several weeks before Christmas there are **candlelight tours of Colonial dwellings**. During the first week of December, Nantucket Island ushers in the season with a **Christmas Shoppers' Stroll**, carol singing, theater performances and craft sales. **First Night**, a New Year's Eve community festival, began in Boston and spread to scores of towns in New England and elsewhere. Each year, for the price of a First Night button, families and friends gain entry to a dazzling array of events. Participants, often wearing elaborate costumes or masks, stroll the streets, listen to jazz, and watch theater, street puppets and art installations.

Snow festivals and ski/snowboard competitions reach fever pitch in January and February at ski resorts. Stowe, Vermont, holds a **Winter Carnival** and Brookfield, Vermont, puts on its annual **Ice Harvest Festival**. Stowe's 10-day **Winter Carnival** has a different theme every year, climaxing with a village-wide ice sculpture exhibition and contest. Dog-sled competitions, ski races and church suppers are highlights. Other festive events keep Vermonters reveling in snow season. There's a masquerade ball at the **Mad River Valley Winter Carnival** and jazz concerts at the **Brattleboro Winter Carnival**.

Galloping Gourmets

New England cuisine, from its beginnings, took inspiration from the good earth's bounty. At the Pilgrims' first Thanksgiving dinner, roast duck and goose, steamed clams, venison, leeks, watercress, wild plums and wines graced the harvest table. Later, immigrants popularized baked beans and boiled dinners. (When I asked a local for his New England boiled dinner recipe he said, "Bah… boil some water and throw everything in the 'fridge into the pot. Let it stay in there for a few hours, then serve it with lotsa vinegah.")

Despite New England's humble culinary history, in the last decade a renaissance has occurred. These days the New England dining scene offers outstanding, innovative cuisine coupled with traditional New England fare. You'll find good **seafood** almost everywhere; some say it's the best in the country. Seafood forms the basis of many local dishes. **Chowders**, made with clams, corn, or white fish, appear on menus in diners and dining rooms everywhere. Boston's annual clam chowder cook-off is a hotly contested event, with the finest regional chefs competing. Restaurants serve **lobster** boiled, baked and stuffed, as part of a salad or a pie, and as the base for lobster bisque.

City food shops dramatize New England's ethnic heritage. You can buy moon cakes made from rice flour at a bakery in Boston's Chinatown, and in Providence's "Little Italy," indulge yourself with cream-filled Neapolitans and rum cakes.

At inland restaurants and country inns, traditional fare still dominates most menus. **Boston baked beans** are rarely served, but **Boston cream pie** and **Indian pudding**, a combination of cornmeal and molasses, are popular menu items. **Apple pan dowdy**, **cornbread**, **mincemeat pie** and other old-fashioned dishes can still be found. **Corn** lovers, who know enough to eat it shortly after it's picked, eagerly await the first crop of fresh corn in July. Connoisseurs look for the "butter and sugar" variety, a blend of yellow and white kernels. **Pumpkins**, harvested

LEFT: Harvesting cranberries in Carver on Massachusetts's south shore. ABOVE: A farm stand in York, Maine, offers a cornucopia of local produce.

before the first frost, are a mainstay of pies. Orchards from Connecticut to Vermont encourage fruit purchases with "pick-your-own" sales, and farm stands display jugs of pressed **apple cider** and bushel baskets of crisp apples (see FAMILY FUN, page 42). New England's apple harvest produces many varieties. Look for Macintosh, Empire, Northern Spy, Cortland, and Paula Reds. **Cranberries**, harvested from Cape Cod's bogs, are served in a tart sauce with turkey dinners or pressed into juice. Maine **blueberries** crop up in pies, scones, sauces, and toppings for pancakes and waffles.

All those Holsteins in Vermont contribute to the state's production of choice **cheddar cheese** and its famous **Ben and Jerry's ice cream**. Try Vermont **maple syrup** on your morning pancakes. Sold in colorful tins, the syrup packs well for further tastings at home.

Conditions for growing grapes are best in southern New England, where some vintners have produced quite palatable **wines**. Chicama Vineyards on Martha's Vineyard, and Sakonnet Vineyards in Little Compton, Rhode Island, produce commendable table wines (see SPECIAL INTERESTS, below). Fruit wines are another regional delicacy. Nashoba Valley Winery, in Bolton, Massachusetts (see FAMILY FUN, page 42), makes delightful wines from pears, peaches and raspberries.

Microbreweries, too, have sprung up around New England. The Boston Brewing Company was one of the first to popularize the brewpub craze by producing Samuel Adam's dark lager. The Brewhouse, in the Lenox Hotel at 710 Boylston Street, Boston, serves six seasonal varieties in addition to its year-round drafts. In summer there is a cherry wheat beer; in late fall Cranberry Lambic is on tap. Elsewhere in New England, New Hampshire has the venerable Portsmouth Brewery, and in Brattleboro there is McNeill's Brewery ☎ (802) 254-2553, 90 Elliot Street, and Greg Noonan's famous Vermont Pub and Brewery ☎ (802) 865-0500, 144 College Street, in Burlington.

Special Interests

New England offers visitors a chance to broaden their knowledge and skills with learning vacations that take in both the cultural and the natural resources of the region. And because it is a magnet for artists and artisans, master chefs and microbrewers, the region has a roster of some fine teachers.

FOOD AND WINE

The **Silo Cooking School** ☎ (860) 355-0300, Upland Road, New Milford, CT 06776, in the Litchfield Hills, was founded in 1972 by Ruth Henderson and her husband, New York Pops founder and director Skitch Henderson. They offer more than 70 classes, from March to December, emphasizing ethnic and regional cuisine and wine selection. Classes are held in a converted barn on their 200-acre (81-hectare) property, Hunt Hill Farms.

Wine and its proper service is the touchstone of the **Master Chef Series** at Sakonnet Vineyards, in the rolling countryside of coastal Little Compton, Rhode Island. October through June, the winery features a regional chef who conducts a full-day demonstration and class. Recent guest chefs have included Casey Riley of the Agora Restaurant in the Westin Hotel, Providence, and Wayne Gibson, executive chef of the Castle Hill Inn and Resort, Newport. Should you want to spend the night in Little Compton, make reservations at **The Roost**, the vineyard farmhouse, renovated as a bed and breakfast inn with three guestrooms (mid-range). Contact both at ☎ (401) 635-8486 TOLL-FREE (800) 919-4637, 162 West Main Road, Little Compton, RI 02837. In New Hampshire, classes of **A Taste of the Mountains Cooking School** are conducted at the Bernerhof Inn ☎ (603) 383-9132 TOLL-FREE (800) 548-8007 FAX (603) 383-0809, PO Box 240, Glen, NH 03838. The three-day and weekend classes are offered in spring and early

winter, and the price includes lodging and meals at the inn. The classes focus on the preparation of contemporary cuisine and favor a "hands-on" approach.

PHOTOGRAPHY

Rockport, Maine is home to the **Maine Photographic Workshops** ☎ (207) 236-8581 TOLL-FREE (877) 577-7700, 2 Central Street, Rockport, ME 04856, founded by writer and photographer David Lyman. The summer program lists 100 one-week workshops and master classes where photographers, filmmakers and photojournalists of varying backgrounds and skills converge for a week or more of intensive learning and networking, instructed by well-known photographers. While Rockport's remoteness lends itself to concentration, it's accessible from Route 1, the tourist route along the Maine coast. The nearby village of Camden offers wonderful dining, shopping, boating and theater. Also a Kodak representative gives three-hour free photographic workshops and walking/shooting hikes almost daily during July and August at **Acadia National Park**. Contact the park for information on ☎ (207) 288-3338.

ART AND CRAFTS

Each summer, the **Woodenboat School** ☎ (207) 359-4651 FAX (207) 359-8920 WEB SITE www.woodenboat.com, PO Box 78, Naskeag Road, Brooklin, ME 04616, teaches the craft of boat building, from canoe repair to sailcraft. Marine photography and coastal seamanship are also in the curriculum.

On Cape Cod, at **Castle Hill Center for the Arts** ☎ (508) 349-7511 WEB SITE www.castlehill.org, Truro, classes take place in a nineteenth-century barn. Some 600 students participate each summer in the classes, lectures and forums taught by professional artists. Painting, photography and writing workshops are offered. Across the Sound on Nantucket, the **Nantucket Island School of Design and the Arts** ☎ (508) 228-9248 WEB SITE www.nisda.org has summer classes for children, teens and adults. Past offerings have included a wide range of activities: mixed media, *plein air* painting, pottery, printmaking, Japanese flower arranging, song writing, polarity yoga and water

The Equinox Resort, Manchester, Vermont, has an unusual array of programs, including a spa, an off-road driving school and courses in falconry.

garden design. Lodging is available for the one-week sessions that run Monday to Friday from 9 AM to 1 PM.

OUTDOOR SKILLS

Urban and suburban dwellers eager to test themselves out-of-doors should check out the **Hurricane Island Outward Bound School** ☎ (207) 594-5548 TOLL-FREE (866) 746-9771 WEB SITE www.hurricaneisland.org, PO Box 429, Rockland, ME 04841, in Penobscot Bay. This training school for wilderness survival skills claims that students should be prepared for the "most miserable, most wonderful days of your life." Two weeks of backpacking, rock climbing, or maneuvering canoes and sailboats past bay islets is standard. Courses last eight days to three months.

Along with their guided trips, the **Appalachian Mountain Club (AMC)** puts out a catalog twice a year listing hundreds of workshops and courses, including outdoor skills such as rock climbing and bushwhacking, natural history courses exploring the mysteries of herbal medicine and mountain weather, and art classes such as nature photography (see THE GREAT OUTDOORS, page 29 for more on the AMC).

Taking a Tour

Those who prefer to leave the planning and driving to professionals can sign up for a guided tour.

ADVENTURE TOURS

New England Hiking Holidays ☎ (603) 356-9696 TOLL-FREE (800) 869-0949 WEB SITE www.nehikingholidays.com, PO Box 1648, North Conway, NH 03860, specializes in country inn-to-inn tours. Two- to eight-day trips, for all levels of experience, take place from May to October. The organization keeps groups to a maximum of 16 people, accompanied by two guides.

Ecological study tours are the specialty of **Earthwatch** ☎ (978) 461-0081 TOLL-FREE (800) 776-0188 E-MAIL info@earthwatch.org, 3 Clock Tower Place, Suite 100, Maynard, MA 01754, whose volunteers assist field researchers in New England and around the world.

For people over the age of 55, **Elderhostel** ☎ (617) 426-7788 TOLL-FREE (877) 426-8056 FAX (617) 426-0701 TOLL-FREE FAX (877) 426-2166, 75 Federal Street, Boston, MA 02110-1941, provides educational adventures in Vermont, Massachusetts, New Hampshire, Rhode Island and Maine.

A host of organizations offer cycling tours of varying lengths and degrees of difficulty, from country rambles to grueling off-road touring. Many of them not only provide experienced guides who lead the way, explaining state sights and sounds, but also carry most of your gear in support vans and make arrangements for overnight lodging and meals. Be sure to inquire about what's included in the touring package.

Backroads ☎ (510) 527-1555 TOLL-FREE (800) 462-2848 FAX (510) 527-1444, 801 Cedar Street, Berkeley, CA 94710-1800, specializes in active adventures in an irresistible backdrop of luxury lodging and gourmet dining. Three New England itineraries are offered: Vermont's Northeast Kingdom, Vermont's

southern river valleys, and a tour of Martha's Vineyard, Nantucket and Cape Cod.

Escape Routes ☎ (802) 746-8943, PO Box 685, Pittsfield, VT 05762, offers mountain adventures for cyclists who desire an out-of-the-ordinary experience. The trips travel backcountry only, including seldom-used dirt roads, old farm lanes, and logging trails. Country inns provide lodging. Two- to five-day tours are available, at beginner and intermediate levels. Mountain bikes required; rentals are available.

COACH TOURS

I've provided contact numbers for the following tour companies; however, you need only contact your travel agent to get information or make arrangements to join one of these tours.

Globus Tours ☎ (303) 797-2800 TOLL-FREE (800) 851-0728, extension 7518, 5301 South Federal Circle, Littleton, CO 80123, is a Swiss-owned company offering deluxe coach tours. Their "Jaunt Through New England" departs from New York, taking in Newport, Boston, Salem, Kennebunkport, North Conway, Montpelier, Stowe and Shelburne, before continuing down the Adirondack chain back to the Big Apple. They offer a similar trip during fall foliage season. With comparable itineraries, their sister company, **Cosmos** (contact Globus) has less expensive motor coach tours with lodging in modest hotels. **Brendan Tours** ☎ (818) 785-9696 TOLL-FREE (800) 421-8446 FAX (818) 902-9876, 15137 Califa Street, Van Nuys, CA 91411, does an eight-day fall foliage tour out of Boston with overnights in York Beach, North Conway, Brattleboro, Sturbridge and Falmouth. **Caravan** ☎ (312) 321-9800 TOLL-FREE (800) 227-2826 FAX (312) 321-9845, 401 North Michigan Avenue, Chicago, IL 60611, also does the tried-and-true leaf-peeping tour. Their motor coach takes Boston as its starting point, heading south to Plimoth Plantation, then on to the Breakers at Newport, Mystic, Historic Deerfield, the Green Mountains, Woodstock, the White Mountains, Portland, Kennebunkport, Walden Pond, Lexington and Concord — all in one week.

OPPOSITE: A pastel cruiser moored at Gloucester on Cape Ann, Massachusetts. ABOVE: A must-see on the American history trail, the North Bridge in Concord, Massachusetts, spans the scenic Concord River.

Welcome to New England

"We're from *old* England," said the elderly British gentleman in the next seat, tapping me on the shoulder. "*Old* Gloucester, to be exact," he continued with a cackle. We were touring Provincetown on Cape Cod, the precise spot where the Pilgrims first set foot on the New World. "Oh?" I replied, "Welcome to *New* England, then!"

My new acquaintance's quip was a reminder: Americans come from somewhere. In this land of fresh starts and constant flux, we not only forget that our roots lie in Europe, Africa, and indeed in every corner of the globe — we forget we have roots at all. Yet, while Americans may tend to think they sprang up fresh and new, history-less, free of the weight (and significance) of ancestry, there remain a handful of remarkable places in this country where history is palpable. New England is foremost among these rare spots — America's strongest link, historically and culturally, to the Old World.

A powerful draw for visitors, this Old World connection is most notable in New England's urban areas — nowhere more so than in Boston, with its meandering streets and its merciful human scale. Throughout the region, cultural memory remains strong, whether it be evidenced in sidewalk cafés, pastoral countryside or, more subtly, in its inhabitants' habit of dropping their "Rs" to "pahk the cah in Hahvahd Yahd."

Yet, New England is also profoundly American — from the tips of its modern skylines to the toes of its busy-busy inhabitants. And for all that, the thread of history continues. New England's maritime past comes alive in Portland, Mystic, Newport and Boston. The story of the first settlers is reenacted each day at Plymouth and Salem. The American Revolution is retold, battle by bloody battle, in Lexington and Concord. New England breathes the stories that built it, evident too in the region's distinguished literary tradition, from colonial-era poet Anne Bradstreet (1612–72) continuing through generations of writers — some native to the region, others drawn here for education and inspiration: Henry Wadsworth Longfellow, Ralph Waldo Emerson, Henry David Thoreau, Louisa May Alcott, Herman Melville, Edgar Allan Poe, Emily Dickinson, Sarah Orne Jewett, Henry James, T.S. Eliot, Wallace Stevens and Robert Frost.

Fortunately for tourists, New England's rich history is packed into a relatively small area, considering the overpowering scale of the rest of the country. Somewhat smaller than Great Britain and less than half the size of California, New England is composed of six states, including five of the original thirteen colonies. It occupies the northeast corner of the United States, bordered by New York to the south and west, and by Quebec and New Brunswick to the north. More consequential than any of these political boundaries is the region's eastern frontier, the Atlantic Ocean, gateway to the world through dozens of ports scattered along the long, crenellated coastline.

This glorious coastline is another good reason to visit New England — just ask the millions of visitors who come each year to revel on the sandy shores of Cape Cod, or the Sunday afternoon sailors in Massachusetts Bay, or island-hopping kayakers in Maine…

Like its coastline, New England's mountainscape has been drawing pleasure-seekers since the eighteenth century. Early visitors to New Hampshire's White Mountains called themselves "rusticators." They took long rambles and stayed in grand hotels. Only a handful of the grand mountain resorts still stand, but the wilderness remains intact, preserved in state forests and parks that continue to draw sightseers and skiers in greater numbers every year. Hikers, especially, love New England for its share of the famed Appalachian Trail, 654 miles (1,046 km) of which run through Connecticut, Massachusetts, Vermont, New Hampshire and Maine.

What is *New* England, really? Having lived over a decade here has only complicated this question for me. So, I leave the parting shot to a native New Englander, overheard one day at Honey Pot Orchards in Stowe, Massachusetts. It was a perfect autumn day, the orchard brimming with amateur apple pickers. The sunlight shimmered, and a breeze rippled the air as we brought our booty back in a wagon stuffed with hay. A woman next to me sighed with contentment. "I love this," she said. "It's so New England-y." And so it was.

Late fall — the afterglow — in New Hampshire's White Mountains.

The
Majestic
Bellowphone

New England and Its People

HISTORICAL BACKGROUND

Around 10,000 years ago, with the end of the last ice age, the first Native Americans, called Paleo-Indians, began to arrive in New England in their migration from the south and the west. Originally, these bands followed the seasonal migration of elk and caribou. Gradually, while northern tribes continued to subsist on hunting, fishing and gathering, southern New England tribes shifted to a semi-nomadic pattern. In summer they grew corn, beans, squash, berries and tobacco, and harvested shellfish, fish and shore animals. In winter they traveled in small clans and hunting groups into the interior and northern watersheds, returning with the moose, caribou and deer.

Across the American continent, native people can be divided into five major linguistic groups; those in the northeast belonged to the Algonquin group. Southern New England had larger numbers of natives than did northern New England, with the Mohegans and Pequots in what became Connecticut, the Narragansetts in Rhode Island, and the Wampanoags in Massachusetts. Northern New England tribes included the Kennebecs, Penobscots, Pocumtucks, Nehantics and Nipmucks. In the early 1600s, some 60,000 Native Americans inhabited the New England region. Barely 70 years later there were just 10,000.

EARLY EXPLORERS

Someday, archaeologists may discover incontrovertible proof that Irish, Spanish or Portuguese sailors reached New England well before Columbus came to the New World in 1492. The earliest evidence indicates that the Norse explored the northeast coast of the continent about 3,000 years ago. They may have established a settlement, called Vinland, but if so, they were expelled by the native inhabitants.

Native Americans were to remain undisturbed for the next two and a half millennia until, in 1492, Christopher Columbus arrived in the New World, the first of a long line of European explorers. Five years later, the English explorer Giovanni Cabota (John Cabot) visited the New England coast and claimed the territory for the King of England, Henry VII. In 1524 Giovanni da Verrazano sailed along the New England coast and named Rhode Island. The first group of colonists, led by Bartholomew Gosnold, landed on Cape Cod and Martha's Vineyard, but their settlement lasted only three weeks. In 1603 Samuel de Champlain established the first European settlement at the Saint Croix River between what are now Canada and the United States, and claimed the coast as far south as Cape Cod for France. Four years later, John Smith arrived on the scene, surveying the New England region and naming it for the first time in *A Description of New England*.

PILGRIMS AND PURITANS

It was four days before Christmas, 1620, when the *Mayflower* weighed anchor off what is now Plymouth, Massachusetts. The settlers had left England on September 16, intending to go to Jamestown. They first reached land on November 19 at Provincetown, on Cape Cod, where they remained but a few weeks. Among the 102 passengers aboard the *Mayflower* were 40 members of a group of Christian separatists, later dubbed Pilgrims. Before heading onward to the mainland and disembarking at what they were to call Plymouth Rock, the group drew up a charter, which they termed the Mayflower Compact. This document established a temporary government based on the principle of the will of the majority: as such, it set the stage for the American Revolution and the writing of the Constitution of the United States 167 years thereafter.

Despite such a lofty beginning, half of the Pilgrims perished from disease and starvation during the first winter. Squanto, a native who had learned English, discovered the survivors, aided them, and negotiated a 50-year peace accord between the settlers and the Wampanoag Indians. Severe adversities notwithstanding, more settlers soon began to arrive; the *Mayflower* had set off a stampede of immigration that forever changed

Still life with fog: A pier in Mystic, Connecticut, is loaded with lobster traps, while a weekender's yacht awaits offshore.

the continent. In 1621, another group of Pilgrims arrived. In 1630, John Winthrop and his Puritans founded the Massachusetts Bay Colony. The settlement, based on theocratic principles, included "the good town of Boston," which rapidly became the hub of New England business, cultural and intellectual life. By 1637, several thousand colonists lived along the Massachusetts coast and as far inland as Concord. By 1640, settlements had spread to Rhode Island, where Roger Williams founded Providence in 1636. In Connecticut, Windsor was founded in 1633, Wethersfield in 1634 and Hartford in 1635.

By 1680, the European colonists had wrested control of the region from the Indians, whose population was devastated by diseases introduced by the Europeans. Armed conflict — most notably the Pequot War in 1637, which wiped out the Pequot tribe, and King Philip's War from 1675 to 1678 — also contributed to the natives' dwindling numbers.

The Changing Landscape

The changes wrought by the European immigrants were to effect not only the human population of the region, but the natural world as well. As migration from Europe turned from trickle to torrent, the ecology of the land changed, and its diversity and bounty were diminished. In sharp contrast to the native view of their world, Europeans had introduced a capitalist ethic that viewed the land and its resources as commodities. Once, flocks of passenger pigeons darkened the sky. Fish were so plentiful in the streams they could be scooped out with a net. The forests were filled with animals that are now legend: caribou, wolves, eastern buffalo and panthers. Greater and greater numbers of humans, the clearing of forests and the grazing of cattle, pigs and sheep disturbed the ecological balance that flourished within the native's caretaking of the land.

The Revolutionary War

As New World settlements grew, British mismanagement of its American possessions created mistrust and anger in the colonies. A stubborn king and a politically maladroit parliament burdened the colonies with unreasonable taxes, exacted to fund England's wars against France and Canada. The Acts of Trade required that the colonies trade only with England and its markets. The Tea Act, the Stamp Act, the Townshend Acts and the Intolerable Acts — all were perceived in the colonies as either oppressive or punitive and aroused increasing defiance. "No taxation without representation" became the rallying cry that moved the colonists towards open rebellion.

By 1775, under the leadership of Bostonians such as Samuel Adams, James Otis and John Hancock, Massachusetts had become a catalyst uniting the 13 colonies. Their speeches provoked protests that eventually exploded into bloody revolution when on April 19, 1775, British soldiers fired on the Minutemen, as the colonial soldiers were termed, on the Lexington Green, Massachusetts — the first time mutual hostility became open warfare. Two months later, on June 17, the Battle of Bunker Hill was fought not on the hill for which it was named but on nearby Breed's Hill. In this battle, British regulars defeated the colonial militia. Nonetheless, the colonists put up a worthy fight, and the battle served to raise the patriots' spirits and strengthened their determination to sustain the long and bloody revolution until independence was achieved with the surrender of General Cornwallis at Yorktown, New York, in 1781.

THE INDUSTRIAL REVOLUTION

With the signing of the Treaty of Versailles, in which Great Britain recognized the independence of the United States, Americans began to trade freely around the world. Fishing, whaling and the china trade made fortunes for seafarers and merchants. When the nineteenth century saw a decline in the maritime economy, those fortunes were, during the industrial revolution, invested in new ventures. New England was a natural location for the textile industry, with its abundance of waterpower, easy access to cotton grown in the South, and cheap labor. From the early 1800s, textile factory towns sprouted along New England's riverways. For the workers in company towns, hours were long, wages ridiculously low, and every aspect of life away from work was rigidly controlled. For the Lowells and the Cabots who created these factory towns, profits were astronomical.

As the Civil War approached, textile factory workers, for the most part young women, proved a receptive audience for the New England abolitionists, and many of them became caught up in the movement.

CIVIL WAR AND THE DECLINE OF NEW ENGLAND

Galvanized in 1851–1852 by Connecticut-born Harriet Beecher Stowe's *Uncle Tom's Cabin*, as well as the essays and oratory of northern abolitionists, New Englanders led the nation in the movement to abolish slavery. While it was becoming more and more repugnant to northerners, southerners saw slavery as essential to their agrarian economy. It was ultimately such social, economic and moral differences between North and South that led to the American Civil War in 1861, when the Confederacy, consisting of 11 southern states, attempted to withdraw from the Union. By 1865 the war was over, slavery had been abolished and the Union preserved.

As the Civil War came and went, New England was changing again. A declining population was the first hint of transformation. Many men did not return from the war, while many others headed off with their families to claim homesteads on the more fertile soil of the West. Whole communities vanished in these years, leaving abandoned farms to melt into the surrounding woodland. Industries vanished too: The discovery of oil in Pennsylvania in 1857 brought an end to the whaling era, as whale-oil lamps gave way to kerosene. Similarly, faster, more capacious steamships docking at the deeper ports to the South replaced New England clipper ships. Textile manufacturers moved to the as-yet nonindustrialized South, where low wages still prevailed. In 1929, the stock market crash was the final blow to the region's faltering economy.

THE HIGH-TECHNOLOGY REVOLUTION

As factors such as cheap labor in the southern states and abroad drew the manufacturing industries away from New England, the region sought out new sources of income. sources of income. Although fishing had been a prime resource since pre-colonial times, post-World War II technology sent fish stocks plummeting and essentially destroyed the industry as an economic staple. Faced with a shortage of both natural resources and cheap labor, Boston switched its economic base from brawn to brains.

The region regained economic stability toward the middle of the twentieth century through a combination of financial services and high technology industries. With the decline of the computer hardware industry in the 1970s, New England looked to its colleges and universities for economic renewal. Drawing on a deep well of technical know-how and a pool of highly educated workers, the area entered the twenty-first century with a robust economy that played to its strengths in software, information and biotechnology.

America's past is alive and well in Boston. Here, a convincing Benjamin Franklin — writer, philosopher, scientist and patriot — greets visitors to the Old South Meeting House on Washington Street.

GEOGRAPHY AND CLIMATE

New England's most prominent geological feature is the Appalachian range, the northern extension of a mountain chain that stretches from Alabama to Newfoundland, running north and south across five of the six New England states. The Appalachians are unspeakably ancient, one of the oldest geological formations on earth. Created 570 to 136 million years ago by tectonic action, and since folded, eroded and uplifted time after time, they were once as mighty as the Himalayas. Their present form, carved by glaciers and eroded over eons, is but a third of their once lavish heights. A mere stump when compared to the peaks of the more youthful Rockies, the highest peak in New England is Mount Washington at 6,288 ft (1,916 m). Even so, it's tall enough for some challenging hiking — not the least because its northerly position has endowed its summit with some of the country's most extreme weather.

Like New England's mountains, its rivers run primarily north to south, swinging east to meet the sea at wide, island-filled bays from Maine's Bar Harbor to Connecticut's Long Island Sound. Many of New England's rivers keep their Native American names — the Merrimac, Penobscot, Kennebec and the 407-mile (655-km) Connecticut. This last runs the length of western New England, separating Vermont from New Hampshire and bisecting Massachusetts and Connecticut before it empties into Long Island Sound at Old Saybrook.

To the north, the New England coastline is shredded into hundreds of bays and promontories. The United States' only fjord, Somes Sound, nearly bisects Mount Desert Island in Maine. Moving south, the red, rocky coastline begins to intermix with sandy beaches. In Massachusetts, sandy Cape Cod is an L-shaped peninsula that juts out into the Atlantic, cradling Massachusetts Bay. The southern part of this sand bar is a glacial moraine (an area marking the end of a glacier where rocks and dirt are deposited), while the northern part is formed by the movement of ocean currents, which have eroded the southern arm of the cape. We can thank the glaciers for the charming islands of Martha's Vineyard and Nantucket, too.

The New England coastline plays a vital part in the region's dramatic weather patterns. Although New England shares the latitudes of Spain, Italy and southern France, its weather, for great portions of the year, is far from balmy. The warm Gulf Stream bypasses New England, leaving the icy Labrador Current to barge in from Greenland — sucked into the vacuum as it were. This set of circumstances is responsible for the northeastern states' legendary winters. Despite the chilling effects of the Labrador Current, coastal areas experience some moderating influences, seeing far less snowfall than do inland areas and experiencing milder temperatures all year long.

The weather is an obsession among New Englanders — perhaps because there's so much of it. In the northern three states, well inland, deep powder blankets the landscape from November to April, providing superb skiing. Along the coast, winter is unpredictable: Sometimes it's an ordeal of sleet, rain and slush; sometimes blizzards blanket the land; occasionally, it turns almost balmy.

Spring, otherwise known as the Mud Season, offers ample compensation for its wet and chill temperament in an explosion of daffodils and narcissus. Late spring is a time for paddling sports, when snowmelt swells rivers and streams. And, lest we forget, those cool spring days are responsible for making the sweet maple syrup flow and the sugarhouses steam.

New England's mild summers draw travelers from southern states to cool mountain trails and refreshing waters. Late summer brings hot days, turning lake and shore beaches into jubilant throngs of sun worshippers. Fishermen cast and troll for trout, salmon, pickerel and bass. The ocean bays fill with sails and spinnakers. Rafters, kayakers and canoeists ride the rivers and hikers wander the hills.

Mother Nature's "must-see," autumn brings shades of scarlet, crimson, vermilion, yellow, gold and orange; as the leaves fall, the white birches and tan beeches and oaks stand out against the darker firs, spruce, tamaracks and pines.

Seasoned travelers know there are no guarantees when it comes to weather. That old saw, "If you don't like the weather, wait a minute," is perhaps nowhere more apt than in New England. But whether you're looking forward to powdery snow, a blanket of autumn color, a spring paddle or the warm buzz of a summer beach, New England has your weather, and in generous quantities.

OPPOSITE: In New Hampshire at Enfield's Shaker Inn, guests stay in a restored Shaker village.
ABOVE: The interior of this West Stockbridge, Massachusetts barn is to become a modern dwelling, but the exterior will remain essentially unchanged, preserving a traditional New England landscape.

Boston

"No other city in the nation so resonates with story, with history," declared a recent *Boston Globe* article. Founded by the Puritans in 1630, Boston played a starring role in America's youthful career as a British colony, and in the nation's battle for independence. A walking tour of the city, the Freedom Trail, connects a series of legendary landmarks — the home of Paul Revere, the Bunker Hill monument — and along it visitors relive the story of the American Revolution. Narrow, colonial-era streets twist and turn through famous neighborhoods — Beacon Hill, the North End, Charlestown. Architecturally, the city is a result of historic preservation and boom-and-bust building cycles. These often-opposing forces have created a skyline where glass and steel skyscrapers alternate with the gold dome of the State House, the glowing stained-glass clock of the Custom House Tower, and the white spire of the Old North Church.

Built largely before the advent of the automobile, Boston was made for walking. Visitors quickly learn that to step out in any direction from the Boston Common is to have a ready-made itinerary: the wide avenues, chic restaurants and shopping of the Back Bay; the cobblestone alleys of the North End; the gaslight-illuminated slopes of Beacon Hill; the raucous sidewalks of Chinatown. Even the yawning pits and towering cranes of the "Big Dig" public works project compel city walkers to stop and stare.

At once charming, cosmopolitan and almost European in style, Boston is also the epitome of Yankee New England, with a stolid, industrious streak that matches its Puritan origins. More conservative than New York, Boston, with a population of 600,000 (three million, if one includes the city's outlying suburbs), is also much smaller than its colossal cousin to the south. Boston has been called the "Athens of America" because of its concentration of colleges and universities. This student population continuously breathes new life into the music scene, which has launched the careers of Aerosmith, the Cars, Jonathan Richman, Boston, and the Pixies, to name but a few. Also called "The Hub," Boston is the undisputed cultural capital of New England, boasting the Boston Symphony Orchestra, excellent university theater, the Museum of Fine Arts and a host of other cultural allures.

Because it is surrounded by water, the heart of Boston is not at the center of the city but at its northeasternmost corner. To the south of this center is Fort Point Channel area, where you'll find the Boston Tea Party Museum, the Boston Children's Museum, and artists' studios. To the north is Boston Inner Harbor, separating the downtown from Logan Airport. To the west is the Charles River Basin, across which is Boston's "Left Bank" neighbor, Cambridge — a crazy-quilt mix of cosmopolitan neighborhoods itself, and with a more casual, rootsy alternative to dining and nightlife. It's also the site of two of the nation's most prestigious universities.

BACKGROUND

THE PURITANS

John Winthrop and his Puritans are said to have "stolen" much of the Shawmut Peninsula from a hermit preacher named Reverend William Blackstone to establish the city of Boston. Following on the heels of the Puritans, settlers in ever-increasing numbers came to Boston, making it the hub of trade and commerce in the English colonies, and the most prosperous city in the English colonial empire. The city owed much of its rapid growth to its fine deepwater harbor and its fishing and merchant fleet which by

LEFT: Boston's State House was designed by Charles Bullfinch and completed in 1795 on land that originally belonged to John Hancock. ABOVE: Fourth of July festivities.

the eighteenth century was the third largest in the English-speaking world. However, when the Crown and Parliament imposed upon the colonies a series of heavy taxes and trade regulations, Boston's patriots led the break from the Mother Country.

Cradle of Independence

Years before the Revolution, the Massachusetts House of Representatives denied the right of Parliament to tax the colonies without representation, and it was Boston's revolutionaries whose speeches at meeting after meeting rallied their compatriots to unite against British oppression.

In March 1770, one such group gathered outside the Old State House, protesting British tax policies and hectoring a stationed troop of British soldiers. The badgered soldiers fired into the crowd, killing five people. News of the Boston Massacre spread through New England, fanning the flames of rebellion.

In meetings at Faneuil Hall and the Old South Meeting House, Sam Otis and Samuel Adams continued to call for independence. One meeting, in December 1773, led to the "Boston Tea Party," when about 90 colonists disguised as Indians boarded English ships by night in Boston Harbor and dumped three hundred chests of tea into the harbor. In retaliation, the English closed the harbor and, in May 1774, sent troops to occupy the city, forcing Boston's citizens to quarter British soldiers in their homes.

The festering anger and resentment came to a head on April 18, 1775, when Paul Revere made his famous "Midnight Ride" to Lexington to warn rebel leaders that British troops were on their way to nearby Concord to confiscate arms stored there by colonists. Bloody skirmishes the next day at Lexington Green and later at Concord gave the colonial militia its first taste of warfare and marked the beginning of the Revolution.

George Washington, previously a colonel in the Virginia militia, assumed command of the Continental forces on the Cambridge Common in July 1775. He proved to be a brilliant commander and politician. In less than a year he had wrested Boston from the British. The city remained free from British control through the end of the Revolution, and thereafter exercised a major role in the affairs of the new nation.

From the time of the Revolution and well into the nineteenth century, Boston's merchant ships reaped mighty fortunes. Wealthy traders transformed Beacon Hill, the Back Bay and the South End into showplaces, populated with splendid mansions and townhouses.

The Immigrant Wave

In the middle of the nineteenth century, Boston's maritime eminence began to fade, and a manufacturing economy gradually took its place. In the same period new waves of European immigrants reached the seaboard states. Thousands of Polish, Irish and Italian workers came to Boston, as well as to other New England cities, eager to begin a new life and to participate in this burgeoning industrial economy. With the rapid influx of people of different customs and nationalities, Boston's population became segregated. Enclaves of Irish or Poles or Italians grew up in older neighborhoods, while the "proper" Bostonians kept to their domains on Beacon Hill and in the Back Bay.

Decline and Revival

By the end of the nineteenth century, Boston and all of Massachusetts had lost much of their manufacturing base to southern states, which offered cheaper labor and lower taxes. The city's decline continued well into the twentieth century.

In the early 1960s, the city fathers, fed up with Boston's image as a blue-haired old lady, decided it was time for a facelift. Immigrant neighborhoods such as the West End were flattened to make way for 40-story apartment towers; seedy Scollay Square was demolished and in its place rose the city, state and federal office buildings of Government Center; and the elevated Southeast Expressway was built, cutting off (and preserving) the North End. This trend of urban renewal (or "slum clearance" as it was called then) transformed almost every major American city throughout the 1950s, 1960s and 1970s. Yet in Boston, the transformation was less complete. Skyscrapers and office complexes mingled with the historic buildings to create a "new" Boston — one of urban sophistication infused with the charm of an earlier era. It was in the 1960s, too, that the area's reserves of "brainpower" at Harvard and the Massachusetts Institute of Technology began to attract high technology industries and research and development. Boston had begun to regain its former splendor.

Today Boston is one of America's most livable cities. It remains the financial, commercial, intellectual and cultural hub of New England. The cobbled streets twist and turn, while the "Emerald Necklace" of parks and greenbelts (designed in the late 1800s by the renowned landscape architect Frederick Law Olmsted) adorns the city. Ethnic communities and independent neighboring cities such as Cambridge and Brookline break up any tendency toward urban sprawl, with each neighborhood having a distinct appeal.

GENERAL INFORMATION

The **Greater Boston Convention and Visitors Bureau** ☎ (617) 536-4100 TOLL-FREE (800) 888-5515 or (888) 733-2678, 2 Copley Place, Boston 02116, will send you its free planning guide in advance of your trip. You can also pick up a copy at their **Boston Common Visitor Information Center** at Tremont and Winter Streets, open weekdays from 9 AM to 5 PM (with seasonal hours Saturday and Sunday), or the **Prudential Visitor Center** in the Prudential Center Plaza, open daily. In the downtown center is the **Boston National Historical Park Visitor Center** ☎ (617) 242-5642, 15 State Street, which manages the Freedom Trail; the office is open from 9 AM to 5 PM.

In Cambridge, make your first stop the **Cambridge Visitor Information Booth** TOLL-FREE (800) 862-5678, just outside the Harvard Square MBTA station entrance, where there is information and maps of Cambridge, as well as public transportation schedules. It's open Monday to Saturday. Also in Harvard Square, the **Harvard Events and Information Center** ☎ (617) 495-1573 FAX (617) 495-0905 E-MAIL info_center@harvard.edu, Holyoke Center Arcade, 1350 Massachusetts Avenue, provides maps and materials on campus highlights; student guides offer campus tours from June through September.

Motorists coming to Boston along the Massachusetts Turnpike (Interstate 90) can take advantage of the services offered by **MassPike Visitor Information Centers** ☎ (508) 248-4581 at Lee (eastbound), Charlton (east- and westbound) and Natick (eastbound).

GETTING AROUND

Much of Boston can be enjoyed on foot. It can be difficult, however, to find your way around the city's labyrinthine older neighborhoods. Take along a good map, and don't hesitate to ask for directions. (If you remember

An encounter on New Congress Street OPPOSITE — in the 1930s and 1940s Bostonians were urged to "vote often and vote early" for their mayor James Michael Curley, memorialized here in bronze. ABOVE: Swan boats await in the Public Gardens.

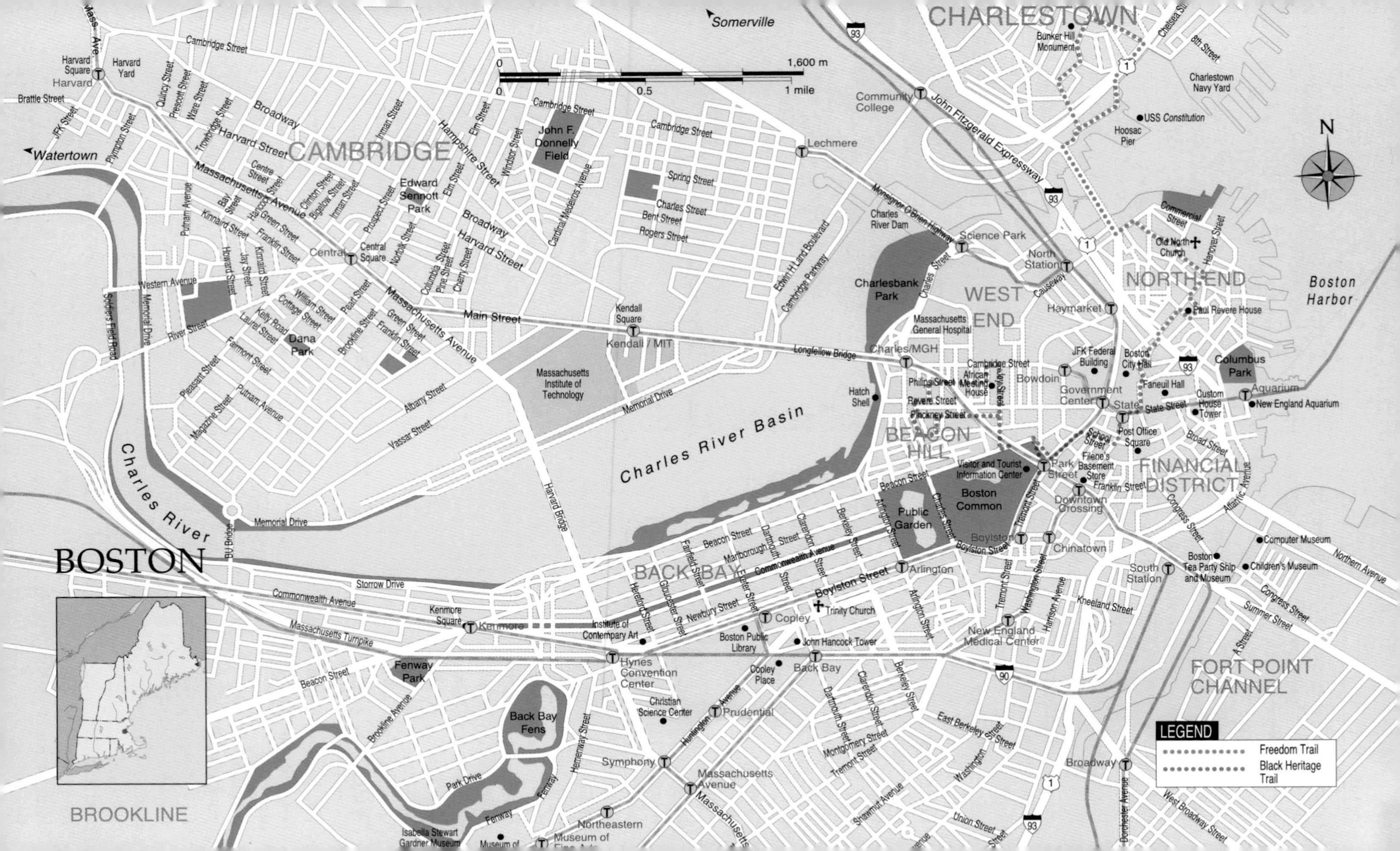
BOSTON
CAMBRIDGE
CHARLESTOWN
BROOKLINE
Somerville
Watertown
N
0
1,600 m
0.5
1 mile
LEGEND
Freedom Trail
Black Heritage Trail
Charles River
Charles River Basin
Boston Harbor
NORTH END
WEST END
BEACON HILL
BACK BAY
FINANCIAL DISTRICT
FORT POINT CHANNEL
Harvard Square
Harvard Yard
Central Square
Kendall Square
Kendall / MIT
Massachusetts Institute of Technology
John F. Donnelly Field
Edward Sennott Park
Dana Park
Lechmere
Community College
Science Park
North Station
Haymarket
Charlesbank Park
Charles River Dam
Massachusetts General Hospital
Charles/MGH
Hatch Shell
Bowdoin
Government Center
State
Aquarium
New England Aquarium
Columbus Park
Paul Revere House
Old North Church
Bunker Hill Monument
Charlestown Navy Yard
USS Constitution
Hoosac Pier
Boston City Hall
Faneuil Hall
Custom House Tower
JFK Federal Building
African Meeting House
Post Office Square
Park Street
Filene's Basement Store
Downtown Crossing
Visitor and Tourist Information Center
Boston Common
Public Garden
Boylston
Arlington
Chinatown
South Station
Boston Tea Party Ship and Museum
Computer Museum
Children's Museum
New England Medical Center
Trinity Church
Copley
Boston Public Library
John Hancock Tower
Back Bay
Copley Place
Institute of Contemporary Art
Hynes Convention Center
Prudential
Christian Science Center
Symphony
Massachusetts Avenue
Northeastern
Kenmore Square
Kenmore
Fenway Park
Back Bay Fens
Isabella Stewart Gardner Museum
Broadway
John Fitzgerald Expressway
Monsignor O'Brien Highway
Longfellow Bridge
Harvard Bridge
BU Bridge
Memorial Drive
Storrow Drive
Commonwealth Avenue
Massachusetts Turnpike
Massachusetts Avenue
Main Street
Soldiers Field Road
Cambridge Street
Boylston Street
Beacon Street
Tremont Street
Washington Street
Atlantic Avenue
Congress Street
Summer Street
Northern Avenue
Huntington Avenue
Dorchester Avenue
West Broadway Street

to say "Mass Av" and "Comm Av," instead of "Massachusetts Avenue" or "Commonwealth Avenue," you might just be taken for a native.)

The Massachusetts Bay Transportation Authority (MBTA), or the "T," is Boston's **subway and bus system** and is the best way to get around when shoe leather wears thin. It's not fast (pardonable, as parts of it are the oldest subway in the world), but it beats battling Boston traffic. After 12:30 AM or so, when the T closes, taxis are everywhere.

The system for getting around on the T is not difficult to grasp if you remember that all lines with the exception of the Blue Line run through Park Street Station on Tremont Street in downtown Boston. Train directions are based on the concept of "inbound" — to Park Street station or "outbound" — traveling away from Park Street Station (see map, page 90).

A ride on the T costs $1, and tokens can be purchased at the stations. If you plan to ride for several days, the **Visitor's Passport** ☎ (617) 222-3200 may be good value for you. It also keeps you out of the token line. Passports are sold at Logan Airport, at several T stations, at the major visitor information centers, and at some hotels and newsstands.

DRIVING AND PARKING

Don't drive in Boston if you can avoid it. Boston's streets were laid out for wandering cows in the late 1600s. One-way streets thwart attempts to get from point to point, and overcrowding can make it maddening to try to park your vehicle. Furthermore, a massive 10-year construction program known as the "Big Dig" or, officially, the Central Artery/Third Harbor Tunnel Project is well under way. The city is doing an admirable job of keeping construction areas passable, and the Big Dig should not be a deterrent to visiting the Hub (indeed some say it's an additional draw, see OTHER ATTRACTIONS, page 85), but it does add to the confusion. For information on general snarls or Big Dig restricted roads, detours and access, call **SmarTraveler** ☎ (617) 374-1234, for up-to-the-minute traffic reports for major Boston routes; or for information on Big Dig detours call the **Central Artery Project** ☎ (617) 228-4636.

NEIGHBORHOODS

BEACON HILL

Beacon Hill has not always been the marvel of architectural splendor it is today. In the late seventeenth century, the Trimount neighborhood (the source of Tremont Street's name) was a wild no-man's land referred to by some Bostonians as "Mount Whoredom." But when the "new" State House was built here in 1798, many of the city's wealthiest families rushed to commission State House architect Charles Bulfinch to design their Federal-style mansions and bow-fronted Greek Revival row houses. Beacon Hill had arrived, and it remains among Boston's most affluent neighborhoods (a single family Beacon Street dwelling recently sold for $9.6 million). A walk around its sloping, cobbled streets, with time to linger in a Charles Street café, is a required part of any visit to Boston.

Ducks crossing Frog Pond in the Public Gardens.

BACK BAY

Flanking the Public Garden and stretching west as far as Massachusetts Avenue is the

Back Bay, a name which often begs the question: "Where's the *bay*?" The answer lies in the city's origins. Once surrounded by marshy coves, Boston was connected to the mainland by a narrow isthmus, marked by present-day Shawmut Avenue. A series of massive landfill projects gave Boston its present form. Starting in the early 1800s, some 50 acres (20 hectares) of wetland became the chic neighborhoods and wide boulevards of the Back Bay. The landfill projects took the better part of a century to complete.

The Back Bay is laid out along three main avenues. Lined with Victorian brick and brownstone row houses, quiet, residential **Commonwealth Avenue** is fashioned after the grand boulevards of Haussmann's Paris. A block north, **Newbury Street** is alive with chic street life, sidewalk cafés, and galleries. It's also the domain of Chanel, Burberry, Versace, Armani and other glossy brand names. Moving west on Newbury Street, the shops devolve downscale, ending with the funky Urban Outfitters and Virgin Records at the corner of Massachusetts Avenue.

Along Boylston Street, you'll find **Copley Square** — named after the painter John Singleton Copley (1738–1815). Copley Square is the heart of Back Bay, with some of Boston's finest nineteenth- and twentieth-century architecture, from Trinity Church to the mirrored "new" John Hancock Tower. Copley Place has more shopping, with Neiman Marcus anchoring this flashy mall.

For purposes of orientation in the Back Bay, remember that the streets that run perpendicular to the Back Bay's three main drags (Boylston Street, Newbury Street and Commonwealth Avenue) are in alphabetical order: Arlington, Berkeley, Clarendon and so on, ending with Hereford Street. They're named after English duchies.

GOVERNMENT CENTER

An arid no-man's-land of poured concrete, Government Center is the result of an urban renewal program that was intended to transform the squalid Scollay Square into a new focus for the city. The centerpiece is City Hall, a massive inverted pyramid resting on a plaza of brick, meant to resemble "an Aztec temple on a brick desert." While some have extolled its post-modern style, others have made comments like, "It looks like the box Faneuil Hall came in." Most people say it's "just plain ugly." Plans are afoot to revamp the windswept plaza that leads up to the "temple."

Surrounding City Hall are several modern buildings that add to the district's dreary, Orwellian aura: the twin towers of the John F. Kennedy Office Building, the Center Plaza Building with its contours that curve to the slope of Beacon Hill, and the State Service Center, whose sharp architectural lines cut the horizon northwest of the Hall. The only nineteenth-century building that survived Government Center's transformation is the Sears Crescent, notable for the huge 200-gallon (900-liter) steaming teapot that hangs out from one corner of the building to mark the site of what was the largest tea store in Boston.

THE FINANCIAL DISTRICT

Rising to sensational heights between the waterfront and Downtown Crossing is Boston's Financial District, with its principal thoroughfare, State Street (called "King Street" before the Revolution). Once a place where the sidewalks rolled up at the end of the business day, the district is attracting more and more restaurants, and its green spaces and small shops make it a worthwhile place to explore.

Hemmed in by an officious group of skyscrapers, **Post Office Square** is the most delightful small park in the city. It's best on sunny weekdays when the suited office workers escape from their cubicles to sprawl over the grass and have their noontime breaks.

Until the early twentieth century, law regulated the height of Boston buildings. The first violation of Boston's skyline was the 496-ft (149-m) **United States Custom House Tower**, distinguishable today among the waterfront high-rises by its peaked roof and multicolored clock. The Italianate tower was added in 1913 on top of the original 1848 Greek Revival building. (There are tours of the Custom House Tower, the interior of which has been converted to luxury timeshare apartments. For tour information, call the Marriott Custom House ☎ 617-790-1400.)

THE HARBORFRONT

"Well, I love that dirty water… oh, oh, Boston you're my home," sang the Standells. The Boston Harbor has been much maligned in recent decades. During his ill-fated run for President of the United States in 1988, former Governor Michael Dukakis had a hard time defending his ecological record when his

OPPOSITE: Quincy Market was a produce center and warehouse until the mid-1970s, when it was turned into a fast-food court catering primarily to tourists. ABOVE: Coleus and cast iron adorn a South End brownstone.

opponent George Bush Snr. poked fun at the deplorable quality of the water in Boston Harbor. Within a decade the harbor was clean enough to swim in. The harborfront has always been the most engaging part of the city — a jumble of commercial buildings, as well as sights, sounds and smells of maritime Boston. The area is more accessible now with the **Harborwalk**, a two-mile (three-kilometer) paved walkway that begins at the National Park Service Visitor Center (on State Street near the Old State House) and ends at the Boston Tea Party Ship and Museum.

Along the way, the walk passes the New England Aquarium (see OTHER ATTRACTIONS, page 85), where an exhibit describes Boston Harbor's polluted past and the successes of recent cleanup efforts.

THE NORTH END

The North End is the city's oldest neighborhood. Until the mid-nineteenth century, these narrow, twisting streets comprised a good half of Boston. When landfill projects created new neighborhoods in the Back Bay and South End, established Boston families moved out of the crowded North End as immigrants moved in. Today it's an animated area full of restaurants offering noontime plates of homemade pasta, sausage and pizza, and cafés where couples linger over espresso and cannoli. It also embraces some revered Freedom Trail shrines (see WHAT TO SEE AND DO, below).

CAMBRIDGE

Not a neighborhood of Boston *per se*, but actually a separate city, Cambridge is defined by its city squares and a diverse population that runs from scores of students to old guard Brahmins to immigrants from around the globe. There are five major squares, all served by the public transportation system (the "T"), with the exception of Inman. They are, from east to west: Kendall, Central, Inman, Harvard and Porter.

Harvard Square has been thoroughly gentrified. The independent coffee shops, music clubs and burger joints that once thrived here have had to make way for The Gap, Starbucks and a host of automatic teller machines, but a few jewels of the old Harvard Square still exist (see SHOPPING, page 97, and WHERE TO EAT, page 102). Formerly little more than the Massachusetts Institute of Technology and its attendant factories, the streets around **Kendall Square** are now also becoming gentrified — though not residential. There are many good, inexpensive restaurants in the area as well as live music venues and movie theaters. Moving back toward Harvard, **Central Square** is a slice of the globe — a rootsy street life characterizes this area — and it is not to be missed if you're interested in cutting-edge music, ethnic food and contemporary art. International cooking is the order of the day, with an especially wide array of Indian cuisines. You'll also find Eritrean, Portuguese, and Haitian Creole cooking — among many others. **Inman Square** is a quiet residential area with some interesting shops and good restaurants. Moving northwest, **Porter Square** is both an upmarket residential area and a shopping district. Here you'll find dozens of good restaurants in all price-categories, and clothing shops where you can adorn yourself as a good Cantabridgian would — natural fibers only (see SHOPPING, page 97, and WHERE TO EAT, page 102).

SOMERVILLE

With the gentrification of Cambridge, artists studios are clustering around the less trendy (read: lower-rent) Somerville. The local arts council claims this area has the highest concentration of artists in the United States. In the heart of Somerville, two stops north of Harvard Square on the Red Line, is **Davis Square**, where a third university, Tufts, turns out more of the intellectual stock of New England.

Along with some good restaurants here and elsewhere in Somerville (see WHERE TO EAT, page 102), Davis Square is home to the caffeine hipster **Diesel Café** — one of the better coffee shops in Greater Boston to bring a book to and sit for hours. Down the street is the grand old **Somerville Theater**, a 1912 vaudeville stage transformed into a cinema where second-run films are projected every day of the week for $2; folk and world music concerts are also staged here.

WHAT TO SEE AND DO

ALONG THE FREEDOM TRAIL

A three-mile (five-kilometer) walking tour maintained by the National Park Service, the Freedom Trail starts at the "new" State House on Beacon Hill and winds through the city and across the Charles River Basin into Charlestown, passing along the way 16 major sites and buildings related to the Revolutionary era. A red line painted on the sidewalk leads the way. It takes about half a day to walk the trail; allow a full day for a thorough survey. Some Freedom Trail highlights are described below. For a complete list go to Boston National Historical Park Visitor Center ☾ (617) 242-5642, at 15 State Street (State Street T station); or the Bunker Hill Pavilion in the Charlestown Navy Yard Visitor Center ☾ (617) 242-5601 (North Station T), where you can pick up free maps and brochures. Both visitor centers are open daily 9 AM to 5 PM.

Whether you're walking the Freedom Trail or not, it's hard to miss the golden dome of the "new" **State House** ☾ (617) 727-3676, on Beacon Street (Park Street T station). Designed by Charles Bulfinch and begun in 1795 on land that originally belonged to John Hancock, its 24-carat dome gleams like the harbor beacon that once topped this hill and gave the neighborhood its name. Bulfinch's building is only a tiny part of the hulking giant that greets the eye today, but it dominates by its brilliant aesthetic. It influenced the design of half the state capitols in the country and served as a model for modifications to the United States Capitol in Washington. Free tours are offered weekdays, departing from the Doric Hall.

In North Square, **Paul Revere House** ☾ (617) 523-2338, 19 North Square (Haymarket T station) was the Revere family home from 1770 to 1800. The brown clapboard building was built in 1680 by a wealthy merchant on the site of Puritan minister Increase Mather's dwelling, which was destroyed by fire in 1676. The medieval-style structure is the oldest wooden house in Boston. While living here, Revere produced his famous "Boston Massacre" engraving, took part in the Boston Tea Party, smuggled revolutionary dispatches to Philadelphia and helped plot many rebel activities. The interior of the house has been restored and many

OPPOSITE: A round of chess with the local wizard in Harvard Square, Cambridge. ABOVE: Paul Revere's house in Boston's North End.

Revere artifacts — including some of his silversmith work, his rocking chair and saddlebags — are displayed. The museum is open daily, except Mondays January through March; an admission fee is charged.

"One if by land and two if by sea" was the signal to be given from the **Old North Church** ☎ (617) 523-6676, 193 Salem Street (North Station T), to advise revolutionaries of the route of British soldiers on their way to seize the rebel armories in Lexington and Concord. On April 18, 1775, a church sexton hung two lanterns in the steeple's highest windows to indicate British troop movements. "Old North" has a 190-ft (58-m) white steeple, a city landmark since the church — the oldest in Boston — was built in 1723. The church bells were cast in Gloucester, England, the first made for Britain's North American empire; they sound now only on Sunday mornings before services.

Across the harbor in Charlestown, a 221-ft-tall (66-m) white granite obelisk stands as a memorial to the men who fought the misnamed Battle of Bunker Hill. The **Bunker Hill Monument** ☎ (617) 242-5641, Monument Square, Charlestown, is actually on Breed's Hill, where the clash took place on June 17, 1775. About 1,200 Americans and 3,000 British troops took part in the battle. The first English attack failed and British troops twice required reinforcements. The American's General Prescott ordered a retreat only after all ammunition had been used. Although the revolutionaries were defeated, the Battle of Bunker Hill proved to the revolutionaries that they measured up well in battle against the British regulars. General Washington said of the clash: "I am content. The liberties of the country are safe."

The monument's spiral staircase has 294 steps (and no elevator), but once at the top your efforts are rewarded by a panoramic view of Boston, the harbor, its islands and the USS *Constitution*. Back on *terra firma*, at the **Bunker Hill Pavilion** ☎ (617) 241-7575 on Hoosac Pier (Community College T station), there's a gripping multimedia presentation, "The Whites of Their Eyes," with 14 screens, 20 life-size figures and dazzling lighting effects. It explains the battle in detail, as well as the events leading up to it. The Bunker Hill Pavilion is open from April to November; an admission fee is charged.

Along the harbor front is the **Charlestown Navy Yard**, one of the first naval shipyards in the nation, operating since 1800, when shipbuilders swarmed over dry docks, rope walks and quays cluttered with maritime equipment. The yard reached peak activity during World War II, when it employed more than 50,000 men and women who built and repaired a record number of vessels (it was closed by the Nixon administration in the 1970s). The centerpiece of the yard is the magnificent **USS *Constitution*** ☎ (617) 242-5670 (North Station T), the Navy's oldest commissioned warship still afloat. When Congress established the United States Navy in 1794 it authorized six new frigates. One of these was the *Constitution*, a 52-gun warship built at nearby Hartt's Shipyard and launched in 1797. The *Constitution* sailed against the Barbary pirates, fought the British in the war of 1812 and engaged in 40 sea battles without a loss. When a British sailor saw cannon balls bounce off the *Constitution*'s planking, he shouted, "Her sides are made of iron!" Thus the ship gained its nickname, *"Old Ironsides."*

The *Constitution* is still a commissioned warship; members of its crew take visitors on tours of the cannon-strewn decks and the captain's quarters below decks — which were evidently built for people five-feet tall and under — and the berthing deck where the crew slept in hammocks. At the rear is the ship's wheel, which required four men to control it. Sailors also climbed the ropes to the "fighting tops" positioned on each mast to direct fire against enemy ships. The ship is open daily for free tours.

Known as the "Cradle of Liberty," **Faneuil Hall** hosted important (and vociferous) protests against British colonial policies. It's open daily 9 AM to 5 PM. It was here that Samuel Adams first urged the colonies to unite against the British. The grasshopper weather vane atop the hall dome was fashioned in 1742, inspired by similar weather vanes on the Royal Exchange building in London. The first floor of the Hall has always been a market; until 1974 the stalls offered fresh meat, vegetables and dairy products to the citizenry. These days the stalls brim with souvenirs and food, catering mostly to tourists.

OTHER ATTRACTIONS

Enthroned, like a king in his court, at the head of Copley Square, the massive and rough-hewn **Trinity Church** ☎ (617) 536-0944, 545 Boylston Street, completed in 1877, was designed by Henry Hobson Richardson (1838–1886), who went on to design Austin and Sever halls at Harvard University. This magnificent French Romanesque-style building is perhaps the best example of church architecture in America. An American Institute of Architects poll voted it the "sixth most important building in America and among the 100 greatest buildings in the world." Inspired by the great cathedrals of France and Spain, it is massive in scale. The interior is broad and open, but the atmosphere is studious, shaded with somber terracotta and green frescoes trimmed in gold leaf, making it look like a library for the saints. The church is at its best during the annual participatory singing of Handel's *Messiah* at Christmas. (Get there early; the line snakes around the block.) The stained glass windows on the north transept, with their rich colors and lacy acanthus leaves, are from the workshops of William Morris & Co.

Across Dartmouth Street is the **Boston Public Library** ☎ (617) 536-5400, with its collection of six million books. You can enter the library through either its nineteenth-century wing along Dartmouth Street — an entry fashioned after a Greek temple and graced with a grand Sienna marble staircase — or through its modern Boylston Street annex. In the old wing, a courtyard with lush greenery and central fountain offers a quiet retreat. Murals, bronzes, and paintings by renowned artists enrich the library. Free one-hour **art and architecture tours** leave from the Dartmouth Street entrance on Copley Square, Monday at 2:30 PM, Tuesday to Thursday at 6 PM, Friday and Saturday at 11 AM, and, October to May, Sunday at 2 PM. The library is open Monday to Thursday from 9 AM to 9 PM, Friday and Saturday from 9 AM to 5 PM, and, October to May, Sunday 1 PM to 5 PM.

The **John Hancock Tower**, 200 Clarendon Street, a striking, glass-covered 788-ft-tall (236-m) skyscraper designed by I.M. Pei, is New England's tallest building. The skyscraper has long been a topic of heated debate among Bostonians, many of who opposed both its style and its height in an area of low-rise brick dwellings. While many people feel its best feature is the vision of Trinity Church reflected in its 10,344 mirrored panels, connoisseurs of modern architecture cite the vanishing trapezoidal form as an exemplar of historically and physically sensitive design. Although its top levels once held a fine observatory deck, security concerns necessitated its closing after September 11, 2001.

Before the John Hancock Tower was built, the **Prudential Center** ☎ (617) 859-0648, 800 Boylston Street, was the city's tallest building. Also a corporate insurance headquarters, its fiftieth-floor **Skywalk** is an observation deck with 360-degree views of the city and accompanying historical displays. The Skywalk remains the best high vantage point from which to gain an overall perspective of the city. Open daily until 10 PM, an admission fee is charged. At street-level, the "Pru" has an indoor shopping mall with a **food court** for quick and inexpensive meals.

Boston's museums offer something for everyone, old or young.

Boston Duck Tours (see TOURS AND EXCURSIONS, below) leave from the Pru as well.

Along Huntington Avenue are the 14-acre (five-and-a-half-hectare) grounds of the **Christian Science Center**, world headquarters for the Church of Christ, Scientist, as well as the offices of the *Christian Science Monitor*, a national daily newspaper. The 1894 Romanesque-style **Mother Church** — an architectural gem made of white New Hampshire granite — is the centerpiece of the Christian Science complex. A domed extension combining Renaissance and Byzantine architectural notions was added in 1906. A reflecting pool runs along Huntington Avenue. After a look around the church building, follow the signs out on the plaza to the Mary Baker Eddy Library for the Betterment of Humanity, which houses the **Mapparium**. Illuminated by hundreds of lights, this antique globe has a bronze framework that holds 600 glass panels. Visitors enter the Mapparium along a bridge and find themselves at the center of the earth. Built in 1935, the political boundaries of this giant glass globe are frozen in time. It's a place to marvel at the political fortunes of the planet (no Vietnam, no Israel). Acoustics are eerie; people whispering near Greenland can be heard distinctly in Australia.

The nucleus of the **New England Aquarium** ☾ (617) 973-5200, Central Wharf (off Atlantic Avenue), is a four-story glass tank filled with sharks, turtles and more than 600 other sea creatures. A ramp spirals up along the tank, leading visitors through various levels of marine life. Besides the big tank, the ground floor has a penguin rookery and an animal hospital with state-of-the-art medical equipment. Upstairs a mesmerizing exhibit demonstrates schooling habits with thousands of silvery herring forming a kind of superfish. At the Edge of the Sea exhibit, small children can touch starfish and sea urchins. One of the newest exhibits, Wired for Sound, demonstrates how noisy the underwater world can be. Dolphin and sea lion shows are offered daily, and the Aquarium sponsors whale-watching cruises to Stellwagen Bank, departing from the Aquarium wharf. The Aquarium's decade-long expansion project has already added a wide-screen IMAX theater and will improve the habitats for marine mammals. Open daily; an admission fee is charged.

While bureaucrats and dignitaries worry about the ill effects of the **Big Dig**, kids (and curious adults) have discovered that the Big Dig is cool. Billed as the largest public works project since the Hoover Dam, the Big Dig aims to alleviate Boston's traffic problems and give the city some much-needed green space along a several-mile-long corridor near the waterfront. A third tunnel has already been built under Boston Harbor, connecting Logan Airport to downtown; soon the rusting eyesore of Boston's elevated Central Artery (the major north–south highway through downtown) will be "depressed" — reconstructed underground. The graceful suspension bridge at the north end of the city, the Leonard Zakim-Bunker Hill Bridge, provides a new signature landmark for Boston.

is that of poet Henry Wadsworth Longfellow (1807–1882). Though born in Maine, Longfellow lived here for 45 years. Built in 1759, the house served as Washington's army headquarters during the struggle to evict the British from Boston. The house contains original books, furnishings and Longfellow's study, where he penned a good many of his poetic masterpieces. The **Longfellow House National Historic Site** ☎ (617) 876-4491, 105 Brattle Street, is open Wednesday to Sunday; tours are held throughout the day, and an admission fee is charged.

Across the Charles River in **Cambridge** there are more historical and architectural sights. Harvard Square and its surrounding neighborhood are the secular complement to the hallowed halls of **Harvard University**, the oldest college in the United States, established in 1636. The campus has more than 400 buildings, including Massachusetts Hall, dating from 1720; its handsome red-brick walls adorned with ivy provided the architectural inspiration for other buildings on the grounds. Tours of the campus are offered year round (see GENERAL INFORMATION, page 77).

Harvard Square's **Brattle Street** is notable for "Tory Row," named for dwellings built by wealthy British sympathizers during the Revolution. The street's most famous house

Sprawling along the river between Central and Kendall squares is the campus of **MIT (Massachusetts Institute of Technology)** ☎ (617) 253-4795, 77 Massachusetts Avenue, famous for its research in science and engineering. The world's first computer was developed here in 1928. Of architectural interest on campus are the triangular-roofed Kresge Auditorium and the moated MIT Chapel, both designed by Finnish-American architect Eero Saarinen, as well as the Dreyfuss and Weisner Buildings, both designed by I.M. Pei. Tours of the campus are offered daily.

Opposite: Denizens of the New England Aquarium capture a boy's attention. ABOVE: Eying a "glory hole." Lunchtime pedestrians on Atlantic Avenue follow progress on the "Big Dig."

MUSEUMS

The **City Pass** will save you 50 percent on Boston's six most popular attractions: the John F. Kennedy Library & Museum, the Skywalk, the Museum of Fine Arts, the Museum of Science, the New England Aquarium and the Harvard Museum of Natural History. It also keeps you out of ticket lines. The cost is $30.50, and it's valid for nine days. It's available at Visitor Information Centers (see GENERAL INFORMATION, page 77).

The **Museum of Fine Arts (MFA)** ☎ (617) 267-9300, 465 Huntington Avenue, was the repository of artifacts gathered by Boston's Brahmins as they traveled the world in the nineteenth century, and those objects still form the core of the museum collections. The 1909 Greek temple-style building contains about 200 galleries. Highlighting the remarkable Japanese collection are Buddhist paintings and sculptures, some dating to the twelfth century. Ceramics, including objects from the Han dynasty (third century), accent the Chinese section. The Egyptian artifacts, the bounty of a 40-year Middle East expedition sponsored by the museum and Harvard University, are a collection of 4,000-year-old antiquities perhaps unparalleled outside Cairo. The European galleries are strong on Monet, and in the American collection are Gilbert Stuart's (1755–1828) portraits of George and Martha Washington. Twentieth-century art is displayed in the museum's new glass-roofed wing. The MFA is open Monday and Tuesday from 10 AM to 4:45 PM, Wednesday 10 AM to 9:45 PM, Thursday and Friday 10 AM to 5 PM (West Wing until 9:45 PM); Saturday and Sunday 10 AM to 5:45 PM. An admission fee is charged, except Wednesday from 4 PM to closing when entrance is "pay as you wish."

A short walk from the MFA is the **Isabella Stewart Gardner Museum** ☎ (617) 566-1401, 280 The Fenway, an elegant 1903 mansion built in the style of a Venetian *palazzo*. Crammed with priceless art, it is the legacy of a charismatic and eccentric heiress, known in her day as "Mrs. Jack." The collection includes old masters and Italian Renaissance paintings, works by Matisse and Whistler, and Titian's *Rape of Europa*, painted for King Philip II of Spain. Other treasures include beautiful tapestries, centuries-old mosaics, and sculpture. The galleries surround a four-story, glass-roofed courtyard, with Venetian-style windows and balconies, flowering plants and trees framing a Roman floor mosaic from Livia that dates from the second century. The courtyard alone is worth the price of admission. Open Tuesday to Sunday 11 AM to 5 PM; an admission fee is charged. There is a Sunday concert series in the Tapestry Room; call for a schedule. The museum café is excellent and has an outdoor terrace; lunch is served until 2 PM.

In Cambridge, the **Harvard Art Museums** ☎ (617) 495-9400, 32 Quincy Street (Harvard Square T), together house more than 150,000 art objects. Works of Van Gogh, Renoir and Picasso can be found at the **Fogg Museum**; in the **Arthur M. Sackler Museum**, across the street, is one of the world's finest collections of Chinese jade; German Expressionists dominate at the **Busch-Reisinger Museum**. Open Monday to Saturday 10 AM to 5 PM, Sunday 1 PM to 5 PM; an admission fee is charged except on Saturday mornings. Also on the Harvard campus is the **Peabody Museum of Archaeology and Ethnology** with exhibits on North American Indians and relics from Lewis and Clark's 1803 explorations. The **Museum of Natural History** is known for its delicate glass flowers depicting 800 different species. The **Museum of Comparative Zoology** collections include a 225-million-year-old egg, a six-million-year-old turtle shell, the 25,000-year-old Harvard Mastodon (found in New Jersey), a 180-million-year-old dinosaur, and a genuine giant sea monster. Call the Harvard Events and Information Center (see GENERAL INFORMATION, page 77) for more information on these Harvard museums.

The **Institute of Contemporary Art (ICA)** ☎ (617) 266-5152, 955 Boylston Street (Hynes Convention Center T stop), has changing exhibits in all media, including film festivals, installations and performance events. The building is a former fire station built in 1880; the tower in the rear of the building was used for drying cotton fire hoses. Next door, the restaurant Barcode is a former police station that now sells $20 hamburgers. The ICA is open Wednesday and Friday to Sunday from noon to 5 PM, Thursday from noon to 9 PM; an admission fee is charged, except Thursday after 5 PM when admission is free.

The ethereal music that greets you at the entrance to the **MIT Museum** ☎ (617) 253-4444, 265 Massachusetts Avenue, Second Floor, in Cambridge, is generated with the use of lasers. Technology is on exhibit at this great little museum, where you'll learn that

OPPOSITE: The Isabella Stewart Gardner Museum blends art, music, architecture, and horticulture to create one of Boston's finest cultural attractions. ABOVE: An aerial view of the Christian Science Center with the Mother Church and reflecting pool.

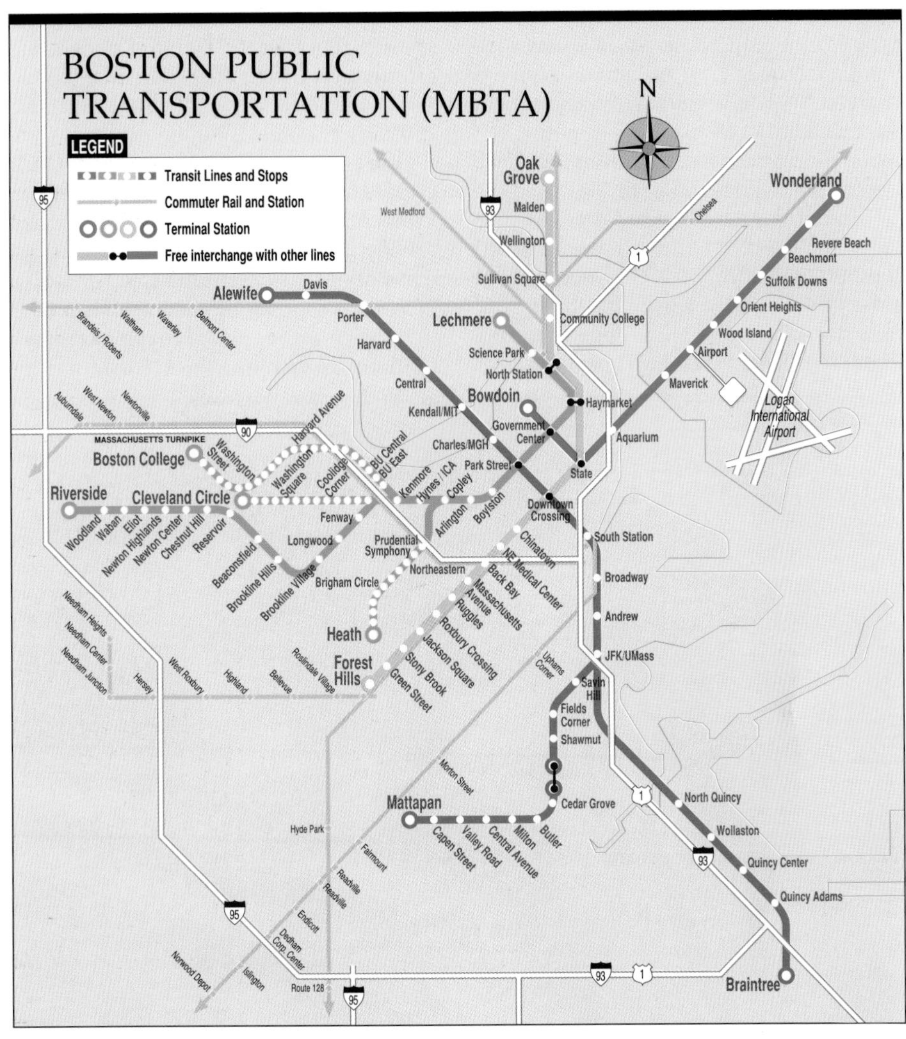

holography is "a way of using laser light to make a single recording of the way an object looks from many different positions." The holography exhibition covers the invention of the hologram as well as a display of holographic art. A 2001 redesign of the museum has stripped away some of the boyish fascination with gadgetry (gone are "slide rules through the ages" and the loving documentation of students pranks, or "hacks") in favor of hands-on robotics exhibits and practical demonstrations of stroboscopic light that amplify the areas devoted to Harold "Doc" Edgerton (1903–90). Edgerton pioneered high-speed and strobe photography, capturing on film such fast-moving objects as bullets, bird wings, and droplets of milk. The museum shop is the place to pick up gadgets and unusual souvenirs. I'm partial to the Jell-O brain mold and the "MIT Nerd Pride" pocket protectors. The museum is open daily; an admission fee is charged. It's about a 15-minute walk from either the Kendall/MIT or the Central Square station.

The **Museum of Science** and the **Charles Hayden Planetarium** ((617) 723-2500, Science Park, Monsignor O'Brien Highway, are built on a dam that once controlled the flow of water between the Charles River and the harbor. A life-sized model of an Apollo space capsule, a 20-ft (six-meter) plastic tyrannosaurus rex and a "lightning-making" machine are among the most popular exhibits. Open Monday to Thursday, Saturday and

Sunday from 9 AM to 5 PM, Friday 9 AM to 9 PM. From July through Labor Day, the museum remains open until 7 PM on Monday to Thursday, Saturday and Sunday. An admission fee is charged.

On Museum Wharf across the Fort Point Channel, the **Boston Children's Museum** ☎ (617) 426-8855, 300 Congress Street, has been called "the country's best museum for kids." Toddlers jump and slide in Playspace; older kids climb like monkeys from platform to platform within a futuristic sculpture; and teens can try out the latest dance steps at the Clubhouse. There are replicas of an Indian wigwam, a village street and a two-story Japanese house. From mid-June through August, open Saturday through Thursday 10 AM to 5 PM, Friday from 10 AM to 9 PM. From September through mid-June, open Tuesday to Saturday 10 AM to 5 PM; an admission fee is charged.

The **Boston Tea Party Ship and Museum** ☎ (617) 338-1773, near South Station on the Congress Street Bridge, is a full-scale replica of the British brigantine *Beaver*. Guides in period costume relate the history of the 1773 Boston Tea Party. Museum artifacts include a tea chest reputed to be among those tossed into the water on that fateful night. Open daily, an admission fee is charged.

The **John F. Kennedy Library and Museum** ☎ (617) 929-4523, Columbia Point, off Morrissey Boulevard (JFK/UMass T stop), is another of architect I.M. Pei's creations, and some consider the sleek concrete and glass structure to be among his best. Nine exhibit halls filled with family and presidential memorabilia encircle a central room containing the president's desk as it was on November 22, 1963 when President Kennedy was assassinated during a motorcade ride through Dallas' Dealey Plaza. A 35-minute film chronicles his life and times. The museum also chronicles his PT-109 days, the Cuban missile crisis, the 1960 Kennedy–Nixon debates, and the Civil Rights movement. It is open daily 9 AM to 5 PM; an admission fee is charged.

A look at the former president's childhood can be had at the **John F. Kennedy National Historic Site** ☎ (617) 566-7937, 83 Beals Street, Brookline. Audiotape segments narrated by Kennedy's mother, Rose, recount the family's life there when JFK was born in 1917. It is open April to mid-November, Wednesday to Sunday; an admission fee is charged.

The **Black Heritage Trail** consists of 14 sites in Boston's Beacon Hill area, including the **African Meeting House**, the oldest Black church edifice in the United States, and the **Robert Gould Shaw and 54th Regiment Memorial**, which pays tribute to the Civil War Union Army's first black regiment. Robert Gould Shaw, a young white officer from Boston, volunteered for its command. The **Smith Court Residences** are five residential structures typical of the homes of Black Bostonians in the nineteenth century. William C. Nell, America's first published black historian, boarded in No. 3 from 1851 to 1865. Nell was also a community activist and a leader in the struggle to integrate Boston's public schools before the Civil War. Free **guided tours** along the Black Heritage Trail are offered daily at 10 AM, noon and 2 PM. The tour takes in the African Meeting House, Abiel Smith School, and George Middleton House, leaving from the Shaw Monument at Beacon and Park streets. Houses on the Black Heritage Trail are not

The John Fitzgerald Kennedy Memorial Library and Museum at Columbia Point, Dorchester.

open to the public, being private residences, but at the African Meeting House you'll find the **Museum of Afro-American History** ☎ (617) 725-0020 WEB SITE www.afroammuseum.org, 8 Smith Court. Exhibits chronicle the history of New England's African-American communities. Open daily in summer, it's closed Sundays the rest of the year; a donation is suggested. For information on guided walking tours of the Black Heritage Trail, contact the museum.

SPORTS AND OUTDOOR ACTIVITIES

Want to start an animated conversation with a Bostonian? Just mention the Red Sox (baseball), the Bruins (ice hockey), the Celtics (basketball) or the Patriots (football). Fervent sports fans rattle off statistics and rankings of their favorite sports teams at the drop of a mitt. The Celtics' glory years are a decade gone, but the Patriots won hearts and minds by taking the 2002 Super Bowl. As for the Red Sox, wait 'til next year....

Watching the **Red Sox** play America's favorite sport from the bleachers in fabled **Fenway Park**, on Yawkey Way, is not to be missed. The oldest and smallest professional sports stadium in the country, Fenway puts you shoulder to shoulder with rabid baseball loyalists. Past Red Sox rosters contain the names of some of baseball's most legendary players: Babe Ruth, Roger "The Rocket" Clemens, Ted Williams and Carl "Yaz" Yastrzemski, as well as current baseball giants such as Pedro Martinez. The first World Series was played in Boston in 1903. Baseball season runs from April to sometime in the fall. (School attendance drops by half on opening day each year.) Guided tours are held April to August Monday to Friday; a fee is charged for the tours (Fenway T station). For schedule information and to purchase tickets call ☎ (617) 267-1700. There is also a 24-hour automated line for credit-card orders ☎ (617) 482-4769, as well as a FAX (617) 236-6640. Finally, you can purchase tickets in person at the Boston Red Sox Ticket Office, 4 Yawkey Way; hours are 9 AM to 5 PM, Monday to Saturday.

The **Boston Bruins** and the **Celtics** (winners of more NBA championships than any other team) share facilities at Fleet Center ☎ (617) 624-1000 (event information), One Causeway Street (North Station T), which replaced the much-loved Boston Garden in 1996. You can tour the team locker rooms and view team memorabilia when games are not taking place.

Both the **New England Patriots** and New England's new professional soccer team, the **New England Revolution**, play between April and September at **CMGI Field** ☎ (508) 543-1776 (box office) ☎ (508) 543-3900 (event information) TOLL-FREE (800) 543-1776 Route 1, Foxboro (Riverside T stop), a 30-minute drive south of Boston.

Intercollegiate sports are as spirited as the professional versions. Tickets to the **Harvard University football games**, especially when their arch-rival Yale comes to town, can be difficult to obtain, but call ☎ (617) 495-2211, or contact the Murr Center, 65 North Harvard Street, Boston 02163, in season, for a home game schedule.

Each Patriot's Day (a Suffolk County holiday celebrated on the third Monday of April), world-class runners line up with amateurs for the opening shot of the **Boston Marathon**, the world's oldest annual marathon, run since 1897. Spectators have a blast cheering runners all along the route, from the starting line in Hopkinton to Wellesley's "Heartbreak Hill" at about the halfway point to the finish line at Boston's Copley Square.

Of all the jewels in Boston's Emerald Necklace, the **Arnold Arboretum** ☎ (617) 524-1718, The Arborway, Jamaica Plain, sparkles the brightest. Founded in 1872 and administered by Harvard University, the arboretum is 265 acres (106 hectares) of beautiful landscape with rare and ancient trees from all over the world. In winter, cross-country skiers and tobogganers make tracks over the gentle hills. Open daily sunrise to sunset; admission is free.

On Boston's Charles River, the Community Boating Company ☎ (617) 523-1038, on the Esplanade, has a complete menu of **sailing** programs and lessons for adults and children from spring through fall. The Boston Sailing Center ☎ (617) 227-4198, The Riverboat, Lewis Wharf (on the Harborfront), also provides beginner and advanced instruction year round.

Bicyclers, joggers and skaters career along the Charles River via an 18-mile (29-km) bikeway that borders both the Cambridge and Boston banks. You can rent a set of wheels from **Back Bay Bicycles** ☎ (617) 247-2336, 336 Newbury Street, Boston 02139. Many hotels provide maps showing routes for joggers and in-line skaters.

TOURS AND EXCURSIONS

Reached by ferry from Long Wharf, a flotilla of islands dots the Boston Harbor. The 34 islands compose the **Boston Harbor Islands National Recreation Area** ☎ (617) 223-8666 WEB SITE www.bostonislands.org. Pack a picnic and voyage out to tour the fortifications on Georges Island, swim at Lovells Island, and take in the city skyline on the return trip. The oldest lighthouse in the Western Hemisphere, the **Boston Light** (1716) is located on Little Brewster Island (see STAY THE NIGHT AT A LIGHT, page 24 in TOP SPOTS). The information booth for the park is at Long Wharf.

Not to be missed, **Boston Duck Tours** ☎ (617) 723-3825, 101 Huntington Avenue, takes its passengers on an exhilarating 90-minute narrated tour of the city and the Charles River aboard vintage World War II amphibious vehicles. Half a dozen standard narrated trolley tours also vie for your vacation dollars, including the **Old Town Trolley Tour Company** ☎ (617) 269-7150. For a single fare, you can complete a tour in two hours, or you can step on and step off throughout the day. I would caution against the late afternoon tours — you risk getting stuck in downtown gridlock while your guide drones on. Old Town also offers occasional theme tours.

Tours with **Boston By Foot** ☎ (617) 367-2345, 77 North Washington Street, feature Boston's architectural heritage on guided city walks. Trained volunteers, who embellish the walk with tales of famous residents and visitors past and present, lead the 90-minute tours. Walks include: The Heart of the Freedom Trail, Beacon Hill, Copley Square, The North End, The Waterfront and Boston Underground.

The **New England Aquarium Whale Watch** ☎ (617) 973-5227 (information) or ☎ (617) 973-5281 (reservations), New England Aquarium, Central Wharf, takes *Voyager II* out on weekends to Stellwagen Bank, with expert commentary. **Boston Harbor Cruises** ☎ (617) 227-4321, One Long Wharf (next to the Marriott), offers whale-watching, Harbor

Retired but still remembered, slugger Wade Boggs signs autographs at Fenway Park.

Islands and narrated sightseeing cruises. **Massachusetts Bay Lines** ☎ (617) 542-8000, 60 Rowes Wharf, does daily whale-watching trips, sunset cruises, and a historic harbor tour on the hour daily. Ships depart from Rowes Wharf, Gate C. **Bay State Cruises** ☎ (617) 748-1428 WEB SITE boston-ptown.com has trips to Provincetown twice daily in summer, departing at 9 AM and noon from Commonwealth Pier; the price is $30, and $10 additional to take your bike along. In Provincetown, call Cape and Islands Travel Agency ☎ (508) 487-4422.

NIGHTLIFE AND THE ARTS

For a list of what's happening around the region, consult the *Boston Globe* Calendar section, or the arts and entertainment weekly, *The Phoenix*; both appear on Thursday.

At BosTix kiosks you can get **half-priced day-of-the-show tickets** to music, theater and dance performances throughout the city. It is also a Ticketmaster outlet. BosTix ☎ (617) 482-2849 (recorded information) has two locations: The Copley Square kiosk is open Monday to Saturday 10 AM to 6 PM, Sunday 11 AM to 4 PM; the Faneuil Hall Marketplace kiosk is open Tuesday through Saturday 10 AM to 6 PM, Sunday 11 AM to 4 PM. Half-price tickets go on sale at 11 AM. For all locations, bring cash; BosTix does not accept credit cards or checks. All purchases must be made in person.

MUSIC AND DANCE

Under the baton of new conductor and music director James Levine, also associated with the Metropolitan Opera, the **Boston Symphony Orchestra** performs familiar and lesser-known classics and hosts world-renowned guest artists. From October through April, concerts take place at **Symphony Hall** ☎ (617) 266-1492 (information) TOLL-FREE (800) 333-2762 FAX (617) 638-9436, 301 Massachusetts Avenue. Keith Lockhart directs the Boston Pops' May through mid-July season, also at Symphony Hall.

The **City Concert Series** sponsors alfresco music throughout the summer with free rock concerts at City Hall Plaza ☎ (617) 635-4000, jazz at Copley Square Park, and world music at Downtown Crossing ☎ (617) 482-2139. Outdoor concerts (Saturday and Sunday) and PG-rated movies (Friday) animate the **Hatch Shell** on the Esplanade; and don't miss the **Fourth of July Boston Pops concert on the Esplanade** — though you'll have to stake your few square feet of turf in the morning to have a seat for the evening concert and fireworks (it's worth it).

Major **rock music venues** include the new Fleet Center ☎ (617) 624-1000 and The Orpheum ☎ (617) 679-0810, One Hamilton Place. Concerts at both of these arenas begin at 7:30 PM. Other venues are CMGI Field ☎ (508) 543-1776 (box office), Route 1, Foxboro and, for outdoor rockfests, Tweeter Center for the Performing Arts ☎ (508) 339-2331, 885 South Main Street, Mansfield (south of Boston).

The **Boston Ballet** ☎ (617) 695-6950, performs at the Wang Center ☎ (617) 482-9393 TOLL-FREE (800) 447-7400, 270 Tremont Street, a 3,800-seat theater that also hosts visiting dance companies. Past guests have included the Alvin Ailey American Dance Theater, the American Ballet Theater, the Bolshoi Ballet Academy, the Mark Morris Dance Group and Twyla Tharp. The **Dance Complex** ☎ (617) 547-9363, 536 Massachusetts Avenue, Cambridge, occupies a historic building designed by H.H. Richardson. Hosting performances and classes, it is the artistic epicenter for independent choreographers and small dance companies.

THEATER

Boston's two leading theater companies are the **American Repertory Theater (ART)** ☎ (617) 547-8300, 64 Brattle Street, Cambridge, and the **Huntington Theater Company** ☎ (617) 266-0800, 264 Huntington Avenue. You can expect top-quality shows from both of these established companies, associated, respectively, with Harvard University and Boston University. The ART leans toward cutting-edge interpretations — staging Shakespeare on a proscenium filled knee-deep with water, and David Mamet premieres — while the Huntington takes a traditional approach to its wide-ranging productions. August Wilson is a favorite and has premiered more than one of his plays here.

In what passes for Boston's **Theater District**, a number of old-time playhouses host long-running musicals and Broadway hits. The **Charles Playhouse** ☏ (617) 426-5225, 74 Warrenton Street, is still trotting out the ever-popular *Shear Madness*, a comedic murder mystery set in a unisex hair salon; **Blue Man Group** ☏ (617) 426-6912 (information) or ☏ (617) 931-2787 (tickets), has lodged itself here as well. The **Colonial Theater** ☏ (617) 426-9366, 106 Boylston Street (at Tremont Street), as well as the **Shubert Theater** ☏ (617) 482-9393, 265 Tremont Street, and the 1,200-seat **Wilbur Theater** ☏ (617) 423-4008, 246 Tremont Street, stage Broadway musicals and plays. The old **Emerson Majestic Theater** ☏ (617) 824-8000, 219 Tremont Street, presents jazz concerts.

Boston has a long tradition of supporting improvisational theater — a type of show whereby audience suggestion provides inspiration for comedy sketches. **ImprovBoston** ☏ (617) 576-1253, 1253 Cambridge Street, Inman Square, Cambridge, has been performing improv sketch shows for some 20 years, albeit with an oft-changing cast. There are no guarantees — sometimes the show is brilliant, sometimes it bombs — but that's improv. Troupes come and go in the Boston, playing at various venues around town. Check the *Globe* Calendar section for the latest crop.

CLUBS AND BARS

Johnny D's ☏ (617) 776-2004, 17 Holland Street, Davis Square, Somerville, with swing dance night beginning with lessons, and a blues jam on Sunday afternoons. The rest of the week is a who's-who of funk, rock and roll, and blues. The room is intimate and open room — a place a woman can feel comfortable going to alone. All that and a good restaurant serving Cajun-style main courses. This is one of the city's best nights out.

Central Square is the focal point of the Cambridge club scene, with both heart and attitude as diverse crowds turn out to see the next great thing: The **Green Street Grill** ☏ (617) 876-1655, 280 Green Street, has local jazz, blues and swing. It's also tops in Cambridge for Caribbean cuisine. A block away, **Man Ray** ☏ (617) 864-0400, 21 Brookline Street, caters to both goth and avant-garde with DJ shows and some live bands. Friday is Fetish Night.

For a more laidback evening, the **Cantab Lounge** ☏ (617) 354-2685, 738 Massachusetts Avenue (Cantab is short for Cantabrigiensis, Latin for Cambridge), packs a melting-pot

Fenway Park is one of four old-style baseball parks remaining in the United States. Owners want to replace it, but fans like it just the way it is.

crowd into its basement dance hall for blues jams, sometimes featuring the ageless Little Joe Cook and the Thrillers. Patrons gyrate nightly to his hit tunes like "Sexy Lady from the Beauty Shop, You Make My Heart Go Bippity Bop!"

The Middle East ☎ (617) 492-9181, 472 Massachusetts Avenue, has been the city's best place to see local rock for the last two decades. The big room downstairs is where national acts are booked. At street level, behind the restaurant, there is a smaller space with local bands on the program. In the bakery, there is belly dancing each Tuesday night, and acoustic music on other nights. Around the corner, **T.T. the Bear's Place** ☎ (617) 492-0082, 10 Brookline Street, is more of a meat-and-potatoes rock club where local and regional music can be heard; Monday nights are reserved for the poetry slam.

Boston has one of the largest Irish communities in the country, and this is mirrored in the number and quality of Irish bars in and around the city. The best (read: most authentically Irish) are probably **F.J. Doyle's Café** ☎ (617) 524-2345, 3484 Washington Street, Jamaica Plain, and **Brendan Behan** ☎ (617) 522 5386, 378 Center Street, Jamaica Plain. In contrast to the these established pubs is a field of newer places, all endowed with rich Guinness, dark rooms and programs of traditional Irish music: **The Burren** ☎ (617) 776-6896, 247 Elm Street, Davis Square, Somerville; **The Field** ☎ (617) 354-7345, 20 Prospect Street, in Central Square, Cambridge, are but two.

A row of clubs on Lansdowne Street, behind Kenmore Square, is the place to ogle big shoes and short skirts. Celebrity disk jockeys and living giants of rock are standard offering. **Axis** ☎ (617) 262-2437, at No. 13, plays house, soul, techno and tribal, and hosts both local and international rock bands. Swanky **Avalon** ☎ (617) 262-2424, at No. 15 is a big, high-tech dance club which also hosts major concerts, and **Karma Club** ☎ (617) 421-9595, at No. 11, takes an enlightened approach to the genre with a decor reminiscent of a Tibetan lamasery.

In Allston, at the **Paradise Rock Club** ☎ (617) 562-8800, 967 Commonwealth Avenue, the music runs from reggae and Euro-techno to retro soul.

Over the years, **Club Passim** ☎ (617) 492-7679, 47 Palmer Street, Harvard Square, Cambridge, has helped launch the careers of such folk greats as Tracy Chapman, Suzanne Vega and Joan Baez. The club is still here, and still hosting the knowns and the soon-to-be-knowns of acoustic music.

JAZZ AND BLUES

Though Boston is no longer the jazz Mecca it was in the 1950s, two high-class clubs still book names from Sonny Rollins to Herbie Hancock, Don Byron to Tito Puente; and there are quite a few smaller venues featuring local talent. The real biggies are **Scullers Jazz Club** ☎ (617) 562-4111, Soldiers Field Road, on the second floor of the Double Tree Guest Suites Hotel, Boston, and the **Regattabar** ☎ (617) 661-5000, in the Charles Hotel, 1 Bennett Street, Harvard Square, Cambridge. Both places seat fewer than 200 at candlelit cocktail tables.

The atmosphere is laid-back at **Ryles** ☎ (617) 876-9330, 212 Hampshire Street, Inman Square, Cambridge, where small jazz ensembles play on the first floor and dance bands from reggae to rock entertain upstairs. Also in Cambridge, the original **House of Blues** ☎ (617) 491-2583, 96 Winthrop Street, serves up jazz and New Orleans-style food to music lovers nightly. When the crowds are packed in, this landmark bar has an intimate living-room feel. The Sunday Gospel Brunch is an institution.

In the South End, jazz comes straight-up without the frills at **Wally's Café** ☎ (671) 424-1408, 427 Massachusetts Avenue. This place has been a jazz purist's hangout since 1947. Not only is the music stellar, but the drinks are cheap and there's no cover charge. At **Bob the Chef's** ☎ (617) 536-6204, 604 Columbus Avenue, Stan Strickland is a regular performer, as are the likes of Toni Washington. The food is as soulful as the music; see WHERE TO EAT, page 102.

Younger jazz lovers gravitate toward trendy nightspots such as the **Wonder Bar** ☎ (617) 351-2665, 189 Harvard Avenue, Allston, **The Good Life** ☎ (617) 451-2622, 28 Kingston Street, Boston, and the **Lizard Lounge** ☎ (617) 547-1228, 1667 Massachusetts Avenue, Cambridge.

SHOPPING

In the Back Bay, **Newbury Street** is the city's equivalent to New York's Fifth Avenue, with its ultra-chic boutiques, clothiers and galleries. Brooks Brothers, Girogio Armani, Louis and MaxMaro offer the latest fashions from cutting-edge designers. Also down the street is Burberry's, makers of the renowned British trench coat that helps to keep Bostonians warm during bitter winters.

At the beginning of Huntington Avenue is the marble-slick **Copley Place**, a $500 million upscale shopping mall. Neiman Marcus department store (nicknamed "needless markup" by Boston wags) — offering a Texas-sized selection of expensive merchandise — sets the lofty tone. (Caution: They don't take Visa or MasterCard.) There are information desks at each entrance. Hours are Monday to Saturday from 10 AM to 8 PM, Sunday from noon to 6 PM. Some stores have extended hours and the cinema and restaurants are open through late evening.

Downtown Crossing is the city's most popular shopping area for all walks of Boston society. Macy's department store has arrived on the scene (in the old Jordan Marsh building), bringing men's and women's clothing and upscale houseware. Then there is Filene's department store, whose basement sales are a Boston tradition. Though still located below Filene's, Filene's Basement Store ☎ (617) 542-2011, 426 Washington Street, is now a separate entity, but the tradition continues unabated; all sorts of designer items are sold at bargain prices, with prices further slashed at regular intervals; unsold merchandise is donated to charity. Don't bother with dressing rooms; join the anarchy and try on those Guess jeans in the aisle.

Snack stands and souvenir kiosks line Quincy Market.

Harvard Square is thick with great bookstores: WordsWorth ☎ (617) 354-5201, at 30 Brattle Street, is a remarkable shop for paperbacks (including foreign editions in English) all discounted 10 percent. WordsWorth is open 363 days a year and late into the evening. Grolier ☎ (617) 547-4648, located on 6 Plympton Street, is the poetry place — a well-stocked hole-in-the-wall that could very well inspire a line or two. The revamped Harvard Cooperative Society ☎ (617) 499-2000, 1400 Massachusetts Avenue, Harvard Square, Cambridge, better known as "the Coop" (pronounced "coop", not "co-op"), is a department store that also houses the official Harvard bookstore, and is the place for all your Harvardiana needs. You may not have a diploma with "Harvard" emblazoned on it, but you can have a pair of Harvard boxer shorts.

A few minutes walk north along Massachusetts Avenue is **Joie de Vivre** ☎ (617) 864-8188, at No. 1792, the ultimate toy store for grown-ups. If you are looking for unusual gifts and souvenirs, it's all here — from electric clocks fashioned out of cans of Spam to Scrabble game-piece earrings. They also have an excellent selection of art postcards.

WHERE TO STAY

Boston hotels are among the most expensive in the country. Several new hotels are either on the drawing board or under construction, but until they materialize the city will continue to have a dearth of hotel rooms, driving up prices and making it essential to make reservations well in advance.

A good source for accommodation bargains is the **Regional Information Complex for Visitors**, on the Massachusetts Turnpike (Interstate 90) at Exit 5. The catch: listed hotels offer discount rates for the same day only, often with a limit of two or three nights lodging. Rates can be as low as 50 percent off, though. Other centers are at Logan Airport and train stations. In all cases, to qualify you must call your chosen lodging from the information complex and tell the reservation clerk the location of the center from which you're calling.

For bed and breakfast reservations, there is the **B & B Agency of Boston** ☎ (617) 720-3540 TOLL-FREE (800) 248-9262 TOLL-FREE IN THE UNITED KINGDOM (0800) 89-5128 FAX (617) 523-5761 WEB SITE www.boston-bnbagency.com, 47 Commercial Wharf, Boston 02110, with listings in Boston, Brookline, Cambridge, some suburbs, and on Cape Cod. (You can even book lodging on a bed-and-breakfast boat in Boston Harbor.) Ask about their winter specials. Bed-and-breakfast lodging can also be arranged through the **Bed and Breakfast Associates Bay Colony, Ltd.** ☎ (617) 720-0522 TOLL-FREE (888) 384-7203 FAX (781) 449-5958, PO Box 57166, Needham 02457. The **Massachusetts Office of Travel and Tourism** ☎ (617) 973-8500 TOLL-FREE (800) 227-6277 WEB SITE www.massvacation.com, 10 Park Plaza, Boston 02116, publishes a list of guesthouses throughout the state in their free *Bed and Breakfast Guide*. Bed and breakfast rates for the area start at around $85 and surge skyward.

THE BACK BAY

Gilded lions guard the entry to the **Fairmont Copley Plaza Hotel** ☎ (617) 267-5300 TOLL-FREE (800) 527-4727 FAX (617) 375-9648, 138 Saint James Avenue, Boston 02116-5002 (luxury), whose ballroom ushers in the seasonal debutantes' cotillion each June. The 373-room hotel on Copley Square offers posh accommodations. The stunningly paneled Oak Room ranks as one of the finest steak houses

in Boston, and the Oak Bar is a top venue for jazz and drinks.

Consistently voted one of the top 20 hotels in the United States, the **Four Seasons Hotel** ✆ (617) 338-4400 TOLL-FREE (800) 332-3442 GUEST FAX (617) 423-0154, 200 Boylston Street, Boston 02116, overlooks the Public Garden and offers top-notch accommodation, dining and entertainment (luxury). Accolades have also gone to its restaurant, **Aujourd'hui** ✆ (617) 351-2071, frequently singled out for its excellence in presentation. The **Bristol Lounge** serves an informal, light breakfast, as well as lunch and dinner (mid-range). Afternoon tea by the fire is a special treat.

The smaller but no less formal **Lenox Hotel** ✆ (617) 536-5300 TOLL-FREE (800) 225-7676 FAX (617) 267-1237, 710 Boylston Street, Boston 02116-2699, has a long history of catering to musical greats; when Enrico Caruso came to town, he stayed here. Within the hotel, **Anago** serves a hearty fusion of Tuscan, Provencal and American cuisines. Downstairs, the **Samuel Adams Brew House** serves passable casual fare and has 12 styles of beer on tap. Guestrooms are elegantly appointed and loaded with facilities to suit both business and leisure travelers (expensive to luxury).

Plunging down the price scale, the **Berkeley Residence/Boston YWCA** ✆ (617) 482-8850 FAX (617) 482-9692, 40 Berkeley Street, Boston 02116, has singles, doubles and triples

Faneuil Hall Marketplace bustles with tourists, snack shops, up-market boutiques and mimes.

BANK OF NEW ENGLAND
287-1900
287-1900
GET ON & OFF
ALL DAY
1 TICKET
SIGHTSEEING
TOURS
BEST TOUR
IN
Beantown

for adult women only (budget). A cafeteria serves inexpensive meals.

A wonderful resource for budget travelers, the 205-bed **Hostelling International (HI) — Boston** ☎ (617) 536-9455 FAX (617) 424-6558 WEB SITE www.bostonhostel.com, 12 Hemenway Street, Boston 02115, has evening lecture and film programs, as well as a kitchen, laundry and game room. Reservations are advised from June to October. Open year-round. The 100-bed **Back Bay Hostel** ☎ (671) 353-3294 or (617) 735-1800 (off-season reservations) FAX (617) 353-4298 (in season), is a second HI facility, at 512 Beacon Street (mailing address: c/o HI-AYH, 1020 Commonwealth Avenue, Boston 02215). Both hostels are located near the Hynes Convention Center T stop, and are open from June 12 to August 16 only.

DOWNTOWN

Adorned with the murals of N.C. Wyeth (the father of Andrew), **Le Meridien Boston** ☎ (617) 451-1900 TOLL-FREE (800) 543-4300 FAX (617) 423-2844, 250 Franklin Street, Boston 02110-2807 (expensive to luxury), is located in the Financial District, near shops and Freedom Trail sights. Guestrooms are irreproachable, and the casual French restaurant, **Café Fleuri** ☎ (617) 451-1900, is noted for its excellent weekend brunch (expensive).

Wedged between Downtown and the Waterfront adjacent to Quincy Market, the **Harborside Inn** ☎ (617) 723-7500 FAX (617) 670-2010, 185 State Street, Boston 02109 (mid-range), occupies a historic granite warehouse. But the interior is warm and inviting, with Victorian furniture and gleaming wood floors, offering the best value in central Boston. Continental breakfast and high-speed Internet access are included in the rates.

THE WATERFRONT

Resembling an upside-down ship's hull, the modern **Marriott Long Wharf** ☎ (617) 227-0800 TOLL-FREE (800) 228-9290 FAX (617) 227-2867, 296 State Street, Boston 02109-2607 (luxury), has an excellent location and 400 comfortable rooms, many of them with spectacular harbor views.

The relatively new **Seaport Hotel** ☎ (617) 385-4000 TOLL-FREE (877) 732-7678 FAX (617) 385-4001 WEB SITE www.seaporthotel.com, 1 Seaport Lane, Boston 02210 (expensive to luxury), is part of the planned Seaport District, the centerpiece of which will be Boston's new Convention Center. Billed as "the next Back Bay" this development is slated for completion by mid-2006, but the Seaport Hotel is up and running in the midst of the construction. There is a health club, heated pool and 24-hour room service.

BEACON HILL

A smart newcomer with contemporary style and an excellent restaurant, **Beacon Hill Hotel & Bistro** ☎ (617) 723-7575 FAX (617) 723-7525, 25 Charles Street, Boston 02114, stands near the Common and Public Garden (expensive). It has limited parking, a rarity in boutique hotels (12 rooms, one suite). The rates include continental breakfast and many high-tech touches.

Well-heeled road warriors, rock stars and sophisticates favor the designer-chic, ultra-contemporary **XV Beacon** ☎ (617) 670-1500 TOLL-FREE (877) 982-3226 E-MAIL hotel@xvbeacon.com, 15 Beacon Street, Boston 02108, at the pinnacle of Beacon Hill, near the State House and corporate law offices, steps from the Common. The 61-room luxury property also includes an excellent New American restaurant for high-rollers, **The Federalist**.

BROOKLINE

It's necessary to leave the center of the city to find inexpensive accommodations of quality. Brookline is a middle-class suburb well-connected to downtown by three branches of the MBTA Green Line, and offers two good value choices. **Beacon Townhouse Inn** ☎ (617) 232-0292 TOLL-FREE (800) 872-7211 FAX (617) 232-5361, 1023 Beacon Street, Brookline 02446-5609, is listed in the National Register for Historic Places. For a mid-range price, it has both modest and larger rooms with private baths. **Brookline Manor Townhouse** ☎ (617) 232-0003 TOLL-FREE (800) 535-5325 FAX (617) 734-5815, 32 Center Street, Brookline

A tourist trolley zips past the impressive Rowe's Wharf building, Atlantic Avenue.

02446-2804, is a four-story Victorian guesthouse on a tree-lined residential avenue. All rooms have private baths. This mid-priced hotel has a few single rooms.

CAMBRIDGE

For nightlife without having to leave the hotel, you can stay at the chic **Charles Hotel** ☎ (617) 864-1200 TOLL-FREE (800) 882-1818 FAX (617) 864-5715, 1 Bennett Street, Cambridge 02138-5707 (expensive to luxury), in Harvard Square, where the Regattabar is one

of the top jazz clubs in Boston (see NIGHTLIFE AND THE ARTS, page 94). Hotel guests receive free entry to all shows midweek and to the late shows on weekends.

Cambridge's new giant on the block is the expensive-to-luxury **Hotel @ MIT** ☎ (617) 577-0200 TOLL-FREE (800) 222-8733 FAX (617) 494-8366, 20 Sidney Street, Cambridge 02139. As might be expected for a hotel associated with MIT, guestrooms are equipped with state-of-the-art technology — including modem connections and ergonomically designed furniture — and technology-inspired touches such as armoires with decorative circuit-board inlays. American cuisine and seasonal specialties are on the card at Sidney's Grille, which also offers 24-hour room service.

In a leafy neighborhood outside Harvard Square, the **Isaac Harding House** ☎ (617) 497-0953, 288 Harvard Street., Cambridge 02139, is a bright, friendly and wheelchair-accessible B&B in a Victorian manse. Continental breakfast and parking are included (budget to mid-range).

WHERE TO EAT

Although you'll be hard pressed to find Boston baked beans or New England boiled dinner on a Boston menu, you will find everything else under the sun. Boston's restaurant scene is sizzling. The choices are varied and the quality is superb. But, like its hotels, Boston's restaurants are pricey. To keep costs down, you can take advantage of lower-priced luncheon menus, offered by many of the restaurants listed below. Also, Cambridge and Somerville restaurants tend to offer more value for the dollar. Reservations are advised for evening meals at all restaurants.

THE BACK BAY

Clio ☎ (617) 536-7200, 370 Commonwealth Avenue, in the Eliot Hotel, is the home kitchen of Ken Oringer, one of America's most celebrated chefs, known for his imaginative reivention of American cuisine (expensive). The wine list is worthy of a baron, and the 11-course tasting menu (nightly) is an epic event. Reserve up to a month ahead.

Stan Frankenthaler continues to amaze with his Malay-tinged fusion cuisine at the ultra-futuristic **Salamander** ☎ (617) 451-2150, 1 Huntington Avenue. Enjoy a baroque feast in the dining room (expensive), or go casual (and cheaper) in the ever-popular satay bar.

The best outdoor scene in Boston is the patio at **Tapeo** ☎ (617) 267-4799, 268 Newbury Street, where Spanish wines and authentic tapas (*real* serrano ham, *machego curado*, stuffed peppers, etc.) are on offer. Poseurs abound on Newbury, but Tapeo is the truly, rather than tragically, hip scene (mid-range).

DOWNTOWN

Downtown at the landmark restaurant **Locke-Ober** ☎ (617) 542-1340, 3 Winter Place, Lydia Shire has made one of Boston's oldest (since the 1870s) elegant dining rooms so celebrated that New Yorkers fly up for dinner — if they can get a reservation. Lunch is less crowded, but reserve ahead for sublimely reinterpreted classic American and French cuisine (expensive).

The Vault ☏ (617) 292-9966, 105 Water Street, has a split personality: New American and Pacific Rim, but both win kudos from sophisticated diners. There's late dining Thursday through Saturday (mid-range to expensive).

Famous for its lobster stew, **Durgin-Park Restaurant** ☏ (617) 227-2038, 5 Faneuil Hall Marketplace, was established "before you were born" — 1827 to be exact. It serves fresh seafood, clam chowder, Boston baked beans and massive plates of prime rib. Durgin-Park does not accept reservations, so arrive early on weekend nights (mid-range to budget).

Established in 1826, **Ye Olde Union Oyster House** ☏ (617) 227-2750, 41 Union Street, is the oldest restaurant in Boston. The oyster bar is fun and the bivalves are delicious, but dine elsewhere unless you want plain food indifferently prepared (mid-range).

Healthy and wholesome, **Milk Street Café** ☏ (617) 542-3663, 50 Milk Street, is Boston's only dairy kosher restaurant. Alas, it only serves lunch, including superb tuna sandwiches and (naturally) chicken soup. The Post Office Square outpost (not strictly kosher) is the ideal spot to assemble a picnic to eat in the park (see THE FINANCIAL DISTRICT, page 80).

Also feeding the Financial District, **Viga** ☏ (617) 482-1113, 291 Devonshire Street, has inexpensive sandwiches and baked pastas. The artichoke pizza is a genuine treat.

BEACON HILL

Beacon Hill, especially along Charles Street, has sidewalk cafés and casual eateries aplenty. There is also the elegant **Lala Rokh** ☏ (617) 720-5511, 97 Mount Vernon Street, just off Charles Street. This Persian delight was recently chosen as one of America's best restaurants by the James Beard Foundation (expensive).

NORTH END

A visit to Boston should include at least one meal in the North End. The competition is stiff, but the best food in the neighborhood is found at **Maurizio's** ☏ (617) 367-1123, 364 Hanover Street, where it's best to get a table by the kitchen and watch the Sardinian chef-owner as he dramatically prepares the fish of the day. Maurizio's takes reservations — so make one. The setting is intimate, the service amiable and the wine list solid and fairly priced (mid-range to expensive).

For more carbo-laden fare, pop around the corner to **Antico Forno** ☏ (617) 723-6733, 93 Salem Street (mid-range), where virtually every dish is kissed by the searing heat of the brick oven. Breads are outstanding — perfect for sopping up the garlicky wine broth that accompanies roasted shrimp and squid.

Only locals know about it (until now) but the finest luncheon fare in the North End is at **Umberto Rosticerria**, 289 Hanover Street. Stand in line and be ready to order quickly for Southern Italian comfort food: pizza, pasta, rice balls and the like (budget).

You'll want to pause for a coffee break on your way through the North End. There are several good places. **Café Vittoria** ☏ (617) 227-7606, 296 Hanover Street, established in 1929, is the oldest Italian café in Boston. It's loaded with Old World charm. The cannoli (from Mike's Bakery) are luscious and authentic.

CHINATOWN

The place for dim sum is **Chow Chau City** ☏ (617) 338-8158, 83 Essex Street, on the top level, where circulating food carts deliver tasty morsels to your table amidst the din of dim sum diners (mid-range).

In Chinatown, you can walk into any Vietnamese restaurant for a cheap, filling and delicious bowl of *pho,* or beef noodle soup. For the chicken version, try **Hu Tieu Nam-Vang** ☏ (617) 422-0501, 7 Beach Street (budget).

SOUTH END

"Glorified chicken with a side of collard greens" are the magic words at **Bob the Chef's** ☏ (617) 536-6204, 604 Columbus Avenue (budget to mid-range). The southern-style cooking includes some delectable desserts, too: save room for a slice of peach

Dining alfresco at Quincy Market.

cobbler, pecan pie or sweet potato pie; take-out or eat-in. There's a jazz brunch on Sunday and live music Thursday to Saturday (see NIGHTLIFE AND THE ARTS, page 94).

Boston's top French bistro is **Hamersley's** ☎ (617) 423-2700, 553 Tremont Street. Characterized by informal chic, this South End eatery has good light fare as well as hearty dinners. The menu changes six times a year and specialties include a grilled mushroom and garlic sandwich. There is outdoor seating in season (expensive).

Le Gamin ☎ (617) 654-8969, 550 Tremont Street, is a casual crêperie across from the Boston Center for the Arts, serving authentic crêpes, both *salée* (savory, and accompanied by a salad of mesclun with vinaigrette) and *sucrée* (sweet). Nothing exotic here — *jambon-fromage* (ham and cheese) tops the card, but there are more daring items such as the goat cheese and turkey crêpe. The dessert crêpes are delicious (budget).

EAST BOSTON

The legendary **Santarpio's** ☎ (617) 567-9871, 113 Chelsea Street, has the best pizza in Boston — hands down, forks up. Order a pie with lamb kebabs on the side for the ultimate under-the-bridge experience (budget).

CAMBRIDGE

French bistro fare with a Cuban accent is the key to **Chez Henri** ☎ (617) 354-8980, 1 Shepard Street, Cambridge. Get in line early, as there are no reserved tables. If all else fails, settle for spicy duck *confit* tamales at the bar, home of one of Boston's liveliest social scenes.

Inman Square is Cambridge's hottest dining scene. The new and lovely **Argana** ☎ (617) 868-1247, 1287 Cambridge Street, Cambridge, serves spicy (if pricey) Moroccan food and boasts a stunning bar and good wine list. Try the chicken *tagine* with preserved lemon and the cumin-laced eggplant compote (mid-range to expensive).

A few doors down, **East Coast Grill** ☎ (617) 491-6568, 1271 Cambridge Street, Cambridge, has lines out the door for Chris Schlesinger's smoky dishes, including whole grilled fish (expensive). The author of *Thrill of the Grill* also prepares an excellent Sunday brunch.

At **Pho Pasteur** ☎ (617) 864-4100, 35 Dunster Street, Harvard Square, fresh orchids decorate the tables and huge bowls of *bun* (noodles) come topped with fresh mint, basil and a choice of grilled meats, shrimp or spring rolls. Service is efficient if a little impersonal. Open all day. There are three other locations around town: 116 Newbury Street, Boston ☎ (617) 262-8200; 682 Washington Street, Boston ☎ (617) 482-7467; and 137 Brighton Avenue, Brighton ☎ (617) 783-2340 (budget).

Iruña ☎ (617) 868-5633, 56 JFK Street, is a long-time Basque favorite of poets, scholars and lovers of casual Iberian cooking. Be prepared for a heady dose of garlic, order the squid, and watch carefully for the sign, as the restaurant is set back from the street (mid-range).

Mr. and Mrs. Bartley's ☎ (617) 354-6559, 1246 Massachusetts Avenue, serves up the best burgers in town, as well as unusual twists on New England standards such as a turkey sandwich with stuffing, gravy and cranberry sauce (recommended). The atmosphere is genial with diners sitting elbow-to-elbow. The lime rickies — sweet soda fountain drinks made with fresh limes — at Mr. and Mrs. Bartley's are without a doubt the best in New England. After a long ramble in the square, get a large rickie and walk down toward the Charles River away from the hubbub of Harvard Square (budget).

ZuZu ☎ (617) 492-9181, 472 Massachusetts Avenue, brings Lebanese bistro with panache to the ethnic-dining Mecca of Central Square. Chef Joseph Halaby's delicious Middle Eastern version of bouillabaisse has enough fish to feed a family. Desserts (mostly chocolate or lemon) are as intense as the Arabic coffee (mid-range).

SOMERVILLE

Washington Square is worth a detour for **Dalí** ☎ (617) 661-3254, 415 Washington Street (corner of Beacon Street), the best tapas restaurant in the city. There is a wide assortment of cold and hot tapas delicious and filling enough to make a meal of — pork sausage with figs, mussels with avocado, and roast duckling with berry sauce. *Platos principales* (main courses) offer a choice of leg of lamb, beef tenderloin, boneless pheasant, or fresh fish (budget to expensive).

On an opposing corner, **EVOO** ☎ (617) 661-3866, 118 Beacon Street, surprises with the sophistication of New American cooking in a true neighborhood bistro run by the chef and his wife. Stop by in the afternoon and you might find the chef smoking some trout or duck in the driveway out back (mid-range to expensive).

When you say "Davis Square" to many Massachusetts residents, they'll likely think of **Redbones** ☎ (617) 628-2200, 55 Chester Street (off Elm Street), Davis Square, Somerville. Inexpensive and informal, Redbones specializes in slow-cooked Memphis-style barbecue. The pulled-pork sandwich is out-of-this-world, and the beer is cold and plentiful, with some 50 varieties on tap. Or try the catfish and a mason jar of homemade iced tea or lemonade. Don't skip the buffalo shrimp starter with blue-cheese dip. A limited late-night menu is available Sunday to Thursday from 10:30 PM to 12:30 AM, Friday and Saturday from 11:30 PM to 12:30 AM.

Tucked away in an unpretentious Somerville square, **Sound Bites** ☎ (617) 623-8338, 708 Broadway, is another worthwhile detour, much loved for its terrific breakfasts and sunny atmosphere. Delicious and fresh omelets, mashed home fries and serve-yourself coffee make this Boston's best breakfast. Lunch is wonderful, too — healthy food with zingy Middle Eastern leanings. It's open from 7 AM to 3 PM.

HOW TO GET THERE

Boston is 208 miles (338 km) northeast of New York city. Interstate 95 leads into Boston from New York and Providence. In the west the Massachusetts Turnpike (Interstate 90) and Route 2 converge on the city; and from the north it's Interstate 93 from New Hampshire and Interstate 95 from Portsmouth, New Hampshire and the Maine coast.

More than 40 airlines serve **Logan International Airport** TOLL-FREE (800) 235-6246 (see TRAVELERS' TIPS, page 341, for a list of airline toll-free numbers), which is located in East Boston, about two miles (three kilometers) outside of downtown. There is a bewildering array of ways to get to and from the airport, including a water shuttle to Rowes Wharf, and the usual assortment of limos and hotel vans. If you're traveling light, the T (see GETTING AROUND, page 77) is a fine way to travel. The drawback is that you must change lines twice. Logan operates a free bus shuttle service to the Airport T station. Taxis are readily available at the airport if you prefer door-to-door service. A cab ride to downtown is about $10. There is the usual array of rental car agencies at Logan (see TRAVELERS' TIPS, page 344, for a list of toll-free numbers), but driving into Boston from the airport during daylight hours is not a recommended experience no matter how steely you think your nerves are. Logan's **ground transportation hotline** TOLL-FREE (800) 235-6426 provides 24-hour information on transportation alternatives to and from the airport.

Amtrak trains ☎ (617) 482-3660 TOLL-FREE (800) 872-7245 leave from South Station in Boston, where you also can catch the MBTA Commuter Rail (to points south) and the Red Line subway. Amtrak offers excursion fares, discounts for children and rail passes good for unlimited travel. In Boston, Amtrak departs from South Station and Back Bay Station. Service to Portland, Maine, with intermediate stops, leaves from North Station. More than half of Amtrak's Northeast Corridor schedule now features high-speed trains (see GETTING THERE, page 341 in TRAVELERS' TIPS).

Eastern and Central Massa-chusetts

While half the population of the state lives in Boston and its outlying suburbs, if you want to know Massachusetts, historically speaking, you'll need to look further afield. Momentous Revolutionary War sites are found northwest of the metropolitan area in the wealthy enclaves of Lexington and Concord. It is history, as well as splendid beaches, that draw day-trippers along the coast to the north of Boston — where the maritime ports like Salem exert a supernatural pull on tourists — and to the south for the hallowed colonial monument of Plymouth, the first New England colony.

Further west, the countryside transforms into a land of lakes and trails, colleges and cornfields — as well as strung-out rust-belt towns attesting to the state's role in yet another "revolution," the American Industrial one. The Connecticut River, watering the student-rich Pioneer Valley, cuts through the center of the state.

THE NORTH SHORE

Salt air, white sand beaches, squawking seagulls — you get the picture: the North Shore is where pallid Bostonians go to get a tan. It's also a good place to soak in some history — and not a few legends, as will attest a trip to Salem, known as much for its seventeenth-century witch trials as its maritime history.

GENERAL INFORMATION

The **North of Boston Convention and Visitors Bureau** ☎ (978) 977-7760 WEB SITE www.northofboston.org, 17 Peabody Square, Peabody 01960, has prepared a wealth of literature on the area's museums and historic houses and public buildings.

MARBLEHEAD

With its gorgeous rocky beach and magnificent harbor, Marblehead is the North Shore at its most scenic. Along the narrow streets, homes bear plaques with the date of construction; many of them date to the Revolutionary War, when Marblehead was a busy shipping center. When you're not touring historic homes, there are scores of little shops selling antiques, jewelry clothing, and boating paraphernalia. Yachting is big in Marblehead and there is sailboat racing all summer long, peaking with **Marblehead Race Week** at the end of July. On summer weekends "Old Town" is jammed with visitors; try to go on a weekday.

Marblehead's **Chamber of Commerce** ☎ (781) 631-2868 WEB SITE www.marbleheadchamber.org, PO Box 76, Marblehead 01945, has a seasonal information booth on Pleasant Street near Spring Street. They publish a 48-page visitors guide, as well as various pamphlets on dining, shopping, and accommodations, and a map of the historic district with walking tours.

SALEM

"At first the girls would not answer, for fear of being discovered. They simply screamed and writhed or did blasphemous things, such as dashing a Bible against the wall. But gradually they began to give names."

Thus begins an inquisitor's account of Puritan Salem's 1692 Witch Trials. The episode was sparked by a well-meaning Barbadian slave named Tituba, a servant of the Reverend Samuel Parris, whose talent for storytelling impressed her charges, Parris' nine-year-old daughter Betty and her 11-year-old cousin, Abigail Williams. The girls soon invited friends to share in the excitement. Hysteria followed when the girls complained of nightmares. When local doctors declared that the girls were witches, people started to believe that the Devil had come to town. In the end, 19 people were hung before Cotton Mather and his father, Harvard president Increase Mather, led the call for tolerance.

What to See and Do

Salem leans on its "bewitching" legacy (its tourism slogan, is "Stop by for a Spell"), but the city is not all hocus-pocus. It's also rich in maritime history. Of Salem's seafarers, native son Nathaniel Hawthorne wrote, "They sailed where no others dared to go, anchored where no one else dreamed of making a trade."

Fishermen's dinghies moored at Rockport on picturesque Cape Ann.

Destination Salem TOLL-FREE (877) 725-3662 WEB www.salem.org, 63 Wharf Street, Salem 01970, can help you plan your trip to the city. A new **Visitor Center** ☎ (978) 740-1650 run by the National Park Service is located at 2 New Liberty Street.

From the early eighteenth century, Salem was an important port and shipbuilding town, home of many wealthy merchants — a legacy that has left the town with many wonderful examples of Federal, Georgian, and Greek Revival architecture. A considerable sampling of them can be seen on the

McIntire Heritage District Walk, a self-guided, one-mile (1.6-km) tour. Maps are available at the National Park Service (above).

Salem's seafaring legacy is beautifully documented at the **Peabody Essex Museum** ☎ (978) 745-9500 WEB SITE www.pem.org, East India Square, begun in 1799 by 22 sea captains. By 1821 they had collected 2,000 items from all over the world; today, the collection numbers more than 300,000 artifacts and works of art exhibited in seven buildings and 30 galleries. Included are ships' figureheads and models, paintings, gold, silver and textiles. There are guided tours daily at 2 PM. Open Tuesday to Sunday, also Monday April to October; an admission fee is charged.

ABOVE: Many visitors mistake this evocative statue of Salem founder Roger Conant (1592–1679) for a witch. OPPOSITE: A boy dressed in seventeenth-century style leads the way to the Salem Witch Museum.

At the nine-acre (three-and-a-half hectare) **Salem Maritime National Historic Site** ☎ (978) 740-1660, 193 Derby Street, you can start your visit by viewing the free "To the Farthest Port of the Far East" (shown every half-hour) at the orientation center. From here, you can wander around Derby Wharf, the West India Goods Store, the Bonded Warehouse, then cross the street to the 1819 Custom House which contains restored offices, including those of Nathaniel Hawthorne. Or you may choose to join one of the well-researched ranger-led walking tours. Open daily year-round from 9 AM to 5 PM, to 6 PM July and August; a fee is charged for tours.

Nathaniel Hawthorne's 1851 novel, *The House of the Seven Gables* was inspired by legends of the 1668 house built by Captain John Turner and later occupied by one of Hawthorne's cousins. **The House of the Seven Gables** ☎ (978) 744-0991, 54 Turner Street, still stands, and a tour is not to be missed. (If you haven't read the book, an audiovisual program fills you in on the plot.) Guides take visitors around the house pointing out six rooms of period furniture and a narrow secret staircase that figures in the story. Open daily for guided tours with costumed interpreters; an admission fee is charged.

More costumed interpreters await at **Salem 1630: Pioneer Village** ☎ (978) 745-0525 or (978) 744-0991, Forest River Park (off West Avenue), a recreation of life in Salem four years after European settlement. There are tours of this Puritan village, craft demonstrations, and farm animals. Open mid-April to November; an admission fee is charged. To get there, take Lafayette Street (Routes 114 and 1A) south to West Avenue, turn left, and follow the signs. Combination tickets are available for the House of Seven Gables and Salem 1630.

At the **Salem Witch Museum** ☎ (978) 744-1692 TOLL-FREE (80) 544-1692, Washington Square North, 13 life-sized stage settings present a historically accurate drama examining the 1692 witchcraft hysteria. It's a visit that is both thought provoking and timeless in its relevance to present-day issues of human rights and tolerance. Open daily; an admission fee is charged.

SALEM
CH MUSEU

You can buy all sorts of potions and powders, crystal balls, magic wands, moonstones and tarot cards at the **Broom Closet** ☎ (978) 741-3669, 3–5 Central Street, and at **Crow's Haven Corner** ☎ (978) 745-8763, 125 Essex Street. The latter is a tiny shop owned by Laurie Cabot, a present day witch. Ms. Cabot gives readings by appointment.

Where to Stay and Eat

As there is much to see and do in Salem, some visitors choose to stay overnight. The **Salem Inn** ☎ (978) 741-0680, 7 Summer Street, Salem 01970, comprises three centrally located historic houses with a total of 39 rooms from large doubles big enough to accommodate families to cozy nooks. The rate (mid-range) includes a continental breakfast. An inexpensive alternative is the **Coach House Inn** ☎ (978) 744-4092 TOLL-FREE (800) 688-8689, 284 Lafayette Street, Salem 01970, a former sea captain's mansion with bright, spacious rooms furnished with antiques and four poster beds (budget to mid-range).

Window boxes adorn a typical clapboard house on Cape Ann's "Painter's Path."

For dining there is the **Lyceum Bar & Grill** ☎ (978) 745-7665, 43 Church Street, serving continental cuisine. It was here that Alexander Graham Bell first demonstrated his telephone. On the Common, the **Tavern at the Hawthorne** ☎ (978) 825-4342 extends a warm fireside welcome with light lunch fare or lobster dinners and entertainment in pub-style atmosphere. The **Peabody Essex Museum Café** ☎ (978) 745-1876, East India Square, overlooks the museum's oriental garden, and offers lunch and Sunday brunch, as well as a Friday evening six-course dinner with live jazz entertainment.

How to Get There

Salem is 16 miles (26 km) north of Boston. Motorists will take Exit 57 off Interstate 95. You can also take a **ferry** from Long Wharf in Boston, with several trips daily between July and October. Contact **Boston Harbor Cruises** ☎ (617) 227-4321. **MBTA buses** run from Haymarket Square (lines #450 or #455) to downtown Salem. The **Commuter Rail** (a 30-minute ride) runs from North Station, on the Rockport/Ipswich Line.

CAPE ANN: GLOUCESTER AND ROCKPORT

The quality of natural light on Cape Ann has long attracted artists and photographers to its picturesque villages. More rustic than Marblehead to the south, the towns of Manchester-by-the-Sea, Gloucester, and Rockport cling to rocky shores brimming with beaches, shops, and casual seafood restaurants. The **Cape Ann Chamber of Commerce** ☎ (978) 283-1601 TOLL-FREE (800) 321-0133 WEB SITE www.capeannvacations.com, 33 Commercial Street, Gloucester 01930, provides informational materials on the region.

Traveling north to Cape Ann from Boston, one first comes upon the village of **Manchester-by-the-Sea**, draped around a picture-perfect harbor. Traces of the town's former life as a nineteenth-century resort community can still be seen. There are some historic residences, and the downtown district has shops and restaurants. The first settlement on Cape Ann, however — and the oldest seaport in the nation (1623) — is **Gloucester**. The statue of the Gloucester fisherman, which faces the sea, is a New England landmark. The statue's inscription mourns, "They that go down to the sea in ships." More than 10,000 Gloucester men have been lost

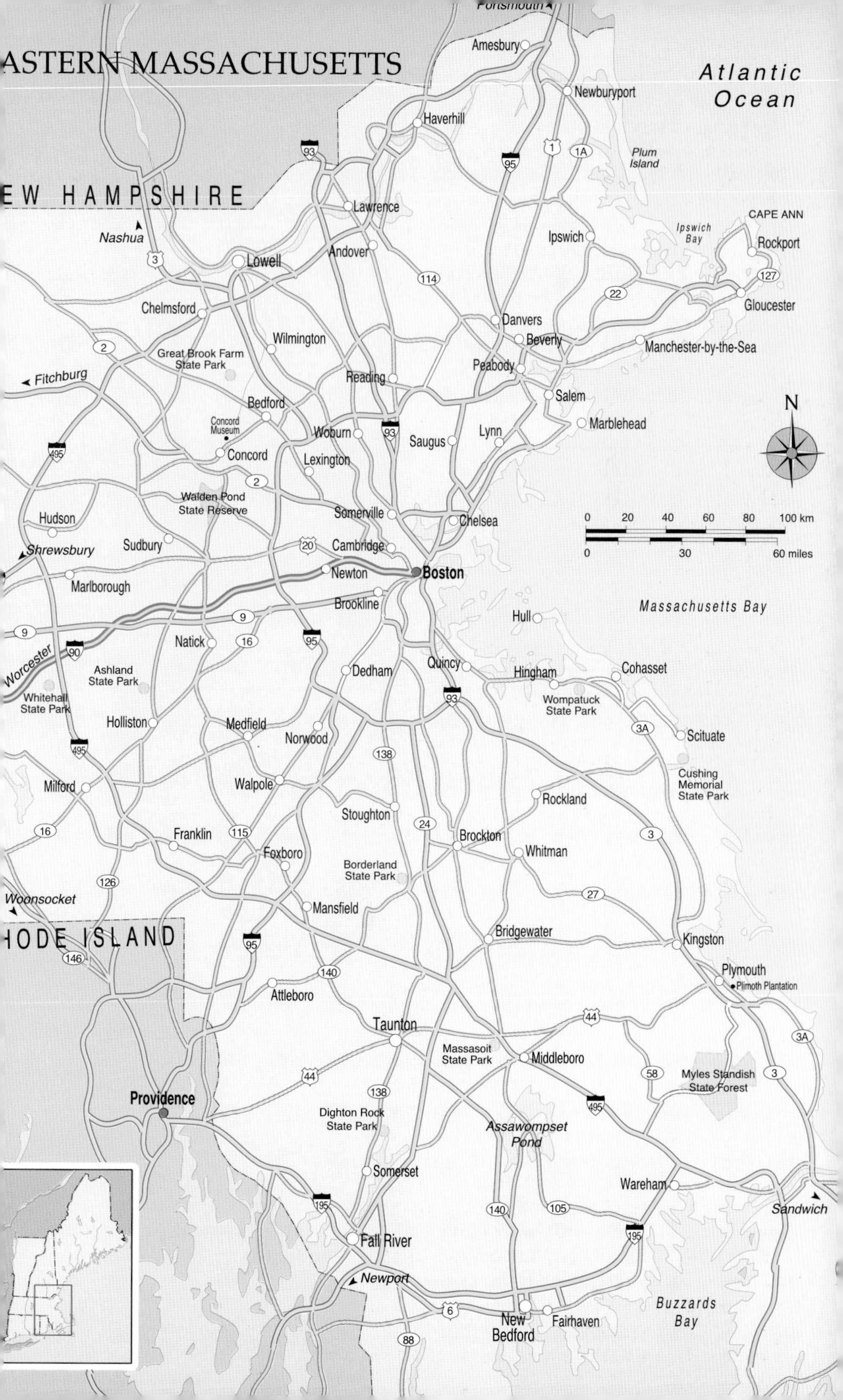

ASTERN MASSACHUSETTS
Portsmouth
Atlantic Ocean
EW HAMPSHIRE
HODE ISLAND
Amesbury
Newburyport
Haverhill
Plum Island
Lawrence
Nashua
Lowell
Andover
Ipswich
Ipswich Bay
CAPE ANN
Rockport
Gloucester
Chelmsford
Wilmington
Danvers
Beverly
Manchester-by-the-Sea
Great Brook Farm State Park
Fitchburg
Reading
Peabody
Salem
Bedford
Concord Museum
Woburn
Saugus
Lynn
Marblehead
Concord
Lexington
N
Hudson
Walden Pond State Reserve
Somerville
Chelsea
Shrewsbury
Sudbury
Cambridge
Newton
Boston
0 20 40 60 80 100 km
0 30 60 miles
Marlborough
Brookline
Massachusetts Bay
Hull
Natick
Worcester
Ashland State Park
Dedham
Quincy
Hingham
Cohasset
Whitehall State Park
Wompatuck State Park
Holliston
Medfield
Norwood
Scituate
Cushing Memorial State Park
Milford
Walpole
Rockland
Stoughton
Franklin
Brockton
Whitman
Foxboro
Borderland State Park
Woonsocket
Mansfield
Bridgewater
Kingston
Plymouth
Plimoth Plantation
Attleboro
Taunton
Massasoit State Park
Middleboro
Myles Standish State Forest
Providence
Dighton Rock State Park
Assawompset Pond
Somerset
Wareham
Sandwich
Fall River
Newport
New Bedford
Fairhaven
Buzzards Bay

in three centuries of fishing. Each June, the **Blessing of the Fleet** ceremony takes place during Saint Peter's Fiesta.

The **Cape Ann Historical Museum** ((978) 283-0455, 27 Pleasant Street, chronicles Gloucester's social and fishing history as well as its luminous place in the annals of American art. The museum's collection of maritime paintings by Gloucester native Fitz Hugh Lane is unparalleled. Considered America's parallel to Britain's Turner, the mid-nineteenth century artist depicted ships and shorelines — but all the while was really painting coastal light. His achievements, little recognized in his own time, later drew Winslow Homer, Milton Avery and Marsden Hartley to paint in Gloucester. The museum is open Tuesday to Saturday 10 AM to 5 PM; an admission fee is charged.

Another fishing village and artists' colony, **Rockport**'s by now clichéd landmark, **Motif No. 1**, is a weathered red lobster shack, a subject for countless painters. It's a recent replica of the original, which was destroyed in a storm a few years ago. Rockport has a bumper crop of galleries, crafts shops, and restaurants crowded into fishing shanties along the winding lanes of **Bearskin Neck**. **Halibut Point Reservation**, along Route 127 in Rockport, is a coastal park filled with old granite quarries and offering views up the Atlantic coast.

Whale watching is a major preoccupation on Cape Ann with cruises sailing out of Gloucester and Rockport to Stellwagen Bank and Jeffreys Ledge. Companies include: Cape Ann Whale Watch ((978) 283-5110, Rose's Wharf, Gloucester; Rockport Whale Watch ((978) 546-3377, 9 Tuna Wharf, Rockport.

Much of the North Shore is rocky, but **Singing Beach** in Manchester-by-the-Sea, is a beautiful crescent of white sand surrounded by rocky headlands. It's named for the sound your feet make as they glide across the quartz granules that form the strand. It's a hot spot since it's accessible by public transportation: take the Rockport commuter rail from North Station, getting off at Manchester Station, walk the half-mile to the beach, or rent a bike from Seaside Cycle ((978) 526-1200.

Rockport harbor with its unavoidable landmark: Motif No. 1, a weathered red lobster shack.

LAURA R.
JUDITH LEE
ROCKPORT, MA.

Gloucester's three beaches are **Stage Fort Park**, at Gloucester Harbor; **Wingaersheek Beach**, on Atlantic Street; and **Good Harbor Beach**, on Thatcher Road. Rockport beaches can be found past Gloucester on Route 127A. **Front Beach** and **Back Beach** are both located in the center of Rockport (metered parking). **Old Garden Beach** is secluded and residential and within walking distance from downtown, but there are no toilets.

There is notable nightlife, too, led by the **Gloucester Stage Company** ☎ (978) 281-4099, 267 East Main Street, founded in 1979 by playwright Israel Horovitz as a workshop and stage for new plays. All performances take place at the Gloucester Stage Company.

When dining out, remember that Rockport is a "dry" town: no alcohol is served or sold. You can, however, bring wine into most of the restaurants that line Bearskin Neck. Seafood is the standard fare and prices are budget to mid-range.

Cape Ann is about 30 miles (48 km) from Boston. Follow either Route 93 or Route 1 north to the intersection with Route 128. Take Route 128 east to its end in Gloucester.

IPSWICH, NEWBURYPORT AND PLUM ISLAND

A colonial town about 21 miles (34 km) north of Rockport on Route 1A, Ipswich still has nearly 50 residences that were built before 1725, with several from the 1600s. One of the finest is the John Whipple House (on Main Street), which dates back to 1640. Ipswich has the splendid Crane Beach with "refreshing" water (read: rather cold) and walking trails. Follow up a swim and a walk with a feast of a regional classic: delectable Ipswich clams, available at any restaurant in the village.

During the eighteenth and nineteenth centuries, Newburyport's large merchant vessel fleet made local sea captains wealthy. Their restored Federal-style mansions line High and surrounding streets. One of the finest is now the **Cushing House Museum** ☎ (978) 462-2681, 98 High Street, built in 1808 for Caleb Cushing, the first United States envoy to China. Tours of the 21-room Federal-style building show artifacts he brought back from his tour of duty in the Orient. The museum is also home to the Historical Society of Olde Newbury. The museum is open May to October Tuesday to Friday 10 AM to 4 PM, Saturday 12 PM to 4 PM; an admission fee is charged.

Maudslay State Park ☎ (978) 465-7223, Curzon's Mill Road, is a 480-acre (194-hectare) park with 16 miles (26 km) of hiking and cross-country skiing trails as well as two sledding hills — one for toddlers, the other for older kids. Set in a natural amphitheater within the state park is the **Maudslay Arts Center** ☎ (978) 499-0050, which offers a diverse musical program. In town there are more cultural offerings at the **Firehouse Center for the Performing and Visual Arts** ☎ (978) 462-7336, Market Square, which houses an art gallery, **visitors' center**, and a 200-seat theater, presenting a yearly season of professional productions.

The five-mile-long (eight-kilometer) white-sand **Crane Beach** ☎ (508) 356-4351 or (508) 356-4354, at the end of Argilla Road on Ipswich Bay, Ipswich, is an expansive stretch of sand and another of the area's best. From here, the Pine Hollow Trail leads hikers on an hour-long trek along the shore and through a red-maple swamp.

Three miles (five kilometers) east of Newburyport is **Plum Island and Parker River National Wildlife Refuge** ☎ (508) 465-5753, off Route 1 and Interstate 95, a national wildlife refuge where more than 250 species of migratory birds stop to rest along the Atlantic flyway each spring and fall. Vistas of the island's dunes, marshes, and its six-mile-long (10-km) beach can be enjoyed from an observation tower. In the fall, wild beach plums and cranberries flourish along the shore. On hot summer days, beach-goers flock to Plum Island; you must get there early to avoid disappointment as rangers limit the number of visitors to this fragile environment. It is closed at least through July 1 to protect the nesting piping plovers (about half the beach is closed year-round for bird-nesting areas).

Always bring an insect repellent to the beach. "Greenheads," stinging flies (at their worst in late July), can ruin a trip to the seashore. Parking costs $5.

Newburyport is about 45 minutes from Boston, and less than six miles (10 km) from the New Hampshire state line. From Boston take Interstate 93 to Interstate 95 and follow it to Exit 57. Look for the **welcome center** at Exit 57.

THE SOUTH SHORE

Plymouth, sight of the first New World colony, celebrates Thanksgiving Day each year with a traditional New England dinner (reservations are taken beginning in August; call Plimoth Plantation, below). Further south in New Bedford, it is the history of the whaling industry that takes the spotlight.

PLYMOUTH

The **Plymouth County Convention and Visitors Bureau** ((508) 747-0100 TOLL-FREE (800) 231-1620, PO Box 1620, Pembroke 02359, provides tourist information.

Every American schoolchild knows about **Plymouth Rock**, the boulder where the Mayflower Pilgrims are said to have alit on December 21, 1620. Said "Rock" is covered by an elaborate Greek Revival pavilion on the Water Street Harbor shore and marked with a plaque. You can't miss it.

Plymouth Rock can be a letdown, but the city's two star attractions — Plimoth Plantation and the *Mayflower II* — are crowd pleasers. **Plimoth Plantation** ((508) 746-1622, extension 210, is a living-history museum that recreates Plymouth Colony, the 1627 settlement of the Pilgrims. Men and women portray the dress, speech and manner of actual residents of the community, bringing to life the routines and activities of seventeenth-century Plymouth. You will get a good overview of the village, with its many thatch-roofed cottages, from the Fort Meetinghouse. The newest exhibit is Hobbamock's Homesite, a reconstruction of a Wampanoag village.

The ***Mayflower II*** (at State Pier) is a full-scale replica of the vessel that brought the 103 settlers from England. Here again, you'll find guides dressed in period costumes and playing the roles of the passengers and crew who made the treacherous crossing. The characters are happy to demonstrate seventeenth-century skills and answer questions about the first colony of Pilgrims. It was

aboard the *Mayflower* that the famous Mayflower Compact was signed, the first act of communal government in America. You can buy a combination ticket to Plimoth Plantation and the *Mayflower II*. Both are open April to November.

Cranberries, those super-sour little fruits, are a specialty of the region. In fact, southern Massachusetts produces more than 50 percent of the nation's cranberry crop. **Cranberry World** ((508) 866-8190, at Edaville Railroad in nearby South Carver, traces the history of the very red berry from colonial

OPPOSITE: Smith's Cove, Gloucester, Cape Ann. ABOVE: Building a house the hard way at Plimoth Plantation, where the seventeenth century comes to life.

times to the present along with tours of working cranberry bogs and cooking demonstrations. Open weekends July to October, daily November to early January; admission is free.

Plymouth is 37 miles (59 km) south of Boston on Interstate 93. For the scenic route to Plymouth, exit Interstate 93 onto Route 3A; take Route 3 for a speedier trip.

NEW BEDFORD

In the second chapter of his classic novel *Moby-Dick*, Herman Melville (1819–1891) says that Nantucket may have been the romantic home of whaling, but it was New Bedford that made whaling an industry. Indeed, New Bedford, a deepwater port on Buzzards Bay, was once the greatest whaling center in the world, providing work for more than 10,000 men. The discovery of oil in Pennsylvania in the late 1850s marked the beginning of the end for New Bedford. With its whaling fleet depleted by the Civil War and losses in Arctic waters, New Bedford's whaling gave way to textile manufacturing.

For informational materials in advance of your visit, contact the **Bristol County Convention and Visitors Bureau** ☎ (508) 997-1250 TOLL-FREE (800) 288-6263 FAX (508) 997-9090.

For 175 years, New Bedford's whalers were known throughout the world. From the **Waterfront Visitor's Center**, on Old Pier Three, it is a short trip up Johnny Cake Hill to the **New Bedford Whaling National Historic Park** ☎ (508) 996-4095, 33 William Street. Established in 1996, the historic park preserves a 13-block, 20-acre (eight-hectare) area of the city much as it was in the heyday of New Bedford whaling. The visitor center offers free tours and a self-guided walking tour map.

The centerpiece of the park is the **New Bedford Whaling Museum** ☎ (508) 997-0046, 18 Johnny Cake Hill, run by the Old Dartmouth Historical Society. It's the largest museum in America devoted to the history of the American whaling industry. Among the museum's highlights are vast skeletons of whales and the half-scale model of the bark *Lagoda*, built in 1915. In the Panorama Room gallery, there are two 50-ft (15-m) sections from a quarter-mile-long (400-m) painting depicting one year aboard an 1847 whaler. The museum theater shows a film of an actual whaling expedition, complete with a "Nantucket sleigh ride," or whale chase. (After being harpooned a whale might have pulled a 10-man dory at top speed for several miles until the animal tired and could be finished off.) Open year-round, 9 AM to 5 PM daily; an admission fee is charged.

Across the street from the museum is the **Seamen's Bethel**, 15 Johnny Cake Hill, the whaleman's chapel of Melville's *Moby-Dick*. Built in 1832, it contains a pulpit resembling the hull of a ship and memorial tablets dedicated to sailors lost at sea.

New Bedford is 54 miles (87 km) from Boston. Take Routes 140 and 24. Interstate 195 connects New Bedford with Providence (about 30 miles or 48 km to the west).

FALL RIVER

On the waterfront at Fall River, **Battleship *Massachusetts*** ☎ (508) 678-1100, Battleship Cove, is a five-vessel complex where you can see and board the USS *Massachusetts*, an enormous battleship that saw action in World War II. Nearby are the smaller USS *Lionfish*,

OPPOSITE: A full-scale replica of the *Mayflower* is moored at Plymouth. ABOVE: The New Bedford Whaling National Historic Park explores the region's seafaring legacy.

the destroyer USS *Joseph P. Kennedy* and the *Hiddensee,* a Russian missile corvette. Open daily 9 AM to 4:30 PM.

Fall River is Lizzie Borden's hometown, made famous in the grizzly nursery rhyme about this unresolved murder: "Lizzie Borden took an ax and gave her mother 40 whacks, and when she saw what she had done, she gave her father 41." The verse remains, despite that fact that Lizzie Borden was acquitted of the murder in 1893. Those with a fascination for the morbid can visit the **Lizzie Borden Museum** ☎ (508) 675-7333, 92 Second Street, situated in the Greek Revival-style mansion that was her family's home. Guided tours also take in the history of Fall River in the 1890s. Open April 7 to December 24. The house is also a **bed and breakfast** inn (expensive).

Fall River is 15 miles (24 km) from Providence (take Interstate 195) and 60 miles (96 km) from Boston (take Route 24).

TOURS AND EXCURSIONS

Captain John Boats ☎ (508) 746-2643 TOLL-FREE (800) 242-2469, 10 Town Wharf, Plymouth 02360, offers ferry transportation from Plymouth to Provincetown from Memorial Day to September. The ferry ride cuts your traveling time in half, making it ideal for day-trippers; a narrated tour of historic Plymouth kicks off the voyage. Once in Provincetown, you can easily explore the town and Race Point Beach on foot or rent a bicycle to go further afield.

LEXINGTON AND CONCORD

"Bloody Butchery by the British Troops!" screamed the headlines of the *Salem Gazette,* describing the fight between 77 colonial militiamen and 700 regular British troops at Lexington Green on April 19, 1775. These were the "shots heard 'round the world."

Revolutionary skirmishes occurred in Concord also, but the town was also home to several figures in the young nation's intelligentsia. Henry David Thoreau, Nathaniel Hawthorne, Ralph Waldo Emerson and Louisa May Alcott called Concord home — at the same time. See LINGER WITH LITERARY LIGHTS, page 15 in TOP SPOTS.

BACKGROUND

Word of the April 19 battle at Lexington Green flamed through the American colonies. Suddenly what had begun as a struggle between English authorities and the people of Massachusetts escalated into a war for independence that lasted more than eight years.

By 1775, Britain's economic policies had transformed America into a powder keg of discontent. The English government suggested that General Thomas Gage, governor

of Massachusetts and commander of the British forces, jail revolutionary rabble-rousers such as Samuel Adams and John Hancock. But Gage decided on what he thought was a less inflammatory engagement: to seize the revolutionaries' arms supplies stored in Concord. Boston's revolutionaries knew of Gage's plan before his troops left the city and sent William Dawes and Paul Revere on horseback to Lexington with news of the advancing soldiers.

In Lexington, revolutionaries gathered at Buckman's Tavern on the Common to await the arrival of the British troops. When the 77 minutemen saw the Redcoats, they formed two long lines. Militia Captain John Parker exhorted his men, "Stand your ground. Don't fire unless fired upon. But if they mean to have a war, let it begin here!"

Soon British officer Major John Pitcairn ordered the patriots to disband; in the face of more than 700 British regulars, there wasn't much else they could do. As the militiamen obeyed, a shot rang out, no one knows from which side. Then British troops, many of them inexperienced in actual combat, began firing at the revolutionaries, ignoring their commanders' orders to stop. When it was over, eight Americans lay dead and the first battle of the Revolution had taken place.

The British continued to Concord where they searched all buildings for arms; what they found they burned or tossed into ponds. When the revolutionaries saw smoke coming from Concord, they thought the British were burning the town and advanced to attack them at Concord's North Bridge. "Fire, fellow soldiers, for God's sake, fire!" yelled revolutionary Major Buttrick of Concord. Having been joined by minutemen from the surrounding countryside, the militia soon outnumbered the English by four to one.

The battle raged on. The British were driven into retreat along the road back to Boston, where they were attacked constantly. One British officer said it "seemed as if there was a musket behind every tree." The heaviest fighting took place at Menotomy, with more than 5,000 troops on both sides. Eventually, the British reinforcements arrived to save Gage's troops from annihilation and they retreated to Bunker Hill in Boston.

England now knew that the American rebellion ran deeper than dissatisfaction over taxes; the American people were prepared to fight.

GENERAL INFORMATION

The **Concord Chamber of Commerce** ((978) 369-3120 WEB SITE www.concordmachamber.org, at 105 Everett Street, Concord 01742, runs an information booth at Heywood Street, one block southeast of Monument Square. Open daily May through October, weekends only in April. **One-hour walking tours**, usually given on weekends and holidays from May to October, begin at the booth.

In Lexington, there is a **Visitor Center** ((617) 862-1450, at 1875 Massachusetts Avenue.

WHAT TO SEE AND DO

The Revolutionary Tour

Nearly 100,000 visitors a year trek Battle Green where British troops and patriots fought. The **Minute Man National Historical Park** ((978) 369-6993, 174 Liberty Street, encompasses the battlegrounds. Your first stop in the park should be at the **Battle Road Visitor Center**, Route 2A, where a film and maps portray the skirmish. During summer months, the National Park Service sponsors reenactments of the battle.

Concord's **North Bridge** is where the American revolutionaries first fired a volley against British soldiers. It is difficult to believe that these beautiful surroundings could have been host to such bloody undertakings. You can walk the battle route and even cross over the North Bridge itself. Daniel Chester French's statue, the *Minuteman*, stands here, a memorial to the citizen-soldiers of 1775 who led the fight for freedom. You get a panoramic overview of the battleground from the **North Bridge Visitor Center**.

The region's dramatic history is also told at the **Concord Museum** ((978) 369-9763, 200 Lexington Road, which traces the stories of the many players from "Algonkian" Indians to Transcendentalist farmers. Highlights of the collection include the lantern hung in the Old North Church steeple on the night of Paul Revere's famous ride; artifacts from the American Revolution; the furnishings from of Thoreau's cabin at Walden Pond; and the contents of Ralph Waldo Emerson's study where he wrote his influential essays.

The Art and Architecture Tour

The neighboring town of **Lincoln** is a woodsy suburb where art and architecture combine with a rural setting perfect for mountain biking and cross-country skiing (see SPORTS AND OUTDOOR ACTIVITIES, below).

The **DeCordova Museum and Sculpture Park** ((781) 259-8355, 51 Sandy Pond Road, Lincoln, is internationally recognized for its collection of modern and contemporary American art. Hours are Tuesday to Sunday

A young Minuteman readies for a revolutionary reenactment at the North Bridge, Minuteman National Park, Concord.

from 11 AM to 5 PM and on selected Monday holidays. An admission fee is charged, except for children under six. The Museum Sculpture Park is open year round during daylight hours and admission is free.

Along with several other fine historical houses in Lincoln, **Gropius House** ☏ (781) 259-8098, 68 Baker Bridge Road is the Bauhaus-inspired 1938 home of the German architect and theoretician, Walter Gropius. The house — which incorporates traditional elements of New England design and modern architecture — is now a museum. Open June to mid-October, Wednesday to Sunday and mid-October to May, Saturday and Sunday 11 AM to 4 PM with tours on the hour; an admission fee is charged.

The Don't-Forget-to-Eat-Your-Vegetables Tour

A visit to a farm stand is yet another Concord and Lexington tradition. But, be warned: Once you've had a ripe red farm tomato you'll never look at a supermarket hothouse variety in quite the same way. Roadside stands abound, all offering a cornucopia of vegetables, herbs, apple cider and homemade baked goods. A couple of the giants are **Verrill Farm** ☏ (978) 369-4494, 11 Wheeler Road, Concord, which provides produce to Hamersley's Bistro and several other top Boston restaurants, and **Wilson Farms** ☏ (781) 862-3900, 10 Pleasant Street, Lexington, with fruit, veggies, flowers, maple syrup and gourmet groceries to boot. The exotic produce is shipped in, but the rest is local.

SPORTS AND OUTDOOR ACTIVITIES

Henry David Thoreau's sojourn at Walden Pond was the beginning of a long tradition of people coming to **Walden Pond State Reservation** ☏ (978) 369-3254, Route 126, Concord, for inspiration and recreation. While it's no longer the secluded wood that it was in Thoreau's time, it's still Boston's best swimming hole, and if you follow the trail around the pond you can usually find a free spot to hang your towel. In the surrounding woods are hiking trails and a replica of Thoreau's cabin. The reserve is open daily from 5 AM to a half hour before sunset. Entrance is free, but there is a parking fee. To avoid the fee, you can park nearby and walk the few hundred yards to the reserve.

When the snow falls, Bostonians head for Lincoln, where there are miles of cross-country trails. **Lincoln Guide Service** ☏ (781) 259-1111, 152 Lincoln Road, Lincoln Center, a well-equipped outdoor gear store, supplies the skis. In summer, the same trails are the domain of mountain bikers, and the Lincoln Guide Service turns to renting mounts, maps and gear.

WHERE TO STAY AND EAT

In Concord it is possible to stay in Henry David Thoreau's former home, now the **Colonial Inn** ☎ (978) 369-9200 TOLL-FREE (800) 370-9200 FAX (978) 371-1533, 48 Monument Square, Concord 01742-1826 (mid-range to expensive). Built in 1760, the inn has an excellent restaurant with continental specialties and home-baked breads.

Nearby in the town of Sudbury, the **Wayside Inn** ☎ (978) 443-1776 TOLL-FREE (800) 339-1776, Sudbury 01776 (expensive), has some strong ties to the literary figures of the region. This colonial structure has creaking floorboards, paneled wood and steep stairs leading to low-ceilinged rooms. Dating from 1716, it is the nation's oldest operating hostelry and got its name when Henry Wadsworth Longfellow's *Tales of a Wayside Inn* was published in 1863. Longfellow stayed here after the death of his wife and the inn was said to have inspired the work. Dine by the fire with its beehive oven. Rooms are budget to mid-range.

HOW TO GET THERE

Lexington, nine miles (14 km) northwest of Boston, is reached via Route 2A or Route 2 from Cambridge through Belmont. Concord, 18 miles (30 km) west of Boston is reached via Route 2. The **MBTA Commuter Rail** offers service to Concord and Lincoln from Porter Square Station in Cambridge.

WORCESTER

Dubbed "Wormtown" by its student population, Massachusetts' second city is a neglected metropolitan area of around 170,000 inhabitants. Yet while Worcester is not a major tourist stopover, it does have some worthwhile attractions, starting with the excellent Worcester Art Museum.

For information, contact the **Worcester County Convention and Visitors Bureau** ☎ (508) 753-2920 TOLL-FREE (800) 231-7557 FAX (508) 754-8560, 33 Waldo Street, Worcester 01608. The **Worcester Cultural Commission** ☎ (508) 799-1400 has recorded information on visual and performing arts in the city, including what's on at the Centrum.

WHAT TO SEE AND DO

The **Worcester Art Museum (WAM)** ☎ (508) 799-4406, 55 Salisbury Street, houses one of the finest collections of art and antiquities in New England. It was the first museum in America to purchase works by Monet and Gauguin. The collection spans centuries, beginning with an array of artifacts from Antioch, dating from the second to the sixth century AD. The museum sponsored a series of Syrian excavations in the 1930s that unearthed these ancient treasures. Open Wednesday to Friday and Sunday from 11 AM to 5 PM, Saturday from 10 AM to 5 PM; an admission fee is charged, although children under 12 enter free.

The **Higgins Armory Museum** ☎ (508) 853-6015, 100 Barber Avenue, is dedicated to arms and armor; one of the more engaging ongoing exhibitions takes a look at armor decoration. Open Tuesday to Sunday; an admission fee is charged.

Worcester is the home of the **Common Outlets** ☎ (508) 798-2581, 100 Front Street (across the street from the Centrum), with Bass, Donna Karan, Nautica, Reebok and London Fog, to name a few of the 100 or so outlets in this indoor complex. Some Boston hotels run free shuttle buses; ask your concierge. Open Monday to Saturday from 10 AM to 7:30 PM, Sunday noon to 6 PM.

Outside of the malls, street-side shopping can turn up surprises, especially on **Highland Street**, which has a sprinkling of shops carrying vintage clothing, junque (a cross between junk and antiques), jewelry and used vinyl.

NIGHTLIFE AND THE ARTS

Main Street in downtown Worcester has a few bars and clubs. **Irish Times** ☎ (508) 797-9599, 244 Main Street, despite its name, is a big brash American bar dominated by an immense television screen making it feel

Sunset on Walden Pond, Concord.

more like a drive-in movie lot than a cozy Irish bar. There's a dining room on the second floor. You won't find shepherd's pie on the menu, but you will find fish and chips. There are frequent Irish pop and folk music concerts. Despite its flaws, it is packed most weekends. **Highland Avenue** is a mellower stretch of sidewalk with late-night cafés, greasy spoons and a sprinkling of street life.

The **Worcester Centrum** ☎ (508) 775-6800, 50 Foster Street, Worcester 01608, hosts blockbuster touring concerts and major theater productions.

WHERE TO STAY AND EAT

Worcester is not the best of places to stay, however there are plenty of interesting lodging options west of town and in the Pioneer Valley (see THE PIONEER VALLEY, page 127).

Worcester's many ethnic groups make for a kaleidoscopic dining scene chiefly consisting of inexpensive, casual places. The Iranian owner of **Café Abba** ☎ (508) 799-9999, 535 Main Street, has been in the business for years, though this current café is newish. Abba, which means "father" in Hebrew and Arabic, is also the name of a certain Swedish rock band; it's meant to reflect the global character of the menu which runs the gamut from Southwest and New Orleans to Italian and Middle Eastern. Portions are huge.

Highland Avenue has a number of eateries that attract a young pre-club crowd. On the corner of Ashland Street, **Tortilla Sam's** ☎ (508) 756-7267, 107 Highland Street, is an inexpensive cantina where you can watch the tortillas being made. Take out or eat in. A few doors down, **Sahara** ☎ (508) 798-2181, 146 Highland Street, is a large stylish café-restaurant serving typical Middle Eastern fare to a youthful clientele. On Monday evenings there's jazz guitar.

HOW TO GET THERE

Worcester is about 43 miles (69 km) from Boston. It lies at the junction of the Massachusetts Turnpike (Interstate 90) and Interstate 395, which connects with Interstate 95 to New Haven and New York. To get there from Boston, take the Massachusetts Turnpike (Interstate 90) West to Interstate 495, head north to Interstate 290 West and get off at Exit 16. From **Logan International Airport** TOLL-FREE (800) 235-6426 in East Boston, there's a limousine service that will take you to Worcester for around $40.

STURBRIDGE

Old Sturbridge Village is 200 acres (81 hectares) of rolling landscape, woodlands, country pathways, a working historical farm and more than 40 historic buildings. Guides in period dress demonstrate nineteenth-century skills and share the customs, work and celebrations of rural Massachusetts with visitors. Near Sturbridge in the town of Brimfield, the Brimfield Fair is of near legendary status. This tri-annual antique show and sale is the largest in New England, gathering 5,000 dealers from all over the country. Dates are around Memorial Day, July 4 and Labor Day weekends, and feature everything from heirloom furniture to Civil War memorabilia to obscure art pottery. For information, contact the Brimfield Antiques and Collectibles Show WEB SITE www.brimfieldshow.com.

A living history museum, Old Sturbridge Village aims to recreate aspects of rural nineteenth-century New England life.

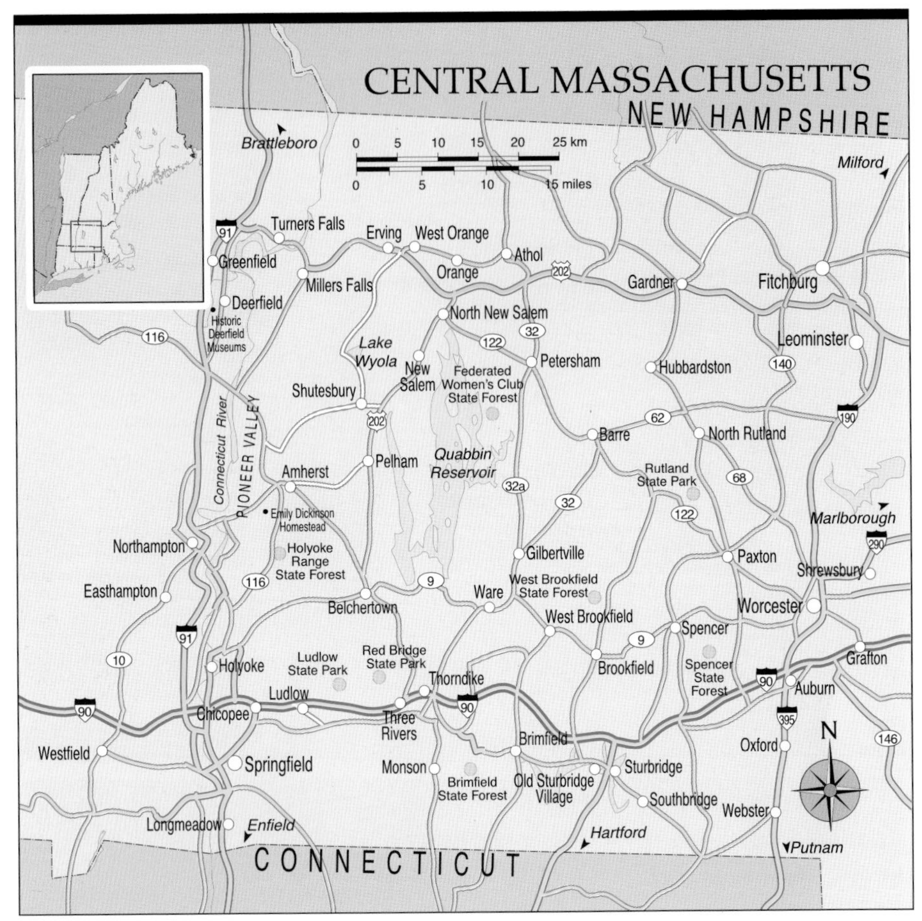

What to See and Do

A recreated 1830s New England village complete with role-playing villagers dressed in period costume, **Old Sturbridge Village** ☎ (508) 347-3362, extension 325, TOLL-FREE (800) 733-1830, Route 20, Sturbridge, is a living-history museum that recreates life in an 1830s rural New England town. There's a banker, a blacksmith, a cooper, a potter, a schoolmaster and a farmer. There are women, too, of course though it's more difficult to pin-down who or what they are. I ran into a pious female churchgoer at the Meeting House and a seamstress in her house on the Common.

Center Village is the heart of Old Sturbridge. Its Common is lined with dwellings such as the rustic 1704 Fenno House, the 1740 Richardson House Parsonage of a saltbox design, and the Center Meeting House, with its Greek Revival columns and tall white-clapboard spire, glowering at the head of the Common.

Take one of the footpaths leading off the Common to the **Pliny Freeman Farm**, which demonstrates typical 1830s community life in New England. It is one of the liveliest spots in the village, with costumed men and women performing daily farmstead tasks. The seasonal rhythms are also evident — with the birth of baby lambs and calves and the plowing and planting of fields each spring, crop harvesting in the fall, and preparations for the long New England winter.

Besides their daily tasks, village residents recreate special events such as the festive Fourth of July celebrations, which include a parade, music and a reading of the Declaration of Independence. The village also conducts regular programs, seminars, and workshops in archaeology, spinning and blacksmithing. Closed holidays and Mondays in December and January; an admission fee is charged. To get there take Exit 9 off the Massachusetts Turnpike or Exit 2 off Interstate 84.

The **Hyland Orchard & Brewery** ℂ (508) 347-7500, 199 Arnold Road, Sturbridge, has a self-guided tour of their brewery, along with free samples. There is also a miniature farm–zoo on the grounds, with unusual breeds such as pygmy goats and wooly Scottish Highlander cows. Open daily June through December (with guided tours at 1 PM and 3 PM on Saturday), but there are no beer sales Sunday by Massachusetts state law.

How to Get There

Sturbridge is approximately 18 miles (29 km) south of Worcester, and 32 miles (51 km) east of Springfield. From the Massachusetts Turnpike (Interstate 90) take Exit 9. From Interstate 84 take Exit 3B.

THE PIONEER VALLEY

The Pioneer Valley was the first interior part of New England to be settled when English colonists moved into the valley in 1633. At that time there were major native communities farming the land. They introduced the English settlers to their crops and foods, and their forest paths became the roads that are traveled today.

A vacation spot since the nineteenth century, the Pioneer Valley drew visitors from New York and Boston to its pleasant towns and Connecticut River scenery. In the 1970s, a new wave of pioneers began to arrive in the valley, setting up restaurants, shops and galleries that now line local streets. The Pioneer Valley also harbors a number of colleges

One of Historic Deerfield's restored eighteenth- and nineteenth-century buildings.

Where to Stay and Eat

The white-columned **Sturbridge Country Inn** ℂ (508) 347-5503, 530 Main Street, Sturbridge 01566, has rooms with fireplace, private whirlpool tub and Colonial-style furnishings. It's within walking distance of shops, factory outlets and restaurants. The rate (budget to mid-range) includes a continental breakfast.

For dinner try the **Whistling Swan** ℂ (508) 347-2321, 502 Main Street, housed in a Greek Revival mansion. Rack of lamb with blue cheese and herbs is a house specialty, and there are classic desserts such as *crème brûlée* and white chocolate mousse to indulge your sweet tooth.

and universities. With thousands of students flooding into the valley each fall, the region is blessed with cultural allures and college-style nightlife.

HISTORIC DEERFIELD

Settled by English farmers in 1669, Deerfield was a frontier outpost that suffered Indian raids well into the 1700s. The restoration of Deerfield's eighteenth- and nineteenth-century structures in the 1950s was the first project of its kind in the United States. Today "The Street," Historic Deerfield's main thoroughfare, has around a dozen houses that are open to the public and some 20,000 early New England objects made or used in America between 1650 and 1850. Guided tours of each of the restored buildings that line the one-mile-long (kilometer-and-a-half) street start each hour on the hour and last 30 minutes. All of the buildings — with the exception of the Dwight house, which was moved here from Springfield — are original to the site. Make sure to see the **Wells-Thorn House**, for it's here that you get a vivid picture of day-to-day life for the gentry of Deerfield between the years of 1725 and 1850. Rooms have been restored to represent different eras within this span of years.

Historic Deerfield's newest attraction is the **Flynt Center of Early New England Life**, a modern construction built to resemble a barn. Downstairs a fascinating exhibition explores the role of status and the practice

of "refinement" in rural New England society from 1750 to 1850. Upstairs, the Visible Storage Gallery displays 2,500 examples of household furnishings. Computer terminals are on hand to investigate the history and origin of many of the objects.

The **Blake Meadow Walk** takes you past a working dairy farm where you can see porkers delighting in their mud puddles, ruminating sheep, and dairy cows being herded off for milking. Interpretive signs along the trail explain the geological history of the region, reminding visitors that though Historic Deerfield seems "timeless" it is in fact ever-changing.

For informational materials contact **Historic Deerfield** ☎ (413) 774-5581 FAX (413) 773-7415, PO Box 321, Deerfield 01342-7415. Open from 9:30 AM to 4:30 PM daily year-round, except on Thanksgiving, December 24 and December 25.

Where to Stay and Eat

There is enough to see in Historic Deerfield to warrant an overnight stay at the white, columned **Deerfield Inn** ☎ (413) 774-5587 TOLL-FREE (800) 926-3865 FAX (413) 775-7221 E-MAIL frontdesk@deerfieldinn.com, 81 Old Main Street, Deerfield 01342 (mid-range), in the midst of the village. This 1880s beauty has 23 guestrooms decorated in Colonial-style finery, including quilts and Queen Anne furniture. Eleven of the rooms are situated in the old inn while the rest are located in the Carriage House, a modern recreation. The rooms come with twentieth-century conveniences including a television, though it is hidden away under a quilted cover. Tea is served each afternoon in the parlor, and there is a terrace café for light meals. The dining room serves breakfast, lunch, and dinner using local ingredients and regional dishes found in vintage recipe books from the village's library (expensive).

How to Get There

From Interstate 91, take Exit 24 North or Exit 25 South; go six miles (just under 10 km) north on Routes 5/10 and turn left for the historic village.

NORTHAMPTON AND VICINITY

Hub of the five-college community (Smith, Amherst, Hampshire and Mount Holyoke colleges, and the University of Massachusetts), Northampton claims to have "more artists, writers and musicians per square foot than any other spot between Soho and Montreal," and has the Pioneer Valley's best nightlife and widest choice of restaurants.

Having graduated from its days of strict New England Puritanism — the western outpost of the 1656 witch hysteria and the home turf of fire-and-brimstone minister Jonathan Edwards — Northampton boomed with the arrival of the railroad in 1845 and remained a commercial and cultural force

Deerfield's Brick Church Meetinghouse was built in 1824 and is, today, an active community church.

for nearly a century. The 1980s saw a new cultural and economic awakening when entrepreneurs began to move into and renovate downtown commercial buildings. Many more galleries, boutiques, music shops and restaurants sprang up, prompting the town's old nickname of "Hamp" to give way to "Noho," reflecting the city's current upscale-bohemian incarnation and significant contingent of ex-Manhattanites nostalgic for the New York scene. The principal activities in Noho are strolling along Main Street, indulging in copious brunches, and shopping for arcane kitchen gadgets. The local music scene played out in bars, coffeehouses and small clubs is impressive, though Northampton has faded from the ranks of rock's avant-garde. It remains, however, a hotbed for acoustic singer-songwriters. The **Northampton Film Festival** ☎ (413) 586-3471, held in early November in the 80-seat Academy of Music, features independent American films.

Informational materials on the region are available at the **Greater Northampton Chamber of Commerce** ☎ (413) 584-1900 FAX (413) 584-1934, 99 Pleasant Street, Northampton.

Northampton is home to Smith College, founded in 1875 to produce "intelligent gentlewomen," but now coeducational. It is the alma mater of poet Sylvia Plath, who graduated in 1955. The **Smith College Museum of Art** ☎ (413) 585-2760, Bedford Terrace and Elm Street, Northampton, is among the finest collegiate museums in the country. The collection contains some 24,000 works representing nineteenth- and twentieth-century American painters, along with an unusually deep collection of graphic art, including prints by Rembrandt, Dürer, Delacroix, Picasso and Degas, as well as collections of photography and ancient art. Open from September to June, Tuesday, Friday and Saturday from 9:30 AM to 4 PM, Wednesday and Sunday from noon to 4 PM, Thursday from noon to 8 PM; July and August: Tuesday to Sunday from noon to 4 PM. Admission is free. The museum is temporarily closed for extensive renovations and is scheduled to re-open in September 2003.

If you are visiting Northampton during the dreary months (November through March), make a point of seeing the Smith College greenhouses on Elm Street, open daily. The extensive Victorian glass houses are continuously abloom with exotic plants, including the most extensive collection of orchids in western Massachusetts.

Nightlife and the Arts

Throughout the Pioneer Valley you'll find live music, cutting-edge art shows, independent films, groundbreaking theatrical performances and avant-garde performance art. For events listings, consult the *Valley Advocate*.

The renovated **Calvin Theater** ☎ (413) 584-2310, 19 King Avenue, hosts jazz and a spoken word series. The **Iron Horse**, 20 Center Street, is a superb place to see bands and dance the night away. Tickets for Iron Horse events may be purchased at the Northampton Box Office ☎ (413) 586-8686 TOLL-FREE (800) 843-8425 or in person at For The Record, 104 Pleasant Street, Northampton. **Pearl Street** ☎ (413) 584-0610 or (413) 586-8686 TOLL-FREE (800) 843-8425, 10 Pearl Street, hosts nationally known musical acts as Black Uhuru, Bob Mould, Porno for Pyros and Roomful of Blues. Once the scene of such theater greats as Ethel and Lionel Barrymore, Sarah Bernhardt, and Rudolph Valentino, the **Academy of Music** ☎ (413) 584-8435, 274 Main Street, is now a cinema screening foreign and independent films. The theater also hosts live theatrical and musical events. **Thorne's Market** ☎ (413) 584-5582, 150 Main Street, opened in 1979 and is now a commercial center and arts venue. The upstairs gallery hosts changing exhibitions and there are dance and theater happenings with excellent local performers.

Where to Stay and Eat

You can stay downtown at the grand **Hotel Northampton** ☎ (413) 584-3100 TOLL-FREE (800) 547-3529 FAX (413) 584-9455, 36 King Street, Northampton 01060. Built in 1927, the five-story red-brick building has a pillared entrance and 77 well-appointed rooms (mid-range). Set in the basement of the inn, Wiggins Tavern is a convincing replica of a New Hampshire tavern that opened in 1786. The terrace is a pleasant lunch spot on a summer's day.

The Autumn Inn ☎ (413) 584-7660 FAX (413) 586-4808, 259 Elm Street, Northampton 01060 (budget to mid-range), faces the Smith College campus. The 30 rooms here are decorated with early-American reproductions and the hotel has a small restaurant and a swimming pool.

In nearby Hadley, the **Clark Tavern Inn** ☎ (413) 586-1900 FAX (413) 587-9788, 98 Bay Road, Hadley 01035 (budget to mid-range), is a Colonial-style inn with three guest rooms, two with fireplaces. A large garden and swimming pool complete the picture.

The smell of roasted garlic wafting out onto Main Street leads many a hungry diner to **Pizzeria Paradiso** ☎ (413) 586-1468, 12 Crafts Avenue (near the corner of Main Street). For starters, try the baked mussels *au gratin*. Then move on the main attraction: pizza, cooked in a wood-burning oven. The atmosphere is two-parts sociable and one-part romance.

A Northampton institution, **Sylvester's** ☎ (413) 586-5343, 111 Pleasant Street, Northampton, is named after Sylvester Graham, the inventor of the Graham cracker, who owned the building that now houses the restaurant. Always jammed with diners, Sylvester's serves breakfast, lunch, and dinner, and bakes its bread on the premises.

The **Haymarket Café and Bookstore** ☎ (413) 586-9969, 185 Main Street, serves "edible masterpieces" including sandwiches of portobello mushroom with gorgonzola cheese, Japanese handrolls, Indonesian *gado gado*, Indian curries and Cuban black beans. Baked goods and coffee are available at the takeout counter, but it would be a pity to miss camping out for a few hours in the rummage sale furniture.

If you have need to check your e-mail, there's the **Java Net Café** ☎ (413) 587-3401, 241 Main Street. Upstairs, six iMacs glow with activity, while downstairs is cozier still with a men's club atmosphere and dark wood paneling. You can relax and read here, or plug your laptop computer into the phone lines for $6 per hour. Try the almond biscotti.

Northampton's restored Calvin Theater brings legends of jazz to town.

AMHERST

Another college town with a literary past, Amherst was home to three celebrated American poets — Robert Frost, Emily Dickinson and Eugene Field. Less self-conscious than Noho's main drag, Amherst's Pleasant Street runs through the heart of town and is lined with hole-in-the-wall boutiques, bookstores, restaurants, and coffee shops. The **Amherst Chamber of Commerce** ☎ (413) 253-0700 FAX (413) 256-0771 E-MAIL info@amherst chamber.com, 409 Main Street, Amherst 01002, provides general information.

From the handsome Amherst Common, walk down Main Street to the **Emily Dickinson Homestead** ✆ (413) 542-8161, 280 Main Street. The Federal-style residence was built in 1813, and was the birthplace and lifelong home of Emily Dickinson (1830–1886). Fewer than a dozen of her poems were published during her lifetime, her work being discovered and published posthumously. The building is used primarily as an Amherst College faculty residence, but there are several rooms and halls open to the public which contain many Dickinson possessions. Hours vary according to season, so be sure to call ahead; an admission fee is charged.

Amherst has three fine university museums. There is a collection of American masters at the **Mead Art Museum at Amherst College** ✆ (413) 542-2335, located at the intersection of Routes 116 and 9 in Amherst. Open during the academic year from Monday to Sunday; summer hours are Tuesday to Sunday (afternoon hours only). Admission is free. The **Hampshire College Art Gallery** ✆ (413) 559-5544, on Route 116, four miles (six and a half kilometers) south of Amherst center, includes an outdoor sculpture collection, as well as changing exhibitions. Open daily during the academic year; admission is free. The University of Massachusetts/Amherst has the **University Gallery** ✆ (413) 545-3670, in the Fine Arts Center, off Route 116, which focuses on contemporary art. Open during the academic year Tuesday to Sunday. Admission is free.

Where to Stay and Eat

Accommodation in Amherst is superior to that in Northampton. **Allen House** ✆ (413) 253-5000, 599 Main Street, Amherst 01002, is a seven-bedroom inn with antiques and down comforters. It's within walking distance to area attractions. The room rate (budget to mid-range) includes breakfast and afternoon tea. The **Lord Jeffery Inn** ✆ (413) 253-2576 TOLL-FREE (800) 742-0358 FAX (413) 256-6152, 30 Boltwood Avenue, Amherst 01002 (mid-range to expensive), is situated in the town center at the head of the Common, Built in 1926, the inn offers 48 smallish guestrooms. Some rooms have private balconies or porches and the rate includes a continental breakfast.

Nancy Jane's ✆ (413) 253-3342, 36 Main Street, serves big breakfasts — griddlecakes with cranberries or chocolate is the house specialty. For lunch there is soup, sandwiches, burgers and hot main dishes. Behind Nancy Jane's you'll find **Bueno y Sano** ✆ (413) 253-4000, 46 Main Street, which translates as "good and healthy," referring to the alt-Mex burritos and quesadillas available at the walk-up counter. Eat in or take out. The **Black Sheep Café/Deli & Bakery** ✆ (413) 253-3442, 79 Main Street, bakes wonderful breads and pastries, including commendable croissants.

SPRINGFIELD

A sprawling industrial city, Springfield is home to more than 200 factories. Each September, the city hosts the massive **Eastern States Exhibition**, or "Big E." This colorful fair has carnival rides, big-name entertainment and displays of the year's agricultural and industrial achievements. For informational materials on the exhibition as well as year-round activities, contact the **Greater Springfield Convention and Visitors Bureau** ✆ (413) 755-1346 TOLL-FREE (800) 723-1548 FAX (413) 781-4607, 1441 Main Street, Springfield 01103.

The **Museums of the Quadrangle** ✆ (413) 263-6800, 220 State Street, are four museums clustered around a green. A single modest admission fee provides entry to all four facilities. The **Connecticut Valley Historical Museum** is the repository of furniture, manufactured goods and toys that tell the story of Pioneer Valley settlers since 1636. The **Museum of Fine Arts'** 10 galleries exhibit American art from the eighteenth through the twentieth centuries. **The George Walter Vincent Smith Art Museum** was the home of G.W.V. Smith and his wife Belle. Built in the style of an Italian palazzo, with stained glass windows by the Louis Comfort Tiffany Company, the house displays the couple's collection of nineteenth-century decorative arts. At the **Springfield Science Museum**, exhibitions highlight natural and human history from dinosaurs to current environmental issues. There is an aquarium and live animal center; a Native American Hall; a 100-seat planetarium and observatory; and an exhibit on the Springfield-based aviation pioneers, the Granville Brothers. The newest permanent exhibit, Underwater World of the Connecticut River, takes visitors below the surface of New England's most important river with photographs and artifacts that explain the biology and history of the river. A new addition to the Quadrangle completed in June 2000, the **Dr. Seuss National Memorial** commemorates Theodor Seuss Geisel, a Springfield native and author of such children's classics as *The Cat in the Hat* and *Horton Hears a Who*. Hours for the Museums of the Quadrangle are Wednesday to Sunday from noon to 4 PM.

In 1891, Dr. James Naismith of Springfield College invented a game whose object was to toss a ball into a peach basket. He called it basketball, and after he realized that removing the basket bottoms would add momentum to the game, it became a passion. Now basketball is part of the American way of life and its heroes and their hours of glory are commemorated in the nation's shrine to hoops, the **Basketball Hall of Fame** ☎ (413) 781-6500, 1150 West Columbus Avenue. It differs from other major sports' halls of fame in that it honors great players from amateur and college as well as the professional ranks. Besides old balls, jerseys, trophies and videos, the hall offers a "shooting gallery" with basketballs delivered on a conveyor belt to visitors who want to shoot some hoops. Open daily; an admission fee is charged.

HOW TO GET THERE

The Pioneer Valley, easily accessible from Boston, is about a 90-minute drive west of the city on the Massachusetts Turnpike (Interstate 90). From New York City, take Interstate 95 to Interstate 91. Buses run regularly from both cities, and trains connect with Springfield. The nearest major airport is Bradley International ☎ (203) 627-3000, Windsor Locks, Connecticut (between Hartford and Springfield).

Rearranging the geraniums at a Pioneer Valley flower market.

The Berkshire Hills

Less than three hours from New York and Boston metropolitan areas, the Berkshire Hills enfold a landscape of lush countryside filled with cultural and visual delights. Nationally famous for music, art, architecture, and history, the green hills and granite crests of western Massachusetts have inspired a host of writers and poets over the years. Herman Melville wrote his epic *Moby-Dick* here; Edith Wharton lived here for close to a decade and built The Mount in Lenox; and Longfellow, Emerson and Thoreau hiked its trails. The Berkshires' extraordinary variety of landscapes — open meadows and rolling farmlands, valleys dotted with shimmering lakes, wooded hills and green mountains, rushing rivers and plummeting waterfalls — is a major ingredient of the region's magic. With cooler temperatures and greater snowfall than the east, this area is also the heart of Massachusetts' ski country.

The Berkshire Hills remained a wilderness until 1725, when pioneer Matthew Noble erected a log cabin in what is now the town of Sheffield. Soon dense forests were cleared for farmland and towns appeared along the Housatonic River. In the nineteenth century, the Berkshires were mined for iron used on the railroads. Marble was also quarried here and transported to construct such edifices as the Capitol dome in Washington, DC. Around the same time, the Berkshires began to attract urban dwellers wishing to "escape" into the country, including some of America's wealthiest families (such as the Carnegies and the Vanderbilts), who built elegant mansions and used them for less than three months of the year.

The bible of these Victorian travelers was *The Book of Berkshire*, the 1887 edition of which sang: "The hills and mountains of Berkshire, now gentle and sloping in their lines, now wild and broken, shelter a well watered, thoroughly cultivated valley, where towns and villages, famous for their beauty, lie among the trees; a region of lakes, mountain torrents, glens, lovers' lanes, rocks and echoes; a region, too, where one may spend the summer and not die of ennui from lack of good and congenial society."

Amazingly, all of this is essentially still true for Massachusetts' Berkshire Hills.

For informational materials contact the **Berkshire Visitors Bureau** ☎ (413) 443-9186 TOLL-FREE (800) 237-5747 FAX (413) 443-1970, Berkshire Common, Plaza Level, Pittsfield 01201. Reservations for accommodations are essential during summer and fall.

LENOX

Lenox was fashionable as a summer resort long before the Boston Symphony Orchestra chose it in 1939 as the site of its annual Berkshire Festival of Music. In the nineteenth century, literary and social figures flocked to this "Inland Newport." In its heyday, the town was surrounded by roughly 100 magnificent mansions, some of which survive, lending the town an air that sets it apart from the rest of the region's villages and towns.

WHAT TO SEE AND DO

Pulitzer-prize winning author of *The Age of Innocence*, *Ethan Frome* and *The House of Mirth*, Edith Wharton (1862–1937) lived in Lenox from 1902 to 1911, designing and overseeing the construction of **The Mount**. Centered around her stately home and gardens, **The Edith Wharton Restoration** ☎ (413) 637-1899 TOLL-FREE (888) 637-1902 FAX (413) 637-0619, EWR at The Mount, 2 Plunkett Street, PO Box 974, Lenox 01240, is one of America's few National Historical Landmarks dedicated to a woman. Guided tours focus on the literary aspects of Wharton's life as well as her role and influence as a decorator and landscape designer. Interestingly enough, Wharton had established her reputation as a decorator long before she ever had a property to decorate, and used The Mount to demonstrate that she knew what she was talking about all along. Although the property is still in the midst of an ongoing restoration, it is open Memorial Day to October daily from 9 AM to 5 PM (last tour at 4 PM); an admission fee is charged.

On Lenox's Main Street is the 1805 **Church on the Hill**. Several other streets offer glimpses of mansions once owned by business and industrial magnates (Harrimans, Biddles, Stuyvesants) who had summer

Picnickers discover one of the Berkshire's many quiet corners.

"cottages" in Lenox. Most of these houses are not open to the public, although one — **Wheatleigh** — is now an elegant country inn and restaurant (see below).

SPORTS AND OUTDOOR ACTIVITIES

North of Lenox center, the **Pleasant Valley Wildlife Sanctuary** ☎ (413) 637-0320, West Mountain Road, Lenox, is a Massachusetts Audubon preserve of native plants and landscapes, including beaver ponds, open meadows and over seven miles (11 km) of walking and cross-country ski trails. Follow Route 7A to West Dugway Road, across from Quality Inn, to West Mountain Road. Open daily dawn to dusk; an admission fee is charged.

NIGHTLIFE AND THE ARTS

A 210-acre (85-hectare) estate where Hawthorne wrote *Tanglewood Tales* and *The House of the Seven Gables*, **Tanglewood** is situated one and a half miles (two and a half kilometers) west of Lenox on Route 183. The summer Boston Symphony Orchestra (BSO) concert series, from June through late August, features performances by some of the world's leading musicians. The main Music Shed, designed by architect Eero Saarinen, seats 6,000, but an expansive lawn allows thousands more to enjoy the performance.

During BSO concert nights, Tanglewood is a mass of traffic and humanity. It is best to arrive early to find a spot in the parking lot and maybe bring along a picnic; it is not unusual for people to arrive more than three hours before a scheduled performance. For information contact **Tanglewood** ☎ (413) 637-5165 (in-season) or (617) 266-1492 (off-season). A number of local agencies offer bus excursions to Tanglewood concerts. Inquire at the Berkshire Visitors Bureau (see above).

You can enjoy, as well, one of the many non-Boston Symphony concerts, recitals and orchestra presentations; nearly 50 of these performances are held throughout the summer. The **Popular Artists' Series** presents a season of jazz, while **Stockbridge Chamber Concerts** at Seven Hills offers a year-round program of music in the estates, halls and churches of the Berkshires. Lenox is also the home of the **National Music Center** ☎ (413) 637-4718, 70 Kemble Street, Lenox, pulling in big name country and jazz acts throughout the summer season.

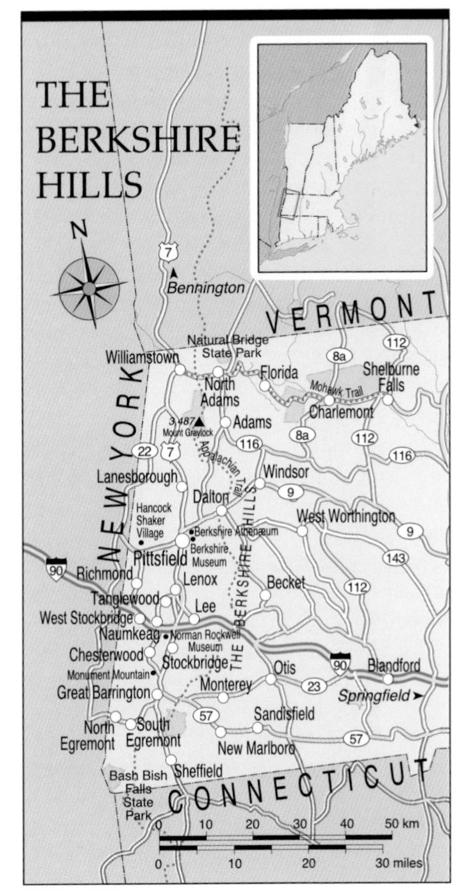

One of the great experiences of the Berkshire summer season, **Shakespeare & Company** ☎ (413) 637-3353 FAX (413) 637-4240 E-MAIL boxoffice@shakespeare.org, 77 Kimble Street, Lenox, present plays by the bard under the artistic direction of Tina Packer. The company has been working with several performance spaces in Lenox as it prepares to construct an exact replica of The Rose, a 1587 London playhouse where some of Shakespeare's plays debuted.

Created in 1933 by modern dance pioneer Ted Shawn, **Jacob's Pillow Dance Festival** takes place in Becket over nine weeks each summer, offering superb contemporary dance performances. Since its inception more than 50 years ago, the program has welcomed a host of renowned choreographers and troupes including Martha Graham, Merce Cunningham, and the Alvin Ailey Repertory Ensemble. Besides main theater performances, the Pillow's "Inside/Out Series" presents a free, hour-long show on an outdoor stage that includes works in progress, discussions with dancers and choreographers and audience questions. For information and tickets contact Jacob's Pillow Dance Festival ((413) 243-0745, PO Box 287, Lee 01238; their season runs June to August.

WHERE TO STAY AND EAT

Owing to its history as a lavishly wealthy summer resort, Lenox has a fair number of swanky inns and resorts to choose from. *Travel and Leisure* magazine has called **Canyon Ranch in the Berkshires** ((413) 637-4100 TOLL-FREE (800) 326-7080 FAX (413) 637-0057, 165 Kemble Street, Lenox 01240, one of the "world's best spas." Guests enjoy superb cuisine in the resort dining rooms (not open to the public). Three- and seven-night packages are available at this super-luxury resort.

Built by rich New Yorker Henry H. Cook in 1892–1893 in the style of an Italian villa, **Wheatleigh** ((413) 637-0610 TOLL-FREE (800) 321-0610 FAX (413) 637-4507, West Hawthorn Road, PO Box 824, Lenox 01240, has splendid views of the surrounding hills. Standard rooms are small (11x13 ft or 3.4x3.9 m), but are nevertheless comfortable and some have cosy fireplaces. Prices go from expensive to luxury. The dining room is one of the best in the area (expensive).

For something a bit more down to earth there is the **Village Inn** ((413) 637-0020 TOLL-FREE (800) 253-0917 FAX (413) 637-9756, 16 Church Street, Lenox 01340. The 32 rooms vary from "superior," with four-posters and fireplaces, to the more basic "economy" style. Rates are mid-range. The restaurant serves afternoon tea and dinner, June to October, while the tavern offers casual meals. Music combos and poetry readings provide weekend entertainment.

Though you shouldn't pass up a chance to splash out on dinner at Wheatleigh (above), there are plenty of other good places to dine in Lenox. The **Church Street Café** ((413) 637-2745, 65 Church Street, is by far the most popular, specializing in vegetarian dishes such as a dinner plate of potato cake, sautéed greens and ratatouille. There is a large outdoor deck for fine weather dining.

A good place to pick up goodies for your picnic, **Suchele Bakers** ((413) 637-0939, 27 Housatonic Street, Lenox, offers muffins, croissants, pastries and whole grain breads.

HOW TO GET THERE

It's a fast and smooth drive from Boston out to the Berkshire Hills on the Massachusetts Turnpike (Interstate 90), though traffic can get heavy at times. The distance is 125 miles (200 km), about a two-and-a-half- to three-hour drive once you escape Boston's orbit. Motorists from New York will take the Taconic State Parkway north to Route 23 east and Route 7 north.

STOCKBRIDGE AND WEST STOCKBRIDGE

Stockbridge is a stately town with fine houses, upscale shops and a spirited arts community. Established as an Indian mission by preacher and theologian John Sargeant — whose 1739 residence, the **Old Mission House** ((413) 298-3239, is open for tours — the town evolved into a grand summer resort and remains a cultural hub of the Berkshires.

A few hills over is the quiet village of West Stockbridge, a former railroad town situated in the Queensboro Pass. West Stockbridge's short Main Street is lined with 1800s-style storefronts housing a couple of galleries and some specialty stores, bordered by the bubbling Williamsville River.

WHAT TO SEE AND DO

Colonial revolutionaries used to meet at the **Red Lion Inn** (see WHERE TO STAY AND EAT, below) to pass resolutions protesting English taxation. The old inn's crest represents the crown of King George III; the green tail painted on the red lion showed sympathy with the colonists' cause. A gift shop and the **Country Curtains** ((413) 298-5565 retail store are found on the first floor.

A prime attraction in the region, the **Norman Rockwell Museum** ((413) 298-4100,

Route 183 (just south of Route 102), contains the world's largest collection of Norman Rockwell illustrations, including such well-known works as *Four Freedoms* and *Triple Self-portrait*. Also on exhibit are Rockwell's studio and archival papers and his *Saturday Evening Post* covers. Open May through October daily 10 AM to 5 PM, November through April Monday to Friday 10 AM to 5 PM. The museum is open year-round, and the studio is open from May to October; an admission fee is charged.

Down the road from the Rockwell Museum is **Chesterwood** ((413) 298-3579, off Route 183, Stockbridge. This was the summer estate of Daniel Chester French, sculptor of the Lincoln Memorial in Washington, DC, and the *Minuteman* in Concord, Massachusetts, among other famous works. French's mansion, studio, barn gallery and period garden are open for guided tours. Nature trails on the grounds offer good views of Monument Mountain. Open May 1 to October 31 daily; an admission fee is charged.

Also west of Stockbridge center is the **Berkshire Botanical Gardens** ((413) 298-3926, 15 acres (six hectares) of intimate landscaped gardens. As you stroll along a woodland trail to the pond garden, you'll pass sculpture exhibits presented by local artists. In May, hundreds of daffodils and flowering cherry trees bloom. Then around Memorial Day the lilacs, peonies and mountain laurel appear. The rose garden is splendid in June. Open daily May 1 to mid-October; an admission fee is charged.

North of town, **Naumkeag** ((413) 298-3239, Prospect Hill, Stockbridge, was the summer home of the Joseph Hodges Choate family. Designed in 1885 by Stanford White, the 26-room estate is noted for its 16 gardens, including the Blue Steps, four flights that twine around reflecting pools. Inside the house, the furnishings are as the family left them. Open daily Memorial Day to Labor Day; the last tour is at 4:15 PM. An admission fee is charged.

NIGHTLIFE AND THE ARTS

Stockbridge is home to one of the nation's top summer theaters, the **Berkshire Theater Festival** ((413) 298-5576 (summer) or (413) 298-5536 (winter) E-MAIL info@ berkshire theatre.org, East Main Street, PO Box 797, Stockbridge 01262, which has taken place here for more than 60 years. Classical works with name actors are staged June through August in the large Playhouse; new plays and children's theater from around the world are set in the barn, as part of the Unicorn Theater Company.

WHERE TO STAY AND EAT

With regard to lodging, Stockbridge is less high-toned than its neighbor Lenox, but is nevertheless equipped to please. The **Red Lion Inn** ((413) 298-5545, Stockbridge 01262 (mid-range with shared bathroom; expensive to luxury with private bath), was built in 1773 on the stagecoach route from Albany to Boston. This Berkshire landmark has 100 antique-filled rooms with feather pillows under canopy beds. The inn's public spaces — a flower-laden courtyard and front porch lined with rocking chairs — complete the picture. Of equal quality, though with smaller rooms, is the **Inn at Stockbridge** ((413) 298-3337, 30 East Street, Stockbridge 01262 (mid-range to expensive).

West Stockbridge is a good place to base yourself for Berkshire explorations, if you are looking for good value without sacrificing convenience and charm. Originally a stage coach stop in the early 1800s, then the home of the inventor Anson Clark, the **Shaker Mill Inn and Tavern** ((413) 232-4600, PO Box 521, West Stockbridge 01266, offers large suites (with kitchenette) and standard rooms loaded with extras. The rate (expensive to luxury) includes a continental breakfast.

Outside of the village center on Route 41 is the **Williamsville Inn** ((413) 274-6118 FAX (413) 274-3539, Route 41, West Stockbridge 01266 (mid-range), with choice lodging and candlelight dining in an 1797 farmhouse in a peaceful country setting at the base of Tom Ball Mountain. On the grounds are a tennis court and pool.

For lunch get off the Group W Bench and head to **Theresa's Stockbridge Café** ((413) 298-5465, 40 Main Street (budget), on the site of the original Alice's Restaurant, brought to fame in the late 1960s by Arlo Guthrie's song of the same name. Or try the **Lion's Den**

☎ (413) 298-5545, at the Red Lion Inn (closed midweek in off-season; budget to mid-range) for a hearty American tavern menu.

Truc's Orient Express ☎ (413) 232-4204 is tucked away behind Main Street in West Stockbridge. The plum wine is mild and sweet and anything you choose from the lengthy menu is bound to be fresh and aromatic. I can't resist the "singing" chicken with its sauce of ginger and garlic. The dining room, decorated with white linens, bamboo curtains and a gas fireplace sets just the right tone.

SOUTHERN BERKSHIRE COUNTY

From West Stockbridge, a short drive south on Route 7 leads to **Great Barrington**, the largest town in the southern Berkshires and in many ways the most interesting, with its vibrant downtown, eclectic mix of restaurants, and interesting shops. South and east of Great Barrington, the little towns multiply along Route 7 and its tributaries. This part of the southern Berkshires delights antique hunters. Curio shops of all sorts throng South Egremont, Great Barrington, Sheffield, New Marlborough, and pop up along the winding back roads of the countryside. Ask for a brochure listing antique shops at the **Southern Berkshire Chamber of Commerce** ☎ (413) 528-1510, 362 Main Street, Great Barrington.

Before the Europeans arrived in Great Barrington, the Mohegans built their "Great Wigwam" at a ford here in the Housatonic River. The village gained prominence in 1774 when its residents seized the courthouse from the British, committing the first act of open rebellion in the colonies against the Crown. And William Stanley (founder of General Electric) helped to light up the town in 1886, making it the first town in the United States to be lit with electricity. Later, Great Barrington was a station on the Underground Railroad transporting fugitive slaves to freedom. W.E.B. Du Bois, the author and editor, lived here, as did James Weldon Johnson, co-founder of the National Association for the Advancement of Colored People (NAACP).

Though it has plenty of history, Great Barrington doesn't have much in the way of historical sights, which leaves the visitor free to enjoy browsing in the many one-of-a-kind shops. Railroad Street is worth a look for the peerless pastries at **Daily Bread** ☎ (413) 528-9610 and the contemporary women's clothing and accessories at **Drygoods** ☎ (413)

Farmland surrounds the village of West Stockbridge. These sturdy steeds are enjoying their pasture after a hard day's work.

528-2950. **The Emporium** ((413) 528-1660, 319 Main Street, is an extensive "group shop" of several dealers in antiques and collectibles. It's one of the better places in the southern Berkshires to look for fine jewelry, china, silver and glass.

Toward the east end of town, **Yellow House Books** ((413) 528-8227, 252 Main Street, Great Barrington, is one of the best used-and-rare book shops in the state. The collections of Native American and regional history, music, art and children's books are particularly wide-ranging. They also have rare vinyl, mostly jazz and rock & roll. You can find listings of local entertainment and events at the corkboard on the verandah.

SPORTS AND OUTDOOR ACTIVITIES

Great Barrington has easy access to the Berkshire's glorious outdoor recreation areas. About five miles (eight kilometers) north of Great Barrington off Route 7, is **Monument Mountain**. Two trails lead to the summit. An easy two- to three-hour round trip offers spectacular views of Squaw Peak. Monument Mountain is the site of an 1850 meeting between Herman Melville and Nathaniel Hawthorne, which began their lifelong friendship.

There are winter revels at the **Butternut Ski Area** ((413) 528-2000 TOLL-FREE SNOWPHONE (800) 438-7669, set in the evergreen glades of East Mountain State Forest. Recognized by *Ski* magazine for excellence in design, the resort offers terrain for experienced skiers and novices, with 22 trails set on 110 acres (44 hectares). Five miles (eight kilometers) of cross-country trails wind through the woods. Butternut is located two miles (three kilometers) east of Great Barrington on Route 23. There's more skiing at **Catamount Ski Area** ((413) 528-1262, Route 23, in South Egremont, where some naturally bumpy trails make for mogul thrills.

About 12 miles (19 km) past South Egremont (off Route 41, then follow the signs almost to the New York state line) is **Bash Bish Falls State Park** ((413) 528-0330, a 200-acre (80-hectare) park and part of the Mount Washington State Forest. The spectacular 275-ft (84-m) Bash Bish Falls plunge down a steep gorge, and there is abundant hiking and fishing (with permit).

One of the most unusual spots in the southern Berkshire's, **Bartholomew's Cobble** ((413) 229-8600, Weatogue Road, Ashley (off Route 7A), is a 278-acre (111-hectare) reservation where tall marble and quartzite "cobbles" — rocky outcrops that rise 100 ft (30 m) from a rolling pasture — border the Housatonic River. Renowned for its native ferns and wildflowers, the reserve has six miles (10 km) of hiking trails skirting the banks of the Housatonic. It also contains a natural-history museum and the Colonel John Ashley House. Open daily, mid-April to mid-October; an admission fee is charged.

NIGHTLIFE AND THE ARTS

Great Barrington has a varied assortment of casual nightlife options. The **Kellogg Music Center at Simon's Rock College** ((413) 528-0771, 84 Alford Road, hosts the summer-long South Berkshire Concert Series, with guest musicians from around the world. At the **Celestial Bar** ((413) 528-5244, in the Castle Street Café, 10 Castle Street, there is live folk and jazz nightly starting at 8:30 PM; no cover charge. Berkshire nightlife extends its reach into the hinterland at the **Old**

Egremont Club ☎ (413) 528-9712, Route 23, West Egremont, which hosts rock, R&B and soul combos. **Barrington Stage Company** ☎ (413) 528-8888, Berkshire School Road, Sheffield, focuses on contemporary drama and musicals, with performances from late June through early August.

WHERE TO STAY

Built on the leafy New Marlborough town green in 1760, and serving variously as inn, tavern, store and post office, the **Old Inn on the Green** ☎ (413) 229-3131, Route 57, New Marlborough 01230 (mid-range to luxury) was renovated in 1979. Today it offers six comfortable guestrooms upstairs and one of the area's finest restaurants on the ground floor. A quarter mile (half a kilometer) down the road, **Gedney Farm**, under the same ownership, is a gorgeous restoration modeled after a nineteenth-century Normandy horse barn with 13 guestrooms decorated in French provincial style. Rooms are small, but marvelously decorated with rich fabrics, plump pillows and comforters, fireplaces and large Jacuzzi tubs. A second barn serves as a gallery and concert hall. Lunch and breakfast are served outdoors, weather permitting. The well maintained grounds include an outdoor sculpture garden. The rate includes a continental breakfast.

If you'd like to base yourself near downtown Great Barrington, there is the **Windflower Inn** ☎ (413) 528-2720 TOLL-FREE (800) 992-1993 FAX (413) 528-5147, 684 South Egremont Road, Great Barrington 01230, located across from the Egremont Country Club on Route 23. Rooms are comfortably arranged, and some are equipped with fireplaces. For warmer months there is an outdoor swimming pool. The rate (mid-range to expensive) includes breakfast.

Hancock Shaker Village is a study in simplicity.

Baldwin Hill Farms Bed & Breakfast ☎ (413) 528-4092, 121 Baldwin Hill Road, Egremont 01230 (mid-range), is a comfortable farmhouse with four guestrooms and wonderful views. Breakfast (included) is served from a menu.

WHERE TO EAT

Plan to linger at **Helsinki Tea Company Café and Bistro** ☎ (413) 528-3394, 288 Main Street, Great Barrington. The one-of-a-kind furnishings — wingback chairs, velvet upholstered booths and throw pillows in rich hues — form a cozy patchwork atmosphere that is effortlessly romantic. Attention to detail marks the menu as well. Garden salads are composed of tender greens and ripe red tomatoes. The iced tea is a redcurrant and blackcurrant brew sweetened with apple juice. Choose from Scandinavian specialties such as gravlax and borscht, or venture out with the café's creative chefs into one of the globally influenced daily specials.

Open for breakfast and lunch, **Martin's** ☎ (413) 528-5455, 49 Railroad Street, Great Barrington, is an old-time diner and a good place to begin your day with blueberry pancakes, stuffed French toast or a big omelet. Don't worry if your day starts late: Martin's serves its hearty breakfasts all day long. For lunch, dieters are well served with salads, but they'll be tempted by the hot and cold sandwiches, thick cheeseburgers, and fries, not to mention the cream pies. Inexpensive daily specials usually include a grilled fish sandwich. It's a cheerful place, and children can pass the short wait for your order drawing with the crayons provided at the table.

The seafood is fresh and well prepared at **Castle Street Café** ☎ (413) 528-5244, 10 Castle Street. At **Bizen** ☎ (413) 528-4343, 17 Railroad Street, organic vegetarian dishes, sushi and seafood are served, lunch and dinner, on the handmade pottery of Michael Marcus.

PITTSFIELD

The Berkshire County seat, Pittsfield, is a small city of 48,500 residents. Though not a major stop on the Berkshire's circuit, it does have a few notable attributes. It was the onetime home of Herman Melville, Amtrak service to Boston and Chicago stops here, and the city even has a Class-A Baseball team, the Berkshire Bears.

WHAT TO SEE AND DO

Herman Melville moved with his family to Pittsfield in 1850, purchasing an eighteenth-century farmhouse, which he named "**Arrowhead**" ☎ (413) 442-1793, Holmes Road (off Route 7). Melville wrote part of *Moby-Dick* here during his 13-year occupancy, where he could gaze out over the Berkshire Hills, which he said reminded him of rolling waves and gray humpback whales. The author's study, with its view of Mount Greylock, contains a few mementos, and the remainder of the house is attractively furnished.

The Melville homestead is also the site of the **Berkshire County Historical Society** (same phone), which offers twice-daily screenings of "The Berkshire Legacy," a film on the Berkshire's cultural history.

Melville fans will also want to visit the **Berkshire Athenæum**, at 1 Wendell Avenue, Pittsfield, where the Herman Melville Memorial Room contains works, first editions, personal effects, photographs and letters of the author.

From the Athenæum look across the town square to the **Berkshire Museum** ☎ (413) 443-7171, 39 South Street, (Route 7), a pleasant regional museum with an outstanding collection Hudson River School paintings and Hawthorne memorabilia, as well as an aquarium for the kids. It's open year round; an admission fee is charged.

A detour off Route 7 onto Route 20 at Pittsfield brings you to **Hancock Shaker Village** (at Routes 20 and 41, Pittsfield), an authentic community of the Shaker religious sect that thrived from 1790 to 1960. It is today a living, working museum of Shaker rural life, on 1,000 acres (405 hectares), and a remarkable window onto nineteenth-century American life with its 20 historic buildings, including a huge, round Shaker barn and working crafts shops.

The Shaker movement started in England in 1747 as an offshoot of the Quakers. Manchester's Ann Lee first led eight followers to the American colony of New York and founded a settlement near Albany. For a time, they were known as "shaking Quakers" because "dances" during religious services made their bodies shake and tremble. Eventually, the Shakers' pronouncements and beliefs in four principal doctrines (separation from the outside world, common property, confession of sins and celibacy, with separation but equality of the sexes) took hold. By the mid-nineteenth century, the Shaker movement reached its zenith, with 19 communities in the United States and some 6,000 believers.

Strolling through the village on a guided tour, you will notice that the buildings are austere but elegant and the craftsmanship outstanding. Shaker ways of coping with the material world are sometimes ingenious, while their keen grasp of the concepts of functionalism raised the design of their buildings, furniture and common utensils to an art form. The village's finest example of Shaker architecture and ingenuity, the magnificently restored **Round Stone Barn**, was built in 1826. The barn's upper level could be accessed by horses and wagons, which unloaded their harvest into a central haymow and then proceeded around a track to another exit. This eliminated the problem of backing hitched teams out of the barn, often a difficult task. Cows were stabled on the ground floor.

Note how the separation of the sexes was carried out: **The Brick Dwelling** (community dining room, sleeping rooms, and kitchen), which housed 100 brothers and sisters, divides neatly in half. Light and airy, its construction includes more than 3,000 windowpanes.

Tours also include nineteenth-century **craft demonstrations** and a walk through the village farm and herb garden (the seed industry was a Shaker specialty). For information contact the Hancock Shaker Village ((413) 443-0188 TOLL-FREE (800) 817-1137 FAX (413) 447-9357, PO Box 927, Pittsfield 01202. Open daily; an admission fee is charged.

Nightlife and the Arts

Pittsfield's concert hall has been the scene of distinguished musical performances since 1918 and is now home to the **South Mountain Concerts series** ((413) 442-2106. Artists who have appeared here include Leonard Bernstein, Leontyne Price, Rudolf Serkin, and the Tokyo Quartet. Concerts are held during late summer and fall. The Albany Berkshire Ballet offers a six-week series of classical, modern and contemporary dance at the **Koussevitsky Arts Center** ((413) 298-5252 or (413) 499-4660, extension 379, 1350 West Street, Pittsfield, on the Berkshire Community College campus.

How to Get There

Pittsfield is 137 miles (219 km) west of Boston, and seven miles (11 km) north of Lenox. **Amtrak** TOLL-FREE (800) 872-7245 operates the *Lake Shore Limited* between Chicago and Boston, with scheduled stops in Pittsfield.

Pricing silver candlesticks, a shopper enjoys the southern Berkshire's sterling reputation as a treasure trove of antiques and *objets d'art.*

WILLIAMSTOWN

Nathaniel Hawthorne called this late-nineteenth-century spa and summer resort, "a white village and a steeple set like a daydream among the high mountain waves." Situated in a hollow of the surrounding Berkshires and in the shadow of Mount Greylock, Williamstown remains one of New England's prettiest villages, home to Williams College, and to some outstanding art museums.

At the **information booth** on Main and South Streets you can obtain a touring map to explore Williamstown's rich past.

WHAT TO SEE AND DO

Williamstown's **Sterling and Francine Clark Art Institute** ☎ (413) 458-2303, 225 South Street, west of the town center, houses one of the world's largest private collections of Renoirs (30 of them), as well as works by other Impressionists. Open Tuesday to Sunday 10 AM to 5 PM and daily in July and August; an admission fee is charged. One of the finest college art museums in the country, the **Williams College Museum of Art** ☎ (413) 597-2429, Main Street, houses some 11,000 works that span the history of art. The neoclassical rotunda of its original structure, an 1846 two-story brick octagon, distinguishes the museum architecturally; Charles Moore designed the extensive additions.

On Main Street, many of the imposing abodes date from the 1750s. One of the most intriguing of the college buildings is Lawrence Hall, part of the Williams College Museum of Art (above), an octagonal Grecian rotunda inspired by Thomas Jefferson's Monticello. While on the campus, you may want to visit **Thompson Memorial Chapel** in a modern Gothic building, **Hopkins Observatory**, and **Chapin Library**, whose collection includes a repository of rare books.

NIGHTLIFE AND THE ARTS

The **Williamstown Theater Festival** ☎ (413) 597-3400, founded in 1955, is an annual celebrity-packed event. The main venue is at the nation's finest summer theater, Williamstown Theater on Main Stage. The festival has featured actors Christopher Reeve and Richard Thomas, director Joanne Woodward, and playwrights such as John Guare. Other venues include Adams Memorial Theater's "Cabaret," which presents an early revue and a late cabaret that often includes stars from the Main Stage; Thespis Productions, now over 15 years old, at the Clark Institute; the Calliope Theater Company; a women's theater group; and the Spring Street Ensemble Theater, with experimental productions.

Where to Stay and Eat

Williamstown lodging tends toward small, intimate inns, where you'll also find the best dining in the area. **The Orchards** ☎ (413) 458-9611, 222 Adams Road, Williamstown 01267 (expensive to luxury), is a luxurious inn situated in a former apple orchard. Some rooms have fireplaces; robes are supplied as well as a host of other conveniences. The **dining room** is one of the area's best; always a special treat.

A modest farmhouse-style inn, **Le Jardin Country Inn** ☎ (413) 458-8032, 777 Cold Spring Road, Williamstown 01267 (mid-range), has eight comfortable guestrooms with private bath and fireplace. The chef owner runs the **dining room**, noted for its classic French specialties such as frog legs. There is a pond on the grounds. Spanish and French are spoken. The rate includes a continental breakfast. Smoking and pets are allowed.

Built in 1881, the **Williamstown Bed and Breakfast** ☎ (413) 458-9202, 30 Cold Spring Road, Williamstown 01267 (budget to mid-range), is a Victorian located within walking distance of local attractions and events. The four guestrooms have private bath and are furnished with antiques. The rate includes breakfast with a hot main course and homemade baked goods.

Field Farm Guest House ☎ (413) 458-3135, 554 Sloan Road, Williamstown 01267 (mid-range), is a modern house in the middle of 296 acres (118 hectares) of protected farmland. Eleanor and Laurence Bloedel built the dwelling in 1948 to house their art collection, parts of which remain here. The five guestrooms are furnished in a 1950s style just as they were when the Bloedels lived here. The grounds offer hiking trails, tennis courts, and a swimming pool. Breakfast includes fresh fruits and homemade pastries as well as a hot main course.

How to Get There

Williamstown lies at the intersection of Route 7 and Route 2, about 145 miles (232 km) west of Boston and 23 miles (37 km) north of Lenox.

OPPOSITE: Thompson Chapel dominates the Williams College campus. ABOVE: Fall colors paint the Mohawk Trail.

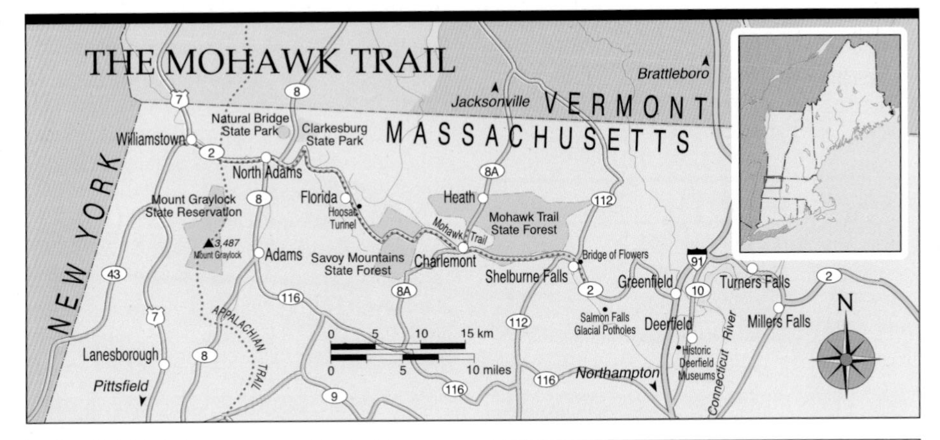

NORTH ADAMS AND MOUNT GREYLOCK

The magnificent granite bulk of Mount Greylock, at 3,491 ft (1,064 m), is the highest point in Massachusetts. From its rocky barren summit, the hiker is rewarded with a fine vista of the Berkshires and western Massachusetts, the Green Mountains of Vermont and the Hudson River Valley of New York. The surrounding peaks and forests have many well-marked hiking trails, including part of the Appalachian Trail, which crosses Mount Greylock. Thoreau climbed to the summit: "I was up early, and perched upon the top of the tower to see the day break. As the light increased, I discovered around me an ocean of mist, which reached up by chance exactly to the base of the tower, and shut out every vestige of the earth, while I was left floating on this fragment of the wreck of a world, — on my carved plank in cloud-laud, a situation which it required no aid from the imagination to render impressive…"

Appalachian Mountain Club's Bascom Lodge ☎ (413) 743-1591, PO Box 1800, Lanesborough 01237, is a rustic lodge on the summit of Mount Greylock. Hearty breakfast and dinner are served AMC-style — in a crowd of amiable hikers enjoying the view. Lunch is served cafeteria style from 10 AM to 5 PM.

In the nearby town of Adams, fans of Americana should stop at the **Miss Adams Diner** ☎ (413) 743-5300, 35 Park Street, where classic diner fare has been served since 1949 in a vintage rail car. Kick off a road trip down the Mohawk Trail with breakfast at the Miss Adams.

ALONG THE MOHAWK TRAIL

The 63-mile-long (100-km) **Mohawk Trail** (Route 2 and 2A) is one of the nation's prettiest highways, winding its bucolic way from the rugged, forested slopes of the northern Berkshires, past farms and orchards, and finally descending into the Pioneer Valley (see THE PIONEER VALLEY, page 127).

Built during the Depression as a WPA project, the road has a series of decorative concrete bridges, each one slightly different than the next. Stop along the way at the marked observation points for views of mountainous portions of Vermont's Green Mountains and northern Berkshires.

The Mohawk Trail follows the trace of an ancient Indian footpath from New York's Finger Lakes to Central Massachusetts. One of the first historical references to the trail notes that the Pocumtuck natives, under pressure from the expanding colonists, retreated from their villages on the banks of the Connecticut River near what is now Greenfield, Massachusetts, in 1663 to invade the lands of the Mohawks, in the area of what is now Troy, New York. In the ensuing war, the Mohawks annihilated the Pocumtucks, wiping out their legacy in North America. Later, pioneers traveled along the Mohawk Trail from the Massachusetts Bay Colony to the Berkshires, then on to Dutch settlements in the Mohawk and Hudson valleys.

The Mohawk Trail became a major path for moving colonial forces to New York to

Mohawk Trail gift shops promise "Indian" souvenirs. Also on sale: pink flamingos, fannies, garden dwarves, and other of life's necessities.

GLOVES
Indian POTTERY
FILM
SOUVENIRS
GIFTS
HONEY
BELTS
RESERVATION
206

defend British outposts during the French and Indian Wars. These troops included a young Paul Revere, then making his first trip away from his Boston home. Soon after Independence, the Mohawk Trail was used by covered wagon trains moving west, as it provided the easiest way over the mountains. In 1786, it became America's first free interstate road. The nineteenth century brought stagecoaches to the trail, as more and more settlers moved westward. But it was not until 1914 that the Mohawk Trail was opened to automobile travel.

GENERAL INFORMATION

For informational materials on this region, contact the **Mohawk Trail Association** ☎ (413) 664-6256 FAX (413) 458-2767, PO Box 722, Charlemont 01339; or the **Franklin County Convention and Visitors Bureau** ☎ (413) 773-5463 FAX (413) 773-7008, 395 Main Street, PO Box 790, Greenfield 01302.

WHAT TO SEE AND DO

Traveling east on the Mohawk Trail from Williamstown, you soon arrive in **North Adams**. Once a busy nineteenth-century mill town, North Adams saw its commercial prominence vanish with the textile industry. It is now a year-round recreation center, with ski areas and abundant summer activities. In early October, the town puts on a Fall Foliage Festival and Parade ☎ (413) 663-3735 (chamber of commerce), when the surrounding hills are a palette of scarlet, gold and crimson. At **Natural Bridge State Park** ☎ (413) 663-6312 (November to April) or 663-6392 (May to October), located on Route 8 North, a 550-million-year-old rock formation leaps a marble chasm 475 ft (145 m) long and 60 ft (18 m) deep. This water-eroded bridge can be traversed from May through October for a small fee (though the rusting chain-link fenced walkway mars the overall effect). North Adams is the site of the **Massachusetts Museum of Contemporary Art** ☎ (413) 664-4481, 87 Marshall Street, North Adams, located in a 28-building former mill complex. Open Wednesday to Monday; an admission fee is charged.

As the Trail ascends from North Adams, slow down for the **Hairpin Turn**, a 180-degree curve memorable for its spectacular views of the surrounding countryside. Off-road parking provides access to an **observation platform** with impressive vistas of the Hoosac Valley, the Green Mountains and Mount Greylock.

Continue through the town of Florida to **Whitcomb Summit**, home of the Elk Memorial on the highest point of the Mohawk Trail, at 2,200 ft (670 m) with a panorama of the Deerfield River and the **Hoosac Range**. This wall of granite (once nicknamed the "Berkshire Barrier") isolated the northern Berkshires until the nineteenth century, when the **Hoosac Tunnel** was blasted through the rock. The four-mile-long (six-kilometer) tunnel took 25 years to complete, and claimed the lives of nearly 200 workers. To reach the tunnel's eastern portal, take Whitcomb Hill Road south to the Deerfield River, then turn left on River Road until you reach the railroad tracks.

Soon after the Hoosac Tunnel, you enter the superb mountain scenery of the **Mohawk Trail State Forest** ☎ (413) 339-5504 and **Savoy Mountain State Forest** ☎ (413) 663-8469, offering excellent hiking trails, including an easy slope to the peak of Forbidden Mountain.

The Mohawk Trail's halfway point, **Charlemont** (settled in 1749) has as its landmark the 900-lb (409-kg) bronze cast statue (at Indian Bridge spanning the Deerfield River), "Hail to the Sunrise," depicting a brave with arms outstretched to the Great Spirit, a 1932 memorial to the long-annihilated Mohawks. There is alpine skiing at Charlemont's Berkshire East ☎ (413) 339-6617, South River Road, Charlemont.

Continue easterly along State Highway 2 to the village of **Shelburne Falls** ☎ (413) 625-2544 (village information center) with its unusual **Bridge of Flowers**, a former trolley bridge that has been maintained as a hanging garden by the Shelburne Women's Club since 1929. The 400-ft (122-m), five-arch concrete bridge was built in 1908 across the Deerfield River to carry trolley tracks between Shelburne and Buckland, but was abandoned in the late 1920s as transportation patterns changed. Flowers cover the bridge from spring to fall. From here, follow

the signs to **Salmon Falls**, where you can see and swim in the **glacial potholes** — an expanse of granite pocked with indentations of various shapes and sizes — reputed to be among the largest in the world. Those in the know point hungry tourists towards the **Copper Angel Café** ☎ (413) 625-2727, 2 State Street, next to the Bridge of Flowers, where rich sauces accompany red-meat-free main courses.

Farther east, **Greenfield** is known for its involvement in the Indian wars and for its fine Colonial architecture. Here in Greenfield, a covered bridge spans the Green River. The **Poet's Seat Tower** on Greenfield Mountain (east on Main Street toward High Street, then follow the signs) affords a panoramic view of the lush Greenfield Valley.

Crossing the Connecticut River east of Greenfield is the **French King Bridge**, 750 ft (228 m) long and 140 ft (43 m) above the water. The northern side of the bridge provides an excellent view of the river and of French King Rock, supposedly the site of the first planting of the French flag in this region by French explorers.

A weathered barn along the Mohawk Trail.

MOUNTAIN

Cape Cod and the Islands

A long spit of sand that curls out into the Atlantic Ocean for about 70 miles (113 km), Cape Cod has some 300 miles (480 km) of sandy beaches, dozens of coastal villages, and isolated islands. A land of shifting dunes, of bird sanctuaries, cranberry bogs and wooded parkland laced with bike paths and hiking trails, the peninsula was a sleepy amalgam of small colonial fishing villages before the advent of the automobile. Then mobile visitors from nearby cities (Boston is only 70 miles or 113 km to the north and New York City is less than 250 miles or 400 km away) discovered its charm. These days the Cape is among New England's prime vacation areas and packed to its gills in the peak months of July and August.

In the late 1800s, Henry David Thoreau made four visits to Cape Cod, rhapsodizing that here "…a sort of chaos reigns still." A century later, Thoreau would hardly recognize the Cape Cod he visited, with the notable exception of the Cape Cod National Seashore. These 43,500 acres (17,400 hectares) of dunes and beaches, salt marshes, pine forests and cranberry bogs protect a remnant of the fragile ecosystems of the Lower Cape.

Sometimes called the "Cape's Cape," the islands of Martha's Vineyard and Nantucket are where Cape Codders get away from it all. Lying south and east of the long arm of the Cape, the islands, like the Cape, are relatively flat and perfect for biking and walking. As on the Cape, there are wonderful opportunities for swimming, bird watching and sailing.

Since Cape Cod and its neighboring islands extend some 30 miles (50 km) into the warm Gulf Stream the weather is much milder here than on the mainland, with summers cooled by sea winds and winters warmed by Gulf Stream air. Summer is of course beach time — but this is New England, and only the hardy swim outside of the period between the July 4 and Labor Day. After Labor Day, the Cape belongs to its residents who, though happy the crowds are gone, are still keen on letting others in on the secret that fall and spring may be the best time of all to visit. In September and October the cranberry bogs are scarlet with berries; in April lawns are carpeted with crocuses and daffodils and the woodlands with wildflowers; in winter… well, come see for yourself.

BACKGROUND

A DISAPPEARING LAND

A succession of glacial deposits and wind and wave erosion formed Cape Cod's present hook shape. This geologic history and ongoing ocean and climatic changes, spell a doubtful future for the Cape, one all too well known to its 175,000 residents. Studies indicate that the roaring sea and northwest winds of the Atlantic are eroding the Cape at an alarming rate, and that the land itself may be sinking into the sea. Generations from now, the Cape may be only a memory, worn away to a few sandy shoals — victim to a geological process that modern-day technology can do nothing to stop.

A greater threat to the Cape is the rise in sea level brought about by the "greenhouse effect" — automobile, power plant, and other human pollution melting polar ice caps. Scientists predict that within the next 40 years, shorelines from Provincetown to Bourne will retreat an average of 100 ft (30 m).

Provincetown, at the Cape's tip, finds itself in a most precarious position; the United States Geological Survey in Woods Hole predicts that the town "is headed for real trouble" which can be measured "in tens of years, not hundreds."

This is happening all over the Cape. The cliffs at Falmouth Heights are washing into Vineyard Sound; West Barnstable recently lost 15 ft (four and a half meters) of Sandy Neck beach in a severe winter storm; even the Wellfleet location where Marconi transmitted along the first transatlantic cable 85 years ago is now more than 200 ft (61 m) out to sea.

EARLY INHABITANTS

Wampanoags inhabited Cape Cod when explorer Bartholomew Gosnold landed in 1602. He named the peninsula for the great schools of cod found in the surrounding waters.

Yachts await the weekend on Cape Cod; while in the background, luxury condominiums sprawl along the shore vying for a view.

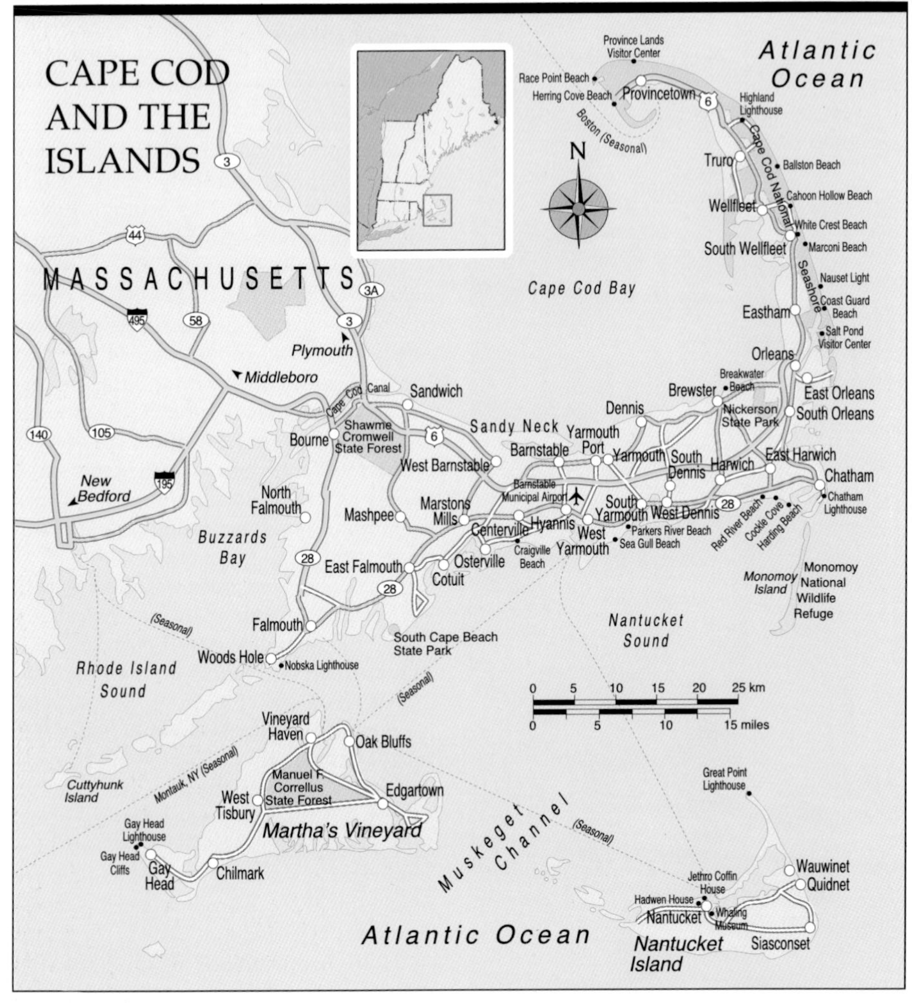

On November 21, 1620, the *Mayflower* Pilgrims landed at what is now Provincetown harbor after 67 days at sea. While anchored here, the group wrote and signed the Mayflower Compact, binding all members to be "straightly tied to all care of each other's good and of the whole by everyone." The Pilgrims stayed on the Cape for more than a month, but finding the soil thin and fresh water scarce, they moved on to Plymouth across Cape Cod Bay.

By the 1630s, settlements had sprung up along the Cape, with fishing the mainstay industry. A whaling industry evolved, lasting into the early twentieth century, and the Cape's fishermen commanded a fleet of vessels that sailed out of the ports of Falmouth, Truro, Wellfleet, Provincetown, and Nantucket Island. In those sailing days, more than 3,000 ships were wrecked on the Cape, with thousands of lives lost.

Today the Cape is famous for its cranberries, its gorgeous scenery and its summer resorts.

GENERAL INFORMATION

For information in advance of your trip, contact the **Cape Cod Chamber of Commerce** ☾ (508) 862-0700 TOLL-FREE (888) 332-2732 E-MAIL info@capecodchamber.org, PO Box 790, Hyannis 02601, at the junction of Routes 6 and 132. The chamber keeps its visitors center open daily during the summer. There you can pick up maps, guides and hotel information.

Getting Around

Cape Cod has miles of heavenly bike trails. For information on **biking** on Cape Cod, contact the membership organization Mad About Cycling (MAC) WEB SITE www.vsp.cape.com/~mac/home.htm. Backpackers and other budget travelers without wheels would do best to take the **ferry** from Boston to Provincetown. Once in "P-Town," as it is called locally, there is much to see and do that can be reached on foot. The **Cape Cod Regional Transit Authority** ✆ (508) 385-8326 TOLL-FREE (800) 352-7155 operates **bus service** linking Provencetown and other Cape towns, including Falmouth–Hyannis and Hyannis–Orleans.

But most people **drive**. Despite the drawbacks of too much traffic and too little parking, the Cape is relatively easy to find your way around on. ("You can't get lost here," a Cape Codder once said to me. After years of visiting the Cape, I would amend that phrase to read: "You can't get lost for long.") Three main routes lead just about everywhere on the Cape: **Route 6** stretches the length of the peninsula and is its main throughway, offering access to all major towns except Chatham and Falmouth. **Route 28** is the Cape's commercial road. The **Old King's Highway (Route 6A)**, running between Sandwich and Orleans, is the slow and picturesque way, and traverses the largest historic district in the United States. Village greens, antique shops, regional museums, galleries, artist's studios, and cafés beckon at every twist and turn. It's been called one of the country's 10 most scenic byways.

How to Get There

Cape Cod is 250 miles (400 km) east of New York City and 70 miles (113 km) south of Boston.

Motorists must contend with heavy traffic, especially on summer weekends. Cars headed for the Cape may be backed up for more than an hour at the bridges spanning Cape Cod Canal, and cars line up bumper-to-bumper along Routes 6 and 6A. If you choose the **Bourne Bridge** at the southern end of the canal, Route 28 will lead you first into the "Upper Cape," that part of the peninsula closest to the mainland, past West Falmouth, Falmouth and Marstons Mill before reaching Hyannis. If you cross at the **Sagamore Bridge**, at the canal's northern end, either continue on the four-lane Route 6, across the "Mid Cape" to Orleans, or on the two-lane Route 6A, a scenic road passing through several Mid Cape towns. Routes 6 and 6A meet near Orleans and continue up the "Lower Cape" to Provincetown as Route 6.

Ferries to Provincetown depart from Boston and Plymouth. For details see TOURS AND EXCURSIONS under these two destinations, page 93 and page 120 respectively.

Slatted wooden fences protect Cape Cod dunes from erosion caused by wind and wayward beach-goers.

Barnstable Municipal Airport ✆ (508) 775-2020 is the Cape's principal landing field. It's centrally located midway along the peninsula in Hyannis (a village near the town of Barnstable). Three airlines serve the airport: Cape Air ✆ (508) 771-6944 TOLL-FREE (800) 352-0714, US Air Express TOLL-FREE (800) 428-4322, and Island Air TOLL-FREE (800) 248-7779. There are usually taxis waiting at the main terminals, and major rental car companies have offices there, including: Avis ✆ (508) 775-2888, Budget ✆ (508) 790-0163, Hertz ✆ (508) 775-5895 and National Car Rental ✆ (508) 771-4353.

THE UPPER CAPE

For years I drove past the Upper Cape on my way to beaches and bike paths further north. Then one day I stopped. I'm glad I did. The "Upper Cape," designating the western part of the peninsula closest to the mainland, has a spectacular coastline that is less crowded and less commercial than the shores of the Outer Cape. Its principal villages of Falmouth and Sandwich retain a flavor of past centuries with their tree-lined village greens and scores of historic houses. And Falmouth offers some of the best lodging values on the peninsula.

General Information

The **Falmouth Chamber of Commerce** ((508) 548-8500 toll-free (800) 526-8532 e-mail info@falmouth-capecod.com, PO Box 582, Falmouth 02541, provides information. You can get a free visitors guide covering **Sandwich**, Bourne and Wareham from the **Cape Cod Canal Region Chamber of Commerce** ((508) 759-6000 fax (508) 759-6965 e-mail execdir@capecod.net, 70 Main Street, Buzzards Bay 02532.

What to See and Do

Falmouth and Woods Hole

Falmouth is the main town on the southwestern "elbow" of the Cape. Incorporated in 1686, it expanded around its **Village Green**, laid out in 1749, where a bell cast by Paul Revere still rings at the First Congregational Church. Here also stands the childhood home of the woman who penned the lyrics to *America the Beautiful*, **Katherine Lee Bates** (the house is privately owned). The **Julia Wood House** and **Conant House**, run by the Falmouth Historical Society, are on Palmer Avenue just past the Green.

On the back road between Falmouth and Woods Hole is the **Nobska Lighthouse**, Church Road, Woods Hole. From the bluff where the lighthouse is positioned you can see boats traveling between Woods Hole and the islands, as well as those *en route* to New York and Boston. The lighthouse has guided vessels since the early 1800s.

Woods Hole is a former whaling town, now a principal Cape port where ferries depart daily for the islands. Stroll its tiny main drag, but don't expect to find parking there. This small fishing village is home to the **Woods Hole Oceanographic Institute** (WHOI) ((508) 289-2663, at Albatross and Water streets, which planned and launched the successful search for the *Titanic* in 1986.

Its neighbor is the **Marine Biological Laboratory** ((508) 289-7623, Water Street (corner MBL Street), where you can visit and learn about current research projects. The tour begins with a slide show, after which a retired scientist leads visitors among the holding tanks and to the lab to watch biologists going about their daily business. Open from June to August at 1 PM, 2 PM and 3 PM; reservations should be made a week in advance if possible. Admission is free.

Lumpfish, blue lobsters and wriggling, live shark embryos are on display at the **National Marine Fisheries Service Aquarium** ((508) 548-7684, Albatross and Water streets. Arrive at 11 AM if you want to observe feeding time for the two harbor seals in the outdoor tank. Fish from native to tropical fill the tanks of the small aquarium. Like the rest of the Woods Hole facilities, this is a working lab, and you are welcome to walk through to see what's up — a look behind the scenes that you don't get at most fancy aquariums. Open daily mid-June to mid-September; from mid-September to mid-June it's open from Monday to Friday only. Admission is free.

Sandwich and Mashpee

Glassmaking made Sandwich. You might guess that it was all of that glorious Cape Cod sand that drew Deming Jarves and his glass shop from Boston to the Cape in the 1820s. In fact, Sandwich sand is too coarse for glassmaking. What attracted the entrepreneur were the trees, which he proceeded to cut down at an alarming rate to feed the furnaces needed to make the molten material for his creations.

The trees are beginning to grow back, and Sandwich glass has become a collector's item. You can visit the **Sandwich Glass Museum** ((508) 888-0251, 129 Main Street, across from the village green, and peruse some 5,000 examples glass art and glassware produced here from 1825 to 1888. There is a small gift shop and a modest glassmaking demonstration in season. Open daily from April through December, and Wednesday to Sunday during February and March; an admission fee is charged.

About a half mile (less than a kilometer) southwest of town center, **Heritage Plantation** ☎ (508) 888-3300 and 888-1222, 67 Grove (corner Pine Street), appeals to both adults and children. On 76 beautifully landscaped acres (30 hectares), a scattering of buildings

The Sandwich Glass Museum.

house a hodgepodge of collections. In the Shaker Round Barn there is a display of antique automobiles, including the 1931 Duesenberg used by actor Gary Cooper. Elsewhere there is a museum of military paraphernalia. The 1912 working carousel features a fancifully carved menagerie as mounts. The complex is open daily from mid-May to mid-October; an admission fee is charged. Call for off-season hours.

Mashpee (sometimes spelled Massipee) means "land grant by the cove." It refers to the first Native American reservation in the country, Mashpee Plantation, established in the early seventeenth century and later incorporated as a town. Here in Mashpee live the surviving descendants of the Mashpee band, part of the Wampanoag tribe, who populated the Cape thousands of years before the first Europeans arrived. The **Old Indian Meetinghouse and Burial Ground** dates back to 1684, making it the oldest meetinghouse on the Cape. To get there from Route 28 West, turn right just before the Seabury Rotary and right again onto Old Meetinghouse Road. From here, continue, bearing right onto Great Neck Road, until just after you pass the Town Hall, turn left onto Main Street (Route 130), and you'll find the small **Wampanoag Indian Museum** ☎ (508) 477-1536, across from Lake Avenue.

SPORTS AND OUTDOOR ACTIVITIES

Beaches

North Falmouth's **Old Silver Beach** on Buzzards Bay and Falmouth's **Surf Drive Beach** on Vineyard Sound are two of the best beaches on the Upper Cape — get there early. Locals know that **Chapoquoit Beach** and **Nobska Point** are prime spots for sunset views. Note that Falmouth beaches require a parking permit, which can be purchased at Surf Drive Beach.

In Sandwich, a boardwalk leads to **Town Neck Beach**, a gravel strand that's good for walking at low tide. **Horizons Beach** is the place to watch boats sailing to and fro in the Cape Cod Canal. There is permit parking at **East Sandwich Beach**. **Sandy Neck Beach** is among the Cape's most scenic. There's a fee for parking.

Walking and Nature Trails

In East Falmouth, the 45-acre (18-hectare) **Ashumet Holly & Wildlife Sanctuary** ☎ (508) 362-1426 off Route 151 has nature trails, guided nature and birding walks, spring seal-watching cruises and summer and fall cruises to Cuttyhunk Island. Open daily from sunrise to sunset; an admission fee is charged. Extensive walking trails through the 2,500-acre (1,000-hectare) **Waquoit Bay National Estuarine Research Reserve**, North Falmouth, offer views of open water, barrier beaches, marshlands and uplands. Access is from Route 151. Within the reserve, **South Cape Beach State P ark** ☎ (508) 457-0495 in Mashpee is a two-mile (three-kilometer) stretch of barrier beach encompassing nature trails, birding walks and a guided evening nature walk.

In Sandwich, **Talbot's Pond Salt Marsh Wildlife Reserve** offers visitors a one-and-a-half-mile (two-and-a-half-kilometer) round-trip walk through one of the largest salt marsh areas on the Cape. Access is from Old Colony Road, off Route 6A. The **Shawme Crowell State Forest**, Route 130, has 700 acres (280 hectares) of forested walking and bicycling trails. The **Green Briar Nature Center and Jam Kitchen** ☎ (508) 888-6870, 6 Discovery Hill Road, East Sandwich, is a 57-acre (23-hectare) spread, with nature trails and wildflower gardens.

Bicycling

The **Shining Sea Bike Path** is a fairly level 7.2-mile (11.5-km) round-trip path hugging the shore from Falmouth to Woods Hole, offering unsurpassed scenery including views of Nobska Light, acres of golden marsh grass, dunes and woodland, not to mention miles of shining sea. It's a beauty. **Art's Bike Shop** ☎ (508) 563-7379 TOLL-FREE (800) 563-7379, at the corner of County Road and Old Main Road, North Falmouth, rents bikes and gear.

Another classic Cape bike trip is the seven-mile (11-km) paved service road that parallels the **Cape Cod Canal** from Sandwich to Bourne. This easygoing route can be accessed at the Sandwich Marina, Pleasant Street in Sagamore, and the United States Engineering Observation Station, Sandwich.

Water Sports

Learn to row at the **Green Briar Nature Center and Jam Kitchen** (above), which offers canoeing lessons for all ages. For those who already know how, kayak rental (with delivery) is available from **Cape Cod Kayak** ☎ (508) 563-9377, Cummaquid Road, Falmouth. Shipwreck divers can rent diving equipment and sign up for instruction and certification at the **Aqua Center** ☎ (508) 888-3444, 2 Freezer Road, Sandwich.

TOURS AND EXCURSIONS

You can visit the island of **Martha's Vineyard** on a day-trip from the Upper Cape. Ferry service runs year-round from Woods Hole, and in summer from Falmouth. See HOW TO GET THERE, page 180 in MARTHA'S VINEYARD.

Also in summer, you can sail from Falmouth to **Cuttyhunk Island** on the Patriot

Party Boats ☎ (508) 548-2626. The same outfit offers trips aboard a replica of a 1750s fishing schooner, as well as Audubon Society seal-watching cruises, sunset trips and moonlight cruises.

Ocean Quest ☎ (508) 385-7656 runs a research vessel giving passengers a chance to learn about oceanographic science. Trips run from mid-May to mid-October and depart from Water Street, Woods Hole.

NIGHTLIFE AND THE ARTS

Because of the presence of its many research institutes, the Upper Cape may have more PhDs per square mile than Cambridge. This educated public supports a medley of artistic ventures. The **Cape Cod Theater Project** ☎ (508) 457-4242, PO Box 410, Falmouth 02541, is a new endeavor bringing professional actors to the Upper Cape for a season of off-Broadway drama. The **Woods Hole Theater Company** ☎ (508) 540-6525, Woods Hole Community Hall, PO Box 735, Woods Hole 02543, presents plays and events year-round.

The **Boch Center for the Performing Arts** ☎ (508) 477-2580, PO Box 1997, Mashpee 02649, has brought in the Count Basie Orchestra, Deborah Henson-Conant and the Vienna Boys Choir. Call for up-to-date scheduling. Most performances take place under a concert tent at Mashpee Commons, intersection of Routes 28 and 151.

WHERE TO STAY

Revolutionary figure Daniel Webster frequented Sandwich's Fessender Inn; in honor of their patriot patron, the inn eventually renamed itself. Today the **Dan'l Webster Inn** ☎ (508) 888-3622 TOLL-FREE (800) 444-3566, Main Street, Sandwich 02563 (remodeled after the eighteenth-century original was destroyed by fire), garners respect both locally and abroad for its 47 elegant rooms and suites and gracious service (expensive).

Several good bed-and-breakfast places hug the Village Green at Falmouth. I recommend **Mostly Hall** ☎ (508) 548-3786 TOLL-FREE (800) 682-0565 FAX (508) 457-1572 E-MAIL mostlyhl@aol.com, 27 Main Street, Falmouth 02540-2652. The 1849 Southern-plantation-style house has a wraparound porch, a garden and a gazebo. Inside are a widow's walk and sitting room (outfitted with television and video player), and six rooms with queen-size canopy beds and 13-ft (four-meter) ceilings. The inn provides a lending library, piano, and bicycles for the use of guests. Off-street parking is available. It is closed during January. The rate (expensive) includes breakfast and afternoon refreshments.

In Sandwich another good bed and breakfast is the **Captain Ezra Nye House** ☎ (508) 888-6142 TOLL-FREE (800) 388-2278, 152 Main Street, Sandwich 02563, an 1829 sea captain's house with five rooms and one suite (mid-range).

There is prime resort-style lodging in Falmouth at **Sea Crest Resort** ☎ (508) 540-9400 TOLL-FREE (800) 225-3110 FAX (508) 548-0556, Old Silver Beach, 350 Quaker Road, North Falmouth 02556 (mid-range).

The **Village Inn** ☎ (508) 833-0363 TOLL-FREE (800) 922-9989 E-MAIL capecodinn@aol.com, 4 Jarves Street, Sandwich 02563, is a restored 1830s Federal-style inn with eight rooms, some of them with fireplaces and queen

OPPOSITE: The Hoxie House, dating from 1637, is the oldest house in Sandwich. ABOVE: The Thornton W. Burgess Museum, also in Sandwich.

beds (inexpensive). Behind the inn is **Sandwich Artworks** which offers five-day workshops in a variety of media lead by accomplished artists. Workshops are available as part of a package with discounted lodging at the inn. Both the Ezra Nye (above) and the Village Inn are located in the heart of Sandwich Village, a short walk away from museums, shops, restaurants or the boardwalk over the marsh to the bay beach.

One of the most dependable and delightful Falmouth B&Bs is **Palmer House Inn** ☎ (508) 548-1230 TOLL-FREE (800) 472-2632

FAX (508) 540-1878, 81 Palmer Avenue, Falmouth 02540, a formal Victorian inn with a hideaway suite behind. Rates run from mid-range to expensive. **Sjoholm Inn** ☎ (508) 540-5706 TOLL-FREE (800) 498-5706, 17 Chase Road, West Falmouth 02574-0430, is a value-oriented bed and breakfast with 15 rooms with private bath as well as a two-bedroom cottage (budget to mid-range).

WHERE TO EAT

In Sandwich, the **Dan'l Webster Inn** ☎ (508) 888-3622 (see WHERE TO STAY, above) has two romantic dining rooms (expensive) serving award-winning cuisine ("best on the Upper Cape" according to readers of *Cape Cod Life*), as well as the Tavern with wood-grilled pizzas (mid-range).

Mediterranean fare is the primary line at **Tra Bi Ca** ☎ (508) 548-9861, 327 Gifford Street, Falmouth, with main courses such as linguine and little necks (soft-shelled clams), Mediterranean ravioli with roasted vegetables, and classic pizzas. Eat in or take out. Service is prompt. Reservations are not accepted (mid-range).

A few minutes' walk from the Woods Hole ferry gangplank, the **Fishmonger Café** ☎ (508) 548-9148, 56 Water Street, is another place with extensive daily specials, such as a starter of asparagus, goat cheese and prosciutto tart; mains may include blackened mahi-mahi or baked stuffed lobster. There's a wide choice for vegetarians including a savory Middle Eastern plate. The stoneware used at the tables is created in Woods Hole by potter Joan Lederman.

A singing proprietor and beer-battered fish and chips draw locals and visitors to **Liam Maguire's** ☎ (508) 548-0285, 273 Main Street, Falmouth. It's your friendly neighborhood Irish pub with standard fare; breakfast is served weekends in July and August (budget).

In Woods Hole, **Shuckers World Famous Raw Bar and Café** ☎ (508) 540-3850 is a good place for a casual outdoor seafood feast. The **Clam Shack** ☎ (508) 540-7758, Scranton Avenue, Falmouth, with its Formica counters and wooden stools, doles out huge portions of fresh fried clams, lobster rolls and fish and chips. Open for lunch and dinner daily (budget).

Ensconced in a vintage dining car brought from Altoona, Pennsylvania, **Betsy's Diner** ☎ (508) 540-0060 or (508) 540-4446, 457 Main Street, Falmouth, opens at 5 AM. Beyond breakfast, there are club sandwiches, meatloaf, liver and onions, frappes (milk shakes) and floats. The turkey dinner feeds a multitude. Take-out is available (budget).

MID CAPE

Encompassing the geographic center of the Cape as well as the bulk of its human population and commercial development are the Mid Cape towns of Yarmouth, Dennis and Barnstable. Within the town of Barnstable are seven villages: Barnstable, West Barnstable, Marstons Mills, Cotuit, Osterville, Centerville and Hyannis. The largest and most central is the village of Hyannis — terminus for island ferries, major bus transportation and airlines.

GENERAL INFORMATION

Serving the seven villages of Barnstable is the **Hyannis Chamber of Commerce** ℂ (508) 362-5230 TOLL-FREE (800) 449-6647 FAX (508) 362-9499 WEB SITE www.hyannis.com. The **Yarmouth Chamber of Commerce** ℂ (508) 778-1008 TOLL-FREE (800) 732-1008 FAX (508) 778-5114 E-MAIL yarmouth@capecod.net WEB SITE www.yarmouthcapecod.com, has a year-round **visitor center** at 657 Route 28.

WHAT TO SEE AND DO

Barnstable and Hyannis

While bucolic Barnstable lounges along the Old King's Highway, Hyannis carries out its bustling role as the Cape's commercial center — a sprawling expanse of tourist attractions and rampant development, the Cape's main vacation and shopping center and a popular base for visits up and down the strand.

National attention focused on Hyannis in the early 1960s when John Fitzgerald Kennedy became president. "I always go to Hyannis Port to be revived, to know again the power of the sea and the Master who rules over it all and all of us," said the President, whose family still owns a large estate (known as the Kennedy Compound) in this exclusive seaside village. The **John F. Kennedy Hyannis Museum** ℂ (508) 790-3077, 397 Main Street, Hyannis, documents the golden era of JFK's life, when the clan would gather at Hyannis Port to vacation. Open daily February through December; an admission fee is charged.

Yarmouth

Originally populated by Wampanoag tribes who called the area "Mattacheese," Yarmouth was settled in 1640 by English farmers. Like Barnstable and Hyannis, Yarmouth evinces the two diverging faces of Cape life: Its north side is bounded by the Old King's Highway (Route 6A) and lined with antique shops and venerable inns, while the south is bounded by Route 28 with its resort motels and shopping malls.

The circa-1740 **Captain Bangs Hallet House** ℂ (508) 362-3021, 11 Strawberry Lane, off Route 6A in Yarmouth Port, is an old-style drugstore in business since the 1800s. You can order a shake at the marble-top soda fountain, and peer into old chestnut drawers. Upstairs there's a small museum where you can learn about the Knowles and Hallet families and the nineteenth-century com-

munity in which they lived and worked. Guided tours are offered on limited days June through September at 2 PM; an admission fee is charged.

The old Custom House, now called the **Trayser Museum** ℂ (508) 790-6270, located on Main Street (Route 6A) at Cobb's Hill, has an engaging display of the town's maritime history.

The ultimate browsers bookseller, **Parnassus Book Service Center** ℂ (508) 362-6420, 220 Route 6A, Yarmouth Port, has volumes stacked floor to ceiling, spilling out of every niche of this former church building.

OPPOSITE: A caricaturist in Hyannis hawks celebrity portraits. ABOVE: A parking attendant looks out for business at a Barnstable beach.

Dennis

Named for its first appointed minister, Reverend Josiah Dennis, the town of Dennis was incorporated in 1793. Street names such as Cold Storage Road and Salt Works Road are remnants of the town's early industries.

The ultimate view of Cape Cod Sound and Bay is from the top of **Scargo Tower**. Built in 1874 as an observatory, it stands atop the tallest hill in the area at 160 ft (49 m) above sea level. Scargo Lake, a kettle pond, is below. To get there, take Old Bass Road off Route 6A, then bear left onto Scargo Hill Road. The **Scargo Pottery** ☎ (508) 385-3894, on Doctor Lord's Road South, displays its earthenware works indoors as well as outdoors among the trees.

The **Armchair Bookstore** ☎ (508) 385-0900, 619 Route 6A, in Dennis, has a good selection of titles on Cape Cod history, travel and lore.

SPORTS AND OUTDOOR ACTIVITIES

Beaches

On the bay side, there is a fine beach on **Sandy Neck**, considered by many to be the Mid Cape's best. This seven-mile (11-km) spit of sand is the peninsula that protects Barnstable Harbor. It's not as crowded during the height of the season as some other beaches, since the beach tends to be gravelly at low tide. Despite the gravel, this is the most beautiful barrier beach on the peninsula — a beach made for walking, where you can see dunes, sand and sea in both directions. There is a fee for parking.

On the sound side, near Centerville, **Craigville Beach** is one of the area's most popular swimming spots; a parking fee is charged. At **Dennis** you can walk out for miles on the sandbars at low tide (but keep a close eye on the tide tables!). The beach is beautiful here and the water is a warm 75°F (24°C). Running south of Dennis to Sandwich, the shoreline is composed primarily of salt marsh. **Dennis Chapin Memorial**, a bay beach, is a good for shelling.

In Yarmouth, the younger set favors **Seagull**. **Parker's River** has a concession stand and outdoor showers, making it a good place to bring the family. **Smugglers** is another good family beach where you can watch the Nantucket ferry come in. The latter two beaches charge for parking.

Walking and Nature Trails

At **Sandy Neck**, the village of Barnstable maintains a nine-mile (14.5-km) round-trip walking trail that takes you along the beach, through the dunes, and past a cranberry bog to the edge of the 4,000-acre (1,600-hectare) Great Salt Marsh. Access is from the beach parking lot, Sandy Neck Road, West Barnstable.

At Yarmouth Port a boardwalk crosses the marsh to **Bass Hole** where there's a beautiful view of Chapin Beach. This is a prime spot for birding during fall and spring migrations, and for sunset watching year-round. There is a large picnic area here.

Bicycling

The Cape's premier bike path is the paved **Cape Cod Rail Trail**, which was created along the right-of-way of the old Penn Central Railroad. The 20-mile-long (32-km) trail begins in South Dennis, passes through **Nickerson State Park** — where there are eight more miles (13 km) of branch trails — and ends at the entrance to the Salt Pond Visitor Center at the Cape Cod National Seashore (where yet more trails await; see below). Access points are: off Route 134 in South Dennis, at Nickerson State Park, on Great Western Road in Harwich, and along Main Street and Rock Harbor in Orleans.

You can rent a bike by the hour or by the day at **Idle Times Bike Shop** ☎ (508) 255-8281, Route 6, North Eastham.

Water Sports

The Cape's vast stretches of briny waterways are a paddler's playground. **Cape Cod Coastal Canoe and Kayak** ☎ (508) 564-4051, offers daily guided tours (weather permitting). You can also contact the **Cape Cod Museum of Natural History** ☎ (508) 896-3867 TOLL-FREE IN EASTERN MASSACHUSETTS (800) 479-3867 FAX (508) 896-8844 E-MAIL info@ccmnh.org WEB SITE www.ccmnh.org, PO Box 1710 Route 6A, Brewster 02631-0016, for information. Museum tours operate May through September; rates are $50 per adult and $35 for ages 7-12; reservations must be made 24 hours in advance.

TOURS AND EXCURSIONS

Ferries for **Nantucket** leave year-round from Hyannis and in summer from Harwich Port. Ferries to **Martha's Vineyard** run in-season from Hyannis. The trip to either island takes about two hours. See HOW TO GET THERE, page 180 in MARTHA'S VINEYARD.

While Provincetown has several whale-watching fleets, the Mid Cape area has only one — however, all boats go to the same spot: Stellwagen Bank. You have a longer boat ride to enjoy if you choose to depart from Barnstable Harbor with **Hyannis Whale Watcher** ((508) 362-6088 TOLL-FREE IN EASTERN MASSACHUSETTS (800) 287-0374, PO Box 254, Barnstable Harbor, Barnstable 02630. On the trip out you'll have views of Sandy Neck and its mansions. The onboard naturalist will explain the impressive habits of the whales.

You can try to spy on the Kennedy Compound from a 1930s coastal schooner with ***Patience* and *Prudence* Harbor Cruises** ((508) 778-2600 from Hyannis Harbor. The **Duckmobile** TOLL-FREE (888) 225-3825 is an amphibious vehicle that takes passengers around the Hyannis area by land and sea. Theme cruises are the specialty of **Hyannis Harbor Cruises** ((508) 778-2600; trips depart from the Ocean Street Docks, Hyannis. You can climb aboard the *Hesperus* for a two-hour cruise on this 1937 wood sloop. ***Hesperus* Sailing Cruises** ((508) 790-0077 depart from the Ocean Street Docks, Hyannis. **Seafari** ((508) 896-2480 takes passengers on a search for indigenous marine life aboard the *Tiger Shark*. Trips depart from the Ocean Street Docks.

In Dennis, ***Freya* Excursions** ((508) 385-4399 offers schooner cruises from Sesuit Harbor, East Dennis, while the **Water Safari** ((508) 362-5555 is a narrated tidal cruise along the Bass River aboard the *Starfish*.

A classic Cape Cod view — dunes, beach grass and wide open sea.

NIGHTLIFE AND THE ARTS

Hyannis is the Cape's nightlife hub. The **Cape Cod Symphony Orchestra** ((508) 362-1111, under the direction of Royston Nash, offers a five-concert season with guest soloists. They perform at the 1,500-seat auditorium at Barnstable High School. The **Cape Playhouse** ((508) 385-3911, in Dennis, is the top summer stock venue for Broadway shows with big-name performers. For pop music concerts (Tony Bennett, Tom Jones,

Diana Ross have all performed here) and stand-up comedy (Joan Rivers, Don Rickles), there is the **Cape Cod Melody Tent** ((508) 775-9100, 21 West Main Street, Hyannis. Performances are held late June through early September in the 2,300-seat theater-in-the-round under the big top. Also look for the children's theater every Wednesday.

Hyannis has a fair number of clubs offering dining, dancing and music well into the midnight hours. You can groove on acoustic music at **Starbucks** ((508) 778-6767, at 668 Route 132; country-and-western at **Bud's Country Lounge** ((508) 771-2505, at 3 Bearse's Way (at Route 132); and blues on Friday and Saturday at **Harry's** ((508) 778-4188, 700 Main Street. You might spot Tony Bennett in the audience at the **Roadhouse Café** ((508) 775-2386, at 488 South Street, Hyannis, which serves up nightly eclectic music, including jazz. For more jazz options, phone the 24-hour hotline of the **Cape Cod Jazz Society** ((508) 394-5277.

WHERE TO STAY

A good choice for families is the **Simmons Homestead Inn** ((508) 778-4999 TOLL-FREE (800) 637-1649 FAX (508) 790-1342 E-MAIL simmonshomestead@aol.com, 288 Scudder Avenue, Hyannis Port 02647. Not only do they welcome children, but they also accept dogs. There are no televisions; but lots of other activities are catered for: bicycles are available and there are fishing poles to take down to the pond behind the property. The 1820s farmhouse inn has 12 guestrooms, including a two-bedroom suite built over the barn (mid-range to expensive).

Harbor Village ((508) 775-7581, 160 Marston Avenue, Hyannis Port 02601, a neat 17-acre (seven-hectare) cottage colony, is a calm retreat from the Hyannis honky-tonk. There are 15 one- to four-bedroom cottages, all with water view. Open April through October (expensive).

I've enjoyed staying at the **Acworth Inn** ((508) 362-3330 TOLL-FREE (800) 362-6363, 4352 Old King's Highway, PO Box 256, Cummaquid 02637. Built in 1860, the house is situated along the Old King's Highway (Route 6A), in the tiny village of Cummaquid. The renovated nineteenth-century Cape house has six sunny rooms, and one luxury suite with double Jacuzzi and a gas fireplace. Innkeepers Jack and Cheryl Ferrel are brimming with ideas for things to do in the area. You can start your day with a walk that begins behind the inn and leads past salt marsh and ponds, with views of Sandy Neck and Cape Cod Bay. Cheryl bakes delicious pastries for breakfast (mid-range).

Over in Yarmouth there's another good bed-and-breakfast inn, the **Captain Farris House** ((508) 760-2818 TOLL-FREE (800) 350-9477, 308 Old Main Street, Yarmouth 02664, is on the National Historic Register, and offers eight rooms, Jacuzzis, fireplaces, and a lavish breakfast (mid-range).

For budget lodging try **Craigville Motel** ((508) 362-3401 TOLL-FREE (800) 338-5610, 8 Shoot Flying Hill Road, Centerville 02632, with 40 rooms, outdoor pool, air conditioning and cable television, or, with similar features, **Cape Haven Motel** ((508) 398-5080, 75 Lower County Road, Dennisport 02639, with nine rooms including apartments.

WHERE TO EAT

Set in a grand old Georgian mansion, the **Regatta of Cotuit at the Crocker House** ((508) 428-5715, 4631 Falmouth Road (Route 28), Cotuit, specializes in seafood preparations such as starters of crispy lobster potstickers with ginger lime glaze, and main courses including pistachio-encrusted pan-seared Atlantic salmon, roasted Long Island duckling, and buffalo tenderloin with a Madeira wine sauce (expensive).

Stylish **Abbicci** ((508) 362-3501, 43 Main Street (Route 6A), between Railroad Avenue and Willow Street in Yarmouth Port, serves good Northern Italian fare. It's pricey, but if you go before 6 PM you can choose from the early menu, which is much better value (mid-range to expensive).

The **Paddock** ((508) 775-7677, West Main Street Rotary, 20 Scudder Avenue, Hyannis, is a casual spot for continental fare, near the Cape Cod Melody Tent (expensive). Local seafood stars in the Cajun cuisine at **Harry's** (see NIGHTLIFE AND THE ARTS, above). The **Cape Sea Grille** ((508) 432-4745, 31 Sea Street (Route 28), in Harwich Port, has excellent seafood, if somewhat pricey (expensive).

Best known for its fine Italian cuisine, the **Roadhouse Café** ☎ (508) 775-2386, 488 South Street, Hyannis, also serves a mean lobster bisque (mid-range to expensive).

You must try the seafood sausage at the **Millway Fish & Lobster Market** ☎ (508) 362-2760, in the marina at Barnstable Harbor. From the takeout window choose from Chef Ralph's delightful fish and chips, clam chowder, clam rolls, clam platter, and lobster-in-the-rough (steamed, with corn on the cob). The proprietor is a graduate of the Hyde Park Culinary Institute (budget).

A visit to the Cape has to include a few trips to the local clam shack: **Captain Frosty's Fish & Chips** ☎ (508) 385-8548, 219 Route 6A, Dennis, serves Chatham cod, gulf shrimp, clam fritters and grilled chicken; while the **Marathon Restaurant** ☎ (508) 394-3379, 231 Route 28, West Dennis, with a similar menu, is noted for its generous portions.

LOWER AND OUTER CAPE

Referring to the part of the peninsula from its southeastern "elbow" to its outer limits at Provincetown, the Lower and Outer Cape encompasses the marvelous shores, dunes and marshland of the Cape Cod National Seashore, as well as Nickerson State Park in Brewster.

GENERAL INFORMATION

At your service are the chambers of commerce in each of the Lower Cape towns, including: **Brewster Chamber of Commerce** ☎ (508) 896-3500 FAX (508) 896-4443; **Chatham Chamber of Commerce** ☎ (508) 945-5199 TOLL-FREE (800) 715-5567 FAX (508) 430-7919; **Eastham Chamber of Commerce** ☎ (508) 240-7211 FAX (508) 240-0345 E-MAIL info@easthamchamber.com.

You can visit the Chatham Chamber of Commerce at their new **Visitor Information Center**, the David T. Bassett House, South Chatham, at the intersection of Routes 28 and 137. The **Eastham Information Booth** is located approximately one and a half miles (just under two and a half kilometers) past the Orleans rotary on Route 6 eastbound, on your right-hand side. It's open seasonally.

WHAT TO SEE AND DO

Brewster

Named for a passenger on the *Mayflower*, Brewster was settled in 1659 and separated from Harwich in 1803. Among Brewster's early industries were packet boat services and milling. A survivor of those days, the **Stony Brook Grist Mill and Museum** ☎ (508) 896-6745, 830 Stony Brook Road, is an active 1873 corn mill where demonstrations take place.

Like the Fisheries Aquarium in Woods Hole the **Cape Cod Museum of Natural History** ☎ (508) 896-3867 TOLL-FREE IN EASTERN MASSACHUSETTS (800) 479-3867 FAX (508) 896-8844 WEB SITE www.ccmnh.org, Route 6A, is a wonderful museum for children and adults — more state-of-the-heart than state-of-the-art. You don't have to worry about kids breaking anything here — everything is made to be touched, explored and used. In the Marsh Room you can observe a beehive at work, watch for life at the bird feeders, or use the binoculars for signs of blue-capped chickadees or Carolina wrens, or the scarlet flash of cardinals. For the youngest kids, there's a "duckling nest" to clamber into. A few live animals are on display, the most impressive of which is the American bullfrog. Behind the museum is a network of trails to outlying tidal marshes and woodlands (see SPORTS AND OUTDOOR ACTIVITIES, below). From October to April, admission is free the first Monday of the month.

Roland Nickerson was a multimillionaire who founded the First National Bank of Chicago. His estate once sat upon a 2,000-acre (800-hectare) forest of hemlock, spruce and pine. Nickerson's wife, Addie, donated the land to the state in 1934 in honor of their son, a victim of the 1918 flu epidemic. **Roland C. Nickerson State Park** ☎ (508) 896-3491, Route 6A, Brewster, is one of Massachusetts' largest state parks. Its topography isn't typical of the Cape — no salt marshes, no dunes. Instead, you'll find eight kettle ponds, Ice Age remnants formed by the glaciers that once covered the land. You can spot many rare species of plants and wildflowers growing on the edges of the freshwater kettle ponds. The choice of activities here is legion:

motorboating or swimming in the beach-edge Cliff Pond, birding, biking or fishing. Nickerson Park is open year-round; winter visitors can ice skate, ice fish or cross-country ski through the woods.

Chatham

The Cape's outermost town, Chatham has been called "The First Stop of the East Wind." There's a radar weather station here, maintained by the United States Weather Service, and if you watch cable television's Weather Channel you might see Chatham Light behind the reporters. In the late 1980s a severe storm broke through a barrier beach here and claimed much shoreline and several waterfront houses. You can see the break on Shore Road across from Chatham Light.

A charming seaside town, Chatham's **Main Street** is jammed with boutiques and craft shops. Look for the signs for the **Chatham Loop**, a five-mile (eight-kilometer) ring that takes in the town sights: Fish Pier, the Chatham Light, the boatyards and the harbor. Access is at Fish Pier or any town parking lot. **Fish Pier**, off Shore Road, is home to the large fishing fleets that unload their catches in the late afternoon.

Not far from the end of Main Street, the **Chatham Light** offers panoramic views of the bay. Just off the coast is **Monomoy Island National Wildlife Refuge**, a 10-mile-long (16-km) sand spit protected as a wildlife refuge, with more than 250 species of birds. Access is by short boat trip from Chatham, and local boat charters are available. See TOURS AND EXCURSIONS, below.

Eastham

The National Seashore's Salt Pond Visitor's Center in Eastham (see below) is often the first stop for visitors to the Cape. Besides its nature programs, the National Park Service runs tours through the **Penniman House**, a partially restored whaling captain's house built in 1868, and the **Three Sisters Lighthouses**, a set of three small wooden lighthouses which functioned as a trio when they were active.

Like the neighboring Highland Light, **Nauset Light** was recently moved back from its eroding bluff. The Nauset Light Preservation Society ☎ (508) 240-2612 offers free tours of the lighthouse, on Sundays from 4:30 PM to 7:30 PM, late June to early September.

Truro and Wellfleet

After 67 days at sea, the Pilgrims were thirsty and famished. It was at Truro that they found their first fresh water. They also found 10 bushels of corn belonging to the Pamet Indians, which they promptly stole.

The **Highland Light** ☎ (508) 487-1121, Lighthouse Road, North Truro, built in 1797, was Cape Cod's first lighthouse (refer to STAY THE NIGHT AT A LIGHT, page 24 in TOP SPOTS). There is a 10-minute presentation on the lighthouse history. Children must be 51 inches (1.3 m) tall; admission is charged; open May to October.

One of the Cape's prettiest towns, Wellfleet was once a great whaling port. It is still home port for a large fishing fleet, and in true seafaring spirit, the downtown church tolls "ship's bells." Also known for its oysters, the town was named after the Wallfleet Oyster Bed in Blackwater Bay, England.

In 1903, Guglielmo Marconi sent the first transatlantic telegraph from the Wellfleet dunes — a message from then President Roosevelt to King Edward VII of England.

Cape Cod National Seashore

Established in 1961, this 43,500-acre (17,400-hectare) stretch of shoreline is a refuge of wind-sculpted dunes, superb ocean beaches, spectacular cliffs and salt pond marshes, as well as pitch pine and scrub-oak forests hugging the seashore from Orleans to Provincetown.

If you're a first-time visitor, start at the **Salt Pond Visitor Center** ☎ (508) 255-3421 or (508) 349-3785, in Eastham. It is open daily 9 AM to 5 PM year-round and can provide literature on the Seashore, schedules for guided nature walks and pamphlets about biking and hiking trails.

The Seashore is a stopover for **hundreds of bird species** making their way up and down the Atlantic flyway. Around wetlands, look especially for snowy egrets, merganser, and bufflehead and common goldeneye. In uplands you may spot red-tailed hawk, towhee, pheasant, and pine and yellow-rumped warblers.

SPORTS AND OUTDOOR ACTIVITIES

Beaches

In Brewster, there is soft sand at **Breakwater Beach**, at the end of Breakwater Road. The waters are calm on this bay-side beach. Harwich has the **Red River Beach**, the only beach in town that allows non-permit parking. In Chatham, **Cockle Cove** is a good choice for families while **Hardings Beach** has challenging surf. In Orleans, **Shaket** is a calm-water bay-side beach where you can walk out into the bay for more than a mile (one and a half kilometers) at low tide. **Rock Harbor's** shallow waters are perfect for wading.

Eastham has **Coast Guard Beach**, a fine National Seashore swimming area, its rough waves making it a sought-after surfing spot. **First Encounter** is a good family beach with shallow waters. The beach at **Nauset Light** is one of the Cape's scenic jewels. Great surf; free parking.

In Wellfleet, **Cahoon Hollow** has sandy shallows where children can play. **Marconi**, another National Seashore beach, has outdoor showers. **White Crest** is a good surfing beach; the only access is over a steep dune. **Indian Neck** is where the windsurfers go.

Truro's family beach is **Ballston**, while shellers favor **Corn Hill**.

Walking and Nature Trails

An easy walk that will introduce you to the Cape's wetland scenery is the 1.3-mile (two-kilometer) **Wing Island Trail** that starts behind the Cape Cod Museum of Natural History (see above). A boardwalk leads over a wide salt marsh, a tiny bridge (almost a stile) leaps a tiny creek, then it's into the beech groves on a fine sandy path and down to the dunes and tidal flats at Bay Beach, where pools of water ripple. From here you can wander the flats gazing into tidal pools and at the horizon spreading out toward the Lower Cape and Provincetown.

In Wellfleet, the Cape Cod National Seashore's seven-mile-long (11-km) **Great Island Trail** is one of the peninsula's more challenging treks, leading hikers through shifting sand and scrub forests.

Bicycling

The **Nauset Bike Trail/Cape Cod National Seashore Bike Path** is a 3.2-mile (five-kilometer) round-trip route that begins in Eastham at the Salt Pond Visitor Center. There is also access to trails in the **Cape Cod National Seashore** at Rock Harbor in Orleans. In North Truro, a four-mile (6.4-km) trail along **High Head Road** passes through dune country to Head of the Meadow Beach. There are **rentals and service** at Bikes and Blades ☎ (508) 945-7600, 195 Crowell Street, Chatham. For competetive prices it's also worth trying **Idle Times Bike Shop** ☎ (508) 255-8211, 4550 State Highway, North Eastham, and the **Little Capistrano Bike Shop** ☎ (508) 255-6515, Salt Pond Road, Eastham, across from the Visitors Center.

TOURS AND EXCURSIONS

The Cape Cod Museum of Natural History ☎ (508) 896-3867 TOLL-FREE IN EASTERN MASSACHUSETTS (800) 479-3867 FAX (508) 896-8844 WEB SITE www.ccmnh.org sponsors **Nauset Marsh Natural History Excursions**. Tours depart from Orleans. The **Massachusetts Bay Audubon Society** ☎ (508) 349-2615, 291 State

Commercial fishing is much diminished on the Cape, but harvesting of certain species continues.

Highway, Route 6, South Wellfleet, offers year-round events such as canoe trips, marine-life cruises and natural history tours. Its **Wellfleet Bay Wildlife Sanctuary** TOLL-FREE (800) 349-2632 sponsors day trips year-round to Monomoy Island, marine-life cruises aboard the *Navigator*, and seal-watch cruises out of Chatham.

NIGHTLIFE AND THE ARTS

An award-winning children's theater, **Harwich Junior Theater** ((508) 432-2002, offers a May-to-December season; many performances are sign-language interpreted. Call for locations. The **Monomoy Theater** ((508) 945-1589, 776 Main Street, Chatham 02659, is the summer stock arena for Ohio State University's theater program. The season runs from mid-June to the end of August. Also in Chatham, the **Chatham Drama Guild** ((508) 945-0510, 134 Crowell Road, presents a major musical each summer in its cedar-shingle 125-seat theater. The **Academy Playhouse of Performing Arts** ((508) 255-1963, at 102 Main Street, Orleans, produces 12 or so shows a year with both local and professional talent, while the **Cape Rep Theater** ((508) 896-1888, Northside Route 6A, East Brewster, presents musicals, American classics and children's theater on two stages, one of them a delightful outdoor theater. At the Town Pier in Wellfleet Harbor, **Wellfleet Harbor Actors Theater** ((508) 349-6835, presents a summer season of new cutting-edge American plays along with world classics. Look for a two-story building that resembles a 1950s-era motel with a sign on the roof that says "W.H.A.T."

First Encounter Coffeehouse ((508) 255-5438, 220 Samoset Road, Eastham, brings in folk and ethnic musical acts from around the region. The **Wellfleet Beachcomber** ((508) 349-6055, 1200 Cahoon Hollow Road, Wellfleet, on Cahoon Hollow Beach, has music and dancing every night of the week from Memorial Day to Labor Day.

WHERE TO STAY

The **Whalewalk Inn** ((508) 255-0617 FAX (508) 240-0017 E-MAIL whalewak@capecod.net, 220 Bridge Road Eastham 02642 (mid-range), is an 1830 Federal-style sea captain's house with 16 rooms — some with fireplace and Jacuzzi-for-two — located in five buildings surrounding gardens and meadows. The rate includes breakfast, afternoon refreshments and evening hors d'œuvres.

A former stagecoach stop, the **Chatham Wayside Inn** ((508) 945-5550 TOLL-FREE (800) 391-5734 FAX (508) 945-3407, PO Box 685, 512 Main Street, Chatham 02633 (mid-range), is now a thoroughly modern place, richly furnished with polished reproductions. The best rooms have balconies overlooking the town bandstand, but all are a treat. The restaurant has both outside and inside tables where New American cuisine is served.

A less expensive option, and an excellent choice for families, is **Cape Cod Claddagh Inn & Tavern** ((508) 432-9628 TOLL-FREE (800) 356-9628 FAX 508-432-6039 E-MAIL info@capecodecladdaghinn.com, 77 Main Street, West Harwich 02671-0667. This 1880 Victorian has an Irish pub-restaurant with poolside dining. It's open April 1 to mid-January; eight rooms (budget to mid-range) with breakfast. Children are welcome and those under 12 stay free. Pets may be permitted in certain cases.

Cyclers and backpackers can stop over in Eastham at **Hostelling International — Mid Cape** ((508) 255-2785 (in season) or (617) 735-1800 (off-season reservations) FAX (508) 240-5598 E-MAIL eastham@cape.com, 75 Goody Hallet Drive, Eastham 02642, located near the Rail Trail. With a kitchen, cabins, and outdoor shower, it's open May 8 to September 13. For off-season reservations, write ENEC Reservations, 1020 Commonwealth Avenue, Boston, MA 02215. Twenty miles (32 km) north is the wonderful **Hostelling International — Truro** ((508) 349-3889 (in season), on North Pamet Road, PO Box 402, Truro 02666, in a former Coast Guard station within the National Seashore, and a five-minute walk from the beach. It is open from June 19 to September 8. Reservations are essential.

WHERE TO EAT

Aesop's Tables ((508) 349-6450, 316 Main Street, in Wellfleet, serves New American cuisine in a delightful old manor next to

Wellfleet's Town Hall. Evenings in the dining room are romantic, and sunny outdoor luncheons are blissful (expensive).

Flawlessly prepared and exquisitely presented New French cuisine keeps diners breathless throughout the three-hour, set-priced seatings at **Chillingsworth** ☎ (508) 896-3640 TOLL-FREE (800) 430-3640, 2449 Main Street (Route 6A), Brewster. Many people consider it the best on the Cape. Prices are high for the main dining room (expensive); the **Greenhouse** bistro presents a casual and less-pricey option (mid-range).

Set in a 1738 farmhouse, **High Brewster** ☎ (508) 896-3636, at the High Brewster Inn, 964 Satucket Road (at Stony Brook Road), Brewster, serves delicious New England cuisine (expensive). From the outside, the **Brewster Fish House** ☎ (508) 896-7867, 2208 Main Street, doesn't look promising, but the food is good, especially the fried oysters, fried artichokes, mixed grill and barbecued squid (mid-range). The runner-up in the seafood class is the **Impudent Oyster** ☎ (508) 945-3545, 15 Chatham Bars Avenue (just off Main Street), Chatham, which serves commendable fish dishes in international styles (mid-range).

Locals favor jovial **Land Ho!** ☎ (508) 255-5165, 38 Main Street at Route 6A, Orleans, where license plates and local business signs hang from the rafters (mid-range to budget).

The **Bay-side Lobster Hutt** ☎ (508) 349-6333, at the foot of Commercial Street, Wellfleet, serves lobster-in-the-rough at picnic tables (mid-range). At **Arnold's Lobster and Clam Bar** ☎ (508) 255-2575, 3580 State Highway, Eastham, you can dine alfresco.

Adrian's ☎ (508) 487-4360, at the Outer Reach Motel, 535 Route 6, in North Truro, has an somewhat uneven reputation for its Italian fare and service, but the sunset views always get rave reviews and brunch is reliably good (expensive).

On the way out to Nauset Beach, there is the long-standing **Kadee's Lobster & Clam Bar** ☎ (508) 255-6184, 212 Main Street, East Orleans, which has been serving up the daily catch since 1975 (budget).

PROVINCETOWN

"P-Town" looks out on the Cape's most spectacular scenery. A sandy spit of land, it is the culminating point both geographically and, perhaps, mentally of all that is Cape Cod. While Provincetown is situated at the outermost reaches of the Cape, it is also, ironically, the most easily accessible from the mainland. Throughout the summer, boatloads of day-trippers from Boston mob the aptly named Commercial Street. The year-round population of 4,000 burgeons to 80,000 in summer.

While the town has a gaudy tourist-trap aspect to it, it remains more humane and less irritating than most American tourist spots, as it still has a distinctive personality. P-Town, one suspects, will always somehow be P-Town, with its *joie de vivre* firmly in tact. Gay life is a given in P-Town, with drag queens and other revelers parading the streets by night.

Rain or shine there's always something to do in Provincetown: shopping, galleries, good food, nightlife, whale watching and trails. And then there is the sea, which no amount of commercialism can overwhelm. Thankfully, the beaches are free of the trappings of tourism, as they are within National Seashore land. I've sat on Race Point Beach

Provincetown's Pilgrim Monument commemorates the early settlers' first landfall.

and watched humpback whales diving out in the gray waves.

As early as the 1500s, Portuguese fishermen camped on the beaches at the northernmost point of the Cape. They came for the bountiful codfish for which the Cape is named. A former fishing town and once the third-largest whaling port in the world, Provincetown still has a significant Portuguese population. But, as are fishing ports all along the Atlantic, the industry is much reduced because of depleted fishing stocks. The Cape's cod are all but extinct. Yet, the background remains in many ways. You'll find some good Portuguese restaurants and will no doubt run into some salty old fisherman in his new life as a parking lot attendant. The town's fishing village legacy continues, albeit in a rather laid-back fashion, with boats arriving during late afternoon at MacMillan Wharf to unload their catches.

In the early 1900s, Charles Hawthorne's Cape Cod School of Art drew artists and writers to this isolated outpost on the Atlantic Ocean. P-Town also figured in the early days of modern American theater, with resident playwright Eugene O'Neill and the Provincetown Players.

GENERAL INFORMATION

The **Provincetown Chamber of Commerce** ☎ (508) 487-3424 FAX (508) 487-8966 E-MAIL info@ptownchamber.com, PO Box 1017, Provincetown 02657, is a useful organization. Visit them at 307 Commercial Street (at MacMillan Wharf).

WHAT TO SEE AND DO

In 1620 the Pilgrims arrived and spent five weeks looking for a suitable site to settle before moving on to Plymouth. Commemorating that landing is the **Pilgrim Monument** ☎ (508) 487-1310, 1 Highpole Road, a 252-ft-tall (77-m) Italianate bell tower; the view from the tower's observation deck takes in all of the Cape as well as the Massachusetts coast at Plymouth. **Provincetown Museum** is located here with exhibits on the Pilgrims, the Lower Cape's maritime history, and the early days of the town's artist colonies. Open daily through November.

At Race Point Beach you can tour the **Old Harbor Lifesaving Museum** ☎ (508) 487-1256, an original 1862 station of the United States Lifesaving Service. Fascinating exhibits feature original lifesaving equipment and videos with rare footage showing lifesaving techniques.

Established in 1914 during the early years of Provincetown's art colony, the **Provincetown Art Association and Museum** ☎ (508) 487-1750, 460 Commercial Street, has along with its collection of 1,700 permanent artworks, four galleries with changing exhibits by Outer Cape artists. An admission fee is charged.

Provincetown streets are lined with **shops** selling everything from snow globe souvenirs to top-of-the-line sporting equipment to fine art. Be sure to take a peek in **Marine Specialties** ☎ (508) 487-1730, 235 Commercial Street. Housed in a former stable, the store is crammed floor to ceiling with oddities. The front of the shop is where you'll find inexpensive souvenirs from run-of-the-mill to freaky and fabulous. Delve deeper and you'll find a large stock of military surplus from around the world — including quite a lot of fascinating USSR military castoffs. Finally, in the rear of the store there's a well-organized camping and fishing supply area. The store is open daily in season, and weekends only from Christmas through mid-March.

SPORTS AND OUTDOOR ACTIVITIES

Beaches

Herring Cove and **Race Point** are Provincetown's two excellent beaches. Both provide spectacular setting for swimming and sun bathing. Herring Cove has calmer waters, warmer waves and is the better swimming beach. It's a well-known gathering spot for "naturists," drawing a largely gay, lesbian and bisexual crowd. The national seashore beaches have a prohibition against nudity, so if you see a park ranger, you should cover up to avoid a potential ticket. At Race Point you can walk out to the dune shacks or sit and watch humpback whales offshore.

Walking, Nature Trails and Bicycling

Known internationally for its research on whales in the area, the **Center for Coastal**

Studies ✆ (508) 487-3622, 59 Commercial Street, a nonprofit organization for environmental research and education, offers field walks, lectures and educational programs year-round.

The one-mile (1.6-km) **Beech Forest Trail** starts at Race Point Road, off Route 6A; while the **Breakwater Trail**, a wide footpath (no bikes allowed), leads to secluded Long Point Beach and views of two lighthouses. Access is from the western end of Commercial Street and Bradford Street Extension. The **Provincelands Trail System** comprises seven miles (11-km) of riding and walking paths with various spurs leading to salt marshes, sand dunes, Herring Cove and Race Point beaches and picnic areas.

Rent bikes and gear by the hour, the day, or the week from **Arnold's** ✆ (508) 487-0844, 329 Commercial Street, Provincetown; **Nelson's Bike Rentals** ✆ (508) 487-8849, 43 Race Point Road, Provincetown; or **P-Town Bikes** ✆ (508) 487-8735, 42 Bradford Street (next to the Community Center). Or reserve online at www.ptownbikes.com.

TOURS AND EXCURSIONS

While many whale-watching outfits compete for your attention in Provincetown, the **Dolphin Fleet** ✆ (508) 349-1900 TOLL-FREE (800) 826-9300, MacMillan Wharf, Provincetown, is the cream of the crop. They have a researcher on board from the Center for Coastal Studies, and a reputation for informed commentary (see WATCH WHALES AT STELLWAGEN BANK, page 25 in TOP SPOTS). Six trips daily starting at 8:30 AM depart from MacMillan Wharf, Provincetown; offered April to October. The trip lasts three to four hours. The ***Portuguese Princess*** ✆ (508) 487-2651 TOLL-FREE (800) 442-3188, at the head of MacMillan Wharf, Provincetown, is a 100-ft (30-m) ship offering three-and-a-half-hour narrated excursions with food and folk music on board. The boat departs from Town Wharf, off Commercial Street at Standish Street. Avoid outfits that claim to have "faster" boats, as they have a reputation for disturbing the whales.

The best way to experience the dunes is to walk out to them (see SPORTS AND OUTDOOR ACTIVITIES, below), but if that's not feasible there is **Art's Dune Tours** ✆ (508) 487-1950 or 487-1050, Commercial and Standish Street, the only outfit authorized on the government-protected dune lands. Contrary to what their advertising brochure states, this

Boat tours, offering a variety of entertainment, vie for your vacation dollars in Provincetown.

is not a "beach buggy" tour but a trip in an enclosed four-wheel-drive station wagon that takes six passengers at a time. The 90-minute tour is a chance to learn about the delicate ecology of the dunes as well as their human history. Artists inhabited and still inhabit the rustic shacks that dot the rippling landscape. Art Costa and, now, his sons have been running these tours for more over 50 years. Trips depart from the corner of Commercial and Standish streets daily from mid-April through October. Reservations are required.

NIGHTLIFE AND THE ARTS

In 1916, the Provincetown Players launched the careers of playwrights Eugene O'Neill, Tennessee Williams and Sinclair Lewis. Continuing that tradition, the **Provincetown Rep Theater** ☎ (508) 487-0600 debuted as a professional theater company in 1995, staging contemporary and classic plays from July to September. Call for location.

P-Town's extravagant club scene starts with one of the nation's leading gay clubs, **The Atlantic House** ☎ (508) 487-3871, 6 Masonic Place (off Commercial Street). Open year-round, it welcomes everyone, gay or straight, except in the leather-oriented Macho Bar upstairs. There's dancing in the Big Room. The **Pied Bar** ☎ (508) 487-1527, 193A Commercial Street (in the town center), is the destination of gay revelers who parade in drag each evening, starting from the boat slip. **Vixen** ☎ (508) 487-6424, Pilgrim House, 336 Commercial Street, is situated in the town's oldest hotel, overhauled in 1995 for this chic new women's bar. There are jazz, blues and comedy acts on the roster.

A couple of good bars: The **Governor Bradford** ☎ (508) 487-9618, 312 Commercial Street (in the town center), features blues all summer, as well as the gender-bending rock band known as Space Pussy. The tiny **Sandbar** ☎ (508) 487-3286, at Sebastian's Waterfront Restaurants, 177 Commercial Street, is a one-of-a-kind place decorated with paint-by-number "chef-d'œuvres," and presided over by the effervescent Larry Wald.

WHERE TO STAY

The **Brass Key Guesthouse** ☎ (508) 487-9005 TOLL-FREE (800) 842-9858 FAX (508) 487-9020, 67 Bradford Street, Provincetown 02657, is probably the town's best bed-and-breakfast spot. The 33 guestrooms and cottages have been equipped with every amenity; some rooms have fireplaces. There are two heated pools on the grounds (expensive to luxury).

Here's something unique: dock yourself on an old fishing wharf. **Captain Jack's Wharf** ☎ (508) 487-1450, 73A Commercial Street, Provincetown 02657 (expensive), has 13 rustic cabins, each with individual character and idiosyncrasies (skylights, claw-foot tubs, sundecks, an enclosed Dutch bed, a spiral staircase). All are comfortable and equipped with linen; housekeeping is provided. During the high season apartments rent by the week, while off-season by the week or day. Pets are welcome in most of the cabins.

The centrally located **Revere Guest House** ☎ (508) 487-2292 TOLL-FREE (800) 487-2292 E-MAIL reveregh@tiac.net, 14 Court Street, Provincetown 02657, is an 1830 Federal-style building with a large common room with fireplace. The eight rooms come with private or shared bath (budget to mid-range); the rate includes a continental breakfast. Open May through October.

Shoestring travelers of all ages can stay in P-Town at the unbeatable price of $14 per night, per person at the **Outermost Hostel** ☎ (508) 487-4378, at 28 Winslow Street, Provincetown 02657. This privately owned hostel has 30 beds in five whitewashed cabins in the center of town on Monument Hill. There is a common living room and kitchen in one cabin and the yard has barbecue grills and picnic tables. The Outermost has no curfew and is open mid-May to mid-October.

WHERE TO EAT

A host of regulars admire the **Dancing Lobster** ☎ (508) 487-0900, 371 Commercial Street, for its excellent seafood — some claim it's the best in P-Town (expensive).

A P-Town institution, **Front Street** ☎ (508) 487-9715, 230 Commercial Street, specializes in Mediterranean fare in a romantic, grotto-like setting. It has an excellent wine list and knowledgeable waitstaff.

Located in a quieter section of town, **Sal's Place** ☎ (508) 487-1279, 99 Commercial Street, serves Southern Italian with outdoor candle-light dining on checkered tablecloths (expensive). While the food is average to good, the by-the-sea setting is unbeatable.

The Moors ☎ (508) 487-0840 TOLL-FREE (800) 843-0840, 5 Bradford Street Extension (mid-range), makes the best Portuguese food in town. Try the *porco em pau* (marinated cubes of pork). Lunch is served in July and August only. Breakfast is heavenly at **Café Edwige** ☎ (508) 487-2008, 333 Commercial Street. It's a sweet place for lunch, too, with good food, wild salads and a cozy, romantic setting; arrive before the lunch rush or you won't get in (expensive).

The funky **Spiritus Pizza** ☎ (508) 487-2808, 190 Commercial Street, has good slices with whole-wheat crust as well as aromatic coffee, espresso and pastries.

HOW TO GET THERE

By car from Boston, you take Interstate 93 south to Route 3; continue south to Route 6 and to Provincetown at the Cape's tip. It is 114 miles (184 km) from Boston to Provincetown, but allow at least three hours to get through the sometimes maddening high-season Cape traffic.

In summer, Provincetown is served by **ferry** from Boston on Bay State Cruises ☎ (617) 723-7800; and from Plymouth on Cape Cod Cruises ☎ (508) 747-2400 TOLL-FREE (800) 242-2469.

Modest white-clapboard beach cottages dot the bay shore at Provincetown.

MARTHA'S VINEYARD

"Island in Troubled Water" screamed a recent headline in the *Vineyard Gazette*, the 151-year-old newspaper that serves Martha's Vineyard, the bucolic island seven miles (11 km) off the Cape Cod coast. The article was written in response to a decision of the state legislature that would allow private developers to run wild over the island's South Beach.

Developers as bogeymen have always been a rallying point for the island's 14,700 year-round residents, who include celebrities such as newsmen Walter Cronkite and Mike Wallace, singers James Taylor and Carly Simon, and cartoonist Jules Feiffer. As a result of the concern expressed by such influential residents, the decision was reversed and the island's spectacular beauty and miles of beaches and woodlands remain comparatively unspoiled.

The explorer Gosnold named the triangular-shaped island in 1602, when he found wild grapes growing everywhere. The grapes are gone, but what remains is a fascinating landscape dotted with little fishing villages and summer resorts.

Architecture buffs have a field day on the Vineyard, where they can see handsome ship captains' houses in Edgartown and a community of several hundred Carpenter Gothic Victorian cottages in Oak Bluffs. The Vineyard is barely 20 miles (32 km) long and 10 miles (16 km) wide, so you can acquaint yourself with its rolling moors, colored cliffs, coves and salt marshes in short order on a day-trip from the Cape, or you can settle down for an extended stay in one of its fine inns. Explore the island by car (although traffic and expense make driving less attractive) or by bike (bring one along on the ferry or rent in Vineyard Haven). Sloops, schooners and dinghies, some available for day rental, beckon in the harbor.

GENERAL INFORMATION

Informational materials are available from the **Martha's Vineyard Chamber of Commerce** ☎ (508) 693-0085 FAX (508) 693-7589, PO Box 1698, Vineyard Haven 02568-1698.

WHAT TO SEE AND DO

Down-Island

The Down-Island towns of Martha's Vineyard are noted for their historical dwellings and excellent restaurants. ("Down-Island" and "Up-Island" are nautical terms referring to longitude.)

In **Edgartown**, the Martha's Vineyard Historical Society and Vineyard Museum ☎ (508) 627-4441, located on the corner of School and Cooke streets, gives history and architecture buffs a head start. The museum complex includes the **Thomas Cooke House**, with ship models, costumes and gear used by whalers and early farmers and the two-story Fresnel lens installed in the Gay Head lighthouse in 1856; and the **Captain Pease House**, with three galleries devoted to Island history. The museum also offers **guided walking tours** of Edgartown.

Another Edgartown historical organization, The Martha's Vineyard Preservation Trust ☎ (508) 627-4440 runs the **Vincent House Museum**. This is the oldest known house on the island, built in 1672. Inside you can get a glimpse of what life on the island 300 years ago.

Oak Bluffs, located between Vineyard Haven and Edgartown, harbors one of the most extraordinary chapters of Martha's Vineyard's history: the story of the annual Methodist revival meetings which took place in what is known as **The Campground**. First held in 1835 in a secluded oak grove in what is now Oak Bluffs, attendance at the meetings burgeoned. In 1868, some 12,000 participants attended the revival. For the first 25 years or so, communal tents provided shelter during the two-week-long emotionally and spiritually charged meeting. Eventually permanent cottages were built. You can see the result if you take a stroll (bikes are not allowed) through "**Cottage City**." More than 300 cottages, reflecting a fascinating, and almost amusing, hybrid Island architecture — part tent, part church, part dollhouse — radiate out from the centerpiece, the Tabernacle, known for its excellent acoustics. Visit the **Martha's Vineyard Camp Meeting Association Cottage Museum** ☎ (508) 693-0525, located within the Campground on the corner of Highland Avenue and Trinity Park, for informational materials.

Along with spiritual regeneration, Oak Bluffs was soon found to provide health and recreational benefits. By the late nineteenth century, a thriving resort community favored by the less well-to-do had formed. The **Flying Carousel**, built during this era, still spins 'round and 'round, and you can admire the homes that were built along Ocean Drive during the resort's heyday. Circuit Avenue remains an animated commercial district with restaurants, shops and movie theaters.

A day at the beach.

A fire in 1883 destroyed the town center, so **Vineyard Haven** does not have the same historical stamp as its fellow Down-Island towns. However, nearby **Williams Street** escaped the blaze, and here you can stroll by an impressive display of Greek Revival houses built during the port's prosperous seafaring times. Along the way, take note of the **Captain Richard G. Luce House**, one of the earliest examples of these dwellings, and the **Seamen's Bethel Museum**, which houses artifacts contributed by seamen who took shelter at the Bethel.

To round out your tour of Vineyard Haven, explore the **West and East Chops** (on two wheels if you like), which flank both sides of the Vineyard Haven harbor. West Chop was first settled as a summer community in the late nineteenth century, and has since become a hidey-hole for actors, writers, television personalities and the like. Your tour will take you past one of the five lighthouses on the Island: the **West Chop Lighthouse**, the Island's last manned beacon. A tour through East Chop culminates in a visit to the **East Chop Lighthouse** where you'll have a wonderful view of Cape Cod. This light was once referred to as the Chocolate Lighthouse because of its cast-iron structure, now painted white.

Up-Island

Three rural towns comprise the area of Martha's Vineyard known as "Up-Island": West Tisbury, Chilmark and Aquinnah (or Gay Head). The small villages that comprise Gay Head are mostly peopled by Wampanoags, descendants of the island's original inhabitants. Chilmark offers excellent views of Vineyard Sound, however, the westernmost tip of the island is the most spectacular. The variegated **Gay Head cliffs** rise 150 ft (45 m) above the Atlantic. Ripples the color of azure, rust and ivory run through the clay, whose strata contain fossils of million-year-old animals. Because of erosion problems, you can no longer walk down the face of the cliffs to the beach below, but a winding path gets you there eventually.

SPORTS AND OUTDOOR ACTIVITIES

Beaches

Oak Bluffs Eastville Beach has calm waters, while the two-mile-long (three-kilometer) **Sylvia Beach** has turbulent surf. The **Oak Bluffs Town Beach** is a short walk from town, near the Steamship Authority Dock.

In Edgartown, **East Beach** is part of the **Cape Pogue Wildlife Refuge**, and **Katama Beach** is a three-mile-long (five-kilometer) strip on the south shore. A pond protects one side of the beach, while the other side has lively surf.

Trails

For island birding, visit **Felix Neck Wildlife Sanctuary** ✆ (508) 627-4850, Edgartown-Vineyard Haven Road, Edgartown, or the **Cape Pogue Wildlife Refuge** ✆ (508) 693-7662, Chappaquiddick.

Martha's Vineyard State Forest, in the center of the island, has hiking paths through dense stands of pines. And the **Manuel F. Correllus State Forest** ✆ (508) 693-2540, Edgartown-West Tisbury Road, has 4,400 acres (1,760 hectares) of hiking trails, bike paths, and an exercise trail. Bicyclers can also take to several dedicated paths, including **Oak Bluffs to Edgartown**, a 12-mile (19.2-km) round-trip path that skirts the waterfront, affording views of Sengekontacket Pond, Joseph Sylvia Beach and Edgartown Beach (follow Beach Road from either town). **Edgartown to West Tisbury** is a 17.2-mile (27.5-km) round-trip passing the State Forest (see above) and connecting with off-road trails.

WHERE TO STAY

Thorncroft Inn ✆ (508) 693-3333 TOLL-FREE (800) 332-1236 FAX (508) 693-5419 WEB SITE thorncroft.com, PO Box 1022, 460 Main Street, Vineyard Haven 02568, is among the island's premier inns, offering 14 guestrooms in a 1918 bungalow and carriage house on three-and-a-half acres (one-and-a-half hectares). Several of the rooms have wood-burning fireplaces, some have two-person Jacuzzis, and two have 300-gallon (1,350-liter) hot tubs. The inn serves breakfast and afternoon tea (expensive to luxury).

As did many Edgartown hostelries, the **Charlotte Inn** ✆ (508) 627-4151, 27 South Summer Street, Edgartown 02539, began life as a sea captain's house, built in 1860. One of the best inns on the island, each of its 25 rooms has a unique character. The inn's L'Étoile Restaurant serves excellent French cuisine (see WHERE TO EAT, below). The inn does not accept children under the age of 14 and is open year-round (luxury).

Dockside Inn ✆ (508) 693-2966 TOLL-FREE (800) 245-5979, PO Box 1206, Circuit Avenue Extension, Oak Bluffs 02557, is painted a combination of ivory, pink and pastel blue, with matching chairs lining its generous front porch. The inn's 22 rooms have air conditioning, private baths and cable television; most rooms have queen-sized beds. There are also three efficiency suites, as well as two larger suites with kitchens. The Dockside, convenient to all the Oak Bluffs activities, is open from April to end of October (mid-range).

At the hospitable **Hobknob Inn** ✆ (508) 627-9510 TOLL-FREE (800) 696-2723 E-MAIL hobknob@vineyard.net, 128 Main Street, Edgartown 02539, start the day with a made-to-order farm breakfast of hot muffins and scones in the sunny tearoom. In the afternoon, enjoy a cup of tea and sample some pastries. This is a delightful and elegant Victorian inn with a convenient location along Main Street — a short walk to the shops along Edgartown's waterfront. There is a fitness center, a sauna and a massage room. Classic beach cruiser bikes are available for rental and a 27-ft (eight-meter) Boston Whaler is available for charter. The inn is open year round (expensive).

Lambert's Cove Country Inn ✆ (508) 693-2298, Lambert's Cove Road, West Tisbury 02575, is where you get away from it all. Off Lambert's Cove Road, an unpaved path leads through wooded wilderness to this place hidden amid tall pines, 150-year-old vine-covered stone walls, rambling gardens, and an apple orchard. The inn has 16 rooms, eight in the original 1790 main building and the remainder in the restored carriage house and converted barn. It serves breakfast each morning, and is home to one of the island's finest dining rooms (expensive).

For $12 (AYH members) to $15 (non-AYH members) a night you can stay at **Manter Memorial HI Hostel** ☏ (508) 693-2665, 40061 Edgartown Road, West Tisbury 02575, a quaint country inn on the edge of Manuel E. Correllus Forest. The hostel has a fireplace in the common room, a volleyball court, a sheltered bike rack and a kitchen. Five dormitory rooms contain 80 bunk beds. The hostel fills up quickly; make reservations (especially during the high-season) at least two weeks in advance. Open from mid-March to mid-November.

WHERE TO EAT

Only in Edgartown and Oak Bluffs are restaurants allowed to serve alcoholic beverages. The other island towns are "dry," but some restaurants allow diners to bring bottles; inquire in advance.

L'Étoile, at the Charlotte Inn (above), is a superb French restaurant starring the artistry of chef/owner Michael Brisson. Main courses include sautéed fresh Dover sole fillets with fried green tomatoes and saffron-poached potato batons and roasted spice-rubbed Australian lamb with artichoke. Dinner is served every evening from June through September, Wednesday through Sunday for the remainder of the year. L'Étoile is closed in January. Reservations are required (expensive).

The **Black Dog Tavern** ☏ (508) 693-9223, Beach Street Extension, Vineyard Haven, resting steps away from the waters of Vineyard Haven Harbor, is a rustic wooden building decorated with nautical items. The windows provide spectacular views of the harbor; but you'll have to arrive early to get a window table (reservations are not accepted). This landmark restaurant serves good pasta and seafood (expensive). Also on the grounds are The Black Dog General Store and the Black Dog Bakery.

The restaurant at **Lambert's Cove Country Inn** (above) is housed in a 1790 building in a romantic country setting at the end of an unpaved woodland path. The restaurant has an elegant dining room, and an outside deck where diners can look out over the apple orchard. Open year round; seven days a week during the summer months. In the off-season, call ahead for opening days and hours. Reservations are suggested but not required (expensive).

Though only seven miles (11 km) off Cape Cod, the island of Martha's Vineyard is a world away.

Since 1931, the **Home Port Restaurant** ☎ (508) 645-2679, North Road, Menemsha, has been offering spectacular views along with commendable seafood. It's located on the Menemsha fishing port, with its weathered shanties lining the harbor (Quint's home port for you *Jaws* fans). The Home Port is open from mid-April to mid-October (expensive).

If you love a good breakfast then tuck in at **Linda Jean's** ☎ (508) 693-4093, 124 Circuit Avenue, Oak Bluffs (no credit cards). This is a year-round family-owned restaurant, beloved of locals and visitors alike. Linda Jean's also serves lunch and dinner; try the seafood platter with clams, scallops, shrimp, haddock, fries and coleslaw (budget).

The **Main Street Diner** ☎ (508) 627-9337, 65 Main Street, Edgartown, is a bit hard to find — approach it from Main Street by following a long, well-lit, flower wallpapered hallway. Along the way you'll pass all sorts of American memorabilia — on the wall at the end is an American flag with 36 states. Take a left and then a quick right, open the door and you're there. The food is good old-fashioned American inexpensive "eats." Main Street Diner serves breakfast, lunch and dinner year round.

How to Get There

The **Steamship Authority** ☎ (508) 477-8600, PO Box 284, Department CVGB, Woods Hole 02543, provides access to Martha's Vineyard, with daily service between Woods Hole and the harbor at Vineyard Haven; the trip takes about 45 minutes. Car ferries fill up quickly, so you should call well in advance to reserve space on the boat. Or you can fly with **Cape Air** and **Nantucket Airlines** (see TRAVELERS' TIPS, page 341), which connect the Vineyard with Boston, Hyannis, New Bedford, and Nantucket year round.

NANTUCKET ISLAND

"Take out your map and look at it. See what a real corner of the world it occupies, how it stands there away off shore… Look at it — a mere hillock, an elbow of sand; all beach, without a background," wrote Herman Melville in *Moby-Dick*. Thirty miles (50 km) southeast of Cape Cod, Nantucket Island was for almost 100 years among the world's great whaling ports.

Today this 15-mile-long (24-km) "elbow of sand" is one of the most charming and picturesque places on the East Coast, its streets lined with well-preserved houses and its landscape graced with long beaches and open green moors. Visitors arriving by ferry from Cape Cod (a three-hour ride) are often confronted with a mysterious, fog-shrouded island seascape that obscures the main port, Nantucket Town. But once

ashore the beauty is astounding. As one writer put it, "This is not just an island; it is an experience."

The Indians taught Nantucket settlers how to harpoon whales from the shore, and soon the settlers were setting out to sea to do their whaling. By the early 1800s, Nantucket Town had more than 10,000 residents. Its cobblestone streets, elegant houses and tall elm trees were testament to the successes of its sea captains, ship owners and merchants. When the new, larger ships could no longer dock in shallow Nantucket Harbor, the island lost many of its whalers to the deep port in New Bedford. After the Pennsylvania oil boom hit in the 1840s, Nantucket's fortunes declined even further, along with the whaling industry's. Today, its year-round population numbers around 3,700.

Nantucket draws visitors year-round, but hordes descend on the island in summer, so those in the know visit off-season in spring and fall when nature's colors strut their stuff. The lighthouse overlooks the harbor from Brant Point and, as if on pilgrimage at Rome's Trevi Fountain, visitors toss coins into the surrounding waters, sending up a fervent wish to return one day. Boats run to the island year-round from Hyannis on Cape Cod, via the Nantucket Steamship Authority.

Pleasure boats in a Nantucket harbor where seventeenth-century whalers once plied their trade.

General Information

For a fee, you can order a copy of the comprehensive *Official Guide to Nantucket* by contacting the **Nantucket Island Chamber of Commerce** ☎ (508) 228-1700 FAX (508) 325-4925, Department I, Nantucket 02554. All guide information is available on the WEB SITE www.nantucketchamber.org.

What to See and Do

Fine seventeenth- and eighteenth-century houses can be seen on Main Street, the local **Historical Association** ☎ (508) 228-1894 provides pamphlets outlining a self-guided walking tour of the town. The **Whaling Museum** on Broad Street powerfully evokes the industry that made the island famous. One of the best-preserved houses is the **Hadwen House** (Main and Pleasant Streets), a Greek Revival mansion built in 1845 for a whale-oil merchant; it contains original furnishings of the whaling era. In 1686 **Jethro Coffin** built the oldest remaining house in the village on Sunset Hill. This saltbox style dwelling is a fine example of seventeenth-century Colonial architecture. The horseshoe-design in the chimney brick was meant to ward off witches and other evil spirits. The **Old Mill**, on Mill Hill, was built in 1746 with wood salvaged from wrecked ships and is still used to grind corn.

Moored at **Straight Wharf**, at the beginning of Main Street, the *Lighthouse Nantucket* is a double-masted lightship formerly used to guide ocean vessels around the island's shoals. The wharf's fishing sheds have been transformed into shops and restaurants.

Just outside the town, the **Nantucket Moors** are tousled hills of bayberry, wild rose, heather and brambles that burst into vibrant color in summer and fall. Tucked among these hills are the villages of Wauwinet, Quidnet and Siasconset.

Wauwinet is the gateway to the **Coatue**, a 10-mile (16-km) sand spit that protects Nantucket Harbor from the more turbulent Nantucket Sound. You can walk along the spit to its northern tip, where the 1818 **Great Point Lighthouse** marks the site of treacherous sandbars in the Sound.

Siasconset sits on the easternmost edge of the island. By the end of the nineteenth century, this village, by then popular with both artists and tourists, was linked to Nantucket Town by a railroad.

SPORTS AND OUTDOOR ACTIVITIES

Beaches

Nantucket beaches offer something for everyone — **Jetties Beach**, located near the channel leading into Nantucket Harbor, has warm Sound swimming and gentle surf. It's a short bike ride from town. **Children's Beach**, with broad shallow flats, is a protected swimming area for bathers.

Surfside, however, is perfect for children, with its tidal pools to splash in. **Cisco Beach** is known its powerful breakers. **Madaket Beach**, at the island's western end, is good for surfcasting.

Bicycling

Several bike paths cross a pastiche of landscapes. The **Madaket Bike Path** is a 12-mile (19.2-km) round-trip path from Nantucket Town winding west alongside moors and over hills to Madaket. The **Sconset Bike Path** is a 14-mile (22.4-km) round-trip passing Milestone Bog, encountering moors and wetlands *en route* to Sconset, while the **Polpis Road Bike Path** is a 16-mile (25.6-km) round-trip outing offering views over ponds and cranberry bogs.

WHERE TO STAY

The **Wauwinet** ☎ (508) 228-0145 TOLL-FREE (800) 426-8718, 120 Wauwinet Road, Nantucket 02584, is a nineteenth-century inn transformed into a resort offering rooms, cottages and suites. This hyper-luxurious resort has all you could ask for including a gorgeous setting (luxury).

The 60-room **Jared Coffin House Nantucket** ☎ (508) 228-2400 TOLL-FREE (800) 248-2405 FAX (508) 228-8549 E-MAIL jchouse@nantucket.net, 29 Broad Street, Nantucket 02554, is an 1845 Greek Revival, restored in 1963. Located in midst of Nantucket's historic downtown, it is convenient to shopping areas and the waterfront. Open all year; rates include breakfast (mid-range to expensive).

The oldest continuously operating guesthouse on the island, **Century House Nantucket** ☎ (508) 228-0530, 10 Cliff Road, Nantucket 02554-0603, is an 1833 late Federal with views of the harbor from its wraparound verandah set with inviting rocking chairs. The 10 rooms are pleasant and the house is convenient to shops, beaches, and dining. Open from May 20 to October 20, the rate includes a continental buffet breakfast and afternoon cocktails served on the verandah (budget to mid-range).

Cottages are another option on the island; **Wade Cottages** ☎ (508) 257-6383, Shell Street, Siasconset 02554 (expensive to luxury) are on the grounds of a former estate and offer the solitude of a private beach. The rooms have private or shared baths and the apartments have one to four bedrooms. The facility is open May to October.

You won't find mid-range priced lodging during high season; however, for cyclists and backpackers the **Star of the Sea Youth Hostel** ☎ (508) 228-0433, 31 Western Avenue, Nantucket 02554-4408, with 72 beds and cooking facilities, is a lifesaver — having literally once been a lifesaving station; the front door still indicates where the lifeboats are located. Open April through October.

WHERE TO EAT

The **Wauwinet** ☎ (508) 228-0145, located at 120 Wauwinet Road, serves outstanding New American cuisine. Open for breakfast, lunch and dinner daily, reservations are recommended (expensive).

At **The Boarding House** ☎ (508) 228-9622, 12 Federal Street, Nantucket Town (expensive), the cuisine has Mediterranean and Asian influences. You can choose from a bistro menu or more formal fare. Seating is in a romantic dining room with low-beamed ceilings or in the comfortable bar area or, in summer, outside on the patio. Lunch and dinner are served year round (expensive).

The cozy atmosphere is one reason to stop off for a pint or a meal at **The Rose & Crown** ☎ (508) 228-2595, 23 South Water Street, Nantucket Town (mid-range). One of the few waterfront pubs that's also hospitable to children, Rose & Crown smokes a mean rack of ribs. Look for island dance music (a little reggae, a little rock) most nights in the summer. Reservations are not taken, so you may have to wait for a table during the season (mid-range).

On a beach vacation, you can't miss with **Provisions** ☎ (508) 228-3258, Straight Wharf, Nantucket Town. This year-round gourmet deli has soups, salads and sandwiches, as well as pâtés, cheeses and French bread. In good weather you can enjoy your lunch on the benches outside. Provisions is open for breakfast, too, and they will pack picnic lunches for you to take away (budget).

A rooftop in the village of Siasconset on the Nantucket Moors.

How to Get There

Regular ferry service throughout the year leaves Cape Cod from Woods Hole and Hyannis. **Hy-line Cruises** ☎ (508) 778-2600 FAX (508) 778-9854 WEB SITE www.hy-lines.com, Ocean Street Dock, Hyannis, and Straight Wharf, Nantucket, offers seasonal passenger-only ferry service from May to October. The trip takes two hours and reservations are not required. Hy-line also offers seasonal service between Martha's Vineyard and Nantucket. The **Steamship Authority** ☎ (508) 477-8600, PO Box 284, Department CVGB, Woods Hole 02543, provides access to Martha's Vineyard, with year-round ferry service for passengers, bicycles, automobiles and pets. Reservations are required for cars, but not for passengers. The trip generally takes a little over two hours. It's expensive to bring your car over, and permits are required for driving on beaches and in conservation areas. Reservations must be made several months in advance.

Flights to Nantucket Memorial Airport are available through a number of carriers, including: Business Express TOLL-FREE (800) 345-3400, Continental Connection (operated by Colgan Air) TOLL-FREE (800) 523-3273, Island Aviation ☎ (508) 325-5548, Nantucket Airlines TOLL-FREE (800) 635-8787 (with 20 flights daily), Island Airlines ☎ (508) 228-7575 TOLL-FREE (800) 248-7779, Colgan Air TOLL-FREE (888) 265-4267, Continental Express TOLL-FREE (800) 272-5488, and US Air Express TOLL-FREE (800) 428-4322.

BECKY THATCHER

Connecticut

Antiques

For more than three centuries, Connecticut has welcomed travelers. George Washington visited the state a number of times — the bedroom his hosts decorated at Webb House for his visit to Wethersfield in 1781 still looks the same today. Mark Twain stopped in Connecticut on business in 1873 and stayed for a good portion of his life, writing such classics as *Tom Sawyer* during his time in Hartford. His flamboyant "Steamboat Gothic" house still stands in Hartford. Even P.T. Barnum, the master of hype, who traveled the world with his Greatest Show on Earth, put all that aside when he returned to his home in Bridgeport. The Barnum Museum there provides entertainment courtesy of the master showman.

Yet despite the state's history of presumably discerning visitors, contemporary travelers on Interstate 95 often pass through Connecticut on their way to vacation spots elsewhere in New England, missing out on a unique part of New England which is best explored along its picturesque back roads. These scenic byways crisscross a roughly rectangular state measuring 90 miles (145 km) by 55 miles (89 km), and bordered by New York on the west, Massachusetts to the north, and Rhode Island to the east. Long Island Sound protects Connecticut's southern boundary with its strands of sandy beaches, historic port towns and wealthy bedroom communities. Both the Connecticut River, which bisects the state, and the Housatonic River in the northwest run through some spectacular scenery. And a string of villages, like rough pearls, dot the Litchfield Hills, which rise in northwest Connecticut.

BACKGROUND

Before European settlers arrived in the sixteenth and seventeenth centuries, tribes of Pequot-Mohegan, Nipmuck, Paugusset, Potatuck and Quiripi populated Connecticut. (Their stories are told superbly at the Mashantucket Pequot Museum and Research Center in Ledyard; see under MYSTIC AND THE SOUTHEAST, page 188.) As did the other Algonquin-speaking groups of southern New England, they followed a semi-nomadic lifestyle, combining the growing of maize, beans, and squash with hunting and fishing.

Adriaen Block, a Dutch navigator, was the first recorded European explorer to sail along Connecticut's coast, in 1614. He traveled up the Connecticut River, where the Dutch later established a trading post near what is now Hartford, for dealing in the region's lucrative beaver pelt trade.

Though the Dutch had their trading post, it was the British who colonized the state. By 1635, English settlers from the already crowded Massachusetts Bay Colony, driven by a search for fertile farmland, began flowing into the Connecticut River Valley

where they established two towns — Wethersfield and Windsor. Not long after that, Hartford was founded by Reverend Thomas Hooker, who had come from Massachusetts searching for relief from the Puritans' restrictive codes and laws. The three towns banded together as the Hartford Colony and proclaimed in 1639 the Fundamental Orders of Connecticut, a statement of citizens' rights that is considered a precursor to the United States Constitution (hence, the state's official nickname, The Constitution State). Meanwhile, the Puritan colony at New Haven adopted *its* Fundamental Agreement, proclaiming the Holy Scriptures to be the supreme law in all civil affairs. Despite their opposing views on the roles of church and state, the two colonies joined in 1662 and together formed one of the more staunchly independent of the original 13 colonies, contributing huge numbers of troops to the Revolutionary War effort.

OPPOSITE: Turn up a treasure in one of Connecticut's antique barns. ABOVE: The state's less-visited northeast corner is a quiet, rural retreat.

Once independence was secured, commerce, trade, and manufacturing took root. Textile and paper mills, along with metal forges and shipyards, were the state's industrial mainstays and attracted immigrants from across Europe, such as the Portuguese who settled in Mystic. Banks were established in Hartford by 1792 and the insurance industry began in Norwich in 1795. Samuel Colt of Hartford developed the Colt revolver (1836); Gideon Roberts made Bristol the clock capital of the United States; everyone wore Danbury hats; and matrons treasured Meriden silver services. In 1775, Connecticut built and launched the first submarine. Pay telephones (1877), hamburgers (1895), Frisbees (1920), lollipops (1908) and color televisions (1948) started here, too.

Connecticut has prospered with the growing importance of service industries, especially insurance. This prosperity has endured for the state's 3.3 million residents, as indicated by the state's per capita income, which is the highest in the nation.

MYSTIC AND THE SOUTHEAST

Mystic (named for the Indian word *mistick* or "tidal river") is the hub for a bounty of coastal and inland entertainments offering the lure of tall ships, seafood, high-stakes gambling, submarine tours, aquarium mammals, and the newest jewel in the crown of this much visited region — the fabulous Mashantucket Pequot Museum and Research Center in Ledyard.

Since the seventeenth century, Mystic has been building boats. At one time Connecticut's most important and prosperous seaport, its elegant clipper ships made it one of the country's top whaling centers — with 20 whalers in its fleet until 1860 when petroleum replaced whale oil. Later, Mystic's vessels formed the backbone of America's Navy in World War II. Today the Mystic Seaport Museum, the state's number one attraction, pays homage to the region's maritime history.

GENERAL INFORMATION

For informational materials about the region, contact **Mystic and More** ☎ (860) 444-2206 or TOLL-FREE (800) 863-6569 WEB SITE www.mysticmore.com.

Visitors to downtown Mystic are invited to stop in at the **Mystic Depot Welcome Center** ☎ (860) 572-9578, 2 Roosevelt Avenue, Mystic, weekdays, for informational materials concerning attractions, lodgings and restaurants. Staff are on hand to answer your questions. There's another drop-in information center at **Olde Mystic Village** ☎ (860) 536-4941, Coogan Boulevard. You can call them in advance for a free copy of their *Discovery Guide*.

WHAT TO SEE AND DO

Mystic

The **Mystic Seaport Museum** is a 17-acre (seven-hectare) living history museum that recreates a typical nineteenth-century New England seaport. Begun in 1929, the Seaport contains more than 60 historic waterfront buildings, 300 ships and boats and artifacts of nineteenth-century maritime America. Interpreters in period dress staff the shops, cook at hearths, and even lead sea chanteys.

The *Amistad* exhibit in the Preservation Shipyard tells the story of the schooner that played an important role in African-American history. In 1839, a group of 53 Africans, who had been kidnapped in what is now Sierra Leone, took control of the Cuba-bound schooner *La Amistad*. The group was eventually captured, jailed, and brought to trial for murder in New Haven, where former President John Quincy Adams undertook their defense. In 1841 they were declared free. Skilled boat-builders and their apprentices used period tools to construct this 81-ft (25-m) replica schooner, which made her maiden voyage in July 2000.

America's sole surviving wooden whaling ship, the *Charles W. Morgan*, is another of the Seaport's master attractions. Visitors may walk the main deck, explore the cargo hold, which still smells of whale blubber, and see where the crew of more than 90 men lived and worked. A fascinating 30-minute program on nineteenth-century whaling at the Meeting House includes rare footage of an actual whaling voyage.

You can explore the decks of many other ships, from the square-rigged *Joseph Conrad*, an iron-hulled Dutch training vessel built in 1882, to the LA *Dunton Fishing Schooner* (1921), which illustrates the days of Grand Banks fishing aboard a two-masted Gloucester schooner. And you can take a cruise down the Mystic River on the coal-fired *Sabino*, a passenger steamboat (1908).

The Seaport is open daily 9 AM to 6 PM, with ships and exhibits closing at 5 PM. An admission fee is charged. For more information, contact the **Mystic Seaport** ☎ (860) 572-5315 TOLL-FREE (888) 9-SEAPORT, 75 Greenmanville Avenue, Mystic 06355.

Recently, a major renovation of the **Mystic Aquarium** has endowed it with a more spacious floor plan and a wider variety of marine life. A new outdoor exhibit provides beluga whales, one-ton Steller's sea lions, seals and other denizens of the Alaskan coast with spacious living quarters. Cascading waterfalls, caves and jagged rocky beach areas create a naturalistic habitat with cutaway views to see the creatures both above and below the water's surface. Further along you can observe the habits of more cold-weather denizens, such as African black-footed penguins.

The aquarium is open daily from 9 AM to 5 PM year-round, except December to mid-March, when it opens Monday through Friday 10 AM to 4 PM. An admission fee is charged. For more information contact the Mystic Aquarium ☎ (860) 572-5955, 55 Coogan Boulevard, Mystic 06355.

OPPOSITE: The sun burns through morning fog at the Mystic Seaport. ABOVE: Steller's sea lions bask in their new outdoor abode at the Mystic Aquarium.

Several tall-ships sail out of Mystic offering **cruises** of varying lengths. On some trips passengers get a chance to lend a hand in sailing the vessel: The 110-ft (33.5-m) *Mystic Whaler* TOLL-FREE (800) 697-8420 is a replica New England schooner offering one-, two-, three- and five-day trips. Voyager Cruises ☎ (860) 536-0416 has morning and afternoon sea trips to Fisher's Island Sound as well as sunset cruises aboard the *Argia*, a recreated nineteenth-century gaff-rigged schooner.

Stonington

Situated on a narrow peninsula jutting out into Fisher's Island Sound, Stonington is one of the prettiest coastal villages in Connecticut. At one time the third largest seaport in the state, whalers and sailors once jammed its streets, going about their fishy business under the stern eyes of sea captains' stately houses. Stonington is still loaded with Colonial charm as well as eighteenth- and nineteenth-century architecture — a place to explore on foot with its narrow streets, restored buildings and numerous shops.

Reminding visitors of Stonington's past as a whaling and sealing port, the **Old Lighthouse Museum** ☎ (860) 535-1440, 7 Water Street, on Stonington Point, has a small museum containing seafaring artifacts. The lighthouse tower affords a view of three states (Fisher's Island, New York; Rhode Island to the east; and Connecticut), as well as vistas across the sound. Open 10 AM to 5 PM daily July and August, closed Monday September through June. An admission fee is charged.

WHERE TO STAY AND EAT

The maritime theme of the area runs to lodging and dining as well. The intimate **Steamboat Inn** ☎ (860) 536-8300, 73 Steamboat Wharf, Mystic 06355, is on the river by the drawbridge in downtown Mystic. Most of the 10 rooms have whirlpool bath and fireplace, and most have water views (luxury). The rate includes continental breakfast and afternoon tea.

You've heard of bed and breakfast; now how about boat and breakfast? **Kittiwake Boat & Breakfast** ☎ (203) 686-1616, 1 Washington Street, on the Mystic River, Mystic 06355, is a 57-ft (17-m) yacht available for one- or two-night stays. There are three staterooms, each with private bath, heating, and air conditioning (call for prices).

Lauren Bacall and Humphrey Bogart honeymooned at **The Inn at Mystic** ☎ (860) 536-9604 TOLL-FREE (800) 237-2415 E-MAIL jdyer@innatmystic.com, at Routes 1 and 27, Mystic 06355. Overlooking Mystic Harbor this inn comes in several parts: the Georgian inn with five rooms, a gatehouse with four rooms and the east wing with 23 rooms with fireplace and Jacuzzi. There is continental fare in the restaurant as well as indoor and outdoor pools, an exercise room, beach access and a boat dock.

Even if you don't stay at the Inn at Mystic, you should dine at its excellent **Flood Tide Restaurant** ☎ (860) 536-9604, Routes 1 and 27, Mystic, with its New England specialties of Long Island roast duck and Maine lobster (expensive).

For international cuisine, there is **J.P. Daniels** ☎ (860) 572-9564, Route 184, Old Mystic, situated in a restored two-level barn (expensive).

Alongside the Seaport is the **Seamen's Inne** ☎ (860) 572-5303, at 75 Greenmanville Avenue, Mystic. Three restaurants in one, the Inne serves New England meals to suit your price range. You can have an inexpensive snack at the pub, an inexpensive meal at the café, or tuck into a more formal, and more expensive, spread in the dining room.

Fans of the sleeper film *Mystic Pizza* will be charmed to know that there is a real **Mystic Pizza** ☎ (860) 536-3700, 56 West Main Street, Mystic, and though the scenes of this Portuguese pizzeria were shot in a nearby warehouse, the pizza is authentic and just as heartwarming as the film.

In North Stonington, **Randall's Ordinary** ☎ (860) 599-4540 FAX (860) 599-3308, Route 2, PO Box 243, North Stonington 06359 (mid-range to expensive) is a Colonial wayside inn with 15 rooms and a "silo suite" with fireplace and Jacuzzi. The guestroom price includes a continental breakfast. The restaurant — which is "anything but ordinary," according to *Bon Appetit* magazine — prepares authentic eighteenth-

Costumed interpreters take their roles to heart at the Mystic Seaport Museum.

GROCERIES
CROCKERY
ICE
CREAM

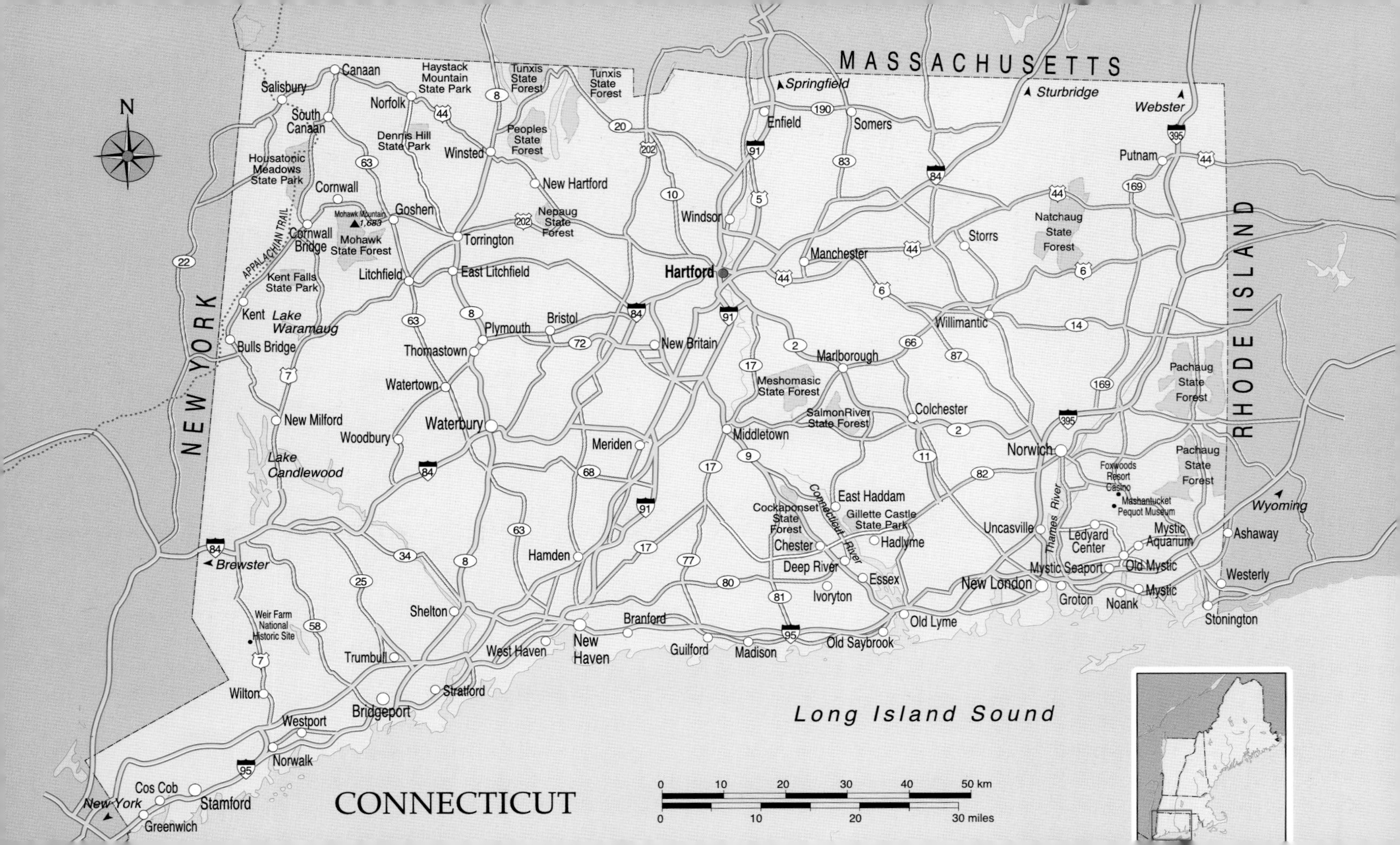
CONNECTICUT
MASSACHUSETTS
NEW YORK
RHODE ISLAND
Long Island Sound
N
Springfield
Sturbridge
Webster
Wyoming
Brewster
New York
Salisbury
Canaan
Norfolk
Haystack Mountain State Park
Tunxis State Forest
Tunxis State Forest
Peoples State Forest
South Canaan
Dennis Hill State Park
Winsted
Housatonic Meadows State Park
Cornwall
New Hartford
Mohawk Mountain 1,683
Goshen
Nepaug State Forest
Cornwall Bridge
Mohawk State Forest
Torrington
APPALACHIAN TRAIL
Kent Falls State Park
Litchfield
East Litchfield
Kent
Lake Waramaug
Bulls Bridge
Plymouth
Bristol
Thomastown
New Britain
Watertown
New Milford
Waterbury
Woodbury
Meriden
Lake Candlewood
Hamden
Shelton
Weir Farm National Historic Site
Trumbull
Wilton
Bridgeport
Stratford
Westport
Norwalk
Cos Cob
Stamford
Greenwich
West Haven
New Haven
Branford
Guilford
Madison
Old Saybrook
Enfield
Somers
Windsor
Hartford
Manchester
Storrs
Natchaug State Forest
Putnam
Willimantic
Marlborough
Meshomasic State Forest
SalmonRiver State Forest
Colchester
Middletown
Pachaug State Forest
Pachaug State Forest
Norwich
Foxwoods Resort Casino
Mashantucket Pequot Museum
East Haddam
Cockaponset State Forest
Connecticut River
Gillette Castle State Park
Hadlyme
Chester
Deep River
Essex
Ivoryton
Uncasville
Thames River
Ledyard Center
Mystic Aquarium
Old Mystic
Mystic Seaport
New London
Groton
Noank
Mystic
Ashaway
Westerly
Stonington
Old Lyme
0
10
20
30
40
50 km
0
10
20
30 miles

century meals that are cooked at the hearth and brought to you by waiters dressed in period costumes. There is a single dinner seating at 7 PM; breakfast is served from 7 AM to 11 PM and lunch from noon to 3 PM.

A little west of Stonington is the famous **Abbot's Lobster in the Rough** ✆ (860) 536-7719, 117 Pearl Street, in Noank, where you get the best buy for your dining dollar (budget). There are no waiters; you order at the window, pay the tab, and wait for your number to be called. Don't forget to wear a bib. If you prefer clam shacks to lobster pounds, the neighboring **Costello's Clam Company** ✆ (860) 572-2779 in the Noank Shipyard (seasonal; budget) has all the right stuff: fried clams, oysters, scallops and lobster rolls.

HOW TO GET THERE

Mystic is situated 108 miles (173 km) from Boston and 130 miles (208 km) from New York. Motorists will take Exit 90 off Interstate 95 onto Route 27 for the Mystic Seaport and the aquarium.

Stonington is east of Mystic, off Alternate Route 1A. **North Stonington** is on Route 2, convenient to the Foxwoods Casino and Mashantucket Pequot Museum (see below).

ALONG THE THAMES: NEW LONDON TO NORWICH

Settled in 1646 by a group of Massachusetts Puritans, New London is one of the Connecticut coast's venerable Colonial towns. The Puritan immigrants named their new home after London, England, and in keeping with the theme, renamed the Monhegan River the Thames.

Once the second-busiest whaling port on the East Coast, New London is still a seafaring town: the United States Coast Guard Academy is based here. Tours of the base are free. There is more martial splendor in Groton, the "submarine capital of the world," at the Submarine Force Library and Museum. Elsewhere in the Thames River region are two of the world's largest gambling and entertainment complexes: Foxwoods and Mohegan Sun.

GENERAL INFORMATION

Regional maps and guides are available from **Connecticut's Mystic and More** ✆ (860) 444-2206 TOLL-FREE (800) 863-6569, 470 Bank Street, PO Box 89, New London 06320.

WHAT TO SEE AND DO

New London

New London's deepwater port is home to the **United States Coast Guard Academy**

✆ (860) 444-8270, Mohegan Avenue (Interstate 95, Exit 3; Interstate 395, Exit 78) one of the nation's four military academies. Here you can see a video presentation on cadet life and take a walking tour of the grounds; the Academy conducts cadet dress parades on Fridays spring and fall. Open daily year-round; admission is free. The training barge *Eagle*, a three-masted square-rigger built in 1936, is open for weekend tours when it is in port.

New London has some notable buildings, including **Monte Cristo Cottage** ✆ (860) 443-0051, 325 Pequot Avenue, boyhood home of Nobel Prize-winning playwright Eugene O'Neill. The house is named for the Count of Monte Cristo, O'Neill's actor father's most famous role. Open Memorial Day to Labor Day, Tuesday to Sunday; an admission fee is charged. You can also visit the **Hempstead Houses** ✆ (860) 443-7949, 11 Hempstead Street, where two restored homes show

A naval officer in Groton, home port of the United States Navy's Atlantic submarine fleet and the Submarine Force Library.

the changes that took place for colonial seafaring families between the seventeenth and the eighteenth century. They are open mid-May to mid-October, Thursday to Sunday; an admission fee is charged.

The **Lyman Allyn Art Museum** ☎ (860) 443-2545, 625 Williams Street, houses a fine collection of contemporary American art. Along with a single gallery of Connecticut Impressionism, there are old master drawings, decorative arts, dolls, dollhouses and toys. Open Tuesday to Sunday; an admission fee is charged.

Groton

Eyeing its sister city from across the wide Thames is Groton, with its **Submarine Force Library and Museum** ☎ (860) 694-3174 TOLL-FREE (800) 343-0079, Naval Submarine Base, 1 Crystal Lake Road, where you can climb aboard the world's first nuclear-powered submarine, the **USS *Nautilus***, built in 1954 by Groton's Electric Boat Division of General Dynamics. The ship's claustrophobic quarters were crammed with crewmen during its journeys, which included cruising under the Arctic ice cap, from the Bering Strait to the Greenland Sea, in 1958. Open mid-May to mid-October, Wednesday to Monday 9 AM to 5 PM, Tuesday 1 PM to 5 PM; November to mid-May, Wednesday to Monday 9 AM to 4 PM. Admission is free.

Norwich

Fanning out from the head of the Thames, Norwich, long economically depressed, is benefiting from the burst of successful tribally-owned-and-operated enterprises in the area, which are bringing capital and jobs to the region. The **Slater Memorial Museum** ☎ (860) 887-2506, 108 Crescent Street, juxtaposes Victorian art reproductions with a collection of contemporary art in a striking Romanesque Revival building with fine stained glass. Open 10 AM to 4 PM weekdays, 1 PM to 4 PM weekends. The **Norwich Rose Garden** on Rockwell Street in Mohegan Park features 2,500 rose bushes in 120 varieties. The bloom peaks in June but continues all summer. Most visitors come to entwine themselves in the voluptuous pleasures of the **Norwich Inn & Spa** (see also WHERE TO STAY, below).

The Casinos

It would be difficult to miss the hype surrounding the region's two tribally-owned-and-operated gambling palaces. The larger and glitzier **Foxwoods Resort Casino** TOLL-FREE (800) 752-9244, Route 2, Ledyard 06339, has 5,000 slot machines and hundreds of gaming tables. You can stay close at hand at one of the resort's three hotels, and if you've brought the family along, there are plenty of distractions for those not yet of age to gamble away their allowances: a movie theater complex, rides, shops, eateries and so forth. A 1,500-seat auditorium hosts crooners of the caliber of Liza Minelli and Paul Anka. Live boxing matches also take place here. **Mohegan Sun** ☎ (860) 862-8000 TOLL-FREE (888) 226-7711, 1 Mohegan Sun Boulevard, Uncasville 06382, on the other hand, is a day-trippers' casino, less crowded and more woodsy than its famous neighbor. (It is, however, the third-largest casino in the country.) Here also you'll find dining and entertainment for adults and children.

Mashantucket Pequot Museum

Opened in August of 1998, the new Mashantucket Pequot Museum and Research Center is a national treasure. Built at a cost of over $193 million, the museum tells the story of the Mashantucket Pequot Tribal Nation, as well as documenting the histories and cultures of other tribes and the region's natural history. An architectural wonder as well as an excellent museum, the building complex symbolizes the tribe's close connection with the land. Visitors enter through the stunning "gathering space," a massive glass rotunda set a few feet from the forest edge; a tower allows museum visitors to gaze out over the reservation land's Great Swamp.

The museum tour begins with a trip back to the Ice Age as visitors descend through a glacial crevasse. From there, a series of galleries take the visitor up to the age of European contact. The colossal 1550 Pequot Village is the centerpiece of the museum, a series of extraordinary dioramas offering a vivid picture of life in a Pequot coastal village at dawn of European contact. Even the scents — crushed leaves, wood smoke — and sounds — seagulls and crows squawking overhead and crickets chirping in the brush — make it feel as if you are observing a living village frozen in time. To each side of the village are galleries with exhibitions on daily life, linguistics, and the structure of Pequot society.

Bracketing this impressive series of galleries are two exhibits on the Mashantucket Pequot tribe itself, with photographic and oral histories of tribe members talking about contemporary issues of family, community, and tradition.

Along with dioramas and interactive computer stations, there are a dozen film theaters,

a library and research center, Native American artwork, and special events. A mezzanine above the gathering space is a **cafeteria** that serves well-above-average fare. The museum is open Memorial Day to Labor Day daily 10 AM to 7 PM, Labor Day to Memorial Day Wednesday to Monday 10 AM to 6 PM; an admission fee is charged. For more information contact the **Mashantucket Pequot Museum & Research Center** ☎ (860) 396-6800 TOLL-FREE (800) 411-9671, 110 Pequot Trail, PO Box 3180, Mashantucket 06339-3180.

TOURS AND EXCURSIONS

It's possible to take a sightseeing cruise on the Thames aboard the ***Captain Bob II*** ☎ (860) 434-5681, PO Box 32, Groton 06469. You will pass the USS *Nautilus* and other submarines at their riverside berths, sight Trident submarines being constructed at Groton, pass the submarine base and Coast Guard Academy, and perhaps even see a submarine or two returning to home port. Cruises sail July to Labor Day; call for schedule.

From New London you can take the ferry to **Block Island** (see BLOCK ISLAND, page 227 in RHODE ISLAND) with Nelseco Navigation ☎ (860) 442-9553 and 442-7891, 2 Ferry Street, PO Box 482, New London 06320, aboard the auto ferry *Anna C*. Sailing time is two hours, and the ferry departs from Ferry Street. There are also ferries from New London to points in New York State.

NIGHTLIFE AND THE ARTS

West of New London in Waterford, the **Eugene O'Neill Theater Center** ☎ (860) 443-5378 or (860) 443-1238, 305 Great Neck Road, Waterford, is an acclaimed playwrights' workshop which has launched the careers of many writers. The theater presents new works in the summer. The **Garde Arts Center** ☎ (860) 444-7373 TOLL-FREE (888) 664-2733, 329 State Street, presents national and international touring companies, Broadway fare, concerts, and dance troupes, as well as an occasional first-run independent film. The renovated theater has received national praise for its excellent acoustics.

WHERE TO STAY AND EAT

High on a bluff over the Thames River, the **Spa at Norwich Inn** ☎ (860) 886-2401 TOLL-FREE (800) 275-4772, 607 West Thames Street (Route 32), Norwich 06360 (expensive), offers a panoply of beauty and health treatments in its expanded and redecorated spa. The main accommodation is a 50-room turn-of-the-century inn, while around the grounds are 80 villas with kitchen, fireplace, and balcony. The restaurant is surprisingly good, especially the "spa menu" whose choices are not only healthy but delicious. This is a comprehensive resort with all sorts

Built as a "house of public entertainment" shortly after 1700, the Leffingwell Inn (348 Washington Street) is the oldest house in Norwich.

of year-round outdoor activities to enjoy in its 40-acre (16-hectare) grounds: indoor and outdoor pools, a complete fitness club and snack bar, jogging and hiking trails, and cross-country skiing.

There are three hotels to choose from at Foxwoods. All have indoor pools and fitness facilities: The **Foxwoods Resort Hotel** TOLL-FREE (800) 369-9663, Route 2, Ledyard 06339, has 312 rooms and suites, and two restaurants (expensive); the larger **Grand Pequot Tower** TOLL-FREE (800) 369-9663, Route 2, Ledyard 06339, has 800 rooms and suites and a coffee shop (expensive); while **Two Trees** ((860) 369-9663 TOLL-FREE (800) 369-9663, 240 Lantern Hill Road, Ledyard 06339, is more of a "country-style" hotel with 280 rooms and suites and a restaurant; the rate includes a continental breakfast.

Glamour aside, the **Stonecroft Country Inn** ((860) 572-0771 TOLL-FREE (800) 772-0774 FAX (860) 572-9161 E-MAIL innkeeper@stonecroft.com, 515 Pumpkin Hill Road, Ledyard 06339, is reason enough to visit the area. A Georgian Colonial surrounded by lawns, gardens, and stone walls, the inn has 10 guestrooms with fireplace and whirlpool tub. The Grange is a converted barn where international cuisine is served either in the dining room or on an outdoor stone terrace. Both inn and restaurant are listed on the National Register of Historic Places.

HOW TO GET THERE

Norwich is 103 miles (165 km) from Boston and 138 miles (221 km) from New York City. Follow Interstate 395 to Route 2. **Groton** and **New London** are 101 miles (162 km) from Boston, 121 miles (194 km) from New York, and they are accessible off Interstate 95. To get to **Foxwoods** from the south take Interstate 95 North to Exit 92 to Route 2 West; from the north follow Interstate 95 south to Exit 92 to Route 2 East or Interstate 395 South to Exit 85 to Route 164 South to Route 2 East.

THE SOUTHWEST COAST

Those entering Connecticut from New York on Interstate 95 may find it difficult to determine when the Empire State ends and the Constitution State begins: the coastal cities and villages, such as affluent Greenwich, Stamford, Riverside and Darien, are as much suburbs of New York City as they are Connecticut towns.

An alternate route tracing a meandering path through the region is the **Merritt Parkway** (Route 15), a 38-mile (61-km) National Scenic Byway. Built during the Depression, the richly landscaped road traverses a series of unique bridges.

GENERAL INFORMATION

Informational materials can be obtained from the **Coastal Fairfield County Convention & Visitor Bureau** ((203) 899-2799 TOLL-FREE (800) 866-7925, 297 West Avenue, Gate Lodge–Mathews Park, Norwalk 06850.

WHAT TO SEE AND DO

Greenwich

Don't try to roller skate, bike, or skateboard on a **Greenwich Avenue** sidewalk: You might be arrested. This relentlessly upscale boulevard, with its pricey boutiques, old-style department stores and fine restaurants, is reserved for more sophisticated pleasures.

Those following the Connecticut Impressionist Trail (see CULTURAL KICKS, page 44 in YOUR CHOICE) will eventually arrive in nearby Cos Cob, where the **Bush-Holley Historic House** ((203) 869-6899, 39 Strickland Road, Cos Cob, was the site of the first Connecticut art colony. The 1732 saltbox became an inn in 1884, and in 1892 artists led by J. Alden Weir began boarding here. Open Tuesday to Sunday March through December, weekends January and February; an admission fee is charged.

Stamford

An eclectic spot, the **Stamford Museum and Nature Center** ((203) 322-1646, 39 Scofieldtown Road, is a 118-acre (47-hectare) working farm with a country store, woodland trails, and a picnic area. An exhibit tells about pond life, and there is a boardwalk with seating niches along a stream. In addition, several galleries exhibit fine art and Americana, as well as interpretive displays of natural history, Native American customs, and a planetarium show. Open daily; an admission fee is charged.

The Stamford Historical Society Museum ℂ (203) 329-1183, 1508 High Ridge Road, offers some insight into the Colonial origins of the community. It also makes arrangements for tours of the 1699 Hoyt-Barnum House. Open Tuesday through Saturday noon to 4 PM; free admission.

Anyone with an eye for the unusual should make the trip to **United House Wrecking** ℂ (203) 348-5371, 535 Hope Street, a huge junkyard of treasures salvaged from estate sales and demolitions. With 30,000 sq ft (2,700 sq m) of antiques, furniture, stained glass, fireplace mantels, plumbing fixtures, lighting fixtures and architectural salvage, it's the state's largest antiques emporium — a fascinating place to poke around whether or not you're in the market for a gargoyle. Open Monday to Saturday from 9:30 AM to 5:30 PM, Sunday noon to 5 PM.

Order up! Boiled lobster, potato chips, drawn butter, slaw… and don't forget the bib.

Norwalk

An increasingly prosperous and trendy area, a rehabilitated **waterfront** has done much to improve South Norwalk. New shops and restaurants are opening at a rapid pace. One of the prime draws is the new **Maritime Aquarium at Norwalk** ℂ (203) 852-0700, 10 Water Street, with marine and maritime life of Long Island Sound. Visitors can see sharks, seals, jellyfish, otters, and 125 other marine species. There are also boat-building demonstrations and restored sailing vessels on show. Open daily year-round; an admission fee is charged.

The **Lockwood-Mathews Mansion Museum** ℂ (203) 838-9799, 295 West Avenue, is a 62-room, circa-1864 estate filled with Victoriana. A walk through the house reveals scores of intricate details such as stenciled walls, inlaid woodwork, and a sky-lit rotunda. Tours are given hourly mid-March to mid-December, Wednesday to Sunday. An admission fee is charged.

The **Norwalk Seaport Association** ℂ (203) 838-9444 provides ferry service to the 1868 **lighthouse** on Sheffield Island. Trips depart from Hope Dock, which is at the intersection of Washington and North Water streets in South Norwalk.

Wilton

Weir Farm National Historic Site ℂ (203) 834-1896, 735 Nod Hill Road, Wilton, has been called the inspirational home of American Impressionist painting (see CULTURAL KICKS, page 44 in YOUR CHOICE). Acquired by J. Alden Weir (1852–1919) in 1882, the farm served as a retreat for other painters (John Henry Twachtman, Childe Hassam, and John Singer Sargent, to name a few). It has been continuously occupied by working artists for more than 100 years. Visitors can buy a brochure and take a walking tour of several spots comparing the landscapes with the artists' conceptions. The Visitors Center is open Wednesday through Sunday 8:30 AM to 5 PM, with studio tours at 11 AM, 1 PM and 3 PM. Admission is free. The farm is next to conservation land where there is fishing, picnicking, and hiking.

Bridgeport

A manufacturing city with a dwindling population (now at 138,000), Bridgeport was once the winter home of P.T. Barnum (1810–91), the circus impresario, creator of the "Greatest Show on Earth," and long-time mayor. The **Barnum Museum** ℂ (203) 331-1104, 820 Main Street, built in 1893, underwent a massive renovation a few years back. Its collection holds materials relating to P.T. Barnum's career and to circus lore. On display are some of the curiosities that made Barnum famous, including personal memorabilia of General Tom Thumb — a Bridgeport native — and Swedish opera singer Jenny Lind. Open Tuesday to Sunday; an admission fee is charged.

WHERE TO STAY AND EAT

If you are looking for luxury, the **Inn at National Hall** ℂ (203) 221-1351 TOLL-FREE (800) 628-4255 FAX (203) 221-0276 E-MAIL nationalhall@relaischateaux.fr, 2 Post Road West, Westport 06880 (luxury), will do nicely. Styled after a European manor, this respected inn has 16 somewhat over-the-top guestrooms and suites with names such as the Turkistan Suite, The Butterfly Room, The Henny Penny Suite and The Raindrop Room; the rate includes a continental breakfast (see LIVING IT UP, page 40 in YOUR CHOICE).

Stanton House Inn ℂ (203) 869-2110, 76 Maple Avenue, Greenwich 06830 (mid-range to expensive), was remodeled and enlarged in 1900 by architect Stanford White — a friend of many American Impressionist painters. Each of the 22 guestrooms has a unique floor plan; the rate includes a continental breakfast.

In Norwalk, the **Meson Galicia** ℂ (203) 866-8800, 10 Wall Street, serves brilliantly prepared Spanish cuisine. A tapas meal is a popular choice. Open Tuesday to Friday for lunch; Tuesday to Sunday for dinner (expensive). Also in Norwalk is **Amberjacks Coastal Grill** ℂ (203) 853-4332, 99 Washington Street (mid-range), where tropical fruits and pungent Asian spices accent the New American cuisine. There is live jazz on Thursdays.

Just off Greenwich's main avenue, the **Elm Street Oyster House** ℂ (203) 629-5795, 11 West Elm Street, Greenwich, is open for dinner and offers daily fish specials along with fried oysters and excellent crab cakes (mid-range).

HOW TO GET THERE

The cities of Southwest Connecticut are reached via Interstate 95 and the Merritt Parkway (Route 15). Mileage from New York City is as follows: Greenwich 35 miles (56 km), Stamford 39 miles (63 km), Norwalk 47 miles (76 km), Wilton 53 miles (85 km), and Bridgeport 60 miles (97 km).

Amtrak TOLL-FREE (800) 872-7245 has convenient connections for Stamford and Bridgeport on its Washington–Boston line, and **Metro North** TOLL-FREE (800) 223-6052 operates several daily trains from New York's Grand Central Station with stops in Greenwich, Stamford, Darien, Norwalk and Westport; its terminus is in New Haven.

NEW HAVEN

Approaching New Haven, the sight that greets the eye is a sad one indeed: a junky waterfront, a halfhearted downtown area, a patchwork of dreary office towers and dilapidated neighborhoods. Yet despite its uninviting initial appearance, New Haven has a much to offer travelers. Theatergoers can enjoy outstanding performing arts for a fraction of the price of a New York production; there are several excellent museums and some tantalizing ethnic restaurants.

Most of what will interest the visitor centers on the tree-lined campus of Yale University, which covers 160 acres (65 hectares) in the central city and dominates New Haven both architecturally and culturally. The distinguished Ivy League school has about 12,000 students. Historically, about 15 graduates each year eventually become United States Congressmen. Renowned alumni include Nathan Hale, William Howard Taft, Noah Webster and George Bush Senior.

The city itself began as a Puritan settlement in 1638. The town was planned in classic fashion with nine squares. The center square today is the **New Haven Green** (the earliest Yale buildings are west of the Green), once a marketplace and pastureland.

It is surrounded by three churches built between 1812 and 1815, all with distinctive architectural styles: Federal, Georgian and Gothic Revival.

From 1703 to 1875, New Haven shared the designation of Connecticut's capital city with Hartford, and legislative sessions alternated between the two cities. After Eli Whitney created an assembly line here for manufacturing his cotton gin in 1794, New Haven gradually became a manufacturing center; that tradition continues.

WHAT TO SEE AND DO

The **Yale Visitor Information Center** ☾ (203) 432-2200, Dwight Hall, offers guided one-hour walking tours of the campus. The Old Campus contains Yale's first buildings, including Connecticut Hall, where Nathan Hale studied. Tours depart Monday to Friday at 10:30 AM and 2 PM, Saturday and Sunday at 1:30 PM. The center is open daily, and tours are free of charge.

In fact, all of the major cultural offerings of Yale are free of charge (donations suggested), including the **Yale University Art Gallery** ☾ (203) 432-0600, 1111 Chapel Street (at York Street). Founded in 1832, it's one of the finest small galleries in the country. Along with a collection of French Impressionist paintings (see CULTURAL KICKS, page 44 in YOUR CHOICE), the gallery exhibits works by patriot painter John Trumbull, as well as signal works by Van Gogh, Copley, Picasso, Hopper, Eakins and Lichtenstein. Open year-round Tuesday to Sunday.

Also on Yale campus, the **Peabody Museum of Natural History** ☾ (203) 432-5050, 170 Whitney Avenue, is a repository of ancient artifacts, with reconstructed dinosaur skeletons, Foucault's pendulum and dioramas telling the story of the Native Americans of Connecticut.

The distinctive architecture of Yale University graces a campus that draws some of the nation's most talented and ambitious students.

In nearby Hamden (about two miles or three kilometers from the New Haven Green), the **Eli Whitney Museum** ☎ (203) 777-1833, 915 Whitney Avenue, traces the history of American technology and invention with salutes to Whitney's (1765–1925) legacy as an inventor and manufacturer, as well as interpretive displays on the toy manufacturer A.C. Gilbert (1884–1961). Open Memorial Day to Labor Day daily from 11 AM to 4 PM, Labor Day to Memorial Day Wednesday, Friday and Sunday noon to 5 PM, Saturday 10 AM to 3 PM.

New Haven **shoppers** gravitate toward Chapel Street where there are a number of smart national chains (Ann Taylor, The Gap, J. Press) peddling the sort of merchandise that would Yale alumnus Brooke Shields might wear. The few small stores selling hip clothing and accessories are worth seeking out. Look for Archetype ☎ (203) 562-6772, at 265 College Street; and Endelman's Gallery ☎ (203) 776-2517, at 1014 Chapel Street.

NIGHTLIFE AND THE ARTS

Three major theaters prosper in New Haven: The venerable, 1,600-seat **Shubert Performing Arts Center** ☎ (203) 562-5666, 247 College Street, where some 200 Broadway shows have premiered over the years, has reemerged after a tough decade with a facelift and a strong artistic calendar. The Shubert presents a series of four or five Broadway shows each year. The **Long Wharf Theater** ☎ (203) 787-4282, 222 Sargent Drive, stages American modern classics (its inaugural show in 1965 was Arthur Miller's *The Crucible*); tickets are inexpensive and the quality of productions is consistently excellent. The **Yale Repertory Theater** ☎ (203) 432-1234, at the corner of Chapel and York streets, is located in a reconstructed Baptist church. The Yale Drama School's intimate 500-seat theater presents both student and professional repertory productions; the emphasis is on experimentation. Yale Rep alumni include actors Sigourney Weaver, Meryl Streep and Henry Winkler, and playwright Christopher Durang.

The **New Haven Symphony Orchestra** ☎ (203) 776-1444 often performs at Yale's Woolsey Hall, College and Grove streets.

Toad's Place ☎ (203) 624-6283, attracts national acts and is open every night with rock, R&B, jazz and blues; Saturday is dance-party night. **Koffee?** (see WHERE TO EAT, below) has an excellent acoustic lineup, while **café nine** ☎ (203) 789-8281, 250 State Street, hosts a weekly blues jam as well as regional rock bands. There are many more music venues. For listings, check the *New Haven Advocate*, a free, weekly arts and entertainment newspaper.

WHERE TO STAY

At graduation and matriculation (May and September), hotels in New Haven fill up early. If your trip will bring you here during these times, make reservations well in advance.

The Victorian-era **Three Chimneys Inn at Yale University** ☎ (203) 789-1201 FAX (203) 776-7363 E-MAIL chimneysnh@aol.com, 1201 Chapel Street, New Haven 06511, offers 10 exquisitely decorated guestrooms and breakfast (expensive).

A $30-million rehabilitation has garnered a Michelin Four-Star award for the 300-room **Omni New Haven** ☎ (203) 772-6664 TOLL-FREE (800) 843-6664 FAX (203) 776-2927, 155 Temple Street, New Haven 06510. You might think such a large, modern hotel would have a swimming pool, but it doesn't. There is, however, a health club with weight-training equipment. The rooftop restaurant overlooks the Green (expensive).

Next to the Yale campus, and thus conveniently located for theater-going, museums and shopping, the **Colony Inn** ☎ (203) 776-1234 FAX (203) 772-2622, 1157 Chapel Street, New Haven 06511, is a smallish hotel with 86 rooms decorated in Colonial style (mid-range). The restaurant serves steaks and seafood, and there is live jazz on Saturdays.

WHERE TO EAT

The best restaurants in New Haven serve ethnic fare. **Tre Scalini** ☎ (203) 777-3373, 100 Wooster Street, offers new Italian cuisine with seafood rather than red sauce (mid-range). For some good Southern Italian *cucina*, there is **Consiglio's** ☎ (203) 865-4489, 165 Wooster Street, a third-generation family restaurant (mid-range).

Galileo's ℂ (203) 974-6858, The Omni New Haven, is a new nineteenth-floor restaurant with views of the New Haven Green and Long Island Sound. The Contemporary American cuisine emphasizes steaks and chops and is a notch or two up from the usual hotel fare (expensive).

Café Pika Tapas ℂ (203) 865-1933, 29 High Street, makes a zingy paella along with its tapas offerings; **Scoozi Trattoria and Wine Bar** ℂ (203) 776-8269, 1104 Chapel Street, serves excellent pasta and adventurous main courses; and **Bangkok Garden** ℂ (203) 789-8684, 172 York Street, has good Thai and savory satays (budget to mid-range).

New Haven has many good pizzerias, including **Modern Apizza Place** ℂ (203) 776-5306, 874 State Street, and **Frank Pepe Pizzeria** ℂ (203) 865-5762, 157 Wooster Street (budget to mid-range).

There are also some quirky and inexpensive places for lunch. As much an attraction as a place to eat, **Atticus Bookstore-Café** ℂ (203) 776-4040, 1082 Chapel Street, serves coffee and pastries, as well as soups and hero sandwiches, in the lofty company of the best selection of books in the state. **Koffee?** ℂ (203) 562-5454, 104 Audubon Street, has daily soup specials along with a mix and match menu of quiches and salads. **TJ's Breakaway Deli** ℂ (203) 865-5946, 24 Whitney Avenue, stacks inventive sandwiches, and the rack of magazines seems an invitation to hang out.

How to Get There

New Haven is 79 miles (127 km) from New York and 141 miles (226 km) from Boston at the junction of interstate highways 91 and 95. For **Amtrak** and **Commuter Rail** connections see under HOW TO GET THERE, page 198.

MID COAST: BRANFORD TO OLD LYME

Motorists on Interstate 95 tend to zip past the seashore communities of Branford, Old Saybrook, Guilford, Madison, and Old Lyme just as the Industrial Revolution bypassed these villages 100 years ago. A handful of lucky travelers, however, have discovered Route 1 which leads through and to the region with its maritime heritage, trim village greens, and its natural beauty: the pristine wetlands of New England's longest river and the sandy beaches, salt marshes and woodlands of Long Island Sound.

General Information

Informational materials can be obtained from the **Connecticut River Valley & Shoreline Visitors Council** ℂ (860) 347-0028 TOLL-FREE (800) 486-3346, 393 Main Street, Middletown 06457.

What to See and Do

Branford

From the shores of Branford the tiny, timbered Thimble Islands are visible on the horizon. Three outfits offer **sightseeing cruises** to the islands with narration detailing their history and pirate lore: Connecticut Sea Ventures ℂ (203) 397-3921, PO Box 3302, Branford 06405, operates from mid-June through Labor Day; Sea Mist Thimble Island Cruise ℂ (203) 488-8905, PO Box 3138, Branford 06405, runs from May through to October; and the *Volsunga IV* ℂ (203) 481-3345,

A green market blossoms at the Florence Griswold Museum in Old Lyme.

PO Box 3284, Branford 06405, runs from early May to early October.

Guilford

A well-preserved village green, the **Guilford Common**, is the chief attraction at Guilford. This expansive square is anchored by the weight of several imposing churches of various denominations. Historic homes, small galleries, and a bistro with lace-curtained windows combine to make the Common an inviting place for a stroll.

South of the Common, the **Henry Whitfield State Museum** ☎ (203) 453-2457, 248 Old Whitfield Street, is billed as the "oldest house in Connecticut and the oldest stone house in New England (1639)." This is misleading as the structure has been almost entirely rebuilt more than once. However, it is a marvelous restoration and well worth a visit. A paean to simplicity of form, the house was a mansion in its time. A low fieldstone wall surrounds the house, and ancient oaks shade its green lawns and herb garden. Within are seventeenth- and eighteenth-century furnishings. It is open February to mid-December, Wednesday to Sunday, mid-December to January by appointment. An admission fee is charged.

Madison

This seaside town of 5,000 inhabitants is the home of Art Carney, the man who played Ed Norton, the New York City sewer worker (or "underground engineer" as he referred to himself) in the *Honeymooners* comedy series.

A couple of more aged celebrities are remembered at two of the town's historic sites. The circa-1685 **Deacon John Grave House** ☎ (203) 245-4798, 581 Boston Post Road, Tuxis Farm, served over the years as a schoolhouse, wartime infirmary, weapons depot, inn, tavern and courtroom. Open summer Wednesday to Sunday; weekend afternoons in fall; winter by appointment. An admission fee is charged. The **Allis-Bushnell House and Museum** ☎ (203) 245-4567 and 245-1368, 853 Boston Post Road (Route 1), is a circa-1785 Colonial house, and the home of Cornelius Bushnell, who financed the building of the *Monitor*, the first ironclad warship, during the Civil War. Visiting hours are limited; call ahead.

Old Saybrook

Old Saybrook's elongated business district trails along Main Street south to Saybrook Point, a peninsula that juts into the mouth of the Connecticut River. The town has its quota of old houses including the 1767 **General William Hart House**, at 350 Main Street (admission free; open afternoons, June to September), headquarters of the Old Saybrook Historical Society ☎ (860) 395-1635. But Old Saybrook is better known as the site of some 400 **antique dealers** clustered in four centers: Essex-Saybrook Antiques Village, 345 Middlesex Turnpike (Route 154); Old Saybrook Antiques Center, 756 Middlesex Turnpike; Essex Town Line Antiques Village, 985 Middlesex Turnpike; and The Antiques Depot at Old Saybrook Train Station, 455 Boston Post Road (Route 1). Happy shopping.

Old Lyme

A must-see on the Connecticut Impressionist Trail (see CULTURAL KICKS, page 44 in YOUR CHOICE), the **Florence Griswold Museum** ☎ (860) 434-5542, 96 Lyme Street, was the site of one of America's most famous art colonies. This National Historic Landmark is a circa-1817 mansion with wall and door panels painted by boarders — including William Metcalfe and Childe Hassam, who perfected the color techniques that defined the style. Open Tuesday to Sunday April to December, Wednesday to Sunday January to March; an admission fee is charged.

SPORTS AND OUTDOOR ACTIVITIES

Jutting out into Long Island Sound, **Hammonasset Beach State Park** ☎ (203) 245-2785, Route 1 (Interstate 95, Exit 62), is a wonderful place to relax as well as to see the region's wildlife. The park's two miles (three kilometers) of sandy beach make for impressive walking, and more hiking trails crisscross the salt marshes and woods. There are excellent opportunities for birding here. The park's 1,000 acres (160 hectares) of marsh, woodland, grassland and seashore are the most diverse bird habitat in the state — 240 different species have been spotted; call for the schedule of weekly birding walks. There are facilities for swimming, saltwater fishing, scuba diving, hiking, and boating. The park

is open year-round from 8 AM to sunset; there is a fee for parking.

SHOPPING

The Guilford Handcraft Center ☎ (203) 453-5947, 411 Church Street (State Highway 77), is a school devoted to fine arts and crafts. Its Mill Gallery hosts seven annual exhibitions and sales of regional crafts including fiber arts, handmade hats, painted silk scarves, contemporary quilts, children's clothing, jewelry, mobiles and more. Open daily, year-round. Admission is free.

Two major new outlet malls draw **shoppers** to the region. The new Clinton Crossing Premium Outlets ☎ (860) 669-3066, at 20 Killingworth Turnpike, Clinton (just off of Interstate 95 on Route 81, Exit 63), has 70 stores representing leading designers and manufacturers such as Nike, Coach, Jones New York, and Lenox; while the Westbrook Factory Stores ☎ (860) 399-8656, Flat Rock Place (Exit 65 off Interstate 95) houses 80 retailers including Reebok, Timberland, Dockers, Corning/Revere, J. Crew, and Jockey. Open daily.

WHERE TO STAY AND EAT

A posh shoreline resort, the **Saybrook Point Inn & Spa** ☎ (860) 395-2000 TOLL-FREE (800)

Sculpted hedges sprout free-form on a patriotic Old Lyme lawn.

243-0212, 2 Bridge Street (Route 154), Old Saybrook 06475, is a complex built around an old inn on the marina (expensive). The 80 rooms decorated in English style are spacious and comfortable with unbeatable views; suites come equipped with Jacuzzis. There is a good restaurant, a lounge, a spa and fitness room, as well as indoor and outdoor pools, and bicycles available for guests' use.

The **Madison Beach Hotel** ☎ (203) 245-1404, 94 West Wharf Road, Madison 06443, is a restored nineteenth-century hostelry with

a small private beach. Having started its life as a boardinghouse for shipbuilders, it retains some of that era's ambiance in the painted wooden wainscoting, but the 35 rooms are otherwise lacking in character. The ocean views and balconies, however, do much to offset the featureless rooms (mid-range to expensive). The rate includes a continental breakfast. The Wharf restaurant — with outdoor dining in season — serves seafood (mid-range); and the hotel lounge offers raucous weekend entertainment. Closed January and February.

Old Lyme has two very good inns. Both charge mid-range rates and both are located in the historic district: The **Old Lyme Inn** ☎ (860) 434-2600 TOLL-FREE (800) 434-5352, 85 Lyme Street, Old Lyme 06371, is an 1850s Victorian mansion with five rooms in the main building and nine in the new addition; and the **Bee and Thistle Inn** ☎ (860) 434-1667 TOLL-FREE (800) 622-4946, 100 Lyme Street, Old Lyme 06371, is a restored 1756 residence on the banks of the Lieutenant River with 11 rooms and a cottage (budget to mid-range). The dining room specializes in seafood and duck dishes.

There is good value at the adorable **Maples Motel** ☎ (860) 399-9345, 1935 Boston Post Road, Westbrook 06498, with its 18 recently redecorated cabin efficiencies. It's a good place for families with its playground, outdoor pool, and beach access (budget).

Under new ownership, **Café Allegra** ☎ (203) 245-7773, 725 Boston Post Road (Route 1), in Madison, serves superb Italian cuisine. I don't mean pasta with red sauce; I mean jumbo shrimp wrapped in bacon, red snapper on a bed of spinach, and caramel cheesecake (if you dare). Reservations are recommended (moderate).

Seafood, pasta and meat dishes are on the card at **Terra Mar** ☎ (860) 395-2000 TOLL-FREE (800) 243-0212, Saybrook Point Inn, at 2 Bridge Street, Old Saybrook (mid-range). The dining room looks out on the marina; open for dinner nightly (expensive). For something more casual, go next door to **Dock & Dine** ☎ (860) 388-4665, College Street, Saybrook Point, Old Saybrook, where you can dock your party at a corner table and dine on a traditional New England shore dinner (budget).

In Guilford, **Cilantro** ☎ (203) 458-2555, 85 Whitfield Street, is a coffee roaster selling delicious deli sandwiches and cakes along with smoothies, juices and great coffee; while **The Place** ☎ (860) 453-9276, Route 1, Guilford, serves grilled seafood, chicken and steak — all cooked over an 18-ft (5-m) fire pit. Roasted clams, corn and lobsters get the same treatment. Seating is outdoors, and if you like you can do as the regulars do and bring a bottle of wine — you can even bring a tablecloth and candles if it's ambiance you want. There's a tent to dine under when the weather is moody. At **The Ribs at Bone Yard** ☎ (860) 388-6056, 1522 Boston Post Road, Old Saybrook, three varieties of tasty ribs are the house specialties.

HOW TO GET THERE

Old Saybrook is 113 miles (181 km) from New York and 138 miles (221 km) from Boston. For **Branford** take Exit 56 off Interstate 95. Follow the signs to Stony Creek, then follow signs to the town dock. Take Exit 58 for **Guilford**, then follow State Highway 77 South. To get to **Saybrook Point** in Old Saybrook take Route 154 off Route 1.

THE CONNECTICUT RIVER VALLEY

Flowing 410 miles (660 km) from the Canadian border to Long Island Sound, and neatly bisecting Connecticut into east and west — the Connecticut River links a cluster of quintessentially New England towns. For centuries, New Yorkers have come here to escape the hurry-scurry of America's largest city. Essex, Ivoryton, Chester and East Haddam, at 10 to 15 miles (16 to 24 km) from Long Island Sound, are within easy reach of the area's most sought-after attractions, and are endowed with restful country inns as well as the state's best restaurants. In summer, reservations are essential.

GENERAL INFORMATION

The **Connecticut River Valley & Shoreline Visitors Council** ☎ (860) 347-0028 TOLL-FREE (800) 486-3346 FAX (860) 704-2340 WEB SITE www.cttourism.org, at 393 Main Street,

OPPOSITE: "The Gris" in Essex. ABOVE: Gillette Castle is a Gothic rock pile.

Middletown 06457-3309, can supply you with armloads of information.

WHAT TO SEE AND DO

Essex

Visitors thronging the narrow streets of Essex seem to have a single idea in mind — to get an eyeful of one of the *100 Best Small Towns in America*, according to the book of the same name by Norman Crampton. Despite the crowds (parking can be difficult), it is a pleasant place to enjoy some fine boutiques, to explore elegant eighteenth-century houses, or to sit on the dock at the marina and watch the yachts coming and going.

While you're at the marina, you might want to check out the **Connecticut River Museum** ((860) 767-8269, 67 Main Street, Steamboat Dock, situated in an 1878 dock house. Focusing on the natural and human history of the river valley, the museum has ship models, prints, paintings and shipbuilding tools. Permanent and changing exhibits include a replica of the first submarine, the 1775 *Turtle*. Open Tuesday to Sunday; an admission fee is charged.

Essex is the point of embarkation for the **Essex Steam Train and Riverboat** ((860) 767-0103, which offers a tour of the river valley aboard a 1920s locomotive, followed by a cruise up the Connecticut River before returning by rail to the Essex Depot. It sounds glorious, but unless you're a railway buff you may be disappointed. The scenery is pleasant enough but the canned narration takes most of the joy out of it. The tour takes two and a half hours. Trips run from May to December. A fare is charged.

Every Friday from 3 PM until 6 PM (July to October), Essex has a **Farmer's Market** at the Main Street Park. It's a good place to pick up some Connecticut cheeses and baked goods.

Chester

More trendy shops, cappuccino bars and bookstores await you in Chester, where many of the shopkeepers are transplanted New Yorkers. Local artists show their works in several galleries. Look for a re-opening of the **Connecticut River Artisans Cooperative** ((860) 526-5575, a long-time stalwart in supporting the work of artists in crafts media.

East Haddam

The 1876 **Goodspeed Opera House** (see NIGHTLIFE AND THE ARTS, below) on the banks of the Connecticut River cuts a dashing figure when viewed from the water; inside, the beautifully restored Victorian auditorium offers acclaimed musicals. A night at the Goodspeed is one of the great pleasures of the region — a happy tradition since the grand old opera house was restored in the 1970s. Before curtain time, it's a thrill to get a peek at the scene shop and rehearsal rooms glowing and bustling with pre-show activity.

If you haven't already noticed, Connecticut abounds with thespians. One of the most celebrated tales in these parts is that of the actor William Gillette, a Hartford native famous for his portrayal of Sherlock Holmes. He built his gaudy fieldstone mansion, dubbed **Gillette Castle**, between 1914 and 1919 on 122 hilltop acres (49 hectares). The quasi-medieval rock pile commands a sweeping view of the Connecticut River and countryside, and is one of the region's most popular tourist attractions. Gillette instructed his executors "to see to it that the property not fall into the hands of some blithering saphead who has no conception of where he is or with what surrounded." In 1943, the state acquired Gillette Castle and designated the surrounding land for public use. **Gillette Castle State Park** ((860) 526-2336, 67 River Road (Route 9, Exit 6 or 7), Hadlyme, is a beautiful old-growth forest where you can walk, picnic and take carriage rides. Look for the impressive 94-ft (28-m)-tall "castle oak" on your right as you enter the park.

The mansion reopened in May 2002 after extensive renovations to restore it to its heyday when Gillette's vision reigned supreme. It is open from late May to Columbus Day, with guided tours daily. An admission fee is charged to tour the house.

NIGHTLIFE AND THE ARTS

Built in 1876 by William Goodspeed, a shipping magnate and theater lover, the **Goodspeed Opera House** ((860) 873-8668, Route 82, East Haddam, has received accolades for its presentation of American musicals. The Goodspeed has earned a reputation for taking the old familiar shows out of mothballs as well as for rethinking and restaging more obscure numbers. The company Equity productions of American musicals run Wednesday to Sunday from mid-April to December.

Its sister company is the **Goodspeed-at-Chester/Norma Terris Theater** ((860) 873-8668, North Main Street, in Chester. This is the place to see new musicals in an intimate country-

The Essex Steam Train and Riverboat excursion is a popular way to explore the area by river OPPOSITE and rail ABOVE.

side theater. In its 15-year history, the Goodspeed-at-Chester has launched 37 musicals. Shows take place in June, August and November from Wednesday to Sunday.

Another respected theater venue, the **Ivoryton Playhouse** ((860) 767-8348, 103 Main Street, Ivoryton, stages performances year-round, including children's theater and a variety of concerts. Summer stock runs from June to September.

WHERE TO STAY AND EAT

The green-shuttered **Griswold Inn** ((860) 767-1776, 36 Main Street, Essex 06426, is a tourist attraction in itself — filled with Antonio Jacobsen maritime art and Currier & Ives steamboat prints. "The Gris" has 16 rooms and 14 suites, some of which have fireplaces. Reservations to stay in the circa-1776 country inn must be made months in advance. To dine on the restaurant's wild game specialties, you will also have to make reservations early. The guest-room price (budget to mid-range) includes a continental breakfast. Each Monday night travelers and townies alike gather in the handsome Tap Room to belt out old sea shanties.

Critics have proclaimed the French restaurant at the **Copper Beech Inn** ((860) 767-0330, 46 Main Street, Ivoryton 06442, one of the best in the state. Named after the marvelous, ancient tree that shades the inn's front lawn, the 1890 country house has 13 rooms with antique furnishings; some rooms have Jacuzzi. The rate (expensive) includes a continental breakfast.

Three miles (five kilometers) from the town center, **The Inn at Chester** ((860) 526-9541 TOLL-FREE (800) 949-7829, 318 West Main Street, Chester 06412, is a late-eighteenth-century farmhouse adjacent to the state forest with access to miles of hiking trails. Here you'll find another of the region's best restaurants along with 42 guestrooms furnished with period antiques and reproductions; the rate includes a continental breakfast. A health club and tennis court complete the picture; pets are welcome (expensive).

Also in Chester, the lace-curtained **Restaurant du Village** ((860) 526-5301, 59 Main Street, Chester, prepares more of the region's best culinary offerings. The fare is French provincial (expensive) and dinner is served Wednesday to Sunday evening; reservations are recommended. **Fiddlers** ((860) 526-3210, 4 Water Street, Chester, has fine seafood for lunch and dinner, with poached, pan-sautéed and mesquite-grilled main courses.

HOW TO GET THERE

Route 9 connects the dots up the Connecticut River Valley. To get to Gillette Castle you can take Route 148 to the free auto **ferry** *Selden III* ((860) 443-3856, which carries eight cars across the Connecticut River from Chester to Hadlyme April to November. The crossing takes about five minutes. You can cross the river more conventionally above Chester on the Route 82 bridge.

THE LITCHFIELD HILLS

Country inns and resorts scattered along blue lakes set the backdrop for travelers in the rolling Litchfield Hills. Motorists come to enjoy the quiet country back roads, touring from one Colonial village to the next (see also THE OPEN ROAD, page 35 in YOUR CHOICE). Hikers arrive to trek part of the Appalachian Trail that stretches from Kent to Canaan, canoeists look forward to adventures on the Housatonic, and winter sports enthusiasts enjoy the gentle slopes and trails in Cornwall and Woodbury.

GENERAL INFORMATION

Informational materials can be obtained from the **Litchfield Hills Travel Council** ((860) 567-4506, PO Box 968, Litchfield 06759.

WHAT TO SEE AND DO

Litchfield

The white-steepled Congregational Church presides over the village green of Litchfield, one of the finest unrestored Colonial towns in the country. The borough of Litchfield has been declared a State Historic District owing to its architectural heritage and a distinguished line of visitors and residents: George Washington and General Lafayette both stayed here, and the homes of three famous Americans — Harriet Beecher Stowe, Ethan

Allen, and Henry Ward Beecher — are found on North Street.

Notable buildings on serene South Street include the 1753 home of Oliver Wolcott, signer of the Declaration of Independence; the birthplace of the revolutionary Ethan Allen; and the **Tapping Reeve House** ✆ (860) 567-8919 (one of the few historic properties regularly open to the public), the first law school in America, founded in 1784. Tapping Reeve claims as alumni two vice-presidents of the United States (Aaron Burr and John C. Calhoun), 101 members of Congress, 34 Chief Justices of the United States, 28 United States Senators and 14 state governors.

Haystack and Dennis Hill State Parks

Six miles (10 km) east of Canaan on Route 44, is **Haystack Mountain State Park**. One mile (one and a half kilometers) north of Norfolk on Route 272 a road leads halfway up the mountain; from there a 30-minute hike gets you to the top. A stone tower at the summit (1,716 ft or 523 m) affords a three-state view with Long Island Sound to the south, the Berkshires of Massachusetts to the north and the Adirondack peaks of New York to the west. Another summit pavilion, in **Dennis Hill State Park**, south of Norfolk on Route 272, looks out over Haystack Mountain, the Green Mountains, and part of New Hampshire. Besides conquering hilltops, visitors to these parks have ample opportunity for hiking and picnicking.

Housatonic Meadows State Park

In the heart of the Housatonic Valley, Housatonic Meadows State Park ✆ (860) 672-6772, Route 7, lies amid rock-strewn hills. Tall pines shade the banks of the river, prized by fly fishermen in-the-know. There is hiking on the Pine Knob Loop Trail, which joins the Appalachian Trail. Picnicking, canoeing and riverside camping are popular activities. Open year-round from 8 AM to sunset.

Kent

On the banks of the Housatonic River, Kent boasts an erstwhile train station in the town center, one traffic light and (at last count): 10 art galleries, eight antique shops, 25 shops and boutiques, a waterfall, a river and three state parks.

The covered **Bull's Bridge** spans the Housatonic four miles (six kilometers) south of Kent, stretching into New York State. North of Kent center, the **Sloane-Stanley Museum** ✆ (860) 927-3849 and 566-3005,

A denizen of a pig farm in Litchfield County.

Route 7, displays handmade tools used by settlers. The grounds include the ruins of the nineteenth-century Kent Furnace. Open mid-May through October, Wednesday to Sunday; an admission fee is charged.

Continuing north on Route 7, you arrive at **Kent Falls State Park** ☎ (860) 927-3288, with its whitewater cascades — one of the most photographed natural areas in the state. A gentle, stepped pathway runs parallel to the waterfalls, offering views at all levels. There are facilities for swimming and picnicking. Open daily 8 AM to sunset; there is a fee for parking.

SPORTS AND OUTDOOR ACTIVITIES

Ski areas in the hills include the Mohawk Mountain Ski Area ☎ (860) 672-6000, off Route 4, Cornwall, and the Woodbury Ski Area ☎ (203) 263-2203, Route 47, Woodbury. **Horseback riding** is a wonderful way to see the countryside: contact Pie Hill Equestrian Center ☎ (860) 491-3444, Pie Hill Road, in Goshen; or Lee's Riding Stable ☎ (860) 567-0785, in East Litchfield. There is **canoeing** and **kayaking** on your own or with guided trips offered by Clarke Outdoors ☎ (860) 672-6365, 163 Route 7, West Cornwall. Opportunities for **hiking** abound, including a pretty section of the **Appalachian Trail**, from Bear Mountain summit near the Massachusetts border to Ten Mile Hill summit at the New York state line. Major access points are in Salisbury, West Cornwall, Cornwall and Kent. See THE GREAT OUTDOORS, page 29 in YOUR CHOICE, for where to get maps and additional information.

WHERE TO STAY AND EAT

The **Mayflower Inn** ☎ (860) 868-9466 FAX (860) 868-1497 E-MAIL mayflower@relaischateaux.fr, 118 Woodbury Road, Washington 06793, is the region's posh address. Guestrooms, furnished with eighteenth- and nineteenth-century pieces, are accented with jewel-hued rugs and canopy beds; most have fireplaces and balconies. A health club, sauna, outdoor pool and tennis courts complete the picture (luxury).

The Colonial-era **Litchfield Inn** ☎ (860) 567-4503 TOLL-FREE (800) 499-3444 FAX (860) 567-5358, 432 Bantam Road (Route 202), Litchfield 06759, has 32 rooms, eight of which are "theme" rooms. The **Tollgate Hill Inn** ☎ (860) 567-4545 TOLL-FREE (800) 445-3903, Route 202 and Tollgate Road, Litchfield 06759, was established as a tavern in 1745 and moved to its present site in 1923. There are 20 rooms and suites, some with fireplaces. The inn accepts pets. Both of these inns serve excellent meals and charge mid-range rates.

The many-columned **White Hart** ☎ (860) 435-0030, Village Green, Routes 41 and 44,

Salisbury 06068, is a nineteenth-century inn (mid-range to expensive) situated in picturesque Salisbury. There are 26 rooms and two restaurants.

When you're not dining at one of the inns, you may want to consider these two standout restaurants: at the **Good News Café** ☎ (203) 266-4663, 694 Main Street South, Woodbury, chef Carole Peck whips up exceptional fare with fresh ingredients (expensive); try the pan-seared shrimp. The café serves lunch and dinner year round; closed Tuesday. Intense flavors are the rule at the **West Street Grill** ☎ (860) 567-3885, 43 West Street, Litchfield, where the ravioli with sweet chard is a favorite. Open year round for lunch and dinner (mid-range to expensive).

HOW TO GET THERE

Litchfield is 99 miles (158 km) from New York and 136 miles (218 km) from Boston. Thirty miles (50 km) from Hartford on Route 202, it is perhaps the best base for a visit to the region. Canaan, on Route 7 near the Massachusetts state line, and Kent, on Route 7 near the New York border, are the northern and southern access points to the region.

HARTFORD

Mark Twain is said to have remarked, "Of all the beautiful towns it has been my fortune to see, Hartford is chief." That was more than 100 years ago. Since then the fortunes of Connecticut's capital city (population 133,000) have fallen and risen and fallen again whilst dealing some hard economic blows. Yet it still offers some worthwhile features, most famously in the form of Twain's eccentric mansion, which still stands on a small green now, surrounded by skyscrapers.

Hartford's riverside location drew early attention. The city began as a Dutch trading post named Fort Good Hope in 1633. Puritans from the Massachusetts Bay Colony settled here two years later and the village eventually formed one-third of the Hartford Colony, its independence guaranteed by the Royal Charter of 1662. Legend says that when the royal governor demanded return of the charter 25 years later, it was stolen and hidden in the trunk of a massive oak tree, the famous "Charter Oak," that stood until felled by a storm in the 1850s. (A plaque now marks the oak's location.) The governor was recalled and the threat to independence overcome.

Hartford has been an insurance center since a ship owner took out a policy on his boat and cargo in the eighteenth-century. When the fire of 1835 destroyed more than 600 buildings in New York City, many insurance companies could not honor claims and went bankrupt. The Hartford Insurance Company's president visited every New York policyholder, assuring them that their claims would be quickly settled. Since then, the stability of its institutions, despite disasters such as the Great Chicago Fire and the San Francisco earthquake of 1906, has sealed Hartford's reputation as the insurance capital of the nation.

GENERAL INFORMATION

For information and assistance before your visit, contact the **Greater Hartford Tourism District** ((860) 244-8181 TOLL-FREE (800) 793-4480, 234 Murphy Road, Hartford 06114. Once in Hartford, contact **Heritage Trails Sightseeing** ((860) 677-8867 WEB SITE www.charteroaktree.com, an educational sightseeing group that offers several different mini-bus tours of historic Hartford, including trips focusing on colonial history, Samuel Colt and Mark Twain.

WHAT TO SEE AND DO

The **Wadsworth Athenæum** ((860) 278-2670, 600 Main Street, is the oldest public art museum in the country. It holds 165 permanent and visiting exhibits, comprising 50,000 art objects. Its collections include Egyptian and Roman artifacts, paintings by masters such as Goya and Rembrandt and a large selection of works by African-American artists and artists of the Hudson Valley School. Open Tuesday to Sunday; an admission fee is charged. Admission is free the first Thursday of each month, and there is free parking on weekends at the Travelers outdoor lot on Prospect Street.

OPPOSITE: The Harriet Beecher Stowe house has a lived-in character that provides insights into the pioneering author's life. ABOVE: Connecticut's State Capitol dome.

Real Art Ways ((860) 232-1006, Arbor Street (across from Pope Park), has expanded its offerings to include video, music and performance series along with annual events such as the winter Gender Bender Ball and a summer jazz festival.

Born and raised in Hannibal, Missouri, on the Mississippi River, Mark Twain (Samuel Clemens) arrived in Hartford in the 1870s. **The Mark Twain House** ((860) 247-0998, 351 Farmington Avenue (at Woodland Street) at Nook Farm, was built in 1874 for $131,000 and reflects the grand imagination of its owner. It is a tangle of gingerbread details, peaked towers, even decorative gems fashioned by Louis Comfort Tiffany. It still contains much of Twain's original furnishings. Twain left the house in 1891 after bad business investments forced him to move to Europe. It is open daily from Memorial Day to mid-October and in December. From January to May and from mid-October to November, it is open Wednesday to Monday.

On the same property is the comparatively modest Victorian **Harriet Beecher Stowe House** ((860) 522-9258, Farmington Avenue (at Forest Street), the final home of the woman who penned the classic and controversial novel *Uncle Tom's Cabin* in 1852. Memorabilia on display relates to Beecher Stowe's family and her work. Guided tours are offered. It is open daily from June to Columbus Day as well as during the month December; open Tuesday to Sunday the rest of the year. An admission fee is charged.

NIGHTLIFE AND THE ARTS

For arts and entertainment listings consult the free weekly, *Hartford Advocate*, available all around town, or check the Friday edition of the *Hartford Courant*. The **Hartford Stage** ((860) 527-5151, 50 Church Street, performs American classics, while **Theatreworks** ((860) 527-7838 delves into new, alternative, and experimental works. The **Bushnell Performing Arts Center** ((860) 987-5900, 166 Capitol Avenue, is the venue for the Hartford Ballet, the Hartford Symphony Orchestra and the Hartford Pops, as well as touring rock bands.

WHERE TO STAY AND EAT

A touch of Old Hartford, the 124-room **Goodwin Hotel** ((860) 246-7500 TOLL-FREE (800) 922-5006 FAX (860) 247-4576, 1 Haynes Street, Hartford 06103, has one of the city's most beautiful façades (expensive). Rooms have high ceilings and the restaurant is good.

The **Mark Twain Hostel** ((860) 523-7255 FAX (860) 233-1767, 131 Tremont Street, Hartford 06105, is a 42-bed Hostelling International facility located in the West End, within walking distance to city sights (budget).

There are a number of Indian restaurants in Hartford owing to its growing community of immigrants from the subcontinent. **Bombay's** ((860) 724-4282, 89A Arch Street, is perhaps the best of the bunch. The exterior isn't promising, but the food is spicy and flavorful.

Max Downtown ((860) 522-2530, 185 Asylum Street, serves chophouse classics and dishes inspired by Pacific Rim cuisines; and **The First and Last Tavern** ((860) 956-6000, 939 Maple Avenue, Hartford, has tasty brick-oven pizza worth going out of your way for.

HOW TO GET THERE

Hartford is located at the junction of interstate highways 84 and 91, approximately 102 miles (163 km) from Boston and 113 miles (181 km) from New York. **Bradley International Airport** ((860) 292-2000, on Interstate 91, at Exit 40 in Windsor Locks, serves the city.

An Alexander Calder sculpture at Wadsworth Athenæum.

Rhode Island

Just over one million people are squeezed into "Little Rhody," the nation's smallest state and one of its most densely populated. Bordered by Massachusetts to the north, Connecticut to the west and the Atlantic Ocean to the east, the land is hilly and rocky — very little of it given over to agriculture, leaving broad tracts of forestland in the interior. But it is to the sea that Rhode Island looks for its identity. Though the state is only 48 miles (77 km) across, it has 400 miles (664 km) of shoreline, and no part of the state is more than 25 miles (40 km) from salt water. Now you know why Rhode Island is called the Ocean State.

It was this seacoast that brought the bluebloods of America to Newport to build their magnificent estates along the ocean cliffs — a harbor town transformed into a haven for the millionaires of what Mark Twain scornfully called "the Gilded Age."

BACKGROUND

The Florentine navigator Giovanni da Verrazano (circa 1485–1528) explored Narragansett Bay in 1524 under commission from the King of France. Some say he named the area Rhode Island because of its resemblance to the island of Rhodes in the Aegean Sea. Another theory advances that it was Dutch explorer Adriaen Block who named the land *Roode Eylandt* for its red clay. In any case, one hundred years were to pass before the first colonists would arrive — from England, not from France. Among the first of these was Reverend William Blackstone, a nomadic preacher who came to Rhode Island when his lands on the Shawmut Peninsula were taken over by Puritan settlers.

Providence and Newport were to become leading seaports and centers of the infamous, "Triangular Trade" in the New World. Their merchants sent ships loaded with rum to Africa, traded the rum for slaves, then sailed to the West Indies where they traded slaves for sugar and molasses, the ingredients from which, in home ports, rum could again be distilled. By 1760, Newport had become New England's major port for slave-trading ships — an ignominious distinction in a colony founded on tenets of religious and individual freedom.

In the same century, Rhode Island's craggy coastline, islands and coves sheltered pirates and privateers who raided ships far out in the Atlantic; later in life, these scoundrels and their crews returned, often to reside ashore in respectable affluence.

In 1772, the resistance of Rhode Islanders to British rule became increasingly overt, as witnessed by the burning of the British ship *Gaspee*. After the Revolutionary War broke out, the colony joined in the long struggle for independence that culminated in the final American-French victory at Yorktown.

Despite its passion for independence (it was the first state to renounce allegiance to the Crown), Rhode Island was the last of the original 13 states to ratify the United States Constitution. The state enjoyed rapid growth and prosperity, becoming a major industrial center. By 1793, a large-scale textile industry had been established in Pawtucket, and by the mid-nineteenth century, it was producing almost 20 percent of the nation's cloth. By the turn of the twentieth century, immigrant workers and their families accounted for almost 70 percent of the state's population. When textile factories were drawn to the south by cheaper labor after World War II, the state was forced to diversify its economy.

Today health services, tourism and manufacturing — of costume jewelry and toys, among other things — are the pillars of Rhode Island's economy. Only one percent of Rhode Island's population is employed in agriculture, making it the nation's most industrialized state.

OPPOSITE: The *Compass Rose* at Bowen's Wharf, Newport Harbor. ABOVE: Ocean State fishermen.

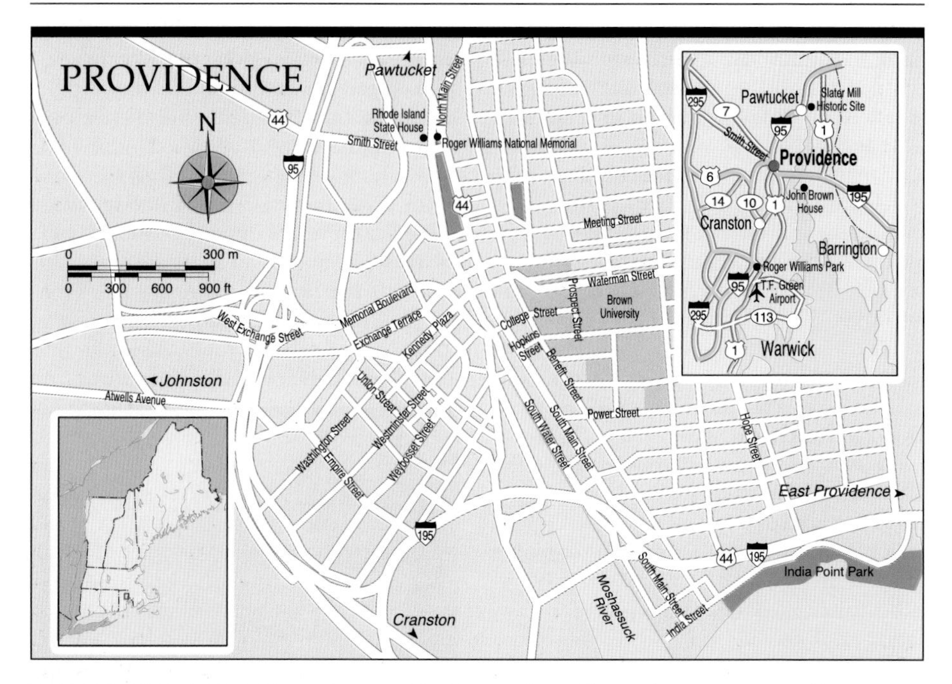

PROVIDENCE

Situated at the north end of Narragansett Bay, Providence is an enjoyable small city blessed with a rich history and plenty of college-town character. Capital of Rhode Island and the second largest city in New England, with a population of around 155,000, it has revamped its once sagging downtown district. *USA Today* dubbed it "Renaissance City," declaring the downtown "a bustling arts and entertainment district." Indeed, with the respected Trinity Repertory Theater and some of the best-preserved Federal-era houses in the country, Providence has much to offer.

BACKGROUND

After clashes with the Puritans forced him out of Massachusetts, clergyman Roger Williams founded Providence in 1636 on land given to him by the native Narragansetts, whom he had befriended. Williams' open-spirited humanity has endured in Providence's sunny streets and attractive dwellings and in the liberal character that gave rise to two of the nations finest schools, Brown University, and the Rhode Island School of Design.

Providence, however, earned its reputation as a seaport in the Triangular Trade (rum, slaves and sugar). When the China Trade opened in 1781, many Providence merchants made a fortune. By 1793, with maritime fortunes declining, Slater Mill (in suburban Pawtucket) became the first American mill to harness waterpower to spin cotton. Textile manufacture brought the city into the nineteenth century and Providence became an important industrial center, as it remains today.

GENERAL INFORMATION

For informational materials on Providence and the vicinity contact the **Providence/ Warwick Convention & Visitors Bureau** ((401) 274-1636 TOLL-FREE (800) 233-1636 FAX (401) 351-2090 E-MAIL information@ goprovidence .com. In Providence, you can drop-in on the **Providence Information Center**, which is within the city center at Waterplace Park.

WHAT TO SEE AND DO

A walking tour of the downtown district can begin at **City Hall** ((401) 421-7740, Kennedy Plaza. One of the focal points here is the new

Fleet Skating Rink, where skaters glide in winter and spin in summer against the backdrop of the Providence skyline. Striking out south of Kennedy Plaza is the **Lederer Theater** at 201 Washington Street, a flamboyant Italianate structure of terracotta arches decorated in white and pale green. Built in 1917 as a vaudeville house, it's now home to the Trinity Repertory Company (see NIGHTLIFE AND THE ARTS, below), one of the finest regional theater companies in the nation. East of Kennedy Plaza, **The Arcade** ☎ (401) 598-1199, 65 Weybosset Street, claims to be "the country's oldest indoor shopping mall." It is the sole survivor of several Greek Revival-style temples of trade built in America in the early 1800s. Today it is a marketplace packed with shops and eateries.

Moving north is the unmistakable profile of Constitution Hill, upon which rests the **Rhode Island State House** ☎ (401) 222-2357, 82 Smith Street (between Francis and Hayes), with its gleaming white marble façade. The capitol was built in 1891 and its cupola is one of the largest unsupported domes in the world. The building houses the original royal Charter of 1663 and, of course, legislative chambers and the governor's office. The gilded figure on top represents *Independent Man*, the state symbol. Inside is an imposing full-length portrait of George Washington, painted by Gilbert Stuart (1755–1828), a Rhode Island native. Self-guided tours are possible on weekdays from 8:30 AM to 4:30 PM; guided tours are available by appointment.

Two hundred yards (218 m) east of the State House, across the narrow Moshassuck River, the **Roger Williams National Memorial** ☎ (401) 521-7266, 282 North Main Street (corner of Smith Street), is the site of the original Providence settlement in 1636. This four-and-a-half-acre (two-hectare) landscaped park honors the colony's founder. You'll find a visitor center in the Antram-Gray House (1730) where there are interpretive exhibits and a video snippet recounting Williams' life; admission is free. A few blocks to the south stands the **Meeting House of the First Baptist Church in America** at 75 North Main Street (corner Waterman Street), a preserved 1775 Colonial church designed by Joseph Brown; Roger Williams established the church in 1638.

At the foot of College Hill (South Water and College streets) is Market House, a red-brick structure built in 1773 that served as the political and commercial center of colonial Providence. It was also the site of the Providence Tea Party, where on March 2, 1775, revolutionaries burned hundreds of pounds of British tea in an act of defiance against the Crown. The house is part of Rhode Island School of Design or RISD (pronounced "RIZ-dee"), one of the country's most prestigious art and design schools. Also part of the school, the **RISD Museum of Art** ☎ (401) 454-6500, 224 Benefit Street (between College and Waterman streets), houses more than 100,000 artworks and stages frequent temporary exhibitions. The collection ranges from Chinese terracotta sculpture and Greek statuary to French Impressionist painting, with Monet, Cézanne, Rodin, Picasso and Matisse all present and accounted for. Connoisseurs of Stuart, Copley and Sargent will enjoy the American wing, with its antique furniture and accessories painted by these three giants of American painting. There are RISD student and faculty exhibitions at the **Woods-Gerry Gallery** ☎ (401) 454-6500, at 2 College Street.

Benefit Street and its so-called "Mile of History" is an impressive concentration of original colonial buildings, beautifully restored eighteenth- and nineteenth-century Federal-era houses, churches and museums. Once a meandering dirt path that led to informal graveyards behind family dwellings, it was straightened and "improved for the benefit" of the people, so the official proclamation reads. The Providence Preservation Society ☎ (401) 831-7440, at 21 Meeting Street, offers booklets outlining a self-guided tour taking in some of the 100 or so dwellings (built by sea captains and colonial merchants) that line Benefit and adjoining streets. The **Providence Athenæum** ☎ (401) 421-6970, 251 Benefit Street, an 1838 building that resembles a Greek temple, is one of America's oldest libraries. The athenæum houses collections of Audubon prints and rare books. It's said that Edgar Allan Poe flirted with Sarah Helen Whitman in these library alcoves. The modest clapboard, 1707 Quaker-style **Governor Stephen Hopkins House** ☎ (401) 451-7067, Benefit and Hopkins Streets, is open to visitors. Hopkins was a signatory of the Declaration of Independence and 10-time governor of Rhode Island. Next is the **First Unitarian Church**, built in 1816, whose steeple holds the largest and heaviest bell cast by Paul Revere & Sons.

The **John Brown House** ☎ (401) 331-8575, 52 Power Street, east of Benefit Street, was described by John Quincy Adams as "the most magnificent and elegant mansion that I have ever seen on this continent." Built in 1786, the three-story Georgian mansion is named after its onetime owner, John Brown, one of four Brown brothers. Another brother, Moses, developed the Slater Mill; Joseph was a noted architect who designed some of Providence's most enduring landmarks; and Nicholas was the founder of Rhode Island College, now Brown University. All of the brothers played important roles in shaping the future of Providence.

North of the Brown House, at Prospect and Cottage Streets, is the 133-acre (54-hectare) College Hill campus of **Brown University** ☎ (401) 863-2703, 45 Prospect Street (near Angell Street). Chartered in 1764, it was named in honor of the Brown family, a generous contributor. The university's John Carter Brown Library holds the world's premier collection of early and colonial Americana. Guided tours of the campus are intended for prospective students, but anyone can join by calling ahead.

Further Afield

About 10 minutes from downtown, the **Roger Williams Park Zoo** ☎ (401) 785-9450 (park) or (401) 785-3510 (zoo), 100 Elmwood Avenue (Exit 17, Interstate 95), is a 430-acre (172-hectare) Victorian-era park that contains a museum of natural history as well as a planetarium, greenhouses, a carousel, a Rhode Island-themed miniature golf course, and a boathouse where visitors can rent paddleboats and miniature speed boats to tour the park's waterways. The zoo's population numbers nearly 1,000 animals, with more than 150 species on display. Most popular are the polar bears, sea lions, giraffes and penguins, along with the birds of the walk-through rainforest and the petting zoo babies — all found in representations of their natural habitats. The park is open daily 7 AM to 9 PM; the zoo is open daily, hours vary.

Site of one of the forerunners of New England's Industrial Revolution, Pawtucket's **Slater Mill Historic Site** ☎ (401) 725-8638, PO Box 696, 67 Roosevelt Avenue, offers guided tours including demonstrations of nineteenth-century machinery. It was the first American mill to harness water power to spin cotton.

SPORTS AND OUTDOOR ACTIVITIES

There's a **river walk** at Waterplace Park ☎ (401) 621-1992, the city's four-acre (one-and-a-half hectare) green space, which has a series of Venetian-style footbridges. The park is open dawn to dusk. You can enjoy more water views as well as fresh salt air along a 14.5-mile (23-km) **walking and bicycling path** which links East Providence to Bristol.

Baseball fans love the spunky Pawtucket Red Sox, or "Pawsox," the farm team for the Boston Red Sox. They play throughout the summer in Pawtucket, a few miles north of Providence, at McCoy Stadium ☎ (401) 724-7300, 1 Columbus Avenue.

NIGHTLIFE AND THE ARTS

Under the artistic direction of Oskar Eustis, the Tony Award-winning **Trinity Repertory Company** ☎ (401) 521-1100 or (401) 351-4242 (box office) FAX (401) 521-0447 E-MAIL info@trinityrep.com, 201 Washington Street, presents classic, contemporary and new works from September to June on two stages in the beautifully restored Lederer Theater. Performances are Wednesday to Saturday at 8 PM with matinees on selected days. The theater sometimes sells half-price tickets the day of the show, and students with valid identification receive a "rush" price of $10.

With Broadway plays and concerts, **Providence Performing Arts Center** ☎ (401) 421-2787, 220 Weybosset Street, is a 1928 theater that was originally Loew's Movie Palace.

Providence has an above-average club scene supporting a handful of hometown bands and bringing in national acts. In the jewelry district, **The Call** ☎ (401) 751-2255 E-MAIL thecall@thecall.com, 15 Elbow Street, and around the corner **The Century Lounge** (same phone), 150 Chestnut Street, hosts bands playing everything from alternative rock to zydeco. The **Met Café** ((401) 861-2142, 130 Union Street, is an active rock venue, as is **Lupo's Heartbreak Hotel** ((401) 272-5876, 239 Westminster Street.

The best thing about Providence nightlife is not its quantity but its quality — one that encourages offbeat enterprises such as **AS220** ((401) 831-9327 FAX (401) 454-7445 E-MAIL info@as220.org, 115 Empire Street, a prolific arts organization hosting nightly entertainment from improv comedy to bring-your-own-drum-and-bang-it nights to artsy television, poetry "zooms" and gotho-industrial-techno dance concerts. Then there is the **Cable Car Cinema & Café** ((401) 272-3970, 204 South Main Street, another one-of-a-kind enterprise, where you can relax on overstuffed couches and watch independent and foreign films. Every Friday night, local artists' slides are projected before show time. On other nights (call for details) there are pre-movie blues, folk and golden-oldies concerts.

WHERE TO STAY

Built in the 1920s, then transformed into a modern hotel, the **Providence Biltmore** ((401) 421-0700 TOLL-FREE (800) 294-7799 FAX (401) 331-0830, Kennedy Plaza, Providence 02903, was designed by the same firm that created New York's Grand Central Station. A princely marble staircase leads the way toward the 244 rooms, suites and efficiency apartments. There is a restaurant and lounge, and all the usual comforts and conveniences (mid-range to expensive).

Located within the Rhode Island Convention Center, the 364-room **Westin Hotel** ((401) 598-8000 TOLL-FREE (800) 937-8461 FAX (401) 598-8200, 1 West Exchange Street, Providence 02903, overlooks Constitution Hill and the historic downtown (expensive). There is a health spa, an indoor pool, lounges and the excellent Agora restaurant (see WHERE TO EAT, below).

There is good value at the **Days Hotel On The Harbor** ((401) 272-5577 TOLL-FREE (800) 528-9931 FAX (401) 272-5577, 220 India Point, Providence 02903. Many of the 136 rooms have views of Providence Harbor (budget to mid-range). A café serves from early to late.

In the historic district you'll find a number of bed and breakfast inns. The circa-1839 **Cady House** ((401) 273-5398, 127 Power Street, Providence 02908, is conveniently

Providence founder Roger Williams observes the skyline of New England's second largest city.

located on College Hill. The house is decorated throughout with antiques and folk art. All rooms have private bath (budget).

Where to Eat

Providence has, arguably, the best dining of any small city in America, thanks partly to chefs who trained at **Al Forno** ☎ (401) 273-9767, 577 South Main Street. Baked pastas are the signature dishes, but be prepared for a long wait to get in (mid-range to expensive).

The Federal Hill neighborhood, Providence's Little Italy (half a mile or under a kilometer west of downtown and Interstate 95), has many serviceable traditional Italian restaurants. Try **Grotta Azurra** ☎ (401) 272-9030, 210 Atwells Avenue (mid-range).

The most formal dining in town is at **Agora** ☎ (401) 598-8011, at the Westin, an award-winning gourmet "gathering place" (expensive) where blonde wood paneling, large ecru armchairs and waiters in gold-trimmed vests give the place a radiant elegance. The emphatically upscale menu attracts the city's politicians, developers and other high rollers.

The **Empire Restaurant** ☎ (401) 621-7911, 123 Empire Street, serves sophisticated Italian-influenced dishes (expensive).

How to Get There

Providence, bisected by Interstates 95 and 195, lies approximately 180 miles (288 km) from New York City and 50 miles (80 km) from Boston.

In Warwick, the **T.F. Green Airport** ☎ (401) 737-8222 is served by international and regional carriers (see GETTING THERE, page 341 in TRAVELERS' TIPS). It's a booming little airport that you should keep in mind when flying to New England. Ticket prices are often substantially cheaper than for flights into Boston Logan. There is an **airport van shuttle** ☎ (401) 737-2868 to downtown Providence and to Brown University; taxis and limousines are available and major rental car agencies are represented. It is a 12-minute drive from downtown Providence, and 25 minutes to Newport.

You can take **Amtrak** ☎ (401) 727-7379 TOLL-FREE (800) 872-7245 from Boston, New York or Washington, DC, on the *Northeast Corridor* line. The new High-Speed rail service whisks visitors to and from Providence Station (adjacent to Waterplace Park at 100 Gaspee Street). Direct **MBTA Commuter Rail** TOLL-FREE (800) 392-6100 service is also available to Boston.

NEWPORT

Home of the rich and famous, former home of the America's Cup and present-day home of the international jazz festival, Newport is also prized for its colonial district. Though the British nearly flattened the city during the Revolutionary War, preservation efforts have revived scores of colonial-era buildings including the Touro Synagogue, the oldest synagogue in the United States and a National Historic Landmark.

Pre-Revolutionary southern plantation owners were the first to discover Newport's summer pleasures as they exchanged the intense heat of the south for refreshing ocean breezes. Following the Civil War, such scions of American wealth as the Astors and the Vanderbilts arrived, building summer "cottages" and entertaining their friends with picnics and parties, caviar and champagne, in keeping with the excesses of the age. Today, no visit to Newport is complete without a tour of at least one of these mansions.

General information

Stop by the comprehensive Visitor Information Center run by the **Newport County Convention and Visitors Bureau** ☎ (401) 845-9123 TOLL-FREE (800) 976-5122 FAX (401) 849-0291 E-MAIL info@GoNewport.com, 23 America's Cup Avenue, Newport 02840, to see an orientation film, rent self-guided cassette tours, consult with travel counselors, or to pick up a pile of useful brochures and maps.

What to See and Do

The Cottages

Although scores of mansions existed at the height Newport's glory, only a dozen or so remain, of which eight are maintained by the **Preservation Society of Newport** ☎ (401) 847-1000, 424 Bellevue Avenue. Tickets,

available at the houses and at the Visitors Center on America's Cup Avenue (see above), range in price depending on the house and the season. The society offers combination admission tickets for all eight houses. Each house tour takes from 45 minutes to an hour. The Preservation Society also maintains the Green Animals Topiary Gardens in nearby Portsmouth.

Largest and most spectacular of the Newport summer cottages, **The Breakers** was built in 1895 for Cornelius Vanderbilt and designed by architect Richard Morris Hunt. It replicates a sixteenth-century northern Italian palace, and has 70 rooms crammed with marble, alabaster, gilding, mosaics and stained glass. Magnificent grounds overlook the Atlantic Ocean. The **Marble House**, on Bellevue Avenue, was built in 1892 as a gift for the wife of William K. Vanderbilt. Also a Hunt design, it was called "the sumptuous palace by the sea" and features a dazzling gold ballroom in the French style. Also on Bellevue Avenue, **The Elms** was completed in 1901 for Pennsylvania coal king Edward Julius Berwind, modeled after the Château d'Asnières near Paris. Another Bellevue Avenue beauty, **Rosecliff**, with its heart-shaped staircase and gardens, was featured in the film *The Great Gatsby*.

The list of cottages goes on, but whatever you do, take time for the **Cliff Walk**, a three-and-a-half-mile (five-and-a-half-kilometer)

The Astors' Beechwood Mansion, one of Newport's pleasure palaces dating from an era that Mark Twain dubbed sarcastically "the Gilded Age."

coastal path that hugs the craggy shoreline along Rhode Island Sound. From its starting point off Memorial Boulevard (near Newport Beach) to its terminus on a side street off Bellevue Avenue, the walk is a narrow strip of public land that separates estates — such as The Breakers, Rosecliff, Marble House — and the campus of Salve Regina College from the sea, offering inspiring views. For additional information on the Cliff Walk call ((401) 845-9123 TOLL-FREE (800) 976-5122.

Other Attractions

The Newport Casino, facing Bellevue Avenue, was America's most exclusive country club in the 1880s. Now it houses the **International Tennis Hall of Fame** ((401) 849-3990, 194 Bellevue Avenue. American lawn tennis started at the casino some 100 years ago, and the first national championships were held on its grassy courts from 1881 until 1915, when the tournament moved to Forest Hills, New York. Hall of Fame exhibits include Davis Cup memorabilia, historical displays, and equipment exhibits. Outside the main building, the Casino's dozen grass courts stretch across to the restored "court tennis" court, where you can see how the "sport of kings" was played in England and Europe during the thirteenth century. The museum is open daily year-round (except during tournaments); an admission fee is charged.

At Fort Adams State Park, America's Cup memorabilia is housed at the **Museum of Yachting** ((401) 847-1018, worth a visit for its spectacular waterfront location on Ocean Drive. Within is a display of Newport's yachting heritage, with small craft, ship models, costumes and photographs. Open daily, mid-May through October.

Among Newport's great treasures is its colonial architecture, especially evident in the Point and Historic Hill neighborhoods. The 1748 **Hunter House** ((401) 847-1000, 54 Washington Street, near the Goat Island Causeway, has been called "one of the 10 best examples of residential colonial architecture in America." Headquarters of the French Navy during the American Revolution, the building now houses period silver, furniture, and portraits. The 1726 **Trinity Church** ((401) 846-0660, Queen Anne Square (Spring and Church Streets) with its tall white colonial spire, is based on a Christopher Wren design and is a landmark visible for miles.

The **Touro Synagogue** ((401) 847-4794, 85 Touro Street, was the first ever built in America (1763). The building stands at an angle because it faces toward Jerusalem, as is the tradition for Orthodox synagogues. On display inside is a 500-year-old Torah. Guided tours are offered year-round; call for hours. Next door at No. 82 is the **Newport Historical Society** ((401) 846-0813, with displays of colonial Newport decorative arts and furnishings. The society offers an **architectural walking tour** at 10 AM on Friday and Saturday mornings from May to October; a fee is charged.

There are dozens of **art galleries** in Newport, as well as many antique and craft shops. Visitors who wish to take home a memento of Newport history should head to "**Antique Alley**," a cluster of antique shops grouped on Thames and Spring Streets; especially good antique hunting is found on Franklin Street in the historic "Hill" section of town a short distance from the extensive waterfront.

Tours and Excursions

Sightseeing cruises set sail daily (May to October) from Goat Island Marina, off Washington Street and other docks. Cruises take you past the mansion-dotted coastline of Newport, the once pirate-infested shores of Jamestown, the towering Newport Bridge and Fort Adams, guardian of the harbor. The *Viking Queen* ((401) 847-6921 offers one-hour cruises around Newport Bay and Rhode Island Sound; the *Spirit of Newport* is a multi-deck cruise ship (contact Newport Navigation ((401) 849-3575, Treadway Inn Marina) with one-hour narrated cruises on Narragansett Bay and Newport Harbor; and Oldport Marine Harbor Tours ((401) 849-2111, America's Cup Avenue, runs one-hour cruises of Newport Harbor aboard the *Amazing Grace*.

A side trip to **Jamestown** (established in 1678), three miles (five kilometers) west of Newport on Conanicut Island, can include a drive along its southern tip; there are superb views across Narragansett Bay from Beaver Trail Lighthouse, including **Fort**

Wetherhill — built on 100-ft-high (30-m) granite cliffs — and Mackerel Cove.

WHERE TO STAY

Newport has an extraordinary number of varied accommodations, many of them wonderful old inns. The city also has more than 60 bed-and-breakfast establishments. To find one that suits your tastes, call **Bed & Breakfast, Newport** ☎ (401) 846-5408; **Bed & Breakfast Registry at Newport** ☎ (401) 846-0362; or **Newport Historic Inns** ☎ (401) 846-7666. You might also consider inquiring at the Visitor Center (see GENERAL INFORMATION, page 222) about lodging in nearby Middletown where rates tend to be lower than in Newport.

The most romantic spot in Newport, the **Cliffside Inn** ☎ (401) 847-1811 TOLL-FREE (800) 845-1811 FAX (401) 848-5850, 2 Seaview Avenue (near Cliff Avenue), Newport 02840, was the home of Beatrice Turner, a reclusive painter who left a legacy of art work, which remains to decorate the common areas (expensive to luxury).

The splendidly situated **Castle Hill Inn and Resort** ☎ (401) 849-3800 TOLL-FREE (888) 466-1355 FAX (401) 849-3838 E-MAIL info@castlehillinn.com, 590 Ocean Drive, Newport 02840, has 10 rooms in a Victorian mansion with beautiful views and fine dining. This handsome retreat rests on 40 acres (16 hectares) of shoreline hugging Narragansett Bay and the Atlantic Ocean. Reservations should be made well in advance. Sunday brunch is heavenly (expensive to luxury).

The Georgian-style **Hotel Viking** ☎ (401) 847-3300 TOLL-FREE (800) 556-7126, in the center of town, 1 Bellevue Avenue, Newport 02840, has been renovated to become a luxury property. Facilities include indoor pool, exercise room and free parking. The rooftop bar looks out over the harbor. It is a member of the Historic Inns of America (luxury).

Newport's Cliff Walk.

WHERE TO EAT

As in every other much-visited New England town, you'll need dinner reservations in Newport. You may also need something that's rarely required elsewhere: formal attire. After dinner, it's time for a stroll along Thames Street.

La Petite Auberge ☎ (401) 849-6669, 19 Charles Street, is one of New England's most appealing classical French restaurants. Built in 1714, the building features a "hide-

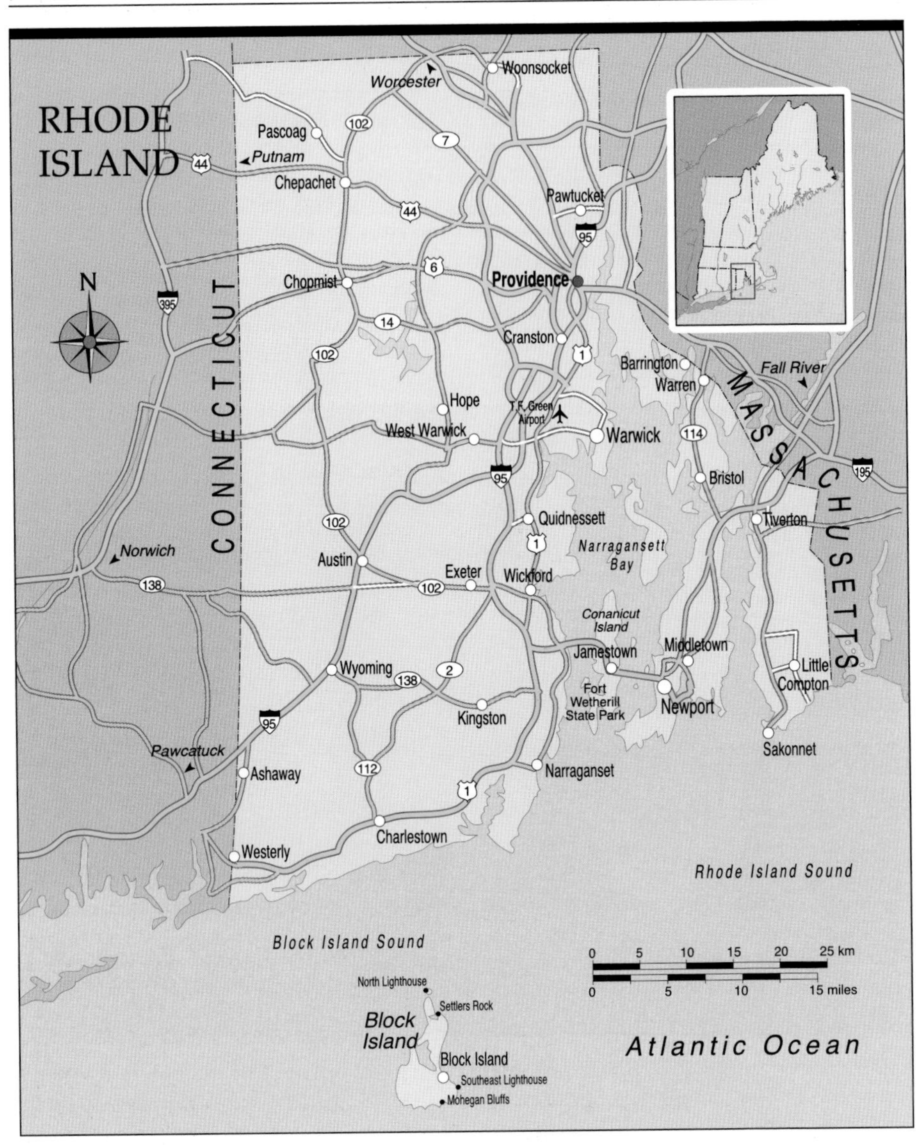

away" side café as well as the main dining areas (expensive).

You can dine in a formal colonial setting at the old **White Horse Tavern** ☎ (401) 849-3600, at the corner Marlborough Street and Farewell streets. Many visitors say a trip to Newport is not complete without a meal here, one of the nation's oldest operating taverns. Jacket required at dinner (expensive).

The **Chart House** ☎ (401) 849-7555, in the harbor area, serves local seafood and steaks. They're famed for the Chart House potpie — a deep dish of lobster, tiger shrimp and sea scallops with vegetables in a sherry cream sauce. There is outdoor seating in season (expensive).

The friendly **Salvation Café** ☎ (401) 847-2620, 140 Broadway, serves an eclectic cuisine that includes many vegetarian options. The authentic Salvation Army decor is a hoot (mid-range).

Via Via II ☎ (401) 848-0880, 372 Thames Street, is Newport's best pizzeria, while the best Italian restaurant is **Puerini's** ☎ (401) 847-5506, 24 Memorial Boulevard, serving both new and classic fare. It's quite popular, but aficionados say it is worth the wait (mid-range).

Sea Shai ☎ (401) 849-5180, 474 Aquidneck Avenue, serves fresh seafood along with Japanese and Korean main courses, and has a sushi bar with local and traditional selections (mid-range).

Diners at **Poor Richard's** ☎ (401) 846-8768, 254 Thames Street, sit in church pews and order delicious sandwiches. Don't pass up the carrot cake (budget).

If you're not up for brunch at the Castle Hill Inn (see WHERE TO STAY, above), you might care to tuck in to a much less expensive meal at the very townie **Franklin Spa** ☎ (401) 847-3540, 229 Spring Street (budget).

The menu at **Muriel's** ☎ (401) 849-7780, on the corner of Spring and Touro streets, brims with temptations, such as Belgian waffle topped with lemon whipped cream, and patrons idle the morning away at wooden booths. The decor is classically New England, lace curtains and all, except for the plastic mannequins gazing at you from the corner. Open for breakfast Monday to Saturday 8 AM to 11:30 AM, Sunday 9 AM to 3 PM (budget).

HOW TO GET THERE

Newport is 115 miles (184 km) northeast of New Haven and 75 miles (120 km) south of Boston. Motorists coming from the north will follow State Highways 136 and 114 through Bristol to Newport. From the south, it's Route 1 to State Highway 38 through Jamestown and over the Narragansett Bay toll bridge.

BLOCK ISLAND

Situated about 12 miles (19 km) south of the mainland off Point Judith, Block Island is a colorful tableau of ocean-side cliffs, shifting sand dunes, perfumed fields of honeysuckle and spectacular annual spring and fall bird migrations. The 11-sq-mile (28-sq-km) island has milder summer temperatures than the mainland. Its miles of beach and hundreds of spring-fed ponds are rarely crowded even at the height of the tourist season, and superb deep-sea fishing can be had in the island's waters. One quarter of the island is preservation land, where rare birds and one-of-a-kind habitats can be observed and enjoyed.

GENERAL INFORMATION

For informational materials in advance of your trip contact the **Block Island Chamber of Commerce** ☎ (401) 466-2982 TOLL-FREE (800) 383-2474 WEB SITE www.blockislandchamber.com, Drawer D, Water Street, Block Island 02807. They have staff on hand, most of whom are year-round residents of Block Island, to help you plan your trip. Once on the island, you can visit them at their office on Water Street or at the information booth at Old Harbor landing.

Getting Around

There is a strict limit on the number of cars that may be brought onto the island. You're best advised to leave the vehicle behind and enjoy this manageable island on foot and on two wheels. **Taxi tours** (pick them up near Old Harbor ferry) are gaining popularity with visitors who want a lift but prefer to leave the driving to someone else. A round trip lasts a bit more than an hour, and drivers will usually let you stop for photographs.

For cyclists, rentals are available at the **Old Harbor Bike Shop** ☎ (401) 466-2029, near the ferry dock. They also rent mopeds, cars, vans, and jeeps. Rentals are available as well at **Block Island Bike & Car Rental** ☎ (401) 466-2297, Ocean Avenue; and **Island Moped and Bike** ☎ (401) 466-2700, Water Street, directly behind the Harborside Inn.

WHAT TO SEE AND DO

Most people who come to Block Island head straight for the beach. Corn Neck Road leads north out of town along the two-mile stretch of **Crescent Beach**, where you'll find the island's best swimming. It's actually a strip of three separate beaches, each with its distinctive personality. The civilized Benson Beach has chair and umbrella rentals, showers and a snack bar. Scotch Beach, a little further on, is more isolated as it is reached by a series of dune paths. Finally, Mansion Beach is located beneath cliffs and the ruins of a former ocean-side estate. The deserted beaches along the western shore are also appealing, but caution should be exercised because of the strong undertow and

rugged surf. Swimmers can also explore some 350 freshwater ponds that dot the island's interior.

A trip to **Mohegan Bluffs** on the island's south shore is a required part of the island experience; multicolored clay cliffs 200 ft (61 m) in height stretch for several miles along the shore, offering a spectacular ocean vista, with steep walking paths to the beaches that rim the coastline below. Not far away is **Palatine Graves**, east of Dickens Point, said to be the burial grounds of eighteenth-century Dutch immigrants. **Settlers' Rock**, resting on the shore of Cow Cove, is the island's Plymouth Rock, commemorating the arrival of the first settlers in 1661. East of the bluffs stands the **Southeast Lighthouse**, which was moved 100 yards (91 m) inland a few years ago to save it from an eroding shoreline. Built in 1874, it was one of the most powerful beacons on the east coast, visible from 30 miles (48 km) out to sea.

Much of the north shore is a bird and wildlife refuge. An old stone lighthouse on Sandy Point can be reached along a sandy path. The restored **North Light** is a prime spot for birding and sunset vigils.

The island is superb **walking and hiking** country. The Greenway, a network of trails that wind through park, conservancy, and private lands starts mid-island and ends on the south shore.

Block Island is well known for its fish-filled waters. Charter boats are available for

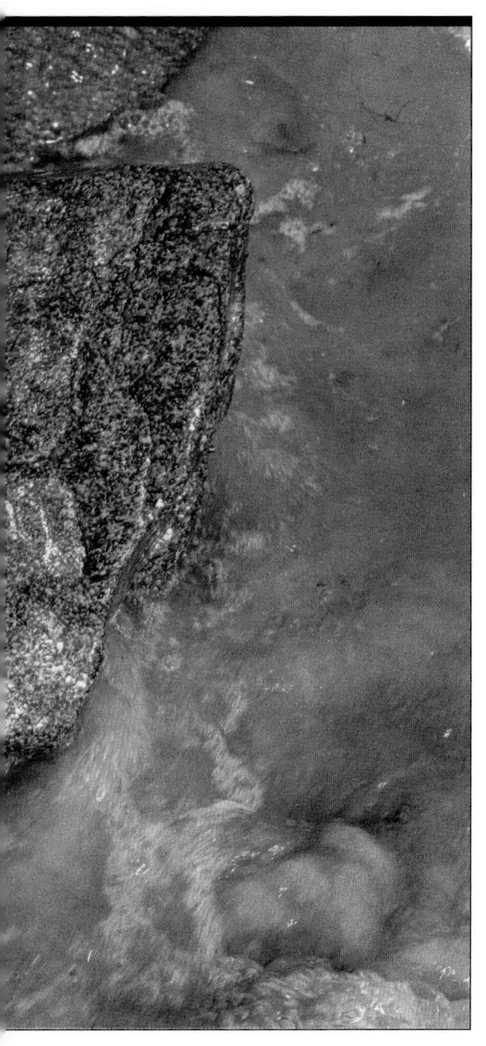

deep-sea fishing or surfcasting off the coast for bass. Freshwater ponds in the interior have bass, perch, and pickerel. You'll need to pickup a license at Town Hall.

WHERE TO STAY

The **Atlantic Inn** ☎ (401) 466-5883 TOLL-FREE (800) 224-7422 FAX (401) 466-5678, High Street, Block Island 02807 (expensive), was built in 1879 and has a sweeping porch on six landscaped hilltop acres (two and a half hectares) with spectacular ocean views. There are tennis courts, a croquet course, horseshoes and Victorian gardens, and it is located near beaches. There is a restaurant and bar. It is open from April to October (expensive). Off-season rates are lower and include a fresh-baked continental buffet breakfast.

The 49-room **Spring House** ☎ (401) 466-5844 TOLL-FREE (800) 234-9263, Spring Street, Block Island 02807, one of the island's best-known hotels, has been greeting visitors since 1852; its wraparound verandah offers a fine view of the Atlantic (expensive to luxury).

WHERE TO EAT

If you're looking for fine dining, try the **Atlantic Inn Restaurant** ☎ (401) 466-5883, High Street, where the cuisine is accompanied by ocean views. The **Hotel Manisses** ☎ (401) 466-2836, Spring Street, uses fresh vegetables and herbs from the hotel garden in its American cuisine. The **Spring House Hotel** ☎ (401) 5844, Spring Street, serves steaks and chops in a dining room that overlooks the ocean.

Block Island also has several good, inexpensive restaurants: **Ballard's Inn** ☎ (401) 466-2231, 42 Water Street, serves Italian and American cuisine; **Harborside Inn** ☎ (401) 466-5504, Water Street, has good seafood and outdoor seating overlooking the Old Harbor; and **Samuel Peckham Tavern** ☎ (401) 466-5458, New Harbor, has lobster specialties, steaks, and outdoor dining (mid-range to expensive).

HOW TO GET THERE

The **Block Island Ferry** ☎ (4010 783-4613 offers year-round service from Point Judith (Rhode Island) and summer service from Newport (Rhode Island) and New London (Connecticut).

Westerly Airport (Rhode Island) provides year-round air service to the island. There are summer flights from East Hampton and La Guardia Airports (New York), and Groton (Connecticut).

Seaspray and golden sunlight wash a section of New England's granite shore.

Vermont

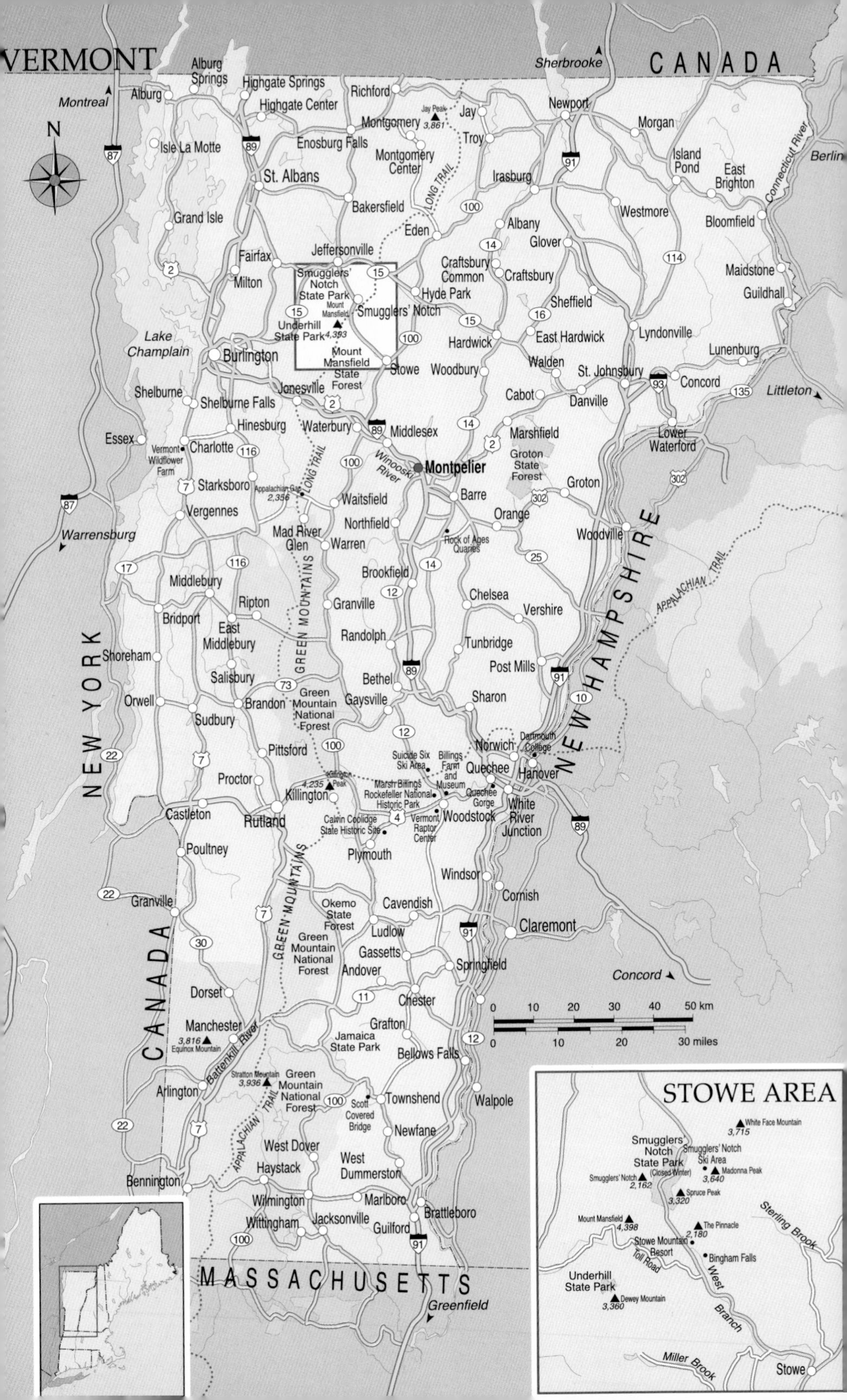

VERMONT
CANADA
Sherbrooke
Montreal
Alburg
Alburg Springs
Highgate Springs
Highgate Center
Richford
Jay Peak
3,861
Jay
Newport
Morgan
Isle La Motte
Enosburg Falls
Montgomery
Montgomery Center
Troy
Island Pond
East Brighton
Berlin
Connecticut River
St. Albans
Bakersfield
LONG TRAIL
Irasburg
Westmore
Bloomfield
Grand Isle
Eden
Albany
Glover
Jeffersonville
Fairfax
Milton
Craftsbury Common
Craftsbury
Maidstone
Guildhall
Smugglers' Notch State Park
Mount Mansfield
Smugglers' Notch
Hyde Park
Sheffield
Underhill State Park
4,393
Hardwick
East Hardwick
Lyndonville
Lake Champlain
Burlington
Mount Mansfield State Forest
Stowe
Woodbury
Walden
St. Johnsbury
Lunenburg
Concord
Cabot
Danville
Littleton
Jonesville
Shelburne
Shelburne Falls
Hinesburg
Waterbury
Middlesex
Marshfield
Lower Waterford
Essex
Vermont Wildflower Farm
Charlotte
Winooski River
Montpelier
Groton State Forest
Starksboro
Appalachian Gap
2,356
Waitsfield
Barre
Groton
Vergennes
Northfield
Orange
Warrensburg
Mad River Glen
Warren
Rock of Ages Quarries
Woodville
Brookfield
GREEN MOUNTAINS
Middlebury
Ripton
Chelsea
Granville
Vershire
APPALACHIAN TRAIL
Bridport
East Middlebury
Randolph
Tunbridge
NEW YORK
Shoreham
Salisbury
Bethel
Post Mills
Orwell
Brandon
Green Mountain National Forest
Gaysville
Sharon
NEW HAMPSHIRE
Sudbury
Pittsford
Suicide Six Ski Area
Billings Farm and Museum
Norwich
Dartmouth College
Proctor
Killington Peak
4,235
Killington
Marsh-Billings Rockefeller National Historic Park
Quechee
Quechee Gorge
Hanover
Castleton
Rutland
Calvin Coolidge State Historic Site
Vermont Raptor Center
Woodstock
White River Junction
Poultney
Plymouth
Windsor
Cornish
Granville
Okemo State Forest
Cavendish
Ludlow
Claremont
CANADA
Green Mountain National Forest
Gassetts
Springfield
Andover
Concord
Dorset
Chester
0 10 20 30 40 50 km
0 10 20 30 miles
Manchester
3,816
Equinox Mountain
Battenkill River
Jamaica State Park
Grafton
Bellows Falls
Stratton Mountain
3,936
Green Mountain National Forest
Arlington
Scott Covered Bridge
Townshend
Walpole
West Dover
Newfane
West Dummerston
Haystack
Bennington
Wilmington
Marlboro
Brattleboro
Wittingham
Jacksonville
Guilford
MASSACHUSETTS
Greenfield
STOWE AREA
White Face Mountain
3,715
Smugglers' Notch State Park
(Closed Winter)
Smugglers' Notch Ski Area
Smugglers' Notch
2,162
Madonna Peak
3,640
Spruce Peak
3,320
Mount Mansfield
4,398
The Pinnacle
2,180
Sterling Brook
Stowe Mountain Resort
Toll Road
Bingham Falls
West Branch
Underhill State Park
Dewey Mountain
3,360
Miller Brook
Stowe

Vermont is a land of small towns, family farms, gentle hills and forested mountains. Taken together the landscape creates a tableau that looks as if it were an illustration for a storybook. The state's pastoral landscapes are relatively free of sizable cities and centers of industry; Burlington, Vermont's largest community, has a population of less than 40,000; the capital city of Montpelier is the smallest capital in the nation. More than 200 covered bridges span rivulets and streams, and its maple groves have given rise to the state's claim to be the maple-syrup capital of the world.

Vermont's Green Mountains divide the Lake Champlain shore in the west from the Connecticut River Valley in the east. The 266,000-acre (90,400-hectare) Green Mountain National Forest, at the center of the state, is an outstanding recreational area. The ski center of New England, these mountains offer downhill and cross-country ski areas ranging from big, brash Killington to the smaller, traditional mountain village at Stowe. Hikers can follow the 260-mile (419-km) Long Trail that tops the Green Mountain ridge all the way from Massachusetts to Canada and intersects with the Appalachian Trail near Killington. The state is a bicycle-rider's dream with long stretches of back roads dotted with wayside inns. Vermont's fall color extravaganza is a major attraction.

Abraham Lincoln and his family, in the mid-nineteenth century, discovered the state's uncommon qualities. They often vacationed in the Green Mountain resort town of Manchester, in southern Vermont. (In fact Lincoln had reservations at Manchester's Equinox Hotel when he was assassinated in 1865.) Noted British historian Lord Bryce was also smitten with Vermont's charm when he called it the "Switzerland of North America."

BACKGROUND

The original inhabitants of Vermont — the Algonquin, Iroquois and Abenaki nations — are echoed in many of the state's place names. The state's name, however, is of French origin. Europeans arrived in Vermont in the early 1600s, when in 1609 French explorer Samuel de Champlain sailed into what is now known as Lake Champlain, describing what he saw from the lake that now bears his name as *les verts monts* (the green mountains). When the French pulled ashore, his Algonquin guides attacked their enemy, the Iroquois, and Champlain was forced to lend aid with his armed troops. *Les verts monts* became a bloody battleground between the French, the Indians and the colonial-minded British for the next 150 years. Only after the English defeated France at Quebec in 1759 did large numbers of colonists begin to settle in the territory.

Colonial Vermont was long embroiled in a territorial dispute with neighboring New York over land beyond Vermont's present borders. Ethan Allen, a patriot of the American Revolution, formed the Green Mountain Boys, a self-styled militia, to defend Vermont's position. The same band of intrepid fighters helped the New World colonists to rid themselves of British rule and proclaim their independence. Vermont then declared itself an "independent nation" in 1777 because of continuing land disputes with New York. Vermont remained independent for 14 years, conducting affairs with the United States as with a "foreign power." Finally, in 1791, it became the fourteenth state.

During the Civil War, Vermont lost proportionately more men than any other state in the Union. When, during the nineteenth century, many of its settlers joined the great westward migration, Vermont seemed destined to remain a small, sparsely populated farm state, albeit a beautiful one.

There's no substitute for the genuine article.

These days, Vermont seems to have latched on to a magic formula of economic strength and ecological husbandry. Small family farms still thrive here. The state legislature has enacted tough land-use, zoning and environmental protection laws, while permitting gay domestic unions (civil unions are a burgeoning business). Most visitors to Vermont come and go, enjoying the state's rustic beauty, without a notion that IBM has a large plant near Burlington, and that Barre is the manufacturing center for Amtrak's super-fast trains. But that's Vermont for you, a gentleman farmer with money in the bank.

BENNINGTON

Surrounded by the Taconic and Green Mountains, Bennington is southern Vermont's commercial center. A pleasant town with a handful of restaurants, Bennington's commercial district is not given over to tourist boutiques, but rather still caters to life's necessities.

Known as the headquarters of Ethan Allen's Green Mountain Boys, the town is also the home of Bennington College, one of the nation's leading experimental colleges.

GENERAL INFORMATION

The **Bennington Area Chamber of Commerce** ☎ (802) 447-3311 FAX (802) 447-1163 WEB SITE www.bennington.com, Veterans Memorial Drive, Bennington 05201, can provide any information you might want about the town and the surrounding area.

WHAT TO SEE AND DO

The **Bennington Museum** ☎ (802) 447-1571, West Main Street (Route 9), has, along with an assortment of Revolutionary War artifacts, the world's largest collection of paintings by "Grandma Moses." Anna Mary "Grandma" Robertson Moses started painting simple country scenes at the age of 70 and achieved instant fame; she continued working until her death at the age of 101. Open daily.

On Monument Circle, the **Old First Church**, built in 1805 with a three-tiered steeple, is an oft-photographed Bennington landmark. Behind the church, a cemetery contains the graves of soldiers who fell in the Battle of Bennington and that of poet Robert Frost (1874–1963), whose simple white marble tombstone is engraved with the epitaph: "I had a lover's quarrel with the world."

The **Bennington Battle Monument** dominates every view of the village. The 306-ft (93-m) blue limestone obelisk was completed in 1889 at a cost of $112,000; it marks the site of an important colonial supply point that was defended in a three-hour clash that was a turning point in the Revolutionary War. From the mountain's observation tower, visitors have superb views of Massachusetts' Berkshires, the Green Mountains, and New York. Not far from this monument is another to the **Old Catamount Tavern** built in 1775 where Ethan Allen's Green Mountain Boy planned the capture of Forts Ticonderoga and Crown Point.

To some, Bennington is synonymous with pottery. With their mission to "put art into the world every day," **Bennington Potters** ☎ (802) 447-7531, 324 County Street (off Route 7), has been producing functional and attractive pottery for nearly 50 years, making it the oldest clayware production house in the United States. Tours are offered from May through October on weekdays at 10:30 AM and 2:30 PM.

NIGHTLIFE AND THE ARTS

Now in its twenty-ninth season, the **Oldcastle Theater Company** ☎ (802) 447-0564 performs at the **Bennington Center for the Arts** ☎ (802) 442-7158, Route 9 and Gypsy Lane. The season runs from March to October with musicals, classics, and new plays on the bill. The art complex also hosts changing exhibits of graphic and sculptural arts.

There's no better way to get to know Vermont and Vermonters than a session of **country line-dancing**. Two Bennington groups offer lessons intended for all levels of experience: Green Mountain Country Dancers ☎ (802) 447-1387, at the First Baptist Church, Monday, 7:30 PM; and Blazin' Boots ☎ (802) 447-2984 or (802) 442-2886, at the Bennington Armory, Monday and Wednesday evening at 7:45 PM.

WHERE TO STAY AND EAT

The **Molly Stark Inn** ☎ (802-442-9631 TOLL-FREE (800) 356-3076 FAX (802) 442-5224 E-MAIL mollyinn@vermontel.com, 1067 East Main Street (Route 9), Bennington 05201-2635 (budget to mid-range), is an 1890 Queen Anne Victorian building with six cozy guestrooms as well as a cottage with a Jacuzzi and a wood stove. The style is homey, with patchwork quilts and braided rugs adorning the rooms.

Renowned for its fine French restaurant (expensive), the **Four Chimneys Inn** ☎ (802) 447-3500 TOLL-FREE (800) 649-3503 FAX (802) 447-3692 E-MAIL judy@fourchimneys.com, 21 West Road, Bennington 05201 (expensive), has 11 luxurious rooms; most have fireplace and Jacuzzi.

The chef-owned **Paradise Restaurant** ☎ (802) 442-5418, 141 Main Street, serves lunch and dinner starring seafood and steaks as well as lighter fare. Meals are served on the garden terrace or by the tavern fireplace.

HOW TO GET THERE

Bennington is located at the intersection of Routes 7 and 9. It is 145 miles (232 km) from Boston and 160 miles (256 km) from New York.

MANCHESTER, DORSET AND ARLINGTON

Stately homes and country inns amid picture-perfect villages and beautiful countryside typify the small southern Vermont towns of Dorset, Manchester and Arlington. Manchester has been a resort for the well-to-do for more than a century. Dorset is another fashionable getaway and artist colony, while Arlington's chief claim to fame is as the home of artist Norman Rockwell.

Manchester and the Mountains Chamber of Commerce ☎ (802) 362-2100 FAX (802) 362-3451 E-MAIL mmchambr@sover.net WEB SITE www.manchestervermont.net, 5046 Main Street, Suite No. 1, Manchester Center 05255-9802, offers informational materials and assistance with lodging and dining choices.

WHAT TO SEE AND DO

A village just about suitable for framing, tucked into the Valley of Vermont between the Taconic and Green Mountains, **Manchester** has been a resort since the 1800s. Illustrious guests include Abraham Lincoln who was drawn here by its beauty and serenity. Mount Equinox, the tallest peak in the Taconic Range, rises high above a town where Federal-style and colonial-style mansions line its shaded streets.

A rural Vermont landscape.

Nearby, Robert Todd Lincoln, the president's son, built a 24-room manor on a large estate where he summered from 1904 until his death in 1926. **Hildene** ☎ (802) 362-1788 commands a splendid view of the surrounding countryside. Many of the original family furnishings remain in his home. Formal gardens surround the property. Open daily, mid-May through October with guided tours from 9:30 AM to 4 PM; an admission fee is charged.

Ernest Hemingway often tried his luck along the **Battenkill River**, one of New England's legendary fly-fishing streams. Fly fishing in America began in Manchester in

1856, and the **American Museum of Fly Fishing** ☎ (802) 362-3300, in Manchester Village, exhibits rods, reels, and other fishing gear along with tales of famous fishermen from Hemingway to Homer (Winslow). An admission fee is charged.

One of the best views in the area is found along the **Equinox Sky Line Drive**, five miles (eight kilometers) south of Route 7A. This six-mile (10-km) paved toll-road climbs from 600 to 3,835 ft (183 to 1,169 m) and offers panoramas from the summit of Mount Equinox.

It was in **Dorset** at Cephas Kent's Tavern that the Green Mountain Boys gathered to watch the founding fathers of Vermont sign the Declaration of Independence from the New Hampshire grants. Today this colonial village, a few miles north of Manchester, is an artists' colony. There are summer theater revels, music festivals, garden and gallery tours, and a number of good restaurants in Dorset. The acclaimed **Dorset Playhouse** ☎ (802) 867-5777, Cheney Road, Dorset 05251, stages a season of plays with Equity actors, annually from June to Labor Day.

Once a gathering place for the Green Mountain Boys, American artist Norman Rockwell made his home in the peaceful little hamlet of **Arlington** for 14 years. The **Norman Rockwell Exhibition & Gift Shop** ☎ (802) 375-6423, Route 7A in Arlington, has hundreds of *Saturday Evening Post* covers and prints on display. The models who posed for his works sometimes lead tours. Open daily year-round; an admission fee is charged.

SHOPPING

The **Vermont State Craft Center at the Equinox** ☎ (802) 362-3321, Historic Route 7A, Equinox Shops, Manchester, features contemporary and traditional Vermont art and crafts in all media as well as changing exhibitions and educational displays. Some 40 brand-name shops can be plundered at the **Manchester Center factory outlets** TOLL-FREE (800) 955-7467. Look for Armani, Brooks Brothers, Calvin Klein, J. Crew, Joan & David, Mikasa, Oshkosh B'Gosh, Polo/Ralph Lauren, Timberland and Gianni Versace, among many others.

SPORTS AND OUTDOOR ACTIVITIES

Nine lifts serve the 42 **skiing** trails at Bromley Mountain Resort ☎ (802) 824-5522 SNOW CONDITIONS (802) 824-5522 TOLL-FREE (800) 865-4786 FAX (802) 824-3659, PO Box 1130, Manchester Center 05255. In warm months, you can take the Bromley's chairlift ride and let gravity have its way with you on the **alpine slide**.

Stratton Mountain ☎ (802) 297-2200 SNOW CONDITIONS (802) 297-4211 TOLL-FREE (800) 787-2886 FAX (802) 297-4300, PO Box 145, Stratton Mountain 05155, has long been known for a European atmosphere and Tyrol-style vaudeville entertainment ("better than Kitzbuhel's"). Snowboarding, which local Jake Burton perfected (some say invented) here, is especially popular. There are 12 lifts serving a total of 90 trails.

From the **Lye Brook Wilderness Center**, hikers can follow a two-mile (three-kilometer) trail leading to the Lye Brook Waterfalls, or pick up the **Long Trail** for a trek among the abandoned marble quarries leading to the 3,186-ft (971-m) Mount Aeolus. The chamber of commerce (above) has maps.

Fly-fishing is taught by Orvis ☎ (802) 362-3750 TOLL-FREE (800) 239-2074, FAX (802) 362-3525 WEB SITE www.orvis.com, from their Manchester headquarters: Historic Route 7A, Manchester 05254. Classes include two and a half days of instruction in classic eastern trout fishing; they run from April through Labor Day. Battenkill Canoe ☎ (802) 362-2800 TOLL-FREE (800) 421-5268, in Arlington, offers guided **canoe** outings including inn-to-inn tours; they also sell waterway maps.

WHERE TO STAY AND EAT

Established in 1769, the **Equinox Resort** ☎ (802) 362-4700 TOLL-FREE (800) 362-4747 FAX (802) 362-1595, Route 7A, Manchester Village 05254 (luxury), is Vermont's most luxurious hostelry. Many guests come to indulge themselves in the sybaritic pleasures of the **Evolution Spa**, which specializes in European-style therapies, including thalassic soaks, herbal wraps and Swedish saunas. Along with the expected round of southern Vermont distractions (golf, hiking, mountain biking, skiing and snowshoeing), the resort offers two out-of-the-ordinary recreation programs. The Land Rover driving school offers courses in off-roading as well as guided four-wheel-drive tours in back-country Vermont. At the resort's British Falconry School participants learn how to handle and fly hawks as well as gaining an appreciation of the role of conservation in preserving these raptors and their natural habitat. Dining options at the Equinox resort run from the casual tavern to an outdoor grill to the elegant Colonnade where New England seafood and fresh Vermont products are served.

A nineteenth-century beauty, **Cornucopia of Dorset** ((802) 867-5751 TOLL-FREE (800) 566-5751 FAX (802) 867-5753 E-MAIL innkeeper@cornucopiaofdorset.com, Route 30, Dorset 05251 (mid-range), is surrounded by verdant English gardens. There are four guestrooms and one cottage suite; most rooms have fireplaces. The rate includes a candlelight breakfast.

In Arlington, the **West Mountain Inn** ((802) 375-6516 E-MAIL info@westmountaininn.com, PO Box 481 Arlington 05250, off Route 313 (mid-range to expensive), was built in the 1840s as a farmhouse and served variously as a gristmill and a lumber mill before being converted into an inn. Kids will be delighted with the innkeepers' menagerie of rabbits and llamas. The chef offers updated New England cuisine such as pumpkin-chestnut bisque and beef tenderloin and shrimp on smoked morel mushroom ragout. Breakfast (included) features homemade bread. Cross-country skiing is popular on the estate's 150 acres (60 hectares).

The **Inn at Manchester** ((802) 362-1793 TOLL-FREE (877) 207-4440 FAX (802) 362-3218, Route 7A, PO Box 41, Manchester 05254 (mid-range to expensive), serves a legendary three-course breakfast. It's included in the room rate, as is afternoon tea. The 14 guestrooms and four suites have mountain views and fireplaces. Manchester also offers the sophisticated **Reluctant Panther Inn and Restaurant** ((802) 362-2568 TOLL-FREE (800) 822-2331 FAX (802) 362-2586 E-MAIL stay@reluctantpanther.com, PO Box 678, West Road, Manchester Village 05254 (expensive to luxury), where five-course dinners, which usually include trout and quail, are served in front of the fieldstone hearth. Guestrooms are luxuriously appointed with two-person Jacuzzi suites and fireplaces.

The proprietor of a country antique store calls off his formidable watch dog.

The **Inn at West View Farm** ((802) 867-5715 TOLL-FREE (800) 769-4903 FAX (802) 867-0468 E-MAIL westview@vermontel.com, Route 30, Dorset 05251 (mid-range to expensive), is an 1870 two-story farmhouse on five acres (two hectares) surrounded by mountains. The 10 rooms with private bath are furnished with rustic antiques; the tavern serves casual fare. The room rate includes breakfast.

HOW TO GET THERE

Arlington, Manchester and Manchester Center are located north of Bennington on Route 7A. Dorset is north of Manchester Center on Route 30.

BRATTLEBORO

With a vital downtown, a thriving arts scene and wilderness in its backyard, Brattleboro is one of the most enchanting small cities in the country. Though a few empty storefronts mar Main Street, a grassroots effort is underway to preserve and improve this small city of 12,000 inhabitants.

Brattleboro is known as the onetime residence of Rudyard Kipling, who married a local woman and lived here (actually in Dummerston) for four years during the 1890s. In his unusual boat-shaped mansion, Naulakha, he wrote *Captain Courageous* and *The Jungle Book*.

People come from all over the region to celebrate **Independence Day** (July 4) in Brattleboro when a colorful parade takes over Main Street. The magnificent **Bach Festival** ((802) 257-4523 is held in October, and in March the **Harris Hill Ski Jump** hosts the annual Olympic-level qualifying matches.

The Creamery Bridge, located west of Brattleboro on Route 9, is a handsome covered bridge built in 1879; from here the Molly Stark Trail (Route 9) leads into high Green Mountain country.

GENERAL INFORMATION

Motorists coming into Vermont on Interstate 91 northbound should look for the new **Vermont Welcome Center** ((802) 254-4593, in Guilford, where they can stock up on maps and other informational materials; open daily year-round from 7 AM to 11 PM. At the Brattleboro Green there is a seasonal information booth open from May to October. The staff at the **Brattleboro Chamber of Commerce** ((802) 254-4565 FAX (802) 254-5675 WEB SITE www.brattleboro.com, 180 Main Street, Brattleboro 05301, is ready with expert advice and stacks of brochures on the region and the state.

WHAT TO SEE AND DO

Located in the 1915-era railway station, the **Brattleboro Museum & Art Center** ((802) 257-0124, Main and Vernon streets (at the Union Railroad Station), has a one-of-a-kind collection of Victorian Estey organs; these reed organs were a nineteenth-century mainstay in those American homes that could afford them.

The **Latchis Hotel** (see WHERE TO STAY AND EAT, below) has changed little since its opening in 1938. Still owned by the family who built it, this quasi-art-deco building's interior includes the original hand-painted murals and terrazzo flooring. Within the hotel is the 800-seat Latchis Theater. While other cinemas of the era were being sliced up into "cinemaplexes," the Latchis lay dormant. In the early 1980s, the owners received a grant to restore it to its 1930s splendor. Now the complex includes the large screen cinema as well as two smaller theaters, a burrito stand, a downstairs restaurant serving casual fare, and an in-house brewery, the Windham, crafting eight or so beers only sold here.

On Main Street, **Vermont Artisan Designs** ((802) 257-7044, 106 Main Street, is a superb gallery showing and selling Vermont and New England art and crafts. Stop in to try out the Vermont rocker or browse the shelves of jewelry, pottery, glassware, weathervanes and more. This is one of the top retailers for American crafts in the country. On Saturday afternoons there is live music at the gallery. Across the street the **Artist's Loft** ((802) 257-5181, 103 Main Street, is a fine art gallery space worth visiting for its rotating shows as well as its 1960s ambiance. There are many more galleries that are worthwhile in Brattleboro. You can get a taste of several by joining a **Gallery Walk** every first Friday of the month. Each month 10 or so galleries host the walk with wine and cheese receptions. For information contact the Artist's Loft.

European ingredients and painstaking attention to detail are the key elements in **Tom and Sally's Handmade Chocolates** (802) 254-4200, 485 West River Road. The factory outlet sells everything from penny candy to gourmet chocolates to whimsical items such as their Vermont "cow pie," and "body chocolate" which comes complete with a brush and instructions to "heat to 98.6°F and enjoy." Join a factory tour to observe the painstaking process of cutting, molding, and enrobing the chocolates. At the end of the tour you'll find out just how deliciously easy it is obliterate all that hard work. Tours are offered Monday to Saturday at 10 AM and 2 PM; admission fee is charged.

Sally, of Tom & Sally's Handmade Chocolates in Brattleboro, demonstrates the life cyle of a bonbon.

SPORTS AND OUTDOOR ACTIVITIES

For **hiking** and **biking** there is the paved West River Trail, which follows along Route 3 and the river. The Brattleboro Bicycle Shop (802) 254-8644, 165 Main Street, rents wheels and can point you in the direction of some backcountry routes. You can hike to the top of Wantastiquet Mountain from downtown. At the summit, you'll have a view of the valley. The Connecticut River Safari (802) 254-5008, in Brattleboro, offers guided **canoe excursions**, including inn-to-inn tours. They also rent canoes and sell maps. When the weather is fine, the Connecticut and West rivers make for fine **swimming**.

Winter outdoor pastimes include **ice skating** at Living Memorial Park Rink (802) 257-2311, where there is also a small ski hill and tow. There is more low-key **skiing** at Maple Valley (802) 254-6083, in West Dummerston. The Brattleboro Outing Club (802) 254-8906, on Upper Dummerston Road (off of Route 30), maintains **cross-country ski trails**.

TOURS AND EXCURSIONS

River excursions on the West River aboard the *Belle of Brattleboro* (802) 254-1263 depart from the marina.

At **Fair Winds Farms** (802) 254-9067, Upper Dummerston Road, Brattleboro, a pair of spirited Suffolk Punch pull sleighs and hay wagons through the farm's surrounding woods. Call ahead for reservations. In summer, the farm offers organic produce from their two-acre (one-hectare) "horse-powered" farm.

NIGHTLIFE AND THE ARTS

Consult the Thursday calendar section of the *Brattleboro Reformer* for area events. The restored **Latchis Theater** (802) 254-6300, at the Latchis Hotel, is a treat in itself with its flamboyant Greek-inspired frescoes, gilded columns and zodiac ceiling designs. It's just the place to see a classic film.

There is rock and blues at the **Marina** (802) 257-7563, 28 Spring Tree Road, and **Mole's Eye Café** (802) 257-0771, 4 High Street, hosts rock bands. **Common Ground** (802) 257-0855, 25 Elliot Street, has live acoustic music.

WHERE TO STAY AND EAT

The Putney Inn (802) 387-5517 TOLL-FREE (800) 653-5517 E-MAIL putneyinn@sover.net, Exit 4, Interstate 91, PO Box 181, Putney 05346 (mid-range), is a 200-year-old house with lodging in an adjacent building, with Queen Anne replica furniture, private entrances, and breakfast. The pleasant dining room, one of the best in the area, serves well-prepared New England food using locally grown produce.

In downtown Brattleboro, the **Latchis Hotel** ℂ (802) 254-6300 FAX (802) 254-6304, at 50 Main Street, Brattleboro 05301, has 30 guestrooms sporting some of its original 1930s furniture and fixtures (budget to mid-range). The rate includes a continental breakfast, delivered to your room. Third-floor rooms have views of the train station and river. Downstairs the **Lucca Bistro and Brasserie** ℂ (802) 254-4747 serves casual fare with booths and tables looking over the gentle Whetstone River.

The **Artist's Loft Gallery** ℂ /FAX (802) 257-5181 E-MAIL artguys@sover.net, 103 Main Street, Brattleboro 05301 (mid-range), is an exhibition space that doubles as a bed and breakfast. In this historic building in the heart of downtown, one large and comfortable two-room suite (shared bath) overlooks the Connecticut River and Wantastiquet Mountain; the rate includes a continental breakfast.

A more traditional style bed and breakfast, **40 Putney Road** ℂ (802) 254-6268 TOLL-FREE (800) 941-2413 FAX (802) 258-2673 E-MAIL frtyptny@sover.net, 40 Putney Road, Brattleboro 05301-2944 (expensive), is perhaps the best in the area. The suite and one of the guestrooms has a gas fireplace. The house is surrounded by inviting grounds and gardens and is within walking distance of the downtown area; the rate includes breakfast.

TJ Buckley's ℂ (802) 257-4922, 132 Elliot Street (mid-range), serves sensational food in a converted railway car. There are typically only a couple of main courses to choose from, but never mind, whatever you order will be fresh, full of flavor and excellently prepared.

Authentic southern cooking has won the inexpensive **Curtis' Bar-B-Q** ℂ (802) 387-5474, Route 5 (off Interstate 91), in Putney, a host of loyal customers. Perched on a hillside and presided over by the affable Curtis, the food is cooked in a tin-roofed shed and served from an old converted school bus. You can order food to go, or settle down for a spell at one of the picnic tables. Open seasonally.

MacNeill's Brewery ℂ (802) 254-2553, 90 Elliot Street (budget), pours gold-medal beer to accompany a menu of casual fare. The **Marina Restaurant & Bar** ℂ (802) 257-7563, Putney Road, at the marina is reliably good (budget).

HOW TO GET THERE

Brattleboro is 102 miles (163 km) from Boston and 194 miles (310 km) from New York. Take either Exit 1 or Exit 2 off Interstate 91. **Amtrak's *Vermonter*** TOLL-FREE (800) 872-7245 (supported in part by the state of Vermont) operates daily between Washington, DC, and Saint Albans with through bus service to Montreal. The baggage car can hold bikes and skis without boxing; Amtrak can supply bike maps for all of its Vermont destinations, including Brattleboro. Inquire about Amtrak's seasonal tours aimed at leaf peepers and skiers.

WILMINGTON AND VICINITY

The attractive village of Wilmington is the gateway to southern Vermont's ski areas Haystack and Mount Snow. Heading north, West Dover is a classic New England jewel with steepled churches and heaps of white clapboard. The acclaimed **Marlboro Music Festival** schedules twelve weekend concerts between mid-July and mid-August on the Marlboro College campus ℂ (802) 254-2394, Marlboro 05344. Informational materials on the region can be obtained from **Mount Snow Valley Chamber of Commerce** ℂ (802) 464-8092 FAX (802) 464-5306, PO Box 3, Page House, Main Street, Wilmington 05363.

SPORTS AND OUTDOOR ACTIVITIES

North of Wilmington on Route 100, loom the **ski slopes** of Mount Snow/Haystack Mountain ℂ (802) 464-3333 TOLL-FREE (800) 245-7669 SNOW CONDITIONS (802) 464-2151 FAX (802) 464-4141. A big draw for **snowboarding**, the area has the East's longest illuminated half-pipe (460 ft or 138 m) served by a dedicated lift. For skiers there are several open snow-field alpine runs with a grand total of 26 lifts serving 134 trails. A five-mile-long (eight-kilometer) cross-country touring trail skirts craggy ridges along six peaks of the Green Mountains; it is the highest cross-country trail in Vermont.

Weekday **mountain biking** on Mount Snow runs through early September; weekends only through mid-October, with 45 miles (72 km) of trails for all levels and abilities.

WHERE TO STAY AND EAT

The **Inn at Sawmill Farm** ☎ (802) 464-8131 TOLL-FREE (800) 493-1133 FAX (802) 464-1130 E-MAIL sawmill@sover.net, Mount Snow Valley, PO Box 367, West Dover 05356 (luxury), has 10 rooms and 10 suites with canopy beds and floral fabrics. A member of the Relais & Châteaux chain, the inn is elegant throughout and the **dining room** is superb. The room rate includes full board.

Honeymoon magazine named the **Deer Hill Inn** ☎ (802) 464-3100 TOLL-FREE (800) 993-3379, Valley View Road, West Dover 05356 (luxury), "the most romantic getaway in the world." Well, all the elements are there: fabulous views, exceptional food, richly decorated rooms. In winter things really heat up with soft flannel sheets to snuggle under, a roaring fire in your room and twinkling white lights in the woodland outside the window. The rest is up to you. Rates includes breakfast.

HOW TO GET THERE

From Boston, take the Massachusetts Turnpike (Interstate 90) to Route 191. Take Exit 2 then turn right onto Route 9 West for Wilmington. To continue to West Dover turn right at the light onto Route 100 North.

NEWFANE AND TOWNSHEND

A National Historic District comprising some 60 buildings, Newfane was first settled in 1774. As the Windham county seat, the town has the splendid 1825 white- and green-shuttered Greek Revival **Windham County Courthouse** on the elm-shaded village green, among the finest Early Republic buildings in the East. Two other handsome buildings flank the courthouse: the Congregational Church (1839) and the Union Hall (1832).

Those following the Route 30 "antique trail" should head for the **Newfane Flea Market** ☎ (802) 365-4000, which takes place each Sunday during the summer. It's located just north of the village center.

Continuing north on Route 30 one reaches the village of Townshend, where historic buildings surround the handsome town green. Townshend's **Scott Covered Bridge**, just off Route 30, is the longest single-span covered bridge in Vermont; built in 1870, it stretches 165 ft (50 m) over the West River.

There is no official information center for this area. Materials are available from the state visitors' center in Guilford south of Brattleboro (see GENERAL INFORMATION, page 238 in BRATTLEBORO).

At **Townshend State Forest** ☎ (802) 365-7500, a steep hiking trail nearly three miles (four and a half kilometers) long leads to the 1,580-ft (482-m) summit of Bald Mountain. A 10-minute drive north brings you up to **Jamaica State Park** ☎ (802) 874-4600, noted for whitewater rafting on the West River.

This area has some of the state's finest inns. The **Windham Hill Inn** ☎ (802) 874-4080 TOLL-FREE (800) 944-4080, West Townshend 05359 (mid-range to luxury), has 13 rooms in the inn and eight larger rooms in the converted dairy barn. All of the rooms are

Newfane's 1839 Congregational Church, proud against a crisp winter sky.

The Old Tavern

whimsically decorated. There are gorgeous views from the grounds and plenty of activities including a skating pond, six miles (10 km) of cross-country trails with lessons and rentals, and a thrilling toboggan run. Room rates include breakfast only.

The 1830 Greek Revival **Four Columns Inn** ☎ (802) 365-7713 TOLL-FREE (800) 787-6633, 230 West Street, Newfane 05345, on the village green (mid-range to expensive), has 12 rooms, a landscaped pool and garden. Rooms have unique architectural details and luxurious touches such as a neck-massaging Jacuzzi. The rate includes an "extended" continental breakfast.

Both of these inns welcome the public to their exceptional dining rooms; another excellent option for dinner is the chef-owned **Old Newfane Inn** ☎ (802) 365-4427, located on the village green at Route 30, Newfane. The dining room, lit by the glow of the immense hearth, looks out on the common. The extensive menu features quality French-Swiss cuisine.

In winter it's a ski lodge, but come summer **Vagabond** ☎ (802) 874-4096, Vermont Route 30, Box 224, East Jamaica 05343, offers hostel-style lodging with 20 beds, with kitchen, game room, and television room. Private rooms are also available. Reservations are advised.

GRAFTON AND CHESTER

Grafton, founded in pre-Revolutionary times under George III, has been called the perfect New England village. Historic buildings, high-steepled churches, old inns, specialty shops (most circa 1805), and a little creek meandering through town make it attractive for photographers and browsers alike.

Grafton's perfect charm, however, is by no means a question of chance. Founded in 1763 as an agricultural settlement, the village developed in the 1800s into a thriving mill town, doddering gracefully into the status of a back road village in the nineteenth and twentieth centuries. It might have remained that way, but for a wealthy businessman named William Mathey, who spent his summers in Grafton. Distressed to see the town falling into disrepair, he established the Windham Foundation in the 1960s, which set about purchasing and restoring the villages' buildings, including the Old Tavern, the Grafton Village Cheese Company, and the Grafton Village Store. These days the Windham Foundation owns two-thirds of the town.

Fans of Victoriana might make a stop just north of Grafton in the village of Chester. Here they can explore two historic districts, Main Street's stately houses along the village green and North Street's Stone Village Historical District, which has more than 25 pre-Civil War houses faced with gneiss stone, also called "glimmerstone" for its glittering surface. Many of these homes (private dwellings and not open for tours) have secret rooms that sheltered escaped slaves moving north during the mid-1800s. Contact the chamber of commerce for more information (below). Chester has a wealth of antique shops and galleries.

GENERAL INFORMATION

The Daniels House, on Townshend Road, is the Grafton **Visitor Center** ☎ (802) 843-2255. It's also a well-stocked gift shop; open year-round. In Chester, contact the **Chamber of Commerce** ☎ (802) 875-2939, on the green, open seasonally.

WHAT TO SEE AND DO

Stock up on film because Grafton is a wonderful place to take pictures. There are no telephone poles and wires (they've been buried). There are no bus tours. Flowers festoon verandahs in summer and snow piles up high in winter, setting the streetscape sparkling.

The **Nature Museum of Grafton** ☎ (802) 843-2111, 186 Townsend Road, offers a "Getting to Know Grafton" tour as well as changing programs each Sunday morning and Tuesday afternoon. There is also a self-guided walking tour detailed in a brochure available at the visitor (see GENERAL INFORMATION, above).

You can peer through the windows to see cheese makers turning huge slabs of curd at the **Grafton Village Cheese Company**

TOP: Townshend's spacious common.
BOTTOM: The Old Tavern at Grafton.

☎ (802) 843-2221 TOLL-FREE (800) 472-3866, Townshend Road, PO Box 87, Grafton 05146. Samples of the award-winning cheddar are available for tasting in the shop. The smoked cheddar is excellent. In summers, tours can sometimes be arranged through the Daniels House (see GENERAL INFORMATION, above). Open daily.

One of the state's most prestigious galleries is located in the village: **Gallery North Star** ☎ (802) 843-2465, Townshend Road. It's situated in an old house with attached barn where there are several rooms showing the works of Vermont painters and sculptors. Closed Tuesday.

There are **music** programs throughout the summer from choral concerts in the nondenominational **White Church** ☎ (802) 843-2346, Main Street, and **Brick Church** ☎ (802) 843-2346, Main Street, to jazz in **Phelps Barn** at the Old Tavern (see WHERE TO STAY AND EAT, below). On summer evenings you might catch the Grafton cornet band giving their traditional open-air concerts in front of the library.

SPORTS AND OUTDOOR ACTIVITIES

Grafton Ponds Nordic Ski and Mountain Bike Center ☎ (802) 843-2400, down the road from the Old Tavern, has a three-mile (five-kilometer) snowmaking system. The facility covers around 1,000 acres (400 hectares) of rural countryside running through forests and grazing pastures (maintained by the local sheep). Ice skating, snowshoeing, sledding and sleigh rides are also part of the winter scene here. For summer mountain biking there are wide open as well as single-track trails with manmade obstacles. Rentals and instruction are available at the lodge. The reserve is also a wonderful place for rambling on foot.

WHERE TO STAY AND EAT

A former stop on the Boston–Montreal Post Road, **The Old Tavern** ☎ (802) 843-2231 TOLL-FREE (800) 843-1801 E-MAIL old-tavern@sover.net, Grafton 05146 (expensive), has been in business since 1801, hosting such prominent guests as Daniel Webster; writers Hawthorne, Emerson, Thoreau and Kipling (who honeymooned here); Ulysses S. Grant, Woodrow Wilson and Teddy Roosevelt — all of whom no doubt spent many an hour relaxing on the same inviting long porch. Rooms are attractive, with modern bathrooms, four-posters, and antiques. There are 14 rooms in the inn itself and an additional 65 rooms spread throughout the town in other historic buildings. You can dine at the inn beneath hand-hewn beams on New England specialties such as lobster pot pie. The room rate includes breakfast and afternoon tea. Guests can

swim in the pond across the street from the inn, and there's tennis, hiking, cross-country skiing or mountain biking.

If you'd like to stay in the heart of Victorian Chester, there is **Chester House Inn** ☎ (802) 875-2205 TOLL-FREE (888) 875-2205 E-MAIL innkeeper@ChesterHouseInn.com, 266 Main Street, Chester 05143 (budget to mid-range), a circa 1780 inn located on the village green with seven rooms, whirlpool baths and fireplaces. A number of other small inns and bed and breakfasts are listed with the local chamber of commerce, including two bed and breakfast places within the Stone Village Historical Site: **Stone Cottage B&B and Collectibles** ☎ (802) 875-6211, North Street, Chester 05143 (mid-range), or **Stone**

Village Bed & Breakfast ☎ (802) 875-3914, North Street, Chester 05143 (mid-range).

HOW TO GET THERE

Grafton is located at the junction of Routes 31 and 121 about 10 miles (16 km) west of Interstate 91. Chester is eight miles (13 km) north of Grafton on Routes 11 and 35.

LUDLOW AND OKEMO

In the Black River Valley of Vermont's Green Mountains, the town of Ludlow is home to Okemo Mountain Resort. Cross-country ski trails radiate from Ludlow and the Green Mountain National Forest ☎ (802) 747-6700 sets the scene for cycling and hiking. The **Ludlow Area Chamber of Commerce** ☎ (802) 228-5830 FAX 802-228-7642, PO Box 333, Ludlow 05149, has an information center at the Okemo Marketplace clock tower.

SPORTS AND OUTDOOR ACTIVITIES

Okemo Mountain Resort ☎ (802) 228-4041 SNOW CONDITIONS (802) 228-5222 TOLL-FREE (800) 786-5366 FAX (802) 228-4558, 77 Okemo Ridge Road, Ludlow 05149, sprawls over more than 500 acres (200 hectares) with 13 lifts serving the resort's 98 trails, including seven mogul runs. "Self's Choice" is Okemo's mega-mogul, with music blasting from speakers on either side of the slope to keep your adrenaline pumping. Okemo, if you hadn't guessed, is a primo boarder's resort.

There is **ice skating** at West Hill Park ☎ (802) 228-2655, West Hill Road.

WHERE TO STAY AND EAT

Jewell Brook Inn ☎ (802) 228-8926 TOLL-FREE (800) 681-4855 E-MAIL jewelinn@ludl.tds.net, 82 Andover Street (Route 100), Ludlow 05149 (budget to expensive), has 10 cozy guestrooms decorated in Vermont country style. Rates include breakfast and afternoon refreshments served by the pond or by the Tavern Room hearth. There is a weekend shuttle bus to Okemo and ski packages are available. In a similar class, the **Andrie Rose Inn** ☎ (802) 228-4846 TOLL-FREE (800) 223-4846, at 13 Pleasant Street, Ludlow 05149 (expensive), has 20 Laura Ashley bedecked rooms as well as some romantic suites with oversize whirlpools, fireplace and steam shower for two. There are also two attractive family suites.

A ski bum's dream, the **Trojan Horse Lodge** ☎ (802) 228-5244 TOLL-FREE (800) 547-7475 E-MAIL thlodge@aol.com, 44 Andover Street, Ludlow 05149 (budget), is close to Okemo and within 25 minutes of nine other ski areas. This 100-year-old carriage house has 18 beds, six bunk beds to a room, a kitchen, and free lockers. Closed in April and from October 20 to November 7. Reservations are essential from December to March.

For slopeside lodging in all price ranges, contact the **Okemo Mountain Area Lodging Service** ☎ (802) 228-2079 TOLL-FREE (800) 786-5366 E-MAIL okemor@ludl.tds.net, 77 Okemo Ridge Road, Ludlow 05149.

Four miles (six and a half kilometers) north of Ludlow, in the village of Mount Holly, look for **Harry's Café** ☎ (802) 259-2996, Route 103 (budget to mid-range), a roadside spot low on atmosphere, but high on flavor. Main courses span the globe, running from grilled sirloin to Thai curry to fish and chips. Creative sauces accompany many of the dishes, and the restaurant bottles some of them for purchase. Reservations are recommended on weekends.

HOW TO GET THERE

Ludlow is located at the intersection of Route 193 and Route 100. From Interstate 93 take Exit 6 and follow Route 103 west toward Ludlow.

WOODSTOCK AND QUECHEE

Designated by *National Geographic* as one of the nation's five most beautiful villages, Woodstock was settled two centuries ago by farmers, millers and merchants. It later became the county seat drawing moneyed professionals who built Romanesque, Greek Revival, and Federal-style estates here. Since the late nineteenth century it has been a year-round resort town. Much of village is

Vermont's recreational paths offer cyclists green corridors for exploring woods and mountains — without the annoyances of automobile traffic.

today designated an Historical District. Fine residences surround the handsome village green. The centerpiece of the village is Woodstock Inn, known for its golf course and ski touring center and its traditional afternoon teas.

Nearby, Quechee is famous for its deep water-carved gorge. An old mill village, Quechee is situated along the Ottauquechee River, and is reached by driving through a covered bridge. Many restored Victorian and Federal houses grace the town, and a bandstand presides over the village green.

GENERAL INFORMATION

The **Town Crier** bulletin board, at Elm and Central Streets, informs residents and visitors of events and activities. The **Woodstock Area Chamber of Commerce** ☎ (802) 457-3555 TOLL-FREE (888) 496-6378 FAX (802) 457-4214 E-MAIL office@wood stockvt.com, is at 18 Central Street, PO Box 486, Woodstock 05091, or stop by their **information booth** located on the village green.

WHAT TO SEE AND DO

You'll want to enjoy a walking tour of Woodstock village. The chamber of commerce furnishes brochures detailing highlights and historical background. Be sure to take in the **Woodstock Historical Society** ☎ (802) 457-1822, 26 Elm Street, housed in the 1807 **Dana House**. Rooms are furnished in Federal, Empire and Victorian styles. Open daily from May to October.

Opened in 1998, Vermont's first national park, **Marsh-Billings-Rockefeller National Historical Park** was named for four influential Vermont conservationists, all of whom once lived on the property that now constitutes the park. George Perkins Marsh, the author of *Man and Nature*, was the first to decry the forest clear-cutting. Frederick Billings, a pioneering conservationist, established a progressive dairy farm and a managed forest on the former Marsh farm. Billings' granddaughter, Mary French Rockefeller, and her husband, Laurence S. Rockefeller, continued Billings' forestry and farming practices on the property over the second half of the twentieth century. The park relates the history of conservation in America with tours of the mansion and its extensive collection of American landscape paintings, and the surrounding 550-acre (220-hectare) forest, one of the oldest managed forests in the nation.

Marsh-Billings-Rockefeller National Historical Park ☎ (802) 457-3368, PO Box 178, 54 Elm Street, Woodstock 05091, is open daily from 10 AM to 5 PM, late May through October. It's located on Route 12, half a mile (under a kilometer) north of the Woodstock village green, and it shares a parking lot and Visitor Center with the Billings Farm & Museum (below). There is no general entrance fee. Guided tours of the Marsh-Billings-Rockefeller mansion, the grounds and gardens of the mansion, and the Mount Tom forest are offered for a fee. Combination tickets are available for park tours and the Billings Farm & Museum.

In 1983, the Rockefellers established the **Billings Farm & Museum** ☎ (802) 457-2355, PO Box 489, Woodstock 05091, a working dairy farm where you can observe farm animals from prize Jersey cows to antique breeds of sheep. It's a fabulous place to take in the Vermont countryside against a backdrop of gentle mountains. Also on the property is a Victorian farmhouse showing Vermont rural home life in the 1890s. Open daily, spring through fall; an admission fee is charged.

When you've had your fill of domesticated animal life at Billings Farm, head up the hill from Woodstock to meet the wildlife at the **Vermont Institute of Natural Science (VINS) and Raptor Center** ☎ (802) 457-2779, Church Hill Road. Here you can see a dozen species of birds of prey from tiny, fist-sized saw-whet owls to immense bald eagles with five-foot (one-and-a-half-meter) wingspans. All of the raptors at the center have been brought here because they were either injured or unable to survive in the wild. The center's mission is to rehabilitate and train the birds and to release them. Naturalists are on hand to answer questions. The center is open daily 10 AM to 4 PM (last ticket sales at 3 PM); an admission fee is charged.

At the village of **Quechee**, a few miles east of Woodstock, there are glassblowing and demonstrations at **Simon Pearce** ☎ (802) 295-2711, The Mill. The sales room glistens with glass objects and pottery.

SPORTS AND OUTDOOR ACTIVITIES

A visit to Woodstock is not complete without a hike to the summit of Mount Tom. The gentle trail starts in Faulkner Park. From the summit there are fine views of the valley and town; follow the trail back down or return via the carriage path to visit Billings Farm (above). The hike to the bottom of **Quechee Gorge**, six miles (10 km) east of Woodstock on Route 4, is more vigorous. The walls of this 165-ft (50-m) chasm sheer down to the Ottauquechee River; a steep one-mile-long (over one-and-a-half-kilometer) hiking trail leads to the bottom of the gorge. Those less energetic can enjoy the view from the roadway (Route 4).

Suicide Six ☎ (802) 457-6661 SNOW CONDITIONS (802) 457-6666 TOLL-FREE (800) 448-7900 FAX (802) 457-3830, 14 The Green, Woodstock 05091, has 22 trails spread out over 100 acres (40 hectares); three lifts serve slopes. For cross-country skiing there is the excellent **Woodstock Ski Touring Center** ☎ (802) 457-6674, at the Woodstock Country Club, south of town on Route 106. The center maintains 36 miles (58 km) of trails varying in elevation by 750 ft (225 m).

Kedron Valley Stables ☎ (802) 457-1480, PO Box 368, South Woodstock 05071, offers riding lessons, pony rides, sleigh rides, and surrey and carriage rides by the hour or by the day.

OPPOSITE: The Simon Pearce restaurant and shop in Quechee. ABOVE: A naturalist at the Vermont Raptor Center, Woodstock, cradles a deep-frozen snowy owl whose feathers may be used to give flight to an injured bird.

NIGHTLIFE AND THE ARTS

Pentangle Council of the Arts ✆ (802) 657-3981 hosts performers from all over the world. For dancing on Friday and Saturday nights, go to **Bentley's** (see WHERE TO STAY AND EAT, below).

WHERE TO STAY AND EAT

Along the village green, the **Woodstock Inn and Resort** ✆ (802) 457-1100 TOLL-FREE (800)

448-7900 FAX (802) 457-6699 WEB SITE www.woodstockinn.com, 14 The Green, Woodstock 05091-1298 (expensive to luxury), is not just a town landmark but also a wonderful place to stay; a savvy combination of country inn charm in a thoroughly modern, comfortable lodging. Rooms are spacious and tastefully appointed, and there are facilities for almost every sport imaginable. Its restaurant is priced in the mid-range. Afternoon tea is a tradition.

South of the town center, **Kedron Valley Inn** ✆ (802) 457-1473 TOLL-FREE (800) 836-1193 FAX (802) 457-4469, Route 106, South Woodstock 05071 (mid-range to expensive), offers lodging in a stagecoach inn. Some guestrooms boast fireplaces, Jacuzzis, queen-size canopy beds and heirloom quilts, and there is fireside dining. Activities include cross-country skiing, horseback riding and swimming at the inn's own pond (see SPORTS AND OUTDOOR ACTIVITIES, above).

One mile (a kilometer and a half) east of the Woodstock village green, and close to ski-slopes, the **Braeside Motel** ✆ (802) 457-1366 FAX (802) 457-9892 E-MAIL info@braesidemotel.com, PO Box 411, Route 4E, Woodstock 05091 (budget to mid-range), includes breakfast in the price of its 12 rooms with views of rolling hillsides; pets $10 extra.

Woodstock's finest French restaurant is the **Prince and the Pauper** ✆ (802) 457-1818, 24 Elm Street, Woodstock (expensive). While **Bentley's** ✆ (802) 457-3232, 3 Elm Street, With its curved, velvet couches and carved wood paneling, has been a culinary mainstay for 20 years. Sunday brunch is a special treat.

HOW TO GET THERE

Woodstock is 13 miles (21 km) west of White River Junction on Route 4. Take Exit 1 off Interstate 89. Quechee is located on Route 4, six miles (nine and a half kilometers) west of the intersection of Interstate 89.

KILLINGTON

One word describes Killington ski resort: BIG. "The Beast of the East" has seven interconnected mountains (Killington Peak is the highest at 4,241 ft or 1,293 m), with hundreds of ski trails and moguls the size of small hotels. In all, there is twice as much skiing here as at any other eastern ski resort. Killington claims the longest ski lift in the world, stretching more than three miles (nearly five kilometers) over the Green Mountains.

GENERAL INFORMATION

Visitors entering Vermont via Route 4A from New York can stop in for informational materials at the **Vermont Welcome Center** ✆ (802) 265-4763 near Rutland; open year-round, from 7 AM to 9 PM.

Killington & Pico Areas Association ✆ (802) 773-4181 FAX (802) 775-7070 E-MAIL info@killingtonchamber.com, PO Box 114, Killington 05751, offers information on recreation, lodging and dining in the area.

SPORTS AND OUTDOOR ACTIVITIES

The numbers speak at **Killington Resort** ☎ (802) 422-3333 SNOW CONDITIONS (802) 422-3261 TOLL-FREE (800) 621-6867 FAX (802) 422-4391 E-MAIL info@killington.com, Killington Road, Killington 05751. There are 205 trails; 33 lifts; two high-speed, eight-passenger gondolas and 12 quad chairlifts; seven mountains, 120 rooms from condos to chalets; and hundreds of restaurants, après-ski and nightclubs. Killington's long ski season is another drawing card. With more than 240 inches (six meters) of snow annually and vast snowmaking capacity, the resort's season often extends from October to June. Bear Mountain is expert terrain, with one trail, Outer Limits, at an incline of 62 percent; it is the steepest in New England. Beginners should try the 10-mile (16-km) Juggernaut trail, the longest Alpine run in the United States. Killington's outstanding ski school and Children's Center attract many families. Besides special programs, activities and day care, its "family ski workshop" allows adults and children to receive lessons and ski together under the tutelage of a single instructor.

In the summer and early fall, it's **mountain biking** season at Killington ☎ (802) 422-6232. There are more than 40 miles (64 km) of trails, the terrain is varied, and there are ample quantities of *après-vélo* activities. Rental, instruction and tours are available.

WHERE TO STAY AND EAT

Active vacationers will love **Cortina Inn** ☎ (802) 773-3333 TOLL-FREE (800) 451-6108 FAX (802) 775-6948 E-MAIL cortina1@aol.com, Route 4, Killington 05751-7604 (mid-range), with its vast array of things to do: cross-country skiing, ice skating, snowmobiling, snowshoeing and more. After all that exertion, you can come back to a pampering massage, a swim and a sauna. Guestrooms are comfortable; some have a fireplace and a Jacuzzi. There is dining on site. Rates include a Vermont breakfast and après-ski social hour.

The Vermont Inn ☎ (802) 775-0708 TOLL-FREE (800) 541-7795, Route 4, Killington 05751 moderately priced, is an 1840 country inn with 18 rooms and an acclaimed restaurant serving New England cuisine. There is a hot tub, a sauna and a games room, and some of the guestrooms have fireplaces.

Killington Resort (above) will book slopeside lodging for you.

Often touted as one of the "top 25 restaurants in America," **Hemingway's** ☎ (802) 422-3886, on Route 4 (expensive), is a classic, serving Vermont lamb and fresh brook trout. It's superb.

HOW TO GET THERE

About 12 miles (19 km) east of Rutland on Route 4, Killington lies just east of the intersection with Route 100 north. Many of the area inns offer shuttle service to Rutland airport. **Amtrak**'s TOLL-FREE (800) 872-7245 *Ethan Allen Express* offers daily service from New York to Rutland with connecting bus service to Killington Resort.

PLYMOUTH

In the early morning of August 3, 1923, in Plymouth (about 30 miles or 48 km east of Rutland on Route 100A), Vice-President Calvin Coolidge was sworn in as the thirtieth president of the United States in the parlor of the Coolidge homestead. These unusual circumstances arose when Coolidge, while visiting his hometown, was notified of President Warren Harding's death. Coolidge's father, a notary public, did the honors.

A visit to Plymouth, a rural Vermont village situated among the Green Mountains, should include a walk through the **Calvin Coolidge State Historic Site** ☎ (802) 672-3773. Here you'll find the Coolidge homestead, the homes of their neighbors, as well as the village church, general store, and community dance hall that served as the 1924 Summer White House office. Ten buildings are open the public. Calvin's son John runs the nearby family cheese factory. Founded by the president's father, it still specializes in the curd cheese so favored by "Silent Cal." In the steep hillside cemetery, Coolidge and six generations of his family are buried.

Vermont kids at work and play in Woodstock.

Stop by the **Visitor Center** for information before starting your tour. The Coolidge homestead is open late May to mid-October daily; an admission fee is charged.

MIDDLEBURY

A classic New England town of 8,000 inhabitants, Middlebury rests between the northern Green Mountains and Lake Champlain, just 34 miles (54 km) south of Burlington. It's a good place to launch a driving tour through the Green Mountains and across the broad, low farmland of the Champlain Valley.

GENERAL INFORMATION

The **Addison County Chamber of Commerce** ☎ (802) 388-8066 FAX (802) 388-6088 E-MAIL info@midvermont.com, 2 Court Square, Middlebury 05753, offers informational materials on Bristol, Middlebury, Vergennes and surrounding villages.

WHAT TO SEE AND DO

Pint-sized Middlebury's village green and historic inn give it a timeless look. The most prominent building in Middlebury is the handsome 1806 Congregational Church on the Common. Old houses and steep streets make wandering around town a pleasure. Inquire at the chamber of commerce (above) for a map to guide you on an informal **walking tour**.

Frog Hollow is the former heart of industrial Middlebury where marble was cut and carved until 1825. Now this assemblage of old stone buildings houses various businesses catering to tourists. Here you'll find the **Vermont State Craft Center at Frog Hollow** ☎ (802) 388-3177, 1 Mill Street, located in a renovated mill, showing and selling the best of Vermont art and crafts, including stained glass, jewelry, woodcraft, and pottery.

You'll want to take time for a drive through the campus of **Middlebury College**, visiting in particular Old Stone Row, which includes Painter Hall (1815) and Old Chapel (1835). The **Middlebury College Museum of Art** ☎ (802) 443-5007 features a small selection of European and American works. It's open Tuesday to Sunday; admission is free.

One and a half miles (two and a half kilometers) north of Middlebury in Weybridge is the **University of Vermont Morgan Horse Farm** ☎ (802) 388-2011, where you can watch more than 50 Morgans being put through training drills. Guided tours take you into the handsome Victorian barns. Open May through October daily; a small admission fee is charged.

About seven miles (11 km) east of Middlebury, on Route 125, is the village of **Ripton**, where poet Robert Frost summered in a rustic log cabin. Frost cofounded the Bread Loaf Writers Conference, a summer writer's school, in a former inn here. The state of Vermont designated Frost their Poet Laureate in 1961, and in 1983 named this section of the Green Mountain National Forest, "Robert Frost Country." Near his former cottage, the **Robert Frost Interpretive Trail** meanders through a wooded setting where seven Frost poems are posted at regular intervals. The trail crosses over Beaver Pond into a birch forest, where, on a plaque, words from Frost's poem, "A Young Birch," breathe the poet's particular vision to life.

SPORTS AND OUTDOOR ACTIVITIES

Middlebury offers easy access to Green Mountain hiking trails. The **United State Forest Service Middlebury Ranger District Office** ☎ (802) 388-4362 is south of town on Route 7; stop by for information on trails, and request their brochure listing day hikes in the region.

The Middlebury College Snowbowl ☎ (802) 388-4356 or (802) 388-7951 FAX (802) 388-2871, Service Building, Middlebury College, Middlebury 05753, has three lifts serving 15 trails. For cross-country skiing there is the **Rikert Ski Touring Center** ☎ (802) 443-2744, at Middlebury's Bread Loaf Campus on Route 125, which has 25 miles (40 km) of groomed trails.

WHERE TO STAY AND EAT

The handsome red-brick Georgian **Middlebury Inn and Motel** ☎ (802) 388-4961 TOLL-FREE (800) 842-4666 FAX (802) 388-4563

The Ottauquechee River continues to carve Quechee Gorge.

E-MAIL midinnvt@sover.net, Middlebury 05753, in the middle of town, has 80 rooms and suites (budget to expensive). I love the vintage Otis elevator and the front porch overlooking the Common. Request a room in the main part of the hotel as the motel addition lacks charm. The rate includes a continental breakfast and afternoon tea. The dining room serves New England cuisine. In summer you can eat on the front porch.

A former stagecoach inn, the appealing 1810 **Waybury Inn** ((802) 388-4015 TOLL-FREE (800) 348-1810, Route 125, East Middlebury 05740 (mid-range to expensive), adjoins the National Forest. Fans of *The Bob Newhart Show* may recognize the exterior; it was the setting for the series. Some rooms are small, but all are charmingly decorated. There is a formal dining room as well as a cozy tavern. The rate includes breakfast.

For home-style New England fare surrounded by the trappings of nineteenth century Labrador and Newfoundland, make a visit to the **Dog Team Tavern** ((802) 388-7651 TOLL-FREE (800) 472-7651, Dog Team Road, Middlebury (budget), a unique experience. Their sticky buns are legendary. It's three miles (five kilometers) north of Middlebury.

How to Get There

Middlebury is located on Route 7, about 46 miles (74 km) north of Rutland and 34 miles (54 km) south of Burlington.

MONTPELIER AND BARRE

A "crunchy granola" town that's also crawling with politicians, a 1960s throw back that is firmly planted in the present, Montpelier is a sophisticated little city of 10,000 residents set in the valley of the Winooski River. The gold dome of the Vermont State House is Montpelier's most obvious landmark. Resplendent in autumn against a backdrop of hills ablaze with fall foliage, the State House is topped by a statue of Ceres, the goddess of agriculture, most appropriate to this state of farms and dairies.

Six miles southeast of the capital, Barre (pronounced "barry") is the center of the country's granite industry, and Montpelier's blue-collar twin. "Granite sheds" here furnished the building materials for Vermont's state house and many church buildings throughout the state. Barre is also known as the birthplace of the Boy Scouts (1909).

General Information

Informational materials on the region can be obtained from the **Central Vermont Chamber of Commerce** ((802) 229-4619 FAX (802) 229-5713 WEB SITE www.centralvermont.com, PO Box 336, Beaulieu Place, Stewart Road, Barre 05641.

What to See and Do

At the golden domed **State House** ((802) 828-2228, you can roam the marble halls on a guided tour, offered Monday to Saturday from July to mid-October. Not far from the State House, the **Vermont Historical Society** ((802) 828-2291, 109 State Street, is housed in a building fashioned to resemble the old Pavilion Hotel, a landmark demolished in 1966. The museum exhibits an eclectic array of artifacts, including a gun used by Ethan Allen and a mount of the last panther shot in Vermont in 1881. In 2003, the society will open a second museum in Barre. Opening times vary; a small admission fee is charged.

For a better understanding of how difficult and dangerous granite mining can be, visit **Rock of Ages Granite Quarries** ☎ (802) 476-3119, four miles (about six-and-a-half kilometers) south of Montpelier on Route 14. These are the world's largest granite quarries, 350 ft (107 m) straight down to the bottom of the open rock mine. Huge machines lift 100-ton granite slabs out of the pit, while at the Craftsmen Center, workers cut and polish the rock, then carve it into memorial gravestones, sculptures, or building blocks. A quarry train offers a 20-minute ride through the mining complex. Open June 1 to October 15, Monday through Friday; an admission fee is charged.

The town's granite legacy can also be viewed at **Hope Cemetery** on the edge of town, where the headstones are said to rival the finest granite carvings anywhere.

WHERE TO STAY AND EAT

The **Inn at Montpelier** ☎ (802) 223-2727, 147 Main Street, Montpelier 05602 (mid-range), is composed of two nineteenth-century Federal buildings; the inviting wraparound porch is a more recent addition. Rooms are comfortable, well furnished, and finely decorated, and some have fireplaces. Located just outside the center, it's a convenient walk to anyplace in town.

The tiny hillside chalet, **Capitol Home Hostel** ☎ (802) 223-2104 (no calls after 9 PM), RD 1, PO Box 2750, Montpelier 05602 (include self-addressed stamped envelope; budget), has three beds and a kitchen. Reservations are essential. The rate includes breakfast.

Don't look for the golden arches; Montpelier is the only state capital in the United States that has no McDonald's restaurant. *Do* look for good-food places. Among many are three New England Culinary Institute restaurants where you can't go wrong: **Main Street Bar & Grill** ☎ (802) 223-3188, 118 Main Street, serving breakfast, lunch and dinner daily; the more formal **Chef's Table** ☎ (802) 229-9202, at the same address, serving lunch and dinner Monday to Friday and dinner only on Saturday; and **La Brioche Bakery & Café** ☎ (802) 229-0443, 89 Main Street, City Center, open daily, for sweet treats and hot java.

Simple souls head to the **Wayside** ☎ (802) 223-6611, 525 Barre Road (just off Interstate 89), Montpelier, a welcoming truck-stop restaurant serving what must be the world's best meatloaf.

HOW TO GET THERE

Montpelier, 182 miles (291 km) from Boston and 301 miles (482 km) from New York, is located on Interstate 84, about 38 miles (61 km) southeast of Burlington. Barre is seven miles southeast of Montpelier at the junction of Routes 14, 62, and 302. **Amtrak's *Vermonter*** TOLL-FREE (800) 872-7245 operates daily between Washington, DC, and Saint Albans (including through bus service to Montreal) with a stop in Montpelier-Barre.

MAD RIVER VALLEY

Mad River Valley is known for its mountainous terrain. Three ski areas and a scenic road leading to the 2,356-ft (718-m) tip of the Appalachian Gap are the major points of interest in the area. Bristol is also home to the only freshwater windjammer cruises in America. You can sail one of these tall-masted ships on Lake Champlain with Vermont's mountains in the background. Informational materials on this and all other aspects of touring the region are available from the **Sugarbush Chamber of Commerce** ☎ (802) 496-3409 TOLL-FREE (800) 828-4748 WEB SITE www.madrivervalley.com, PO Box 173, Waitsfield 05673.

Two Vermont icons — the gold-domed state capitol OPPOSITE and Ben and Jerry's ice cream ABOVE.

Sports and Outdoor Activities

For a pleasant walk, take the **unpaved recreation path**, in Waitsfield, which follows the Mad River.

Mad River Glen ✆ /FAX (802) 496-3551 SNOW CONDITIONS (802) 496-2001 TOLL-FREE (800) 828-4748, PO BOX 1089, Waitsfield 05673, has 44 trails served by four lifts. Here you'll find New England's most challenging mogul runs as the mountain gets loads of snow and the resort does very little grooming.

Sugarbush ✆ (802) 583-2381, off Interstate 89, Warren, has long been known for bumpy terrain. Its 1995 purchase by the giant American Ski Company has resulted in a $28-million spruce up, including a two-mile (three-kilometer), high-speed chairlift that links the resorts two ski areas.

The **Icelandic Horse Farm** ✆ (802) 496-7141, PO Box 577, Waitsfield 05673, specializes in tours on this small sturdy breed. Daylong and half-day rides are available, but to really get a feel for the countryside, sign up for one of the multi-day trips.

Where to Stay and Eat

The **Inn at Round Barn Farm** ✆ (802) 496-2276 FAX (802) 496-8832 E-MAIL roundbarn@madriver.com, East Warren Road, Waitsfield 05673 (mid-range to luxury), is the place to put some fire in your romance. Set in beautifully landscaped gardens, the inn has 12 elegantly appointed guestrooms. There are 45 miles (75 km) of cross-country ski trails on the property as well as an indoor lap pool. The rate includes a breakfast of Belgian waffles and rum raisin scones.

Inn at Mad River Barn ✆ (802) 496-3310 TOLL-FREE (800) 631-0466 FAX (802) 496-6696 E-MAIL madriverbarn@madriver.com, Route 17, PO Box 88, Waitsfield 05673 (budget to mid-range), is a classic ski lodge built of knotty pine. The 15 guestrooms with basic furnishings have private bath, most with queen-size bed. Meals are served family style in the rustic common room. There is a beautiful pool in a grove of birches. Rates include breakfast.

The **Common Man** ✆ (802) 583-2800, in nearby Warren, has been in the food business for more than 30 years. The setting is a nineteenth-century barn complete with cozy hearth; the cuisine is European, and the wine list long.

How to Get There

Take Interstate 89 to Exit 10 (Waterbury) and drive south on Route 100 for 14 miles to Waitsfield. Continue south for another five miles (eight kilometers) for Warren.

STOWE

At the foot of Mount Mansfield, Vermont's highest peak, lies Stowe, a first class resort community and one of New England's most scenic villages. A skier's dream, the resort has more than 350 miles (564 km) of well-groomed alpine skiing terrain and 100 miles (160 km) of cross-country trails. Stowe is also magical in summer, with the "gondie" ride up Mount Mansfield and miles of hiking trails in the surrounding protected land. Year-round, dining and lodging are superb both in quality and variety.

Visitors from the United Kingdom have discovered that skiing Stowe is every bit as enjoyable as skiing the Alps, and without the long lines and elbowing. They come in large numbers each year, and their presence lends a cosmopolitan flare to the town. Each fall, the **British Invasion** festival features a British car rally and rugby and polo matches.

General Information

The **Stowe Area Association** ✆ (802) 253-7321 TOLL-FREE (800) 247-8693 FAX (802) 253-2159, PO Box 1320, Stowe 05672, has a welcome center in the village.

What to See and Do

"Stowe" may rhyme with "snow," but this Vermont valley town has much to offer in any season. During summer months motorists can climb the **Mount Mansfield Toll Road** off Route 108, a five-mile (eight-kilometer) gravel road leading to a lookout point near the summit; from there you can follow a two-mile (just over three-kilometer) hiking path to the top. Mount Mansfield's

gondola ride is not to be missed with its near-summit panoramas. It's at the Midway Base Lodge; open daily, June to early September; Saturday and Sunday from September to October. Neighboring Spruce Peak has an **alpine slide**, a warm-weather luge with wheels, that barrels down the slopes along an aluminum chute.

The headquarters of **Ben & Jerry's** ☎ (802) 244-5601 TOLL-FREE (866) 258-6877 all-natural ice cream is in nearby Waterbury. Guided factory tours start with a short "mooovie" about the company. From there you swept off the to mezzanine for a view of the production room. By the end of the tour, you'll be primed for your sample scoop. A small fee is charged for the tour. To get to the factory take Exit 10 off of Interstate 89 in Waterbury, then take Route 100 north towards Stowe. It's about a mile up the road on the left. The tours run daily year-round (though there is no ice cream production on Sundays and holidays).

More dairy dreams are just up the road at the **Cabot Cheese Annex** ☎ (802) 244-6334 TOLL-FREE (800) 881-6334. Samples of all the various Cabot cheeses and other products are available, along with a chance to taste Lake Champlain chocolates in the same building.

SPORTS AND OUTDOOR ACTIVITIES

Stowe is justifiably proud of its paved **recreation path**. Leading five miles (eight kilometers) from the Stowe Community Center, up the valley toward the mountain, the path ends behind the Topnotch Tennis Center.

The best Mount Mansfield hiking trails begin at **Underhill State Park** ☎ (802) 899-3022. Trails are marked, but if you're planning on taking more than a casual stroll, you'll need the Green Mountain Club's *Long Trail Guide* (see RECOMMENDED READING, page 353, or contact the **Green Mountain Club** ☎ (802) 244-7037 E-MAIL gmc@greenmountainclub.org, GMC Headquarters, Waterbury Center 05677).

Umiak Outdoor Outfitters ☎ (802) 253-2317, in Stowe, offers guided **canoe tours** and, for independent paddlers, waterway maps.

"There is always snow at Stowe," is an oft-repeated refrain. One of New England's premier ski areas, **Stowe Mountain Resort** ☎ (802) 253-3000 ☎ SNOW CONDITIONS (802) 253-3600 TOLL-FREE (800) 253-4754 FAX (802) 253-3406, 5781 Mountain Road, Stowe 05672, was built in 1933 by Civilian Conservation Corps

An early-morning crew prepares the slopes at Stowe Mountain Resort.

workers, who carved out a trail on Mount Mansfield, Vermont's highest peak (4,393 ft or 1,339 m).

Mount Mansfield's fabled "Front Four" have been called "the toughest expert proving grounds in the East." Beginning at elevations of 4,000 ft (1,339 m), with vertical drops of 2,350 ft (716 m), these slopes challenge a skier's ability with steep, mogul-filled, tree-lined chutes. "Goat" and "Star" are two of the steepest mogul trails in the east. Plenty of intermediate slopes provide wide-open touring and a cross-country system offers more than 100 miles (161 km) of interconnected backcountry trails. Stowe has several beginners' trails, so new skiers need not be scared away by its "expert" reputation. New skiers quickly graduate from short runs around the base lodges to the scenic four-mile-long (six-kilometer) "Toll Road."

Be sure to take advantage of activities offered to the public by inns and lodges. Old-fashioned **horse-drawn sleigh** rides circle the hills around Stowehof Inn; the Trapp Family Lodge puts on **wagon rides** for 20. You can **ride horseback** at Edson Hill Manor or take **tennis lessons** from a professional at Topnotch Resort (see WHERE TO STAY, below).

NIGHTLIFE AND THE ARTS

The **Stowe Theater Guild** ☎ (802) 253-3961, Town Hall Theater, PO Box 1381, Main Street, Stowe 05672, is a repertory company that presents a summer season with a few Equity actors to flesh out the local talent. An annual presentation of the story of the Von Trapp family, a stage version of *The Sound of Music*, is always a big hit.

There are changing exhibits featuring area and national artists at the **Helen Day Art Center** ☎ (802) 253-83528, School Street, which also presents an annual film series and an outdoor sculpture show from July through October.

Stowe has après-ski activities to suit every taste. Locals pack the **Rusty Nail** ☎ (802) 253-6245, Mountain Road, nightly for live music, dancing and socializing. A somewhat younger crowd frequents **The Matterhorn** ☎ (802) 253-8198, Mountain Road, beginning from après ski until 2 AM when Stowe rolls up the sidewalks. Those seeking a quiet moment by the fireside can enjoy the Swiss-style atmosphere of the lounge at the Stowehof (see WHERE TO STAY, below).

WHERE TO STAY AND EAT

The Michelin-star-spangled **Topnotch at Stowe Resort and Spa** ☎ (802) 253-8585 TOLL-FREE (800) 451-8686 FAX (802) 253-9263 E-MAIL topnotch@sover.net, 4000 Mountain Road, Stowe 05672, is Stowe's most luxurious resort hotel (expensive to luxury). It's located on 120 acres (48 hectares) at the foot of Mount Mansfield, with a massive spa, and a year-round tennis facility.

The mountaintop **Trapp Family Lodge** ☎ (802) 253-8511 TOLL-FREE (800) 826-7000 FAX (802) 253-5740 E-MAIL info@trappfamily.com, 700 Trapp Hill Road, Stowe 05672, is a Tyrolean-style inn built by the family on whose story *The Sound of Music* is based (expensive to luxury). Located off Route 108, the 93-room lodge also has timeshare condominiums available for rent on a weekly basis. The room rate does not include meals at the excellent restaurant.

A 1940 estate in a beautiful rural setting, **Edson Hill Manor** ☎ (802) 253-7371 TOLL-FREE 800-621-0284 FAX (802) 253-4036, 1500 Edson Hill Road, Stowe 05672-4132, is a museum piece itself with brick walls from the old Sherwood Hotel in Burlington, an antique fireplace from Holland, and living room beams from Ethan Allen's barn (luxury). On the property are cross-country and bridle trails. The rate includes breakfast. The dining room consistently receives rave reviews.

The Gables Inn ☎ (802) 253-7730 TOLL-FREE (800) 422-5371, 1457 Mountain Road, Stowe 05672-4750, is quite comfortable, and located conveniently right on the main drag that connects the village and the mountain; a delicious breakfast (included) is served on the open porch or lawn in summer (budget to expensive). Some 25 dishes are on the menu every morning.

The red-clapboard **Green Mountain Inn** ☎ (802) 253-7301 TOLL-FREE (800) 253-7302 FAX (802) 253-5096, PO Box 60, Stowe 05672, is an 1833 colonial on the National Historical Register (expensive to luxury). It's located in the heart of the village.

The tranquil hamlet of East Orange.

The film location for *Four Seasons* (starring Alan Alda), the hilltop **Stowehof Inn** ☎ (802) 253-9722 TOLL-FREE (800) 932-7136 FAX (802) 253-7513, Edson Hill Road, Stowe 05672 (mid-range — price includes breakfast), exudes European charm. Decorated in Swiss-Austrian style, guestrooms have panoramic views, canopy beds, fireplaces and balconies. The dining room is superb and there is fireside entertainment in the Tyrolean-style bar, sleigh rides on the hilly wooded property and cross-country skiing at your doorstep.

From Stowe Resort's Midway Base Lodge you can hike or take the gondola up to the **Cliff House** ☎ (802) 253-3665 where Swiss fare is served at lunch spring and fall and at lunch and dinner mid-summer. Spectacular — the alpine views I mean, not the Linzer torte, although you won't want to miss that either (expensive).

Miguel's is famous all over the East for its tortilla chips. Here in Stowe it's the convivial cantina, **Miguel's Stowe Away** ☎ (802) 253-7574, 3148 Mountain Road, *and* the chips that draw crowds. The crab enchiladas are a highlight of the Mexican and Texas fare (mid-range).

Mes Amis ☎ (802) 253-8669, 311 Mountain Road, is a newcomer to the Stowe cuisine scene. A local French couple runs this likable bistro-café (mid-range).

Named after a beloved pet and decked with dog memorabilia, **Gracie's** ☎ (802) 253-8741, Carlson Building, Main Street, has delicious sandwiches served on breads made there. It's a cozy place, especially in winter when the fireplace sets the little basement space aglow. Desserts are homemade, too, of course. There are wonderful pies, and the "dog bone" — a delicious chocolate pecan brownie with vanilla ice cream and fudge sauce (budget).

HOW TO GET THERE

Stowe is located north of Waterbury on Route 100. In summer, Stowe can be reached via Smugglers Notch on Route 108.

Amtrak's *Vermonter* TOLL-FREE (800) 872-7245 serves Waterbury.

ABOVE THE NOTCH

Traveling west from Stowe on Route 108 takes you through some spectacular scenery. Once you enter **Smugglers' Notch State Park** ☎ (802) 253-4014, you will be negotiating hairpin curves along sheer cliffs and ledges leading to the 2,162-ft (659-m) "notch," named after the nineteenth-century outlaws who smuggled contraband from the United States into Canada through the natural pass in the Green Mountains. This is rock climbing country as well as an excellent place for hiking. Route 108 is closed during the winter (see HOW TO GET THERE, under STOWE, above). Informational materials on the area can be obtained from the **Smugglers' Notch Area Chamber of Commerce** ☎ (802) 644-2239, PO Box 364, Jeffersonville 05464.

Smugglers' Notch Resort ☎ (802) 644-8851 SNOW CONDITIONS (802) 644-1111 TOLL-FREE (800) 451-8752 TOLL-FREE IN GREAT BRITAIN 0800-169-8219 FAX (802) 644-1230, Route 108, Smugglers' Notch 05464, is a year-round recreation resort. In winter the main attraction is **Madonna**, 3,668 ft (1,118 m) high with a vertical rise of 2,610 ft (796 m). Smugglers' is, in short, expert skier territory. Yet the resort is consistently rated best for families by major ski magazines. Its children's center offers day care, ski schools, and camps — there is even a Club Med-type program headquartered in the new Village Center with a swimming pool, health club, shops and dining.

BURLINGTON

Burlington is a college town, much like any other, but with an outstanding difference: Lake Champlain and its dramatic backdrop, the Adirondack Mountain Range. Vermont's northern mini-metropolis of 40,000 inhabitants follows the shore of Lake Champlain, and a walk to downtown Battery Park reveals a setting that impressed even Rudyard Kipling.

Surrounded by remarkable scenery, Burlington offers brilliant autumn colors making it a favorite stopping-place on the **fall foliage** stampede. Each year, the **Vermont Mozart Festival**, presented by the University of Vermont (UVM) in July and August, draws an audience from around the region. Concerts are held in scenic outdoor settings, including Shelburne Farm (below) and the Trapp Family Lodge at nearby Stowe. During the 10 days leading up to Labor Day, the **Champlain Valley Fair** takes place. This traditional New England agricultural fair has all the proper trappings from prize hogs to blue-ribbon pies, as well as big-name performers.

GENERAL INFORMATION

Canadians entering Vermont via Interstate 89 can stop in for informational materials at the **Vermont Welcome Center** ☎ (802) 868-3244 near Highgate; open daily year-round from 7 AM to 11 PM. Another **Vermont Welcome Center** ☎ (802) 254-4593 is located along Route 2 at Alburg; open daily year-round, from 7 AM to 5 PM. The **Lake Champlain Regional Chamber of Commerce** ☎ (802) 863-3489, PO Box 453, Suite 100, Burlington 05401, runs a **tourist center**, at 60 Main Street, near the waterfront. It's open daily from Memorial Day to Labor Day. There is an extension of the center along Interstate 89 northbound between Exit 11 and 12.

WHAT TO SEE AND DO

On Burlington's overhauled waterfront, **Battery Park** is where American guns defeated the British during the War of 1812; the park affords sweeping views of the Lake Champlain. Also on the waterfront, the **Center for Lake Champlain** ☎ (802) 864-1848, at the foot of College Street, has been undergoing extensive renovation and expansion with a planned reopening in 2003.

Founded in 1791 the University of Vermont (UVM) is located at the top of a hill on the eastern edge of town. UVM (which stands for Université des Verts Monts) has a student population of around 15,000. The **Robert Hull Fleming Museum** ☎ (802) 656-0750 or (802) 656-2090, 61 Colchester Avenue, is the university's fine arts and anthropology exhibit space with permanent and changing shows. Call for hours; an admission fee is charged.

The heart of the downtown shopping and strolling district is the pedestrian-only **Church Street** where you'll find **Lake Champlain Chocolate** ☎ (802) 864-5185, 61 Church Street. Their **factory** ☎ (802) 864-1807, 750 Pine Street, offers weekday tours 9 AM to 2 PM to watch candies being made. Back on Church Street, don't miss the **Vermont State Craft Center on the Marketplace** ☎ (802) 863-6458, at No. 85. Every Saturday

The general store at Peacham, a charming village south of St. Johnsbury.

during the summer there is a **farmers' market** on College Street. Down along the waterfront area, **Battery Street** has several funky shops and delicatessens.

If deep discounts are what you're after you'll want to visit **Essex Outlet Fair** ☎ (802) 657-2777, 21 Essex Way, Essex Junction (about 15 minutes west of the city) with Polo Ralph Lauren, Jones New York, Levi's, Adidas, Dockers, Jockey, Nine West, and it's growing.

The region's finest offerings lie in the village of Shelburne, south of the city. **Shelburne Farm** ☎ (802) 985-8686, a beautiful nineteenth-century manor farm on the shores of Lake Champlain, is a working experimental farm and learning center. This 1,400-acre (560-hectare) National Historic property has a gorgeous restored inn and restaurant. On the grounds, visitors can enjoy the formal gardens, the handsome barn and cheese factory, a bakery, and a children's petting farm. Guided, driven tours are offered. The Shelburne Farms Visitors Center is on Harbor Road, off Route 7 in Shelburne. An admission fee is charged.

Nearby is the marvelous **Shelburne Museum** ☎ (802) 985-3346 TOLL-FREE (800) 253-0191 FAX (802) 985-2331, Route 7, PO Box 10, Shelburne (five miles or eight kilometers south of Burlington). Founded by Electra Havermeyer Webb in the 1950s, this "Smithsonian of New England," spreads out over 45 acres (18 hectares) with 37 buildings brought here from locations throughout the northeast: a horseshoe-shaped barn which houses a fanciful scale model of a quarter-mile-long circus parade; the 1783 Stagecoach Inn with its collection of American folk art; the 1840 Dorset House with more than 1,000 hand-carved duck decoys; and Lake Champlain's 1906 side-wheeler steamboat *Ticonderoga*, docked alongside the old Colchester Reef Lighthouse. The *Ti* has undergone an extensive five-year restoration and now gleams from top to bottom with polished wood, brass fixtures and imported etched-glass. You can tour the boat with docents or sit in a stateroom and listen to taped oral histories of people who rode the *Ti* reminiscing about Lake Champlain's steamboat days. The museum is generally considered one of the top collections of American folk art anywhere in the world. Tours focusing on various aspects of the property are offered, including a 1 PM daily tour telling the story of Mrs. Webb, the museum's founder. Owl Cottage is a family activity center where kids can dress up in 1890s clothing and play period games. The Shelburne Museum is open year-round, and reservations are recommended for the 1 PM tour. The admission fee allows entrance for two consecutive days.

Continue south on Route 7, and you'll arrive at the multicolored barn and silo of the **Vermont Teddy Bear Factory** ☎ (802) 985-3001, extension 1800, 2236 Shelburne Road

(Route 7), where you can take a tour and find out how the pricey plush toys are made. VTBF is famous for their "bear-grams," but here at the factory the bears are available for purchase. The creatures come decked out in one of hundreds of costumes: Ballerina? James Dean look-alike? Snowboarder? There's even a black and white spotted "cow-bear" in honor of Vermont's dairy denizens. Each bear comes boxed with a chocolate "snack" and the sales clerk punches a "breathing hole" in the box. The 13-inch (33-cm) bears run from $38 to $52.

Further south in Charlotte (pronounced "char-LOT"), the **Vermont Wildflower Farm** ☎ (802) 951-5812, has six acres (two and a half hectares) of fields blooming with wildflowers and crossed by walking trails. The shop and visitor center sells wild flower seeds suitable for all areas of North America.

SPORTS AND OUTDOOR ACTIVITIES

A paved **recreational path** runs for seven miles (11 km) along an old rail bed along Lake Champlain. The **Lake Champlain Community Sailing Center** ☎ (802) 864-2499 (at the old Moran Plant on the waterfront), rents sailboats and offers instruction. And then there are the Lake Champlain **beaches**.

The farm team for the Montreal Expos baseball club, the **Vermont Expos** ☎ (802) 655-4200 play their home games at Centennial Field, located on the UVM campus; the season runs from June to September. I hear the UVM **ice hockey** ☎ (802) 656-4410 (box office) games are the hottest ticket in town.

TOURS AND EXCURSIONS

You can sail Lake Champlain on the ***Spirit of Ethan Allen III*** ☎ (802) 862-8300, a sternwheeler. The 90-minute voyage, with magnificent view of Vermont's Green Mountains in the east and New York State's Adirondacks to the west, is especially dazzling in autumn.

The regional ferry service company, **Lake Champlain Transportation Co.** ☎ (802) 864-9804 FAX (802) 864-6830 E-MAIL lct@ferries.com WEB SITE www.ferries.com, offers three different crossings of Lake Champlain. One of the more scenic, but shorter trips departs Charlotte for an 18-minute ride to Essex, New York, a charming nineteenth-century town. The one-hour sojourn from Burlington to Port Kent, New York, makes an excellent scenic tour in the fall. They also offer regular dinner and music cruises from Burlington.

NIGHTLIFE AND THE ARTS

For events listings, pick up a copy of the free arts weekly *Seven Days*; it appears on Wednesday. The 1,400-seat **Flynn Theater** ☎ (802) 863-5966 offers concerts, plays, musicals and dance performances; while the **University of Vermont Lyric Theater** ☎ (802) 656-4528 (information) mixes local talent and New York pros in Broadway-style productions; and the **George Bishop Lane Series** ☎ (802) 656-3131 brings drama and music of many genres to city venues.

There is a robust rock scene in Burlington. A number of bands have gotten their start at **Nectar's** ☎ (802) 658-4771, 188 Main Street, including the pop rock band Phish who first played here in 1984. Open every night, every day of the year. Food is served; don't miss the house specialty, fries and gravy.

Jazz has a foothold in Burlington as well, with **Red Square** ☎ (802) 859-8909, 136 Church Street, as one of the newer venues. Burlington's **Discover Jazz Festival** takes place the second week of June when the city explodes with musical performances in practically every club and restaurant in town. There's even music on the city buses and ferries. Festival tickets can be purchased through the Flynn Theater Box Office ☎ (802) 863-5966, 153 Main Street, Burlington 05401.

WHERE TO STAY

Besides the accommodation listed below, there are a half dozen or so chain hotels and motels in South Burlington. Contact the chamber of commerce (see GENERAL INFORMATION, above) for a brochure listing bed and breakfast accommodations; prices range from budget to expensive.

The building is uninspiring, but inside the **Radisson Hotel Burlington** ☎ (802) 658-6500 TOLL-FREE (800) 333-3333 FAX (802) 658-4659 E-MAIL burlington@radissonvt.com, 60 Battery Street, Burlington 05401 (expensive), is all you would expect from this chain, and many rooms have fabulous views of Lake Champlain. Children stay free.

Eight miles (13 km) outside of downtown Burlington, the **Inn at Essex** ☎ (802) 878-1100 FAX (802) 878-0063 TOLL-FREE (800) 727-4295 E-MAIL innfo@innatessex.com, 70 Essex Way, Essex 05452 (expensive), is a newer property that aims to create the atmosphere of a country inn. It succeeds to some extent because of the friendliness and helpfulness of the staff. The 120 guestrooms are comfortable and spacious, if a bit stiff. Some "Country Inn" rooms recently built have kitchens, Vermont-made quilts, wood stoves and rocking chairs. Eighteen acres of lawns and

A piglet in her element at Shelburne Farms.

gardens surround the hotel. A fitness facility is available for an additional daily fee, but you must board a shuttle bus to get there.

The gorgeous **Inn at Shelburne Farms** ☎ (802) 985-8498, 102 Harbor Road, Shelburne 05482 (mid-range to luxury), is a late nineteenth century mansion with 24 rooms, each furnished in period antiques. Once the family home of William Seward and Lila Vanderbilt Webb, it sits on Saxton's Point overlooking Lake Champlain and the Adirondack mountains. On the property, a 1,000-acre (405-hectare) working farm supplies the inn with fresh produce. The inn and its two dining rooms are open from mid-May to mid-October.

WHERE TO EAT

The New England Culinary Institute runs two excellent restaurants at the Inn at Essex (see above). NECI (pronounced "necky") was founded in 1980 to teach both the business and the art of cooking. The menu changes daily at **Butler's** (mid-range to expensive), where you can enjoy perfectly prepared venison, salmon, and pork. If the dessert crêpe is on the menu, order it. Reservations are essential. At **The Tavern** (budget to mid-range), you can live it up without blowing your budget on lighter fare as well as full dinners and nightly specials. Both restaurants have beautifully constructed salads and wine lists where you can't go wrong. Both offer excellent value.

Contemporary American cuisine and a 1,000-bottle wine cellar have won accolades for the **Inn at Shelburne Farms** (see WHERE TO STAY, above; mid-range to expensive). **Pauline's** ☎ (802) 862-1081, 1834 Shelburne Road, South Burlington, serves seafood and home-style cooking at affordable prices. For steak and seafood on a terrace overlooking Burlington's ferry dock, there is the **Ice House Restaurant** ☎ (802) 864-1800, 171 Battery Street (budget to mid-range).

The **Oasis** ☎ (802) 864-5308, 189 Banks Street (budget), is a vintage rail car serving classic diner fare. **Henry's** ☎ (802) 862-9010, 155 Bank Street (budget), isn't as authentically situated, but serves the same type of honest fare. **Bove's Café** ☎ (802) 864-6651, 68 Pearl Street, is an affordable Italian eatery where students lineup every night for carbo-loading.

The **NECI Commons** ☎ (802) 862-6324, 25 Church Street, is a stylish, casual restaurant that serves pizza and calzones from the hearth, and uncommon salads such as wild rice and warm duck with mesclun greens and a raspberry vinaigrette. Desserts are as artistically rendered and delicious.

If you haven't already overdone it at NECI Commons, get some goodies at **Mirabelle's** ☎ (802) 658-3074, 198 Main Street, a fabulous pastry shop. For picnic supplies, or simply to marvel at Vermont's bounty, stop by the **Cheese Traders** ☎ (802) 863-0143, 1186 Williston Road, in South Burlington.

HOW TO GET THERE

Burlington is 226 miles (364 km) from Boston and 263 miles (420 km) from New York City. There is daily service aboard **Amtrak's *Vermonter*** TOLL-FREE (800) 872-7245, which operates between Washington, DC, and Saint Albans (with through bus service to Montreal).

The city is served by **Burlington International Airport** ☎ (802) 863-1889 in South Burlington with direct flights from Boston, New York, Philadelphia, Pittsburgh, Washington, DC, and Chicago.

Three **ferries** cross Lake Champlain to New York State: Grand Isle–Platzburg, Port Kent–Burlington, and Charlotte–Essex.

THE NORTHEAST KINGDOM

Three counties and some 2,000 sq miles (5,000 sq km) of hills and farmland comprise Vermont's Northeast Kingdom. Called "the Vermonter's Vermont," this roughly triangular area of lakes and mountains stretches from the Connecticut River in the east to the Green Mountains in the west. A land of fiddlers' festivals, country dances, smoked hams, country fairs, flea markets and church suppers — some people call it the essence of Vermont. It's also a paradise for outdoor recreation.

Dozens of hilly farms and pretty white clapboard towns and villages define the Northeast Kingdom's landscape. Near **Saint Johnsbury**, you'll find New England's largest cheese factory, the Cabot Creamery ☎ (802) 229-9361 TOLL-FREE (800) 837-4261, Main Street, in Cabot Village, about 15 miles (24 km) west of Saint Johnsbury. Tours are offered daily late May through October, weekdays the rest of the year. **Danville**, west of Saint Johnsbury, is the headquarters of the American Society of Dowsers, whose water-witching fall convention draws lots of attention. In **Newport** there are boat cruises on Lake Memphremagog. **Lyndonville**, in the green hills of the Passumpsic River valley, has five covered bridges within village limits, the earliest dating from 1795. **Cavendish** was the decade-long refuge of Russian novelist Alexander Solzhenitsyn and his wife. **Glover** is home to Bread & Puppet Museum Theater ☎ (802) 525-3031. Their annual festival is sadly defunct, but the wonderful museum remains, set in an old barn where

their larger-than-life puppets are arranged in dioramas telling stories with social and ecological morals and great humor.

During the fall foliage season, the woods of the Northeast Kingdom are ablaze with color and villages make merry with harvest festivals. Winter brings skiers to Jay Peak's slopes. Spring is mud season throughout the north, but in Craftsbury a can't-beat-'em-join-'em attitude prevails when the **Mud and Ice Quadrathlon** takes place in March. Participants compete in mud-skiing, mud-biking, mud-canoeing and mud-running. Whatever....

GENERAL INFORMATION

For information on the region contact the **Northeast Kingdom Travel & Tourism Association** ☎ (802) 723-9800 TOLL-FREE (888) 884-8001 FAX (802) 525-4387 E-MAIL info@travelthekingdom.com, The Historic Railroad

OPPOSITE: A covered bridge at Waitsfield.
ABOVE: A farm nestles in the rolling hills of the Northeast Kingdom.

Station, Main Street, PO Box 355, Island Pond 05907-0355. Visitors entering Vermont via Interstate 93 from New Hampshire can stop in for informational materials at the **Vermont Welcome Center** ☎ (802) 748-9368 near Saint Johnsbury; open year-round, from 7 AM to 11 PM.

SPORTS AND OUTDOOR ACTIVITIES

Eight miles (13 km) south of the Canadian border is **Jay Peak Resort** ☎ (802) 988-2611 SNOW CONDITIONS (802) 988-9601 TOLL-FREE (800) 451-4449 FAX (802) 988-4049, PO BOX 152, Jay 05859. Spread out over more than 375 acres (150 hectares) are the resort's 64 trails, served by seven lifts.

Every half hour the **Jay Peak Tramway** ☎ (802) 988-2611, Route 242, in Jay, carries goggle-eyed passengers to the summit for a panoramic view of the surrounding countryside. It's a treat in any season, but the view will knock your socks off in the autumn. To get there take Route 242 from Montgomery Center. Hours vary according to the season. A fare is charged with reductions for families.

Craftsbury Outdoor Center TOLL-FREE (800) 729-7751, Craftsbury Common 05827, is my favorite cross-country ski area. Wax up your skis at the wood-stove heated shed and take off on the 90 miles (150 km) of trails ranging in elevation from 700 to 2,000 ft (210 to 600 m). Rentals and instruction are available. In summer the trails host a platoon of off-road bikers.

WHERE TO STAY AND EAT

The Northeast Kingdom offers some beautiful getaways. **Rabbit Hill Inn** ☎ (802) 748-5168 TOLL-FREE (800) 762-8669 FAX (802) 748-8342, Lower Waterford 05848 (luxury), has 21 guestrooms and suites with stunning architectural details and lots of extras. Some rooms have fireplace and whirlpool for two. The room rate includes a candlelight breakfast buffet and afternoon tea. Five-course gourmet meals are served in the dining room.

Montgomery Center, at the junction of Routes 118 and 242, is the dining and lodging hub for Jay Peak. The **Inn on Trout River** ☎ (802) 326-4391 TOLL-FREE (800) 338-7049,

PO Box 76, Main Street, Montgomery Center 05471-0076 (mid-range), has cheerful Victorian rooms, and the rate includes breakfast. You can have dinner on the premises at **Lemointe's** (expensive), where the menu features seafood and grilled meat dishes.

Situated on 145 private acres (58 hectares) by Great Hosmer Pond, the **Craftsbury Outdoor Center** TOLL-FREE (800) 729-7751 FAX (802) 586-7768 E-MAIL crafts@sover.net, PO Box 31, Craftsbury Common 05827, offers hearty meals, simple and comfortable rooms (no phone, no television) and lakeside cottages for 90 guests year-round. The surrounding woods are crossed by trails. There's a pond for swimming. Canoes and kayaks (free) and mountain bikes (rental) are available.

The **Black Lantern Inn** ((802) 326-2024 TOLL-FREE (800) 255-8661 FAX (802) 326-4077 E-MAIL blantern@together.net, Route 118, Montgomery Village 05470, has 10 rooms in an 1803 brick house and six modern suites in an adjacent building (budget to expensive). The rate includes breakfast. The dining room's signature dish is grilled leg of lamb.

A bit south in White River Junction, the **Hotel Coolidge** ((802) 295-3118, 39 South Main Street, maintains an AYH-HI-affiliated hostel wing with shared baths and kitchen. Reservations are essential.

Zack's on the Rocks ((802) 326-4500, Route 58, Montgomery Center, is a one-of-a-kind restaurant. Small and funky, the two-level dining room sports decor to go with the season. The eclectic menu (written on a paper bag) features main courses such as crispy duckling and tournedos béarnaise. Open Tuesday to Sunday for dinner (expensive). Reservations are required. Also in Montgomery Center, **J.R.'s** ((802) 326-4682, Main Street, has exalted the humble sandwich to an art (budget).

How to Get There

St. Johnsbury lies at the junction of Interstates 91 and 93. Interstate 91 continues northwest as far as Derby Line where it becomes Highway 55 as it heads into Quebec province in Canada.

All is evidently well in this remote Vermont village.

New Hampshire

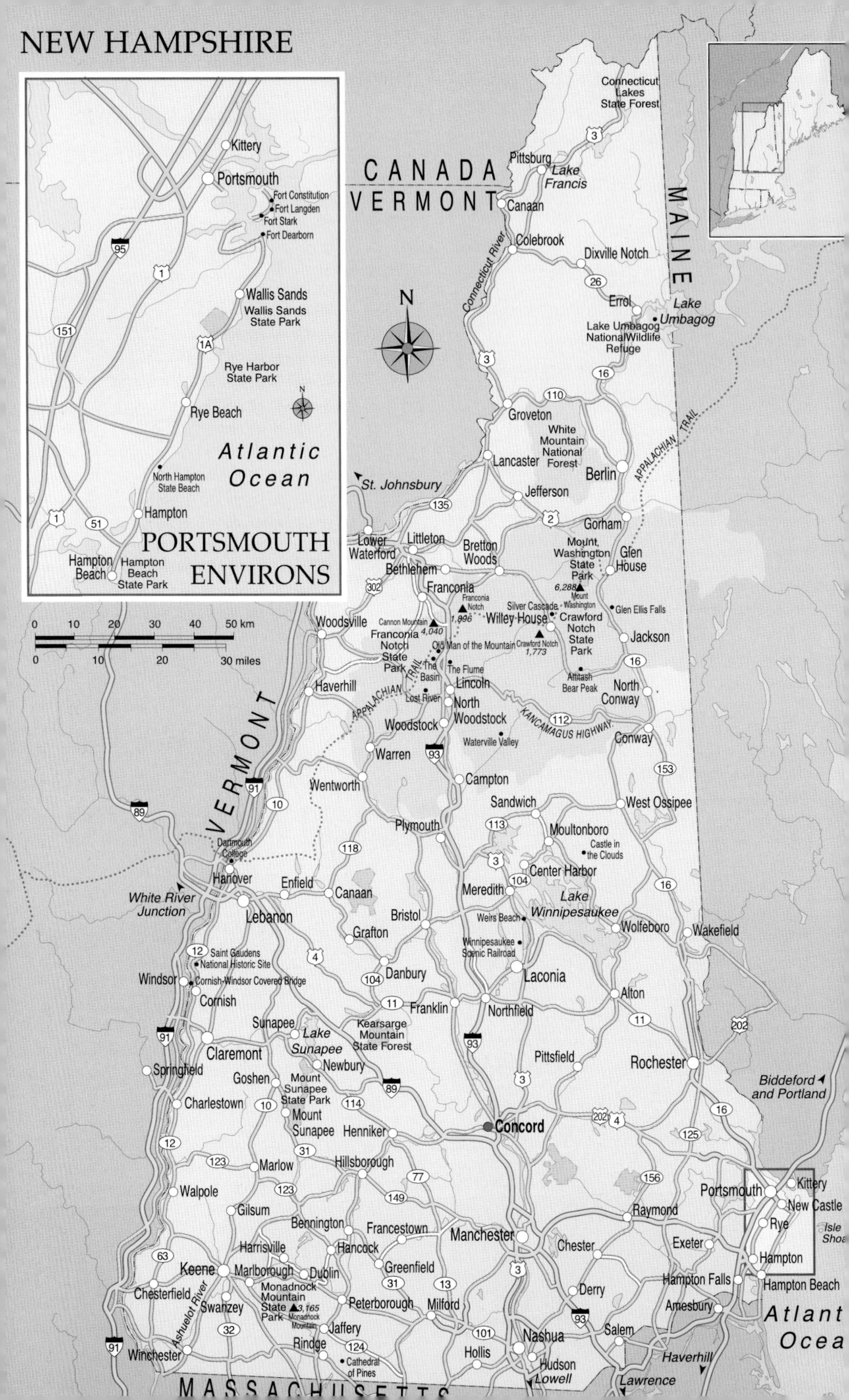
NEW HAMPSHIRE
PORTSMOUTH ENVIRONS
Kittery
Portsmouth
Fort Constitution
Fort Langden
Fort Stark
Fort Dearborn
95
1
Wallis Sands
Wallis Sands State Park
151
1A
Rye Harbor State Park
N
Rye Beach
Atlantic Ocean
North Hampton State Beach
Hampton
51
Hampton Beach
Hampton Beach State Park
0 10 20 30 40 50 km
0 10 20 30 miles
CANADA
VERMONT
MAINE
Connecticut Lakes State Forest
3
Pittsburg
Lake Francis
Canaan
Colebrook
Connecticut River
Dixville Notch
26
Errol
Lake Umbagog
Lake Umbagog National Wildlife Refuge
16
110
Groveton
White Mountain National Forest
Lancaster
Berlin
APPALACHIAN TRAIL
St. Johnsbury
Jefferson
135
2
Gorham
Lower Waterford
Littleton
Bretton Woods
Mount Washington State Park
Glen House
Bethlehem
302
Franconia
6,288
Mount Washington
Glen Ellis Falls
Franconia Notch
1,896
Silver Cascade
Willey House
Crawford Notch State Park
Woodsville
Cannon Mountain
4,040
Franconia Notch State Park
Old Man of the Mountain
Crawford Notch
1,773
Jackson
The Basin
The Flume
Attitash Bear Peak
Haverhill
Lincoln
North Conway
Lost River
North Woodstock
KANCAMAGUS HIGHWAY
112
Woodstock
Conway
Waterville Valley
Warren
93
153
Campton
Wentworth
91
Sandwich
West Ossipee
10
89
Plymouth
113
Moultonboro
Castle in the Clouds
118
Dartmouth College
Hanover
Center Harbor
Enfield
Meredith
104
White River Junction
Canaan
Lake Winnipesaukee
Lebanon
Bristol
Weirs Beach
Wolfeboro
Wakefield
Grafton
12
Saint Gaudens National Historic Site
Winnipesaukee Scenic Railroad
4
Windsor
Cornish-Windsor Covered Bridge
Danbury
Laconia
Cornish
11
Franklin
Northfield
Alton
Sunapee
Kearsarge Mountain State Forest
202
Lake Sunapee
Claremont
Pittsfield
Rochester
Newbury
Springfield
Goshen
Mount Sunapee State Park
Biddeford and Portland
Charlestown
114
Mount Sunapee
Henniker
Concord
125
31
123
Marlow
Hillsborough
77
156
Walpole
149
Portsmouth
Kittery
New Castle
Gilsum
Raymond
Rye
Bennington
Francestown
Manchester
Isle
Harrisville
Hancock
Chester
Exeter
63
Keene
Marlborough
Dublin
Greenfield
Hampton
Monadnock Mountain State Park
Hampton Falls
Hampton Beach
Chesterfield
13
Derry
Swanzey
3,165
Monadnock Mountain
Peterborough
Milford
Amesbury
Ashuelot River
Atlant
32
Jaffery
101
Nashua
Salem
Winchester
Rindge
124
Hollis
Hudson
Haverhill
Cathedral of Pines
Lowell
Lawrence

Just specimens is all New Hampshire has,
One each of everything as in a showcase,
Which naturally she doesn't care to sell…

—Robert Frost

Travelers to New Hampshire quickly discover what the poet meant. Despite its small size — 180 miles (290 km) from north to south and 100 miles (160 km) at its widest point — New Hampshire has a splendid variety of scenery from its short but pretty seacoast to the highest mountain peaks of New England, from the fertile farmland of the Connecticut River Valley to dense north woods and well-preserved villages. And don't forget the shopping. New Hampshire draws bargain hunters from nearby states for its factory outlets and tax-free items.

New Hampshire was the only one of the thirteen colonies not invaded by British troops during the Revolution. The people of the state had then, and still retain, a determined sense of independence and have embraced conservative democracy with a particular fervor. One of New Hampshire's major newspapers, *The Manchester Union-Leader*, has in its editorial policies and news coverage one of the most ferocious right-wing stances in the nation. Although many New Hampshire residents would disagree, such attitudes seem to have filtered down into the daily attitudes of segments of the population.

New Hampshire's political leanings manifest themselves in other substantive ways. New Hampshire has no state income tax or sales tax. State revenues are generated through so-called "sin" taxes on lottery tickets, liquor and cigarette sales. Most notably, the state's Bill of Rights recognizes "revolution" as a legitimate means of carrying out the will of the people, hence the state motto, "Live Free or Die," found on its license plates.

Political awareness and self-determination are also evident in New Hampshire's form of local government: the town meeting. Established early in New England's history, the town meeting was, in a sense, the genesis of American democracy, giving each member in the community an equal voice in local affairs. Town Meeting Day remains an important element of that process throughout New Hampshire. In the state government, more than 420 legislators constitute one of the largest legislative assemblies in the world.

New Hampshire's presidential primary, the nation's first in a presidential election year, has become the forecast of success or failure for candidates for that office, a mega-media event that has somehow achieved "make or break" status on the political scene. Candidates who might otherwise have difficulty pointing out New Hampshire on a map of the United States descend quadrennially upon the state to offer political platitudes to this independent people.

Remembrance: an Independence Day memorial, erected 48 years after the fact.

But platitudes do not seem to work in New Hampshire. Its residents are straightforward, unpretentious Yankees who cut to the political quick of issues. They also have an uncanny record of reflecting the national mood. Around 75 percent of the time, New Hampshire Primary winners have become presidential candidates of both the Republican and Democratic parties.

It is not surprising that New Hampshire residents relish their role as tough independents. Ever since a small group of English fishermen made the dangerous journey across the Atlantic, landing at Odiorne Point (the town of Rye) in 1623 to establish a fledgling fishing industry, independence and self-reliance have been traits vital to survival.

BACKGROUND

European settlers experienced severe hardships. The rocky land had only a thin layer of topsoil. Clearing dense forests demanded months of hard labor before food crops could be planted. And winters were bitter, with subzero temperatures and mounds of snow.

Apart from subsistence farming, there were two other economic activities in the new settlement. Fishing fleets set sail from the state's only deepwater port — now Portsmouth — to seek cod on the west Atlantic, while loggers cut down New Hampshire's 1,000-year-old pines for use as masts and shipbuilding timber.

By 1641, the struggling settlements had agreed to consolidate with the flourishing Massachusetts Bay Colony to the south. But the year-long King Philip's War (named for a Wampanoag chief) caused much disruption when it began in 1675 and the settlements did not recover until just before the American Revolution.

New Hampshire received its "independence" from Massachusetts in 1679, when King Charles II declared it a royal province. John Wentworth, a successful merchant, was appointed to govern the colony in 1717; it prospered for a time, with Portsmouth taking on an English elegance that is still apparent.

Later, the colony became caught up in the fervor for independence and Wentworth was forced to leave Portsmouth in 1775. One year later, on January 5, 1776, New Hampshire drew up its own constitution and declared its independence from England, six months before the Declaration of Independence of July 4, 1776.

In the 1800s, New Hampshire evolved from a logging, fishing and farming center into a cotton and wool-manufacturing hub, while the nineteenth century saw the development of the textile and shoe industries.

Manufacturing continued to grow well into the twentieth century, attracting thousands of French Canadians from poor farms across the border. Many factories, including the Amoskeag Manufacturing Company, then one of the largest mills in the country, drew immigrant workers from around the world who toiled long, grueling hours. The mills are said to have produced more than one mile (1.6 km) of cloth every working minute. However, the Great Depression, labor strikes and the changing economy combined to deal New Hampshire's economy a serious blow.

Today, a revived (and diversified) manufacturing industry combines with tourism, a relaxed lifestyle and a favorable tax climate to make New Hampshire an attractive place in which to live and work.

PORTSMOUTH AND THE SEACOAST

New Hampshire's only seaport, Portsmouth was once the capital of the state and homeport to a long-lived dynasty of merchant seamen. Great riches were amassed from their trade, which then were used to build handsome houses befitting their status, bringing to the settlement a veneer of refinement and culture. The city's "Golden Age" has passed, but the modern city of Portsmouth still glows with superb historical attractions, a sparkling nightlife with theater and music that is both of the highest quality and affordable, and many excellent restaurants.

GENERAL INFORMATION

The **Greater Portsmouth Chamber of Commerce** ✆ (603) 436-1118, at 500 Market Street, PO Box 239, Portsmouth 03802-0239, can provide information on the Portsmouth and Seacoast region and offers a free visitors' guide. Look for the big **welcome center** as you enter New Hampshire from Massachusetts on Interstate 95. Once downtown, there is an **information kiosk** in Market Square; open daily 9 AM to 5 PM from Memorial Day Weekend through Labor Day, weekdays only the rest of the year.

WHAT TO SEE AND DO

Travelers can sample a bit of Portsmouth's colonial past by following the **Portsmouth Trail**, a self-guided tour that takes in the city's finest seventeenth- and eighteenth-century dwellings, the waterfront and gardens. A brochure entitled "The Portsmouth Trail: An Historic Walking Tour" is available free from the city's information centers (see above). Homes tend to be open June to October.

On Market Street is the **Moffatt-Ladd House**, built in 1763 by Captain John Moffatt as a wedding gift for his son, Samuel, and noted for its elegant furnishings and eighteenth-century architectural style. Visitors are also welcome in the formal gardens, where peonies blossom in colorful splendor each June.

The **Warner House** (next to the Town Hall on Daniel Street), built in 1716 by another wealthy sea captain, was occupied by the old salt's descendants as late as 1930. Called "one of the finest urban brick residences of the first quarter of the eighteenth century," it is one of New England's most beautiful Georgian houses, with several antique murals hanging in their original positions along the staircase. The lightning rod on the west wall was installed under the supervision of Benjamin Franklin in 1762.

George Washington called the **Governor John Langdon House**, on Pleasant Street, "the handsomest house in Portsmouth." Built in 1784 for a prominent Revolutionary War political leader who was a three-term governor of New Hampshire and first president *pro tempore* of the United States Senate, this elegant Georgian mansion remains one of the finest eighteenth-century houses in New England. The exterior proportions are enormous, while the gracious interiors contain fine hand carving. The gardens have been restored to their original state, with rose and grape arbors, perennial garden beds, and a handsome gazebo. Washington, Lafayette, and other statesmen of the time were entertained here.

Other houses on the tour include the 1758 residence of famed American naval leader **John Paul Jones** (who, when beckoned by the British to surrender during one high-seas battle, uttered the renowned line, "We have not yet begun to fight"); the grand 1807 Federal-style mansion called the **Rundlet-May House**; and the 1760 **Wentworth Gardner House**, whose grand woodcarvings are said

to have kept a master craftsman busy for more than a year.

Named for the wild strawberries that grew here in abundance when settlers arrived, **Strawbery Banke Museum** ☎ (603) 433-1100, Hancock and Marcy streets, is a 10-acre (four-hectare) outdoor museum in downtown Portsmouth. The museum preserves the waterfront neighborhood that was the site of the original Portsmouth settlement. About 35 buildings, dating from 1695 to 1940 and furnished with period antiques, are being

OPPOSITE: The state motto, "Live Free or Die," underlines another imperative, "visit," on a New Hampshire license plate. ABOVE: Strawberry Banke, an outdoor museum and restored neighborhood, tells the story of Portsmouth.

restored. Many of them are completed and open to the public, including the 1780 Captain John Wheelwright House. Also recently restored is the 1766 William Pitt Tavern, a former stagecoach stop and hotbed of Revolutionary politics. George Washington often came here when visiting local state officials. The Shapiro House depicts the life of a Russian-Jewish family during World War I, and a grocery store illustrates rationing measures during World War II.

Not only can you stroll among the historic structures (in many cases watching actual

restoration taking place), but you can also participate in a number of activities. Several of the houses have been transformed into workshops, where programs for all age levels offer seminars on colonial crafts (including hands-on demonstrations), lectures and special events such as the December candlelight tour through the "village." Other houses contain craft shops of working artisans who display their handiwork. Even landscapes have been recreated, including eighteenth-century herb and vegetable gardens. Set your own pace; visits are self-guided. Open daily May through October; an admission fee is charged.

If you drive south of the city, nearby **New Castle** offers views of the Isles of Shoals from Fort Constitution, as well as scores of beautiful colonial homes to admire.

TOURS AND EXCURSIONS

The Isles of Shoals first harbored pirates, and later literary figures such as James Whittier, Nathaniel Hawthorne and Harriet Beecher Stowe. There are **Narrated boat tours** to the beautiful little islands with Isles of Shoals Steamship Co. ((603) 431-5500 TOLL-FREE (800) 441-4620, 315 Market Street, Portsmouth 03801. Once there you get a chance to explore.

The company also offers whale-watching tours, lighthouse cruises and foliage excursions to the Great Bay Wilderness Area. Also in the business is Portsmouth Harbor Cruises ((603) 436-8084 TOLL-FREE (800) 776-0915, at Ceres Street Dock.

Hampton State Beach ((603) 926-3784, campground (603) 926-8990, Route 1A, Hampton, is about eight miles (13 km) south of Portsmouth.

NIGHTLIFE AND THE ARTS

The vintage **Music Hall** ((603) 436-2400, 104 Congress Street, presents dance, music and theater throughout the year. The **Seacoast Repertory Theater** ((603) 433-4472,

125 Bow Street, and the **Pontine Movement Theater** ☎ (603) 436-6660, 135 McDonough Street, are both highly acclaimed companies.

WHERE TO STAY

Sise Inn ☎ (603) 433-1200 TOLL-FREE (800) 267-0525, 40 Court Street, Portsmouth 03801, in the heart of the historic district, is a Queen Anne-style town house reminiscent of nineteenth-century Portsmouth. Rooms have queen-size bed; the rate (expensive) includes a continental breakfast.

Portsmouth's only hotel with harbor views, the **Sheraton Harborside Portsmouth** ☎ (603) 431-2300 TOLL-FREE (800) 325-3535, 250 Market Street, Portsmouth 03801 (expensive), is within walking distance of the historic center and shopping; parking is free.

You could hardly find more central lodging than the **Bow Street Inn** ☎ (603) 431-7760 FAX (603) 433-1680, 121 Bow Street, Portsmouth 03801 (mid-range), built into a waterfront mill building directly over the Seacoast Repertory Theater. Nine guestrooms have river views, queen-size beds, and reading chairs; the rate includes a generous continental breakfast.

A more modest option is available at the **Port Motor Inn** ☎ (603) 436-4378 TOLL-FREE (800) 282-7678, Route 1 Bypass at Portsmouth Traffic Circle, Portsmouth 03801 (budget); some rooms have refrigerator and microwave oven. The rate includes a continental breakfast. The heated pool is open spring through fall.

WHERE TO EAT

The dining capital of the state, Portsmouth has loads of small restaurants — more than 50 at last count — and the prices won't break your budget.

The Portsmouth waterfront has some of the best. **The Oar House** ☎ (603) 436-4025, 55 Ceres Street (mid-range) is the priciest choice (expensive). Dine onboard the tugboat *John Wannamaker* at **Dunphy's John Wannamaker** ☎ (603) 433-3111, One Harbor Place, No. 10. Good food and a unique setting make this restaurant popular with locals as well as travelers (expensive). **Lindbergh's Crossing** ☎ (603) 431-0887, 55 Ceres Street (mid-range), is a wine bar and French provincial bistro where, on a cold night, the lentil, tomato and mussel soup will help you shake the chill (expensive).

OPPOSITE: Lobster LEFT by the pound and popcorn RIGHT by the scoop. ABOVE: Tugboats await the call to duty in Portsmouth harbor.

Don't look for fancy food at the **Press Room** ☎ (603) 431-5186, 77 Daniel Street, but do expect good company and a thriving acoustic music and jazz scene. One of New England's stalwarts on the singer-songwriter circuit, the Press Room serves better casual food than most coffeehouses and cheaper drinks than most lounges.

The **Portsmouth Brewery** ☎ (603) 431-1115, Market Street, serves good pub food in a room decorated with natural wood, but the star is the beer. There are many varieties, with Shoals Pale Ale and Old Brown Dog Ale being two of the best (budget).

If you're looking for a breakfast place, **Café Brioche** ☎ (603) 430-9225, 14 Market Square, serves fresh-baked pastries, with outdoor seating in a pleasant central square (budget).

HOW TO GET THERE

Portsmouth is 55 miles (88 km) from Boston. Motorists arriving from the south will take Interstate 95 to Exit 7.

Forty miles (64 km) from Portsmouth and within an hour's drive from many of the state's resort areas, **Manchester Airport** ☎ (603) 624-6539, is located adjacent to Interstate 93, Interstate 293, Route 101 and Route 3. It is served by US Air and US Air Express TOLL-FREE (800) 428-4322, United Airlines TOLL-FREE (800) 241-6522, Comair TOLL-FREE (800) 345-3400, Business Express TOLL-FREE (800) 345-3400, Continental Express TOLL-FREE (800) 525-0280, and United Express TOLL-FREE (800) 241-6522.

Rental car agencies at Manchester Airport are: Avis ☎ (603) 624-4000 TOLL-FREE (800) 331-1212, Budget ☎ (603) 668-3166 TOLL-FREE (800) 527-0700, Hertz ☎ (603) 626-1890 TOLL-FREE (800) 654-3131 and National ☎ (603) 627-2299 TOLL-FREE (800) 227-7368.

HANOVER AND VICINITY

The town of Hanover has a crisply starched look, but behind the preppy sheen there is plenty of local character, with bookstores, restaurants and shops lining its streets. There is also ready access to outdoor recreation, including the Appalachian Trail, which passes through the campus. South of Hanover, along Route 120, a region of lakes, picturesque villages and gentle mountains unfolds along the Connecticut River Valley. This area is the last bastion of New Hampshire small-farm activity where there are family-run orchards and dairies as well as a number of small enterprises producing specialty foods. For maps and information contact the **Hanover Chamber of Commerce** ☎ (603) 643-3115, Hanover 03755.

WHAT TO SEE AND DO

Hanover

The cultural anchor for the region is **Dartmouth College**, chartered in 1769 by Rev-

erend Eleazar Wheelock "for the instruction of the Youth of Indian tribes." It now attracts youths of every persuasion from all over the country. Dartmouth's handsome campus retains much colonial flavor, with stately Federal and Georgian buildings and a wide village green. **Dartmouth Row**, located on the east side of the Green, has several white brick buildings dating from 1784, and the **Baker Memorial Library** displays frescoes by the Mexican artist Orozco. Guided campus tours are offered during summer months.

Next to the Hanover Inn (see WHERE TO STAY AND EAT, below), the **Hood Museum of Art** ☎ (603) 646-2808, Wheelock Street, contains one of the oldest and largest college art collections in the country. Most impressive are the group of Assyrian reliefs, dating from 883 to 859 BC, that dominates the central gallery. There is also a fine collection of nineteenth-century American landscapes.

Next door you can walk through the **Spaulding Center** and observe students at work making jewelry and woodcrafts. Handiwork from throughout the state is shown and sold at the **League of New Hampshire Craft Shop** ☎ (603) 643-5050, at 13 Lebanon Street.

Enfield

In 1793 a group of Shakers established a community along the western shore of Mascoma Lake, where they practiced the Shaker tenets of equality of the sexes and races, celibacy, pacifism, and communal ownership of property. The fellowship thrived here until 1923 when they were forced to close their community because of declining membership. They sold the land and buildings to an order of Catholic priests who established a seminary and continued to farm the land until 1985 when the buildings and grounds were purchased by a group of private investors. Today the **Enfield Shaker Museum** ☎/FAX (603) 632-4346 WEB SITE www.shakermuseum.com, 24 Caleb Dyer Lane, Enfield 03748, preserves the legacy of the Shakers who lived and worked here for 130 years. Visitors can view 13 buildings on a self-guided tour, wander among the exquisite Shaker Gardens and see demonstrations of traditional crafts and exhibits of the Shaker furniture, tools and clothing. The Great Stone Dwelling, once the living quarters of the community, has been converted into a splendid inn (see WHERE TO STAY, below). Next to the village is the workshop of the **Dana Robes Wood Craftsmen** TOLL-FREE (800) 722-5036, where you can see and buy Shaker-inspired furniture and woodcrafts. Open daily May through October, weekends the rest of year.

Cornish and Windsor

South of Hanover, the village of Cornish was home to the famed **Cornish Colony** of artists and writers; set up in 1885, it lasted for 50 years. J.D. Salinger, the reclusive author of *The Catcher in the Rye*, still lives in this town. Cornish also has the longest remaining covered bridge in the United States, the **Cornish–Windsor Bridge**. Built in 1866, it stretches 460 ft (140 m) over the Connecticut River to Vermont. For more about covered bridges, see KISS ON A COVERED BRIDGE, page 17 in TOP SPOTS.

Also in Cornish, the **Saint-Gaudens National Historic Site** ☎ (603) 675-2175, RR 3, PO Box 73, Cornish 03745, preserves the summer cottage and gardens of the Dublin-born sculptor Augustus Saint-Gaudens (1848–1907). America's foremost sculptor at the turn of the century, Saint-Gaudens came to New Hampshire in 1885 and converted an old tavern into his estate and studio. Much of Saint-Gaudens' work is located throughout

the attractive grounds. Open late May to late October; an admission fee is charged.

In **Windsor**, you can see master glassblowers and potters at work at the **Simon Pearce Glass Factory & Pottery** ☎ (802) 674-6280. Other crafts are on show, including handcrafted furniture, linens and baskets, woolens, tweeds, sweaters and leather goods.

SPORTS AND OUTDOOR ACTIVITIES

There is **skiing** at Mount Sunapee ☎ (603) 763-5561, Mount Sunapee State Park, outside Newbury (on Route 103). At the Dartmouth

OPPOSITE: The Green at Dartmouth College, Hanover. ABOVE: Midwinter thaw at Enfield near the Shaker Museum.

Skiway ☎ (603) 795-2143, 15 minutes north of Hanover in Lyme Center, a quad lift serves 16 trails; they guarantee you won't have to stand in a lift line. There's more alpine skiing near Windsor at Vermont's Ascutney Mountain Resort ☎ (802) 484-7711 SNOW CONDITIONS (802) 243-0011 TOLL-FREE (800) 243-0011 FAX (802) 484-3117, Route 44, PO Box 699, Brownsville, VT 05037, where four lifts serve a total of 47 trails.

In summer months, Mount Sunapee has **chairlift rides** up to the mountain's 2,700-ft (823-m) summit, with panoramic views of

Lake Sunapee, the Green Mountains in the distance to the west and the White Mountains to the northeast. The lake is known for its fine salmon and lake trout **fishing**.

In Cornish, you can rent a **canoe** for a bucolic trip on the Connecticut River from North Star Canoe Rentals ☎ /FAX (603) 542-5802, RR2, Route 12A, PO Box 894, Cornish 03745. They'll also arrange for shuttle service for half-, full- and multi-day trips.

NIGHTLIFE AND THE ARTS

Drop by the Dartmouth Bookstore, where events are posted on the corkboard at the entrance; or look for the *Wicked Good Calendar*, a monthly arts and entertainment publication for the region.

At Dartmouth College, the **Hopkins Center** ☎ (603) 646-2422 is a superb year-round forum for concerts, dance performances and film festivals. There's not much late-night revelry, but if you've got insomnia, there's a pub on campus in the Collis building that's open until 2 AM.

WHERE TO STAY

The finest accommodation in Hanover is the 100-year-old **Hanover Inn** ☎ (603) 643-4300 TOLL-FREE (800) 443-7024 FAX (603) 643-4433, PO Box 151, Hanover 03755, at the corner of Main and Wheelock streets (expensive to luxury). Located on the Dartmouth campus, this inn offers rooms and suites decorated with Georgian-style antique reproductions of polished walnut. Beds are covered with handmade quilts, each of them unique. There are views of the green campus from most rooms. Within the inn are two good restaurants offering room service and alfresco dining (see WHERE TO EAT, below). Afternoon tea is served on Tuesday and Thursday.

The recently opened **Shaker Inn at the Great Stone Dwelling** ☎ (603) 632-7810 TOLL-FREE (888) 707-4257, 447 Route 4A, Enfield 03748 (mid-range), is part of the Enfield Shaker Museum (above). Guestrooms in this exquisite inn are the community's original sleeping quarters with the addition of a private bathroom. A careful renovation has retained the Shaker simplicity leaving handsomely decorated rooms. Fresh New England flavors are emphasized in the dining room, and many of the dishes, accented with herbs from the museum garden, are influenced by hearty, healthy Shaker recipes, such as the fragrant rosemary biscuits and vegetable stew.

Next door is the **Mary Keane House** ☎ (603) 632-4241 TOLL-FREE (888) 239-2153, PO Box 5, Lower Shaker Village, Enfield 03748 (budget to mid-range), an elegant Victorian with spacious, sunny suites and a private beach on Mascoma Lake. At breakfast you'll find out why they pride themselves on their oatmeal scones.

WHERE TO EAT

At the Hanover Inn (above), the ecru-on-white elegance of the **Daniel Webster Room** makes a delightful setting for lunch or dinner. There's a sunny terrace for outdoor dining in summer (mid-range to expensive). Half-glasses of wine are available at lunch, a casual affair, but nevertheless served with flare: your consommé is poured from a teapot. Dinner is formal. Also at the inn is the brand new art-deco inspired **Zins**, an ocean of undulating blonde wood. This smooth wine bistro serves more than 50 labels by the glass along with an extensive menu of New American cuisine (mid-range).

This is a college town so there are plenty of cheap eats with character. Through a door reminiscent of a hobbit's portal, **5 Olde Nugget Alley** ☎ (603) 643-5081, 5 Olde Nugget Alley (budget), is a grotto-like restaurant-bar with exposed brick walls. Try the pesto cod. **Lou's** ☎ (603) 643-3321, 30 South Main Street (budget), is a traditional diner with a loyal clientele. The pies are terrific.

How to Get There

Hanover is situated slightly north of the junction of Interstates 89 and 91 on Route 10 or Route 120. It's approximately 125 miles (200 km) from Boston. Enfield is located on Route 4A, 12 miles (19 km) south of Hanover.

MONADNOCK

This small region in southwest New Hampshire shares its border with Massachusetts to the south and the Connecticut River and Vermont to the west. Many of New Hampshire's 54 covered bridges can be found here.

The region's eighteenth-century towns and villages offer tranquil touring against the backdrop of Mount Monadnock: **Keene** has a 172-ft-wide (52-m), tree-lined Main Street, believed to be the widest paved street in the world, while **Francestown** has colonial houses dating back to the town's 1772 beginnings. **Gilsum** has a stone arch bridge and offers maps of 56 local abandoned mines. **Jaffrey Center's** Old Town Burying Yard is where novelist Willa Cather is buried. And **Hancock** is known for its Revolutionary War graves in Pine Ridge Cemetery and a splendid covered bridge spanning the Contoocook River. In **Milford**, an 1802 Paul Revere bell in the town hall tower tolls every hour. **Dublin** is a resort colony that once attracted Mark Twain and other literary figures. It is the highest town in the region, at 1,439 ft (439 m) above sea level. **Swanzey** has four covered bridges and its theater continues to perform annually the 100-year-old play *Old Homestead*. Nearby, **Winchester** has two covered bridges. And **Harrisville** has been called the "most paintable, photogenic mill town in the United States." On Route 119 in Rindge, you will find the **Cathedral of the Pines**, a pine-forest memorial dedicated to a son lost in World War II.

The area also provides some of New Hampshire's best hiking country, with trails of many shapes and descriptions. Following a high ridge from Mount Watatic in Massachusetts to the 2,280-ft (695-m) North Pack Monadnock near Greenfield, the **Wapack Trail** offers spectacular vistas along a 21-mile (34-km) path marked by yellow blazes.

Using Keene as a hub, the Monadnock has several bicycle trails on roads with little or no traffic. One of the best follows the **Ashuelot River** and crosses many covered bridges. The **Keene Chamber of Commerce** ☎ (603) 352-1303, Keene 03431, has regional biking trail maps.

Monadnock State Park (off Route 124, west of Jaffrey, then follow the signs) offers several trails leading to the summit of **Mount Monadnock**, one of the most-climbed moun-

OPPOSITE: Casting for salmon and lake trout. ABOVE: Fly-fishing purists head out from their posh digs at the Mount Washington Hotel for a day of river-runs-through-it revels.

CRAFT
NH 2812A

tains in the world. It is about a three- to four-hour round trip to the 3,165-ft (965-m) summit where you will be rewarded by a commanding view of the surrounding region. Among those who have climbed Monadnock are Emerson and Thoreau. The summit is quite barren, the trees and bush having been burned off in the 1820s by farmers. **Mount Monadnock State Park Visitor Center** ((603) 532-8862, off Route 124, Jaffrey, has maps of the park.

THE LAKES REGION

It is the 130 lakes and ponds in east-central New Hampshire that gives the Lakes Region its name. With their deep fish-filled waters, good harbors and country lanes, the lakes invite an unhurried pace. Neat-as-a-pin motels, bustling resorts and elegant lakeside inns offer accommodations to suit every taste. Visitors can enjoy several restaurants overlooking the lake. And when not on the water, they can splash out at the local artisans' studios and factory outlet stores.

GENERAL INFORMATION

New Hampshire Lakes Region Association ((603) 774-8664 TOLL-FREE (800) 605-2537 FAX (603) 253-8516 WEB SITE www.lakesregion.org, PO Box 589, Center Harbor 03226, has information about recreation, lodging, and dining in the area. During the summer there is a staffed **information booth** at Weirs Beach.

WHAT TO SEE AND DO

From an Indian word meaning "smile of the great spirit," Lake Winnipesaukee covers 72 sq miles (186 sq km), with 283 miles (456 km) of shoreline and 274 islands, some of which are inhabited. Eight towns cling to its shores.

On Route 28 between Lake Winnipesaukee and Lake Wentworth, **Wolfeboro**, the heart of the Lakes Region stakes its claim as the country's oldest summer resort. Governor John Wentworth built a summer mansion here on Lake Wentworth in 1771.

The largest town of the region is Laconia, on Route 3 to the southwest of Lake Winnipesaukee. Here in Laconia **Weirs Beach** offers a taste of Atlantic City with its assortment of band concerts, fireworks, boat races, seaplane rides, water-skiing shows, arcades, miniature golf links, slot cars, a water park, and a 325-ft (99-m) water slide where revelers plummet down flumes to the pool below.

From Lincoln to Laconia, the **Winnipe saukee Scenic Railroad** ((603) 279-5263, is a 24-mile (39-km), two-hour round-trip train tour along Lake Winnipesaukee's southeastern shore behind a chugging antique steam engine. Trains depart Meredith Station daily at 10:30 AM, 12:30 PM, 2:30 PM and 4:30 PM, with additional 6:30 PM departures on Wednesday and Saturday. Departures from Weirs Beach Station in Laconia are every hour on the hour from 11 AM to 5 PM. The train operates daily from June 26 to Labor Day, weekends only from May 24 to June 12, and weekends only from Labor Day through the fall foliage season.

This is, of course, boating country, whether you charter, rent, or take a public cruise. The largest boat on the lake is the 230-ft (70-m) **MS *Mount Washington***, with narrated cruises departing from Weirs Beach and ending at nearby Wolfeboro. There are also breakfast, lunch, dinner and moonlight cruises and several "theme trips" — Fabulous Fifties, Hawaiian Luau, Buccaneers Ball and Irish Fling, to name but a few. Weirs Beach also offers cruises on the **SS *Mailboat***, which makes two-hour mail trips to islands on the western side of the lake. For information and booking for the above cruises call Mount Washington Cruises ((603) 366-5531 TOLL-FREE (888) 843-6686 FAX (603) 366-2007, PO Box 5367, Weirs Beach 03247.

At **Center Harbor** on the northern end of the lake, professional musicians gather for six weeks each summer, as they have since 1952, to perform orchestral concerts, chamber music and original commissioned pieces at the **New Hampshire Music Festival** ((603) 524-1000, 88 Belknap Road, Gilford 03246.

North of Center Harbor on Route 25 is Moultonborough, where a winding road leads up to **Castle in the Clouds** TOLL-FREE (800) 729-2468, Route 171, a 6,000-acre (2,430-hectare) mountain top country estate built in 1910 by the eccentric millionaire

Pontoons and pleasure boats line a pier.

Thomas Gustav Plant at a cost of $7 million. Set on a hill overlooking Winnipesaukee with a 75-mile (121-km) panorama of Lake Winnipesaukee, the estate offers tours of the mansion, of the Castle Springs water bottling plant, and of the new microbrewery. In a converted barn on the property there is a cafeteria-style restaurant where you can dine in the old horse stalls or outside on the terrace. Facilities for horseback riding can be found here, as well as moderate hiking around the wooded estate.

WHERE TO STAY AND EAT

The lakeside town of Meredith has three very good inns under the same ownership: The **Inns at Mill Falls** ☎ (603) 279-7006 TOLL-FREE (800) 622-6455, Routes 3 and 25, Meredith 03253 (mid-range), offer guestrooms with lake and mountain views fireplaces, and whirlpools, as well as an indoor pool, shops, and package vacations. Each of the three inns has a good restaurant, the newest of which is **Camp**, decked out like a fishing camp complete with open rafters and Lakes Region memorabilia.

The **Wolfeboro Inn** ☎ (603) 569-3016 TOLL-FREE (800) 451-2389, 90 North Main Street (mid-range to expensive), has 44 guestrooms and the rate includes a continental breakfast and a spin on the lake. There is a private beach, and two restaurants serve excellent New England dinners.

Dine on the shady verandah at **Hickory Stick Farm** ☎ (603) 524-3333, 66 Bean Hill Road, southeast of Laconia (mid-range), a three-star restaurant renowned for its roast duckling (they also have two bed-and-breakfast rooms). In downtown Laconia, the **Stone Coast Brewery** ☎ (603) 528-4188, 546 Main Street (mid-range), is another branch of the Portland, Maine, brew pub and restaurant, with earthy decor, pool tables, and live entertainment three nights a week.

HOW TO GET THERE

Take Interstate 93 north and follow it to Exit 23 in New Hampton. Make a right turn at the end of the ramp onto Route 104 to Meredith. From Meredith take Route 3 to the junction of Route 25 North towards Center Harbor.

WHITE MOUNTAIN NATIONAL FOREST

The White Mountain National Forest extends over 768,000 acres (307,200 hectares) and includes the highest point in the Northeast, the 6,288-ft (1,916-m) Mount Washington. More than 100 miles (160 km) of roads give access to the region's whitewater rivers, 650 miles (1,048 km) of fishing streams, dense forests with mountain lakes, ponds and deep valleys. But more than anything, the White Mountains are a hiker's paradise, with more than 1,000 miles (1600 km) of trails. Besides Mount Washington, seven other peaks in the Presidential Range rise to more than one mile (1,609 m) high and 22 others reach more than 4,000 ft (1,219 m).

Despite their imposing statistics, the White Mountains are not that difficult for the traveler to negotiate. Most highways are well maintained, including the 90-minute round-trip Mount Washington Auto Road. For the hiker, however, mountain weather can be treacherous. Even in the middle of summer, violent blizzards and freezing temperatures do occur; and the strongest winds ever measured in the world have been recorded at the summit of Mount Washington. Unless you are an experienced, well-supplied hiker, it is advisable to keep to the short, heavily used trails.

The White Mountains provide the best skiing, both alpine and cross-country, in the state. Ten "Ski the White Mountains" resorts offer a full panorama of slopes and cross-country ski trails set against a backdrop of snowcapped peaks and serene New England scenery.

GENERAL INFORMATION

The Appalachian Trail snakes across the White Mountains' spectacular scenery, including several of the tallest peaks in the East. Located on Route 16, the **Appalachian Mountain Club, Pinkham Notch Visitor Center and Lodge** ☎ (603) 466-2721 (mailing address: PO Box 298, Pinkham Notch, Gorham, NH 03581), on Route 16, in Pinkham

Fall in the White Mountains.

Notch, provides guidebooks, maps, trail supplies and information about hikes and lodging along the trail, as well as free guided day trips and evening lectures. This is also the place to get information and make reservations for the **Appalachian Mountain Club Huts**, a series of mountaintop accommodations located a day's hike apart.

The **White Mountain National Forest Supervisor's Office** ((603) 528-8721 is located at 719 Main Street, Laconia 03246. Other ranger stations include Ammonoosuc Ranger Station ((603) 869-2626, PO Box 239, about half a mile (just under a kilometer) south of US Highways 3 and 302 on Trudeau Road, Bethlehem 03574; Androscoggin Ranger Station ((603) 466-2713, 300 Glen Road, about half a mile south of Route 2 on Route 16, Gorham 03581; Pemigewasset Ranger Station ((603) 536-1315, RFD 3, PO Box 15, Route 175, Plymouth 03264; and Saco Ranger Station ((603) 447-5448, 33 Kancamagus Highway, about 100 yards (91 m) off Route 16 on the Kancamagus Highway, Conway 03818.

NORTH CONWAY AND THE SACO VALLEY

For some visitors this bustling area is the ultimate goal — statistics spread about by the local chamber of commerce give an idea of the area's essential character. They claim: a dozen "family attractions," 90 holes of golf, seven downhill ski areas, six ski touring networks, 75 lodgings, 50 restaurants and 200 shops and outlets. Other vacationers pass through as quickly as possible, running the gauntlet of North Conway's Main Street along which Mount Washington beckons in the distance.

The Saco River Valley (also called the Mount Washington Valley) is a major **fall foliage** stopover. While the weather can play havoc with the change of seasons, the most colorful period is the first two weeks in October. More than a half-million people jam New Hampshire's roads each year to have a glimpse of nature's annual color extravaganza. Traffic can be heavy from Conway Village through North Conway. Take this into account when calculating travel time. Delays are likely on weekends year-round. Informational materials are available from the **Mount Washington Valley Chamber of Commerce** ((603) 356-3171 TOLL-FREE (800) 367-3364 WEB SITE www.mtwashingtonvalley.com, Main Street, PO Box 2300, North Conway 03860.

In North Conway, board the **Conway Scenic Railroad** ((603) 356-5251 TOLL-FREE (800) 232-5251, PO Box 1947, at the Main Street depot, a canary yellow building built in the 1870s. Steam locomotives puffing billows of black smoke pull restored turn-of-the-century coach cars through the Saco River Valley on one-hour train rides. The 11-mile (18-km) round trip also offers first-class service and dining on an 1898 Pullman observation car. A second trip takes passengers through Crawford Notch. Both routes offer jaw-dropping scenery. Call for the current schedule and fares.

You can hardly come to North Conway without a little **outlet shopping**; this town has one of the largest collections of outlets in the Northeast. Most of the true outlets are located just south of North Conway village, but there are a few along Main Street.

The **League of New Hampshire Craftsmen** ((603) 356-2441, Route 16, North Conway, offers handmade crafts from the state's best artisans. It's located just south of the Conway Scenic Railway. Across the street in the Handcrafters' Barn is **A Taste of New England** ((603) 356-8996, where you can select from a cornucopia of regional specialties from smoked meat to salsa. See SPECIAL INTERESTS, page 56 in YOUR CHOICE, for cooking class options in the area.

Accommodations of all persuasions abound in North Conway and environs. The **Cranmore Mountain Lodge** ((603) 356-2044 TOLL-FREE (800) 356-3596, PO Box 1194, Kearsarge Road, North Conway 03860 (mid-range to expensive), attracts families with its 40-ft (12-m) pool and dozens of recreational facilities, including tennis courts, farm animals, and hiking and biking trails on eight acres (three hectares). In winter, there is a lighted skating pond, cross-country trails, and tobogganing. Ten rooms in the old lodge have shared baths and are thus less expensive. The remaining seven are in the renovated barn loft; the rate includes breakfast.

Recently renovated, the **Eastern Slope Inn** ((603) 356-6321 TOLL-FREE (800) 862-1600,

Main Street, Route 16, North Conway 03860, is next door to a summer stock theater and has clay tennis courts, a health spa, lawn sports, and an indoor heated pool. The restaurant and pub feature New England fare, which you can enjoy in the glass-enclosed courtyard along with entertainment and dancing on weekends.

A Revolutionary War-era center-chimney structure, the **1785 Inn & Restaurant** ☎ (603) 356-9025 TOLL-FREE (800) 421-1785 FAX (603) 356-6081 WEB SITE www.the1785.com, Route 16, North Conway 03860-1785 (expensive), retains its hand-hewn beams and original 200-year-old fireplaces. There are 17 rooms, 12 with private bath and five with shared baths. Situated on six acres (two and a half hectares) with mountain views, there are 50 miles (80 km) of cross-country trails for winter antics, and a pool for hot summer days. Rates include breakfast and dinner.

Located in a farmhouse in Conway Village the **Albert B. Lester Memorial Hostel** ☎ (603) 447-1001 FAX (603) 447-3346 E-MAIL hiconway@nxi.com, 36 Washington Street, Conway 03818 (budget), has 45 beds, and the price includes a continental breakfast. Reservations are always advisable; closed during November.

The inns all have dining rooms that are open to the public, but there are other fine restaurants in the area.

The **Scottish Lion** Inn & Restaurant ☎ (603) 356-6381, 3378 White Mountain Highway (mid-range), has been recognized with *Wine Spectator* magazine's Award of Excellence. The restaurant serves an international menu as well as a popular Sunday brunch. It's about a mile (1.6 km) north of North Conway Village.

Recommended by *Bon Appetit*, **Stonehurst Manor** ☎ (603) 356-3113 TOLL-FREE (800) 525-9100, Route 16, North Conway (mid-range), offers casual, elegant dining, with wood-fired pizzas a house specialty.

Horsefeather's ☎ (603) 356-2687, on Main Street in the center of North Conway (budget to mid-range), is a popular eatery serving light fare in a casual atmosphere. **Bellini's** ☎ (603) 356-7000, 33 Seavey Street, North Conway, has homemade Italian bread, pastries, and main courses of veal and seafood. There is outdoor seating in season.

There are a couple of options for those coming from Boston and vicinity. The **scenic route** would be to take Interstate 93 north and follow it to Exit 23 in New Hampton. Take a right at the end of the ramp for Route 104 to Meredith, then take Route 3 to the junction of Route 25 North towards Center Harbor. Follow this road to Tamworth and the junction of Route 16 North. Follow Route 16 north to North Conway. The **fast route** is to take Interstate 95 north to Hampton and at Exit 5 take the Spaulding Turnpike to Route 6 then to Route 16. Follow to North Conway.

Local outfitters offer gear for White Mountain adventurers.

LINCOLN AND WOODSTOCK

The Pemigewasset Valley towns of Lincoln and Woodstock are situated on the southern edge of the White Mountains, where the **Kancamagus Highway** meets Interstate 93. Popular and accessible, these towns of around 1,000 inhabitants each are somewhat overshadowed by the area's two large resorts, Waterville Valley and Loon Mountain. Both resorts offer dozens of year-round attractions and accommodations. Along with the resort offerings, there is hiking, snowmobiling, and cross-country skiing on the National Forest trails.

The **White Mountains Visitors Center** ☎ (603) 745-8720 TOLL-FREE (800) 346-3687 E-MAIL info@visitwhitemountains.com, PO Box 10GB, North Woodstock 03262, is located off Exit 32 of Interstate 93. They offer a free vacation-planning kit that includes several brochures, a map and the *Official White Mountains Travel Guide* magazine. The **Lincoln/Woodstock Chamber of Commerce** ☎ (603) 745-6621 WEB SITE www.bestskitown.com, PO Box 358, Lincoln 03251, is another good source of information in the White Mountains. The office is located off Interstate 93 at Exit 32. Their brochures and maps detail hiking routes in the national forest, trail by trail.

The **Lost River** ☎ (603) 745-8031 and the **glacial caves**, west of Lincoln in North Woodstock (on Route 112), owe their existence to the passage of glaciers that gouged out depressions and then receded north, leaving unique boulder-strewn ravines and tunneling caves. A self-guided tour allows visitors to explore the rock formations following the river as it appears and disappears through the gorge, and to learn about the natural history of the region and the plant life. Located on Route 112, Kinsman Notch, the attraction is open mid-May to mid-October, weather permitting.

A year-round resort in the midst of the White Mountain National Forest, **Waterville Valley Resort** ☎ (603) 236-8311 SNOWPHONE (603) 236-4144 TOLL-FREE (800) 468-2553 WEB SITE www.waterville.com, Route 49, Waterville Valley 03215, is popular with families because of its village atmosphere and children's programs. There is tennis on 18 clay courts (two of which are indoor), a nine-hole golf course, swimming and boating in a six-acre (two-and-a-half-hectare) pond, in-line skating and a skateboard park. It's well known by mountain biking aficionados. The tracks here are set on 65 miles (104 km) of cross-country ski trails. Rentals and instruction are available, and biking runs through mid-October. In winter, alpine and cross-country skiing take over.

There is more alpine and cross-country skiing at **Loon Mountain** ☎ (603) 745-8111 SNOWPHONE (603) 745-8100 TOLL-FREE RESERVATIONS (800) 745-5666 E-MAIL info@loonmtn.com, RR 1, PO Box 41, Kancamagus Highway, Lincoln 03251. It's also a major alpine biking center with an extensive network of trails along with rentals and guided tours to the swimming hole at Franconia Falls. Families have a world of activities to choose from here. The **Wildlife Theater** ☎ (603) 745-8111, located in a barn near the Base Lodge, houses a small zoo. Daily or weekend performances (depending on the season) feature birds and beast of the region displaying their natural talents (a fee is charged). The **Skyride** is a one-mile (one-and-a-half-kilometer) gondola trip to the summit of Loon Mountain. At the top there are more activities, such as the lumberjack show and the jungle-gym-like glacial caves. A combination ticket for the Wildlife Theater and the Skyride is available.

Listings and reservations for lodging in the area can be obtained from the **Lincoln-Woodstock Lodging Bureau** TOLL-FREE (800) 227-4191, PO Box 358NHG, Lincoln 03251, which is run by the chamber of commerce. If you want a small hospitable inn, try one of the following.

The **Woodstock Inn** ☎ (603) 745-3951 TOLL-FREE (800) 321-3985, 80 Main Street, Box 118, Route 3, North Woodstock 03262 (budget to mid-range), has 24 rooms with either private or shared bath; the rate includes breakfast. Dinner is served in the dining room and there is a bar-restaurant with an extensive menu for casual dining, with entertainment nightly. Also on site is the inn's brewery and pub. The **Colonel Spencer Inn** ☎ (603) 536-3438, Route 3, Campton 03223, offers good value, particularly for families. This 1760s center-chimney Colonial building has antique furnishings, four fireplaces, views of Pemigewasset River and White Mountains, hewn beams and wide pine floor boards. It also offers special rates for stays of three or more days; children and teens stay free in their parents' room. Open all year, it has six rooms and one efficiency apartment, all with private baths; the rate (budget) includes breakfast.

Lincoln and Woodstock are 150 miles (240 km) from Boston on Interstate 93.

On Mount Washington's eastern slope, Glen Ellis Falls can be reached from the parking area on Route 16, about one mile (one and a half kilometers) south of the Pinkham Notch Visitor Center. The gravel path to the falls is 0.3 miles long (half a kilometer) with stone steps and handrails.

JACKSON

"Jackson, N.H.," reads the sign tacked to the covered bridge. Located just off Route 16, but somehow a world away from the commercial bustle of its near neighbors, Jackson is a tiny resort village and a cross-country-skiing Mecca. Thanks to the Jackson Ski Touring Foundation, the town has the largest trail system in the east with over 97 miles (157 km) of trails for all abilities with 60 miles (97 km) groomed to Olympic standards. Rental shops in the village can outfit you; instruction, clinics and events are also available. Those same trails lead summer wanders on rambles around the village and surrounding countryside. The **Jackson Ski Touring Center** ☎ (603) 383-9355 TOLL-FREE LODGING INFORMATION (800) 866-3334, Jackson 03846, maintains this renowned trail system — ranked as among the best in the world.

There is alpine skiing at **Wildcat** ☎ (603) 466-3326 TOLL-FREE SNOWPHONE (800) 643-4521 TOLL-FREE (888) 225-6439, Route 16, Jackson, which has the longest vertical drop (2,100 ft or 640 m), the highest lift-served summit, and the greatest lift capacity in the Mount Washington Valley.

Jackson Chamber of Commerce ☎ (603) 383-9356 TOLL-FREE (800) 866-3334, PO Box 304, Jackson 03846, will make lodging reservations for you; or you can contact one of the following inns directly.

The seven-room **Nestlenook Farm on the River** ☎ (603) 383-9101 TOLL-FREE (800) 472-5207, PO Box Q, Dinsmore Road, Jackson 03846, is a 200-year-old Victorian gingerbread-style inn set in 65 acres (26 hectares). Besides giving you easy access to Jackson's touring trails, there are additional recreation facilities at the inn: horse-drawn carriage rides, a heated pool, mountain biking, rowboats on the farm's pond, and in winter, sleigh rides, ice skating and snowshoeing. The rate (mid-range to luxury) includes breakfast and afternoon wine and cheese.

In the center of Jackson Village, the **Wentworth Resort Hotel** ☎ (603) 383-9700 TOLL-FREE (800) 637-0013 FAX (603) 383-4265 WEB SITE www.wentworth.com, Route 16A, PO Box M, Jackson 03846 (expensive), has 58 no-nonsense rooms in a cluster of Victorian-style buildings. There is an 18-hole golf course, clay tennis courts, an outdoor heated pool, and of course miles of cross-country skiing at the doorstep. The dining room features regional cuisine.

Both of these inns welcome non-guests in their dining rooms. You might also try the ginger-cured pork tenderloin with cranberry chutney at **The Inn at Thorn Hill** ☎ (603) 383-4242 TOLL-FREE (800) 287-8790, Thorn Hill Road (upper-range); or hefty portions of lasagna, steak, seafood or chicken at the **Wildcat Inn and Tavern** ☎ (603) 383-4245, Main Street (mid-range).

PINKHAM NOTCH AND MOUNT WASHINGTON'S EASTERN SLOPES

"A 400-million-year-old spike of metamorphic rock," "home of the world's worst weather," an "arctic island in a temperate climate," "The Rockpile" — descriptions such as these give some indication of the mystique that surrounds New England's tallest peak, the 6,288-ft-high (1,916-m) Mount Washington. Spectacular vistas, cooling waterfalls, deep gorges, rushing streams and peaceful valleys reward those who choose to hike to the summit. While many of the national forest hiking trails accommodate even the casual stroller, those leading to the Mount Washington summit require more than a few hours of moderate to tough hiking.

Local authorities urge extreme caution for those who plan to climb Mount Washington. And if you do go, foul-weather gear, even on the most benign days, is essential. Because of a funnel effect, the mountain bears the brunt of three continental storm fronts. The highest winds ever measured were recorded on its peak at 231 mph (372 km/h); a mild breeze down below can become a gusty 75-mph (120-kph) howler at the top. The **Pinkham Notch Visitor Center** ☎ (603) 466-2721 FAX (603) 466-3871, Route 16, Pinkham Notch, run by the Appalachian Mountain Club (AMC), has information on trail and weather conditions, voluntary registration for backcountry winter camping, books and maps including those from the AMC's

The trail to the summit of 2,850-ft (869-m) Mount Willard, of the Willey Range in Crawford Notch.

excellent collection, and last-minute gear and safety items in the retail store (see WHERE TO STAY AND EAT). The visitor center is the major trailhead on the eastern side of Mount Washington. Free parking is available. The **Tuckerman Ravine Trail**, the **Lost Pond Trail** and the **Old Jackson Trail** start here, and each of these trails access many more. There are also ski touring trails.

In Pinkham Notch, the 90-minute round-trip **Mount Washington Auto Road** ☎ (603) 466-3988, Route 16, leads to the summit. The eight miles (13 km) of braking on the way down can be tough on some cars. Vehicles that make it to the top can sport the "This car climbed Mount Washington" bumper sticker. On a clear day the summit view includes the Atlantic Ocean off the Maine coast; Stowe, Vermont; and the Adirondacks. The road is open early May to late October daily from 8:30 AM to 5 PM; a toll is charged.

If you have any doubts about driving, leave your car at the foot of the mountain and take the "**Stagecoach**" ☎ (603) 466-3988 or (603) 466-2222, a chauffeured van service to the top. Narration along the way is of the entertaining variety and there is a half-hour stopover at the summit. It runs early May to late October daily from 8:30 AM to 5 PM; a fare is charged; the van departs from across from the toll-road entrance in Gorham.

Until recently the trip up Mount Washington was a summer-only phenomenon. New in 1999, the "**Snocoach**" at Great Glen Trails (see below) is a van equipped with caterpillar-type wheels that takes eight people above the tree line on Mount Washington. Along the way there is narration on the geography, ecology and history of the area, and a chance to spot wildlife such as fox, deer and wild turkey. The cost is $35 per person with reductions for children age five to 12, and trips run on demand.

The Pinkham Notch area offers first-rate cross-country skiing at **Great Glen Trails** ☎ (603) 466-2333, Route 16, Pinkham Notch 03581-0300, with 25 miles (40 km) of paths, about half of which are groomed. The Base Lodge houses the largest cross-country retailer in the state, as well as a demo center where you pay a small fee to take a pair of skis out for a test run before you buy them. Also in the Base Lodge, there is a cafeteria and lots of room to picnic and socialize in front of the stone hearth. There are programs for a range of sports spanning all levels of ability and a three-times-daily ski school, for which reservations are not required. In summer a bike trail network runs through the same countryside under the brooding countenance of Mount Washington.

Hikers and budget travelers are well served by **The Joe Dodge Lodge** ☎ (603) 466-2721, PO Box 298, Pinkham Notch, Gorham 03581, at the Pinkham Notch Visitors Centers. The lodge accommodates 100 guests in comfortable four-bed bunkrooms, triples or doubles. Amiable, rustic and just plain cool, the lodge gives you access to miles of trails outside your door. Hearty meals are served family style, a time for swapping tales with fellow hikers and travelers.

Pinkham Notch is located along Route 16 between Gorham and Jackson. **Concord Trailways** ☎ (603) 228-3300 operates daily service to the Pinkham Notch Visitor Center from Logan Airport and South Station in Boston. During the summer, the Appalachian Mountain Club runs a **hikers' shuttle bus** from the Visitor Center to principal trailheads in the White Mountains; contact the center (above).

CRAWFORD NOTCH AND MOUNT WASHINGTON'S WESTERN SLOPES

Crawford Notch is the site of the first attempt at a tourist industry in the White Mountains. It is named for Abel and Ethan Crawford, who in 1819, blazed the first footpath to the summit of Mount Washington, and then advertised their services as tour guides and lodging arrangement for visitors.

This narrow, rugged mountain pass, off Route 302 north of Bartlett, offers some incomparable views of the Presidential Range, including the 4,052-ft (1,235-m) Jackson Mountain. The Saco River also runs through the Notch, creating some of the tallest and most spectacular waterfalls and cascades in New Hampshire. **Arethusa Falls**, the state's highest, are a 50-minute walk from the trailhead along Route 302; **Silver Cascade**, a 1,000-ft (305-m) cataract, is visible from the highway. A plaque marks the site of **Willey House**, a stopover for bygone wagon teams traveling between northern New Hampshire and the seacoast. The Willey family was killed here in 1826 when they fled their house during a rockslide; ironically, the building was untouched. From Willey House you can take the easy to moderate footpath to **Kedron Flume**. It's a two-mile (just over three-kilometer) hike that takes about one and a quarter hours.

Since the mid-nineteenth century, the **Mount Washington Cog Railway** ☎ (603) 278-5404 TOLL-FREE (800) 922-8825 WEB SITE www.thecog.com, has hauled tourists to the summit of the White Mountains' tallest peak — the highest north of the Carolinas and east of the Rockies. Hailed in 1869 as a marvel of "modern" technology, it was the world's first mountain-climbing cog railway. The "cog" is a notched wheel that latches on to a center track, pulling and lowering the train up and down the mountain. Today the train, powered by steam locomotives, climbs three miles (five kilometers) to the summit on the second-steepest railway track in the world. (Only a track in the Swiss Alps beats it.) One trestle, "Jacob's Ladder," registers an incredible 37 percent grade. Each locomotive consumes a ton of coal and 1,000 gallons (3,785 liters) of water while making the one-hour climb to the top. On clear days the view from the summit's observation center spans four states. Often, however, the mountain is shrouded in gray clouds and thick mist and the train climbs through the fog. But, rain or shine, the railway runs daily from mid-May to late October; a fare is charged. The train departs from the Base Station, which is located one mile (one and a half kilometers) north of Crawford Notch on Route 302.

Along Route 302, 12 miles (19 km) north of Bartlett, **Crawford Notch State Park** ☎ (603) 374-2272, Route 302, Harts Location 03812, is crossed by **hiking trails**. Several stables in the region offer **guided trail rides**, most notably along 75 miles (121 km) of bridle paths belonging to the venerable Mount Washington Hotel & Resort (see below).

At **Above the Notch Motor Inn** ☎ (603) 846-5156, Bretton Woods 03575 (budget), the views from the slopes are unsurpassed and the base lodge, though packed with conveniences, retains a human scale. Bretton Woods is a good place for families with small children. The resort's "Hobbit" program combines daycare with instruction for three- to five-year-olds. The "wonder carpet" lift, like an escalator, carries kids up a tiny slope.

In summer **Attitash Bear Peak** ☎ (603) 374-2368 TOLL-FREE (800) 223-7669, on Route 302, in Bartlett, has water and alpine slides; in winter there's skiing on two mountains boasting the largest snowmaking capacity in the state — covering more than 200 acres (80 hectares). The "Grandstand" trail hosts mogul competitions throughout the ski season.

An engineer on the Mount Washington Cog Railway.

The sight of the gleaming white, twin-towered **Mount Washington Hotel & Resort** ☎ (603) 278-1000 TOLL-FREE (800) 258-0330, Route 302, Bretton Woods 03575, set against the backdrop of Mount Washington, never fails to impress. A National Historic Landmark, the hotel was built in 1902 as one of America's premier resorts. In 1944 the Bretton Woods Conference that established an international monetary system for the postwar era was held here. Its spectacular 2,600-acre (1,053-hectare) property embraces 27 holes of PGA golf, meandering bridle paths, 12 clay tennis courts, indoor and outdoor pools, and play areas. From the hotel's 900-ft-long (274-m) verandah, the view encompasses the entire Presidential Range. A fine dining room, a welcoming lobby with a working fireplace, and renovated, comfortable rooms and suites, make this grand resort a place where you will feel on top of the world. Do make a trip down to the **Cave Lounge** for a pre- or postprandial drink; this stonewalled grotto was a wine cellar and a speakeasy during the Prohibition. The resort is open year-round, with room rates in the luxury category that include breakfast and dinner.

Besides the grand hotel, the resort offers a range of accommodation to suit most budgets. The **Bretton Arms Country Inn** ☎ (603) 278-1000, Route 302, Bretton Woods 03575 (mid-range; open year-round), has spacious, if somewhat characterless, rooms. The tavern serves cocktails, but you're more likely to find a tousled-headed family taking part

in a sing-a-long there. The dining room is superb. Call ☎ (603) 278-1000 TOLL-FREE (800) 258-0330 to make reservations for the grand hotel and the inn, as well as the **Bretton Woods Motor Inn** and the **Townhomes at Bretton Woods**.

The Appalachian Mountain Club's **Crawford Notch Hostel** ☎ (603) 466-2727, Route 302, is open year-round as of spring 2003, following extensive renovation. There are two 12-bunk heated cabins, kitchen facilities, hot showers, a library, and resident staff offering trail information and weather reports. During the summer hiking season, the **Crawford Notch Depot Visitor Center** (no phone) dispenses information as well as selling maps and guidebooks.

There is fine dining at the **Bretton Arms Dining Room**, Bretton Arms Country Inn, where you'll find game meats such as pheasant, quail, and venison on the card as well as some more standard main courses. The **Slopeside**, at the Bretton Woods Base Lodge, is a large sunny dining room offering casual dining with views of the busy slopes, as well as good burgers and quesadillas. The Base Lodge also has a cafeteria and plenty of picnic-style seating on three levels. Also on the slopes is the **Top o' the Quad**, with mountaintop dining at the top of the quad chairlift. On a sunny day diners can enjoy priceless views of Mount Washington from the restaurant's terrace. **Darby's**, in the Bretton Woods Motor Inn, US Highway 302, offers "family dining in a rustic atmosphere" (mid-range). **Fabyan's Station**, on Route 302, also part of the Bretton Woods resort, is a restored train depot packed with railroad memorabilia. Seafood and steaks are the fare (mid-range), and there is nightly entertainment in the lounge. Call ☎ (603) 278-1000 for any of these restaurants and operator will direct your call.

Crawford Notch is around 160 miles (256 km) from Boston. Route 302 runs through Crawford Notch, making it accessible from North Conway in the east from Route 16 and from Franconia Notch in the west from Interstate 93/Route 3.

FRANCONIA NOTCH

Another New England tourist shrine, and well worth a visit, Franconia Notch is a deep 6,440-acre (2,580-hectare) valley cut between the towering peaks of the Franconia and Kinsman mountain ranges, with the granite-walled, 4,200-ft-high (1,280-m) Cannon Mountain on the east and the twin 5,000-ft (1,524-m) peaks of Mounts Lafayette and Lincoln to the west. This much-visited valley also contains some of the region's most recognizable landmarks. Most of the area's attractions lie within **Franconia Notch State Park** ☎ (603) 823-8800 (no postal address). Call the park office for additional information about the area.

ABOVE: A steam engine on display at Clark Trading Post, Franconia. RIGHT: The Mount Washington Hotel, among the last of the state's grand hotels.

The spectacular **Flume Gorge** ☎ (603) 745-8391, extends for 800 ft (244 m) at thhe base of Mount Liberty, down which cascades the Pemigewasset River flanked by 90-ft (27-m) granite walls. Close-up views (accessible by stairs and walkways) yield glimpses of rare mountain flowers and luxuriant mosses that cling to the moist walls. Nearly a half-million travelers visit the gorge annually.

The **Old Man of the Mountain**, also called "The Great Stone Face," is a natural granite profile that resembles a man's face jutting from a sheer cliff 1,200 ft (366 m) above glistening **Profile Lake**. Carved by nature over millions of years, it is formed by five separate ledges of granite and measures 40 ft (12 m) from jutting brow to bearded chin. You may notice that this guy follows you everywhere you drive in New Hampshire. The rock is that squiggly box that frames the state-route signs.

Panoramic views of the mountains and distant valleys are provided by the **Aerial Tramway** ☎ (603) 823-8800, Cannon Mountain Ski Area, Franconia Notch State Park, which carries tram cars more than a mile (1.6 km) at an average height of 2,022 ft (616 m) to the summit of Cannon Mountain at 4,180 ft (1,263 m).

South of the Notch are three other natural phenomena. At the base of a waterfall, **The Basin**, a deep glacial pothole, measures 20 ft (six meters) wide. **Indian Head** is a 98-ft-high (30-m) profile carved by the elements in granite; its scowling visage is said to resemble that of an Abenaki chief.

The Frost Place ☎ (603) 823-5510, Ridge Road, Franconia 03580, was the summer home of the poet Robert Frost and his family from 1915 until 1920. You can tour the house and see a video produced by Robert Frost's great-grandson about the Pulitzer-prize winning poet's life and work. On the property is a woodland trail where Frost's lines come to life as you move from station to station reading snippets of his verse on small placards tucked amongst the greenery, wildflowers, and ancient trees. The Frost Place is also an active literary center, with summer

Walkways give visitors a chance to marvel at the mountain flowers and luxuriant mosses that cling to the moist walls of the spectacular Flume Gorge, which extends for 800 ft (244 m) at the base of Mount Liberty.

guest lectures, a writers' conference, and evening readings. Open from Memorial Day to Columbus Day Wednesday to Monday from 1 PM to 5 PM; an admission fee is charged.

Franconia Notch State Park is a year-round recreation area offering 100 miles (160 km) of trails connecting with the Appalachian Trail system. **Artist's Bluff and Bald Mountain Trail** (1.5 miles or 2.4 km) is an easy hike with fine views. The hike takes about one and a quarter hours. Access is from Route 18. Starting from The Basin (see above), the **Basin-Cascades Trail** (two miles or just over three

kilometers), ascends along Cascade Brook, ending at Cascade Brook Trail. The trip takes about one and a half hours.

In winter, the Notch's star attraction is **Cannon Mountain** ☎ (603) 823-8800 SNOW-PHONE (603) 823-7771, Franconia Notch State Park, the last of the state-owned ski areas. Cannon is known for what was described to me as "ultrasonic steeps," in other words, extreme skiing on expert terrain. Cannon's aerial tramway was the nation's first, and its slopes were also the site of the first World Cup ski races.

The **Bungay Jar Bed and Breakfast** ☎ (603) 823-7775 TOLL-FREE (800) 421-0701 FAX (603) 444-0100 E-MAIL info@bungayjar.com, Easton Valley Road, Franconia 03580 (mid-range), is a converted eighteenth-century barn situated on 15 acres (six hectares) with mountain views, woodland trails, and beautiful gardens. There are six guestrooms and suites, sauna, and a two-story common room with a fireplace. The rate includes breakfast, served outside (weather permitting) in view of the Appalachian Trail.

The white-clapboard **Franconia Inn** ☎ (603) 823-5542 TOLL-FREE (800) 473-5299 FAX (603) 823-8078, 1300 Easton Valley Road (Route 16), Franconia 03580 (mid-range), is an 1866 inn on 107 acres (43 hectares) with 34 rooms and suites and a verandah with mountain views. The inn serves French and American cuisine in the dining room, which is open to the public. In the same class is the **Sugar Hill Inn** ☎ (603) 823-5621 TOLL-FREE (800) 548-4748, Sugar Hill Road (Route 117), Franconia 03580 (mid-range), a 1789 farmhouse with wide pine and maple flooring, fireplaces and exposed beams. Stenciled walls, antiques, handmade quilts and rugs accent many of the 16 guestrooms; a country breakfast (not included in the rate) with hot muffins is available.

A 10-minute drive from Cannon Mountain, **Pinestead Farm Lodge** ☎ (603) 823-5601 or 823-8121, 2059 Easton Road (Route 116), RFD 1 (call for rates), with nine rooms, is a good base for skiers. This is a working farm, and guests are welcome to wander around and observe the many activities, from maple-sugaring in late winter to cattle-raising. Each of the nine rooms has a double and single bed.

Interstate 93 runs through Franconia Notch, making it the most accessible part of the White Mountains region. It is about 150 miles (240 km) north of Boston.

THE NORTH COUNTRY

New Hampshire's North Country is bound together by culture, tradition, landscape and economics, with the 26-million acre (10.4-million-hectare) **Northern Forest** that stretches from Maine's North Woods to Vermont's Northeast Kingdom and New York's Adirondacks. This land of woodlands, mountains, rivers, lakes and streams is the largest stretch

ABOVE: Robert Frost's mailbox at his old summer home in Franconia. RIGHT: The meeting house at Sugar Hill, near Franconia.

of undeveloped forestland east of the Mississippi River. Its diverse habitats are home to a wide range of wildlife, but wild areas are disappearing at a rapid rate because of development and logging. Information on lodging, dining, moose-watching and more is available from the **North Country Chamber of Commerce** ☏ (603) 237-8939 TOLL-FREE (800) 698-8939 extension 1, PO Box 1G, Colebrook 03576.

Thanks to a recent act of Congress, one area of North Hampshire's Northen forest at least is preserved as the **Lake Umbagog Wildlife Refuge**, where there is excellent eagle viewing, as well as osprey and otter. Great Glen Trails (see under PINKHAM NOTCH, page 288) and Saco Bound ☏ (603) 447-2177 E-MAIL rivers@sacobound.com, Box 119, Conway Center 03813, both run guided excursions to Lake Umbagog.

It took $20 million to resurrect the **Mountain View Grand** ☏ (603) 837-8884 TOLL-FREE (800) 438-3017 FAX (603) 837-8884 E-MAIL info@mountainviewgrand.com, Mountain View Road, Whitefield 03598 (luxury), to its circa-1900 glory as a White Mountain grand resort, and the money was well-spent. The original 200 rooms were opened up into 145 more spacious and gracious accommodations with deeply cushioned mahogany furniture. An 18-hole golf course spreads across the ample acreage and a bevy of restaurants, bars and lounges are sprinkled throughout the property. Unlike other grand resort hotels of the region, the Mountain View is *not* an all-inclusive, making the rooms a considerable bargain, especially mid-week (mid-range).

Situated on a private 15,000-acre (6,000-hectare) estate high in the White Mountains, the **Balsams Grand Resort Hotel** ☏ (603) 255-3400 TOLL-FREE OUT OF STATE (800) 255-0600 TOLL-FREE IN STATE (800) 255-0800 FAX (603) 255-4221 WEB SITE www.thebalsams.com, Dixville Notch 03576, is an oasis of gentility in the state's remote northernmost reaches. Travelers coming up from Errol through Dixville Notch can take in the spectacular setting of this grand hotel. Rooms are large and decorated in somewhat over-the-top floral patterns with antique reproductions and wicker furniture. There is a breakfast buffet that seems to stretch for miles and events all day, with a naturalist leading hikes and programs. The **Balsams Mountain Bike and Nature Center** ☏ (603) 255-3921 has 29 miles (48 km) of marked trails, and offers rentals, sales and repairs on site; guided and self-guided tours for all ages and abilities are also available. The resort is an hour's drive north of Mount Washington. You may experience some sticker shock when you see the price of your room, but all things considered, the package is excellent value.

Route 3 is the region's principal thoroughfare. Dixville Notch is accessible from Bethel, Maine, via Route 26, and from Gorham, New Hampshire, via Route 16.

OPPOSITE: Rock around the clock at the Balsams Grand Resort Hotel in New Hampshire's North Country. ABOVE: This stony ledge protruding off 4,100-ft-high (1,250-m) Cannon Mountain is known as the Old Man of the Mountain, popularized as "The Great Stone Face" in a story by Nathaniel Hawthorne.

Maine

MINOAN
ROCKPORT
CONFIDENCE

In his 1846–57 journals of exploration, *The Maine Woods*, Henry David Thoreau termed Maine the last remaining wilderness east of the Mississippi. Even then, however, most of the towering white pines that gave the state its nickname had been cut down for British ship masts. Today, nearly 90 percent of Maine remains virtually uninhabited fir, spruce and pine forests, which are nonetheless heavily logged by the paper industry, furnishing, as one Maine conservationist complained, "half of America's toilet paper."

Comprising 33,125 sq miles (84,800 sq km), the state of Maine is as big as the five other New England states combined, encompassing some 6,000 lakes and ponds, 32,000 miles (51,200 km) of rivers and streams, 17 million acres (6.8 million hectares) of forestland, 5,500 miles (8,850 km) of coastline and 2,000 islands.

For those willing to take the time and effort, Maine's extensive northern river system offers perhaps the best long-distance canoeing in the lower 48 states. Some of the East's finest scenery and most rugged terrain await adventurers in recreation areas such as the 98-mile (157-km) Allagash Wilderness Waterway and Baxter State Park with its mile-high Mount Katahdin (5,271 ft or 1,607 m).

Easily accessible from the urban hubs to the south, Maine's lower coast is dotted with quaint villages overflowing with antique shops and historic inns. Further north, Rockland, Camden and Rockport are the windjamming capitals of the northeast (see CRUISE ON A WINDJAMMER, page 18 in TOP SPOTS). Portland is Maine's metropolis, a small city loaded with street-life and excellent restaurants. To the west there is superb skiing as well as unparalleled hiking and freshwater fishing opportunities. Rafting is another Maine passion, with thrills and spills awaiting the adventurous on fast northern rivers.

Travelers interested in visiting the state's more popular and accessible spots — Bar Harbor, Portland, Kennebunkport and Acadia National Park — should consider visiting off-season. These areas are glorious in the autumn, even into late October, and free of the crowds that pack into them at the height of the summer and early fall.

BACKGROUND

Vikings may have explored Maine's coastline 1,000 years ago, but the first European known to have set foot in Maine was the explorer John Cabot in 1497. In the 1600s, colonists began to move north from what is now Massachusetts, and the French started to travel south from Acadia into Maine. Soon, frequent skirmishes arose between British-held Maine and French Canada, which led in part to the French and Indian War of the 1760s.

Initially governed as part of Massachusetts, Maine became a state in its own right in 1820, when it entered the Union under the Missouri Compromise — in which Maine joined the United States as a free state and Missouri entered as a slave state. The young state quickly distinguished itself in its opposition to slavery, its commercial power and the contribution its regiments made in several major Civil War battles.

Throughout the nineteenth and into the twentieth centuries, Maine prospered on the strength of its shipyards. These days, shipbuilding continues to play an important role

OPPOSITE: Rockport harbor on Maine's mid coast. ABOVE: Local color at the Fryeburg Fair.

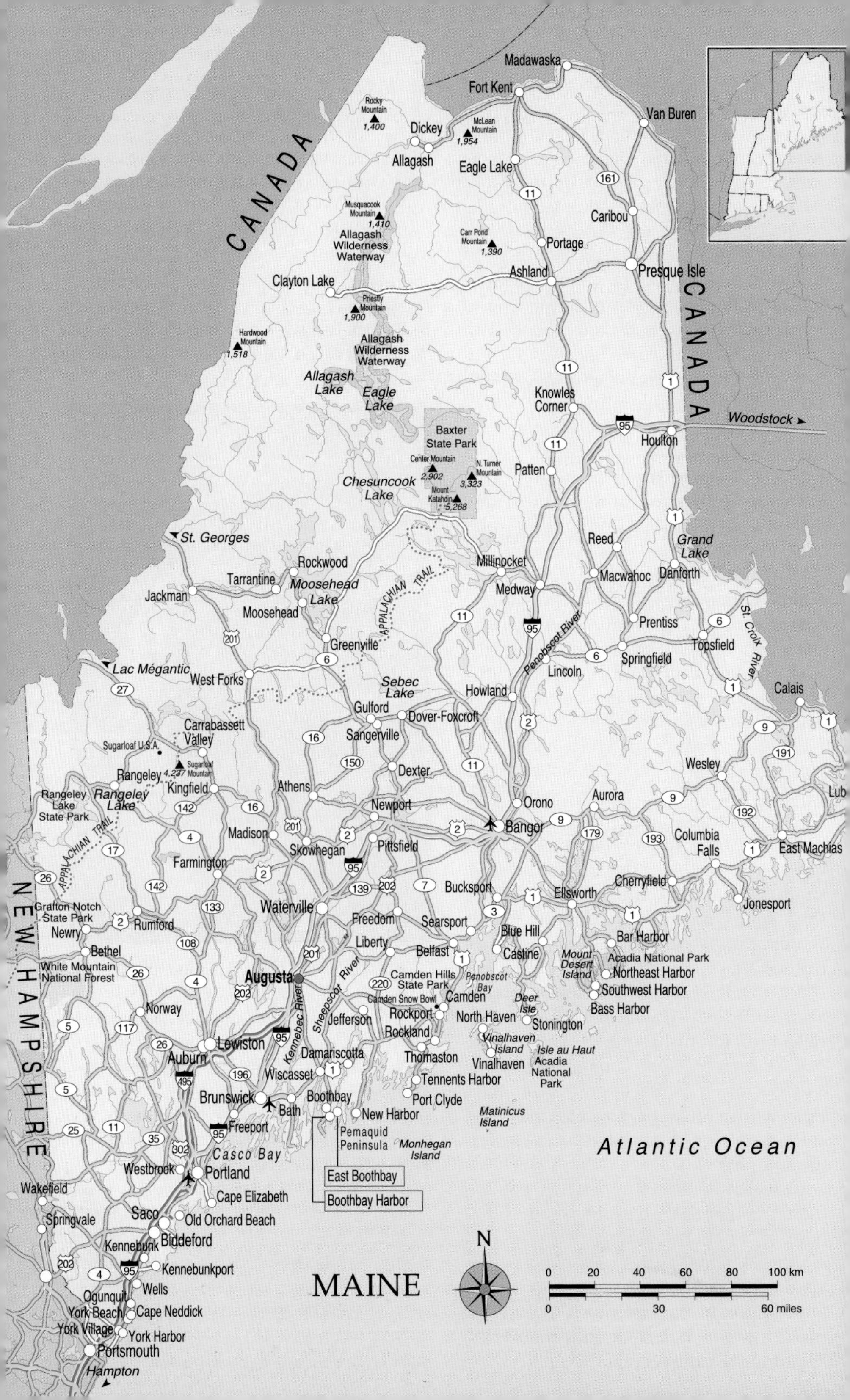
MAINE
CANADA
CANADA
NEW HAMPSHIRE
Atlantic Ocean
Madawaska
Fort Kent
Van Buren
Dickey
Allagash
Eagle Lake
Caribou
Portage
Ashland
Presque Isle
Clayton Lake
Rocky Mountain 1,400
McLean Mountain 1,954
Musquacook Mountain 1,410
Carr Pond Mountain 1,390
Priestly Mountain 1,900
Hardwood Mountain 1,518
Allagash Wilderness Waterway
Allagash Lake
Eagle Lake
Knowles Corner
Woodstock
Houlton
Baxter State Park
Center Mountain 2,902
N. Turner Mountain 3,323
Mount Katahdin 5,268
Patten
Chesuncook Lake
St. Georges
Reed
Grand Lake
Rockwood
Millinocket
Tarrantine
Moosehead Lake
Jackman
Medway
Macwahoc
Danforth
Moosehead
APPALACHIAN TRAIL
Prentiss
Greenville
Penobscot River
Topsfield
Springfield
Lincoln
St. Croix River
Lac Mégantic
West Forks
Sebec Lake
Howland
Calais
Gulford
Dover-Foxcroft
Carrabassett Valley
Sangerville
Sugarloaf U.S.A.
Sugarloaf Mountain 4,237
Rangeley
Kingfield
Dexter
Wesley
Rangeley Lake State Park
Rangeley Lake
Athens
Newport
Orono
Aurora
Lub
Bangor
Madison
Skowhegan
Pittsfield
Columbia Falls
East Machias
Farmington
Bucksport
Ellsworth
Cherryfield
Jonesport
Grafton Notch State Park
Waterville
Rumford
Newry
Freedom
Searsport
Blue Hill
Bar Harbor
Bethel
Liberty
Belfast
Castine
Mount Desert Island
Acadia National Park
Northeast Harbor
White Mountain National Forest
Augusta
Camden Hills State Park
Penobscot Bay
Southwest Harbor
Kennebec River
Sheepscot River
Camden Snow Bowl
Camden
Deer Isle
Bass Harbor
Norway
Jefferson
Rockport
North Haven
Stonington
Rockland
Vinalhaven Island
Isle au Haut
Lewiston
Auburn
Damariscotta
Thomaston
Vinalhaven
Acadia National Park
Wiscasset
Tennents Harbor
Brunswick
Bath
Boothbay
Port Clyde
New Harbor
Matinicus Island
Freeport
Pemaquid Peninsula
Monhegan Island
Casco Bay
Westbrook
Portland
East Boothbay
Boothbay Harbor
Wakefield
Cape Elizabeth
Saco
Old Orchard Beach
Springvale
Biddeford
Kennebunk
Kennebunkport
Wells
Ogunquit
York Beach
Cape Neddick
York Village
York Harbor
Portsmouth
Hampton
N
0 20 40 60 80 100 km
0 30 60 miles

in the economy. Lumber and fishing also make significant contributions to the state's revenue, but the largest part of the economic pie is furnished by the state's small business owners and entrepreneurs from bakers to boat-builders.

THE SOUTH COAST: THE YORKS TO THE KENNEBUNKS

The sea chills out as one moves northeast, so if you plan to swim in Maine, you may want to stop in the south. Besides, this 60-mile (96-km) stretch of coastline has almost all of Maine's sandy beaches.

The state's early history is evident in the architecture of these coastal communities. European colonists, who were repeatedly driven out by Indians, eventually managed to establish settlements along the coast. They were followed by shipbuilders and merchants, whose grand houses attest to the prosperity of those years. Later, wealthy nineteenth-century city dwellers built their coastal summer "cottages," only to be followed by middle-class vacationers and their modest beach bungalows.

THE YORKS

The Yorks comprise four distinct communities: York Village (often referred to as "Old York"), York Beach, York Harbor and Cape Neddick. For information materials, contact **The Yorks Chamber of Commerce Visitors Center** ☎ (207) 363-4422 E-MAIL info@yorkme.org, located at 571 Route 1, York 03909.

York Beach has a long stretch of white sand surrounded by dunes, marshes and modest vacation cottages. It also has the Wild Kingdom Zoo and Amusement Park ☎ (207) 363-4911, Route 1, and a never-ending strip of fried-fish restaurants. Fairs and special activities take place year-round, including the weeklong York Days, held each summer.

York Harbor is York Beach's upper-crust hillside neighbor, boasting antique shops, galleries, a snug harbor and green lawns surrounding Victorian houses; while at York Village there are historic buildings, a colonial-period cemetery, and the oldest jail in America, the Old Gaol. The Old York Historical Society ☎ (207) 363-4974, PO Box 312, York 03909, offers tours.

For swimming and sunning there is honky-tonk York Beach, as well as the somewhat secluded **Cape Neddick Beach**. Nearby, **Long Sands Beach** is an extended narrow stretch of sand. A two-mile (3.2-km) drive parallels the beach.

There are some fine bed-and-breakfast inns in the area. Atop a bluff overlooking the blue Atlantic, **York Harbor Inn** ☎ (207) 363-5119 TOLL-FREE (800) 596-4926, US Alternate 1, PO Box 573, York Harbor 03911, may look

familiar to L.L. Bean catalogue browsers — it was once pictured on the cover. The inn has 40 luxurious rooms, some with hot tub, fireplace, deck, and ocean view. The dining room (expensive) has been recognized by *Food & Wine* magazine.

The Yorks are located along Alternate Route 1 off the Maine Turnpike (Interstate 95).

OGUNQUIT

Ogunquit means "beautiful place by the sea." The name is well suited, as the beach here is a three-mile (five-kilometer) stretch of white,

Poppies brighten a York Harbor yard.

inviting sand. With its fine colonial architecture, cliffs, and peaceful backdrop of rolling dunes, it is no surprise that Ogunquit became a destination for artists at the end of the nineteenth century. A number of small art galleries (along with a jumble of shops) can be found in the village. Contact the **Ogunquit Chamber of Commerce** ☎ (207) 646-2939, PO Box 2289, Route 1 South, Ogunquit 03907, for informational materials.

From the center of town, the legendary **Marginal Way**, a one-mile-long (1.6-km) path, winds along the ledges high above the

Atlantic, providing walkers with superb vistas of the ocean and shoreline tidal pools. Follow the path as it crests the 100-ft (30-m) peak of Bald Head Cliff and then meanders into the fishing port of **Perkins Cove**, an intriguing hodgepodge of lobster shacks and craft shops where you can tread the only **foot drawbridge** in New England. There is two-hour free parking in the public lot; once that's full there is a private lot that charges $5. The little cove abounds with casual restaurants (see below) and **deep-sea fishing charters**, such as the *Bunny Clark* ☎ (207) 646-2214, Perkins Cove Road, Ogunquit 03907.

There are Equity shows at the **Ogunquit Playhouse** ☎ (207) 646-5511, State Road. The oldest theater in Maine, the Playhouse stages a different show each week during the tourist season. Launched half a century ago in a local garage, it has become one of the premier summer stock theaters on the East Coast.

Ogunquit has snug motels, graceful inns and superb dining. The **Cliff House** ☎ (207) 361-1000 FAX (207) 361-2122, PO Box 2274, Shore Road, Ogunquit 03907, has 94 rooms (mid-range to expensive), most of which have sea views. Arguably the state's finest restaurant, **Arrows** ☎ (207) 361-1100, Berwick Road, Ogunquit, specializes in innovative American cuisine, with a menu that changes daily. Dining in this colonial farmhouse surrounded by splendid gardens is a treat for the senses (expensive).

Barnacle Billy's ☎ (207) 646-5575, in Perkin's Cove, serves fresh-off-the-boat seafood; lobster is a specialty. The restaurant is highly recommended.

Ogunquit is about 85 miles (136 km) north of Boston on Route 1.

THE KENNEBUNKS

With Victorian-style sea captains' mansions, fishing harbors where lobster boats still go out year-round, antiques and art, fine restaurants and inns, the Kennebunks are a vastly popular vacation spot. George Bush

Senior and his family summer at their Kennebunkport compound, and locals will assure you that they are "just regular members of the community." For visitor information and assistance with lodging, contact the **Kennebunk-Kennebunkport Chamber of Commerce** ☎ (207) 967-0857 TOLL-FREE (800) 982-4421 E-MAIL info@visitthekennebunks.com, 17 Western Avenue (Route 9), Lower Village, Kennebunk 04043.

Kennebunk, or "The Village," was settled in 1650 and was once the shipbuilding capital of York County. As the boatwright trade declined, the town became a fishing and tourism center. What remains of those affluent days are some imposing houses, towering trees and graceful New England churches, including the First Parish Church (on Main Street), built in 1772.

Kennebunkport, at the mouth of the Kennebunk River, is transformed into a vacation boomtown each summer. Quaint shops, beautiful old inns and fancy private estates abound. Aside from Dock Square's trinket shops, there are a number of dedicated antique shops and galleries well worth exploring.

Though the seawater never gets warmer than 65°F (18°C), the Kennebunks have some of Maine's best beaches for walking and sunning. At low tide, the three-mile-long (five-kilometer) **Goose Rocks Beach** becomes a wide swathe of smooth sand. **Gooches**, **Mother's** and **Kennebunk** beaches are generally more crowded than Goose Rocks. Mother's, with its little playground, is favored by families. Many of the beaches require a parking permit ($7 to $10), which you can get at Town Hall.

Aside from the beaches, the Kennebunks don't offer much for children, but the delightful **Seashore Trolley Museum** ☎ (207) 967-2800, on Log Cabin Road just north of town, is an exception. Some 150 antique streetcars from the United States and abroad are on display (the largest collection in the world), and there are trolley rides through the surrounding woods in a vintage trolley. Open daily 10 AM to 5 PM, May to November, limited hours in spring and fall; an admission fee is charged.

There are three **whale-watching cruises** to choose from, one takes visitors out on the 65-ft (20-m) *Nautilus* ☎ (207) 967-5595. Or you can opt to float by the Bush compound and other summer cottages on the *Elizabeth II* ☎ (207) 967-5595, a narrated **sightseeing cruise**. Both of these trips leave from the Arundel Shipyard.

During high season, make reservations for lodging in the Kennebunks two months in advance (though you may get lucky and find a last-minute opening). Topping a long list of fine accommodations, the **White Barn Inn** ☎ (207) 967-2321 FAX (207) 967-1100 E-MAIL whitebarn@relaischateux.fr, 37 Beach Street, PO Box 560 C, Kennebunkport 04046 (luxury), has 17 small but completely charming rooms and seven suites, all flawlessly adorned; many have fireplaces and Jacuzzis. The restaurant is superb (see LIVING IT UP, page 40 in YOUR CHOICE).

The Colony ☎ (207) 967-3331 E-MAIL info-me@thecolonyhotel.com, Ocean Avenue, Kennebunkport 04046 (luxury), is a splendid, green-shuttered estate. The grand old building, new aluminum siding notwithstanding, is still one of the best-loved places to stay on the Maine coast. There are gorgeous views from many of the 120 antique-filled rooms, and panoramas as well from the heated saltwater swimming pool. Aside from daily dining, the restaurant also offers a Sunday jazz brunch and evening dancing and entertainment.

A beautiful old bed-and-breakfast inn infused with the fresh enthusiasm of new owners, **Crosstrees** ☎ (207) 967-2780 TOLL-FREE (800) 564-1527 FAX (207) 967-2610 WEB SITE www.crosstrees.com, South Street, PO Box 1333, Kennebunkport 04046-1333 (mid-range to expensive), has four sunny, treetop guestrooms, adorned each day with fresh flowers from the garden and supplied with fresh-baked cookies or other treats. Some rooms have working fireplaces, and there is a king suite with separate entrance, gas fireplace, gigantic sleigh bed, peaked ceilings with skylights and exposed beams. The hosts serve a full cooked breakfast each morning. The inn is open year-round.

Some reliable mid-range choices are the motel-like **King's Port Inn** ☎ (207) 967-4340 TOLL-FREE (800) 286-5767, junction of Route 9

A wood cabin peaks out of the forest.

and Route 35, PO Box 1070, Kennebunkport 04046, within walking distance of the heart of region; and the **Lodge at Turbat's Creek** ((207) 967-8700, Turbat's Creek Road, PO Box 2722MI, Kennebunkport 04046 (mid-range), in a quiet wooded setting a few minute's drive from the village center. Both of these places offer good value.

Diners have a world of choices here. The **Cape Arundel Inn** ((207) 967-2125, 207 Ocean Avenue, Kennebunkport, is situated across from the Bush estate with a presidential view of the water; go during a full moon for the ultimate effect (mid-range to expensive). It doesn't look promising from the outside, but a local innkeeper assured us that the **Grissini Trattoria & Panificio** ((207) 967-2211, 27 Western Avenue, Lower Kennebunk Village, is one of the best Italian restaurants he's ever come across (mid-range to expensive).

Locals and tourists alike crowd the benches each night at **Nunan's Lobster Hut** ((207) 967-4362, 9 Mills Road (Route 9), Cape Porpoise, where two one-and-a-quarter-pound (600-gram) lobsters go for around $15. Nunan's doesn't take reservations; look for the tiny black and yellow shack. If someone in your party doesn't want lobster, you could opt for **Mabel's Lobster Claw** ((207) 967-2562, Ocean Avenue, where the lobster is also good, but the menu is more varied.

The Kennebunks are about 90 miles (145 km) from Boston. Follow Interstate 95 North to the Maine Turnpike (Interstate 95); then take Exit 3 onto Route 35. Kennebunkport is seven miles (11 km) further along.

PORTLAND AND CASCO BAY

With a population of 65,000, Portland is Maine's largest city and the state's commercial and cultural center. Safe, clean and easygoing, Portland is — according to the *Utne Reader*, which cited its liberal politics and generous social programs — one of the most "enlightened" cities in the United States. For visitors, Portland's Old Port shops, its working fishing wharves, excellent museums, nightlife and restaurants add up to a fascinating and enjoyable place to visit.

Portland occupies a long peninsula jutting into magnificent Casco Bay. At both ends of the city, the land slopes upward, forming the Eastern and Western promenades, excellent viewpoints from which to see the bay's hundreds of islands to the east and the hills and mountains to the west.

BACKGROUND

First settled in 1631, Portland was burned to the ground three times — by raiding Indians in 1676, by invading British troops in 1775, and by accident in 1866. Longfellow commented that the smoldering ruins of 1866 resembled the rubble of Pompeii.

From its beginnings, the city was an important commercial and shipping center, its natural deepwater harbor being 100 miles (160 km) closer to Europe than any other port in the United States. From Portland's docks sailed many of the finest sailing vessels and clipper ships built in the United States; in the eighteenth and nineteenth centuries the city was a major center for lumber export, fisheries and the West Indies molasses and sugar trade. The Bath Ironworks has established a ship-repair facility in Portland which has a constant stream of United States Navy vessels in its dry-docks.

Overfishing of Atlantic fisheries and lobster beds, however, has cut into Portland's trade and many of the docks along the port have been turned to other uses. But the city continues to grow and diversify. The early 1960s saw the beginning of Portland's preservation movement that resulted in the city's current look, and in the 1970s the Old Port became an area of artist's studios and retail shops.

GENERAL INFORMATION

An excellent resource for information on Portland and beyond, the **Convention and Visitors Bureau of Greater Portland** ((207) 772-5800 WEB SITE www.visitportland.com, 305 Commercial Street, Portland 04101-4641, has a walk-in information center with a staff ready to answer all your questions and racks of informational materials.

Around downtown, look for the **Downtown District Guides**, recognizable by their safari hats and purple shirts. They are out and about during the summer tourist season to help visitors find directions, shopping, events and restaurants.

If you are heading onward to Nova Scotia (see TOURS AND EXCURSIONS, below), you can take advantage of the services of Portland's **Nova Scotia Tourism Information** ✆ (207) 772-6131, 468 Commercial Street; call for hours.

WHAT TO SEE AND DO

A walk around the **Old Port** is part of the Portland experience. This area has been beautifully restored to form a thriving commercial and tourist center that has lost none of its nineteenth-century charm, with original buildings, brick sidewalks and attractive cafés, bookstores and boutiques amid lawyers' offices, ship chandlers and seamen's bars. For a taste of Portland's salty past that persists into the present, try to catch the early morning fish auctions at Long Wharf. Greater Portland Landmarks ✆ (207) 774-5561 gives guided **walking tours** of this district and other of Portland neighborhoods. The organization also produces a pamphlet describing a self-guided walking tour.

A few blocks up the hill from the Old Port is Congress Street, where a renaissance of sorts has taken place in the last several years. Several new arts establishments, cafés and retail stores have popped up — including a new L.L. Bean Factory Store ✆ (207) 772-0431, 542 Congress Street, legendary purveyors of outdoor gear and casual clothing. Congress Street is also the location of the **Maine Historical Society** ✆ (207) 879-0427, at No. 489, a repository of artifacts and information on four centuries of Portland life. Within the Society's grounds are some exquisite old houses, including the 1785 boyhood home of the poet Henry Wadsworth Longfellow. Next door to the Longfellow House is the Maine History Gallery with permanent and temporary exhibits. A diminutive and delightfully peaceful garden is tucked away amongst the buildings. The Society is open daily, June through October; an admission fee is charged.

Even if you're not an architecture buff, you'll enjoy the extravagant **Victoria Mansion** ✆ (207) 772-4841 at 109 Danforth Street, a few blocks southwest of Congress Street. An Italianate villa built in 1858, it is one of the country's most significant Victorian buildings. Behind the brick and brownstone façade is a fantastically decorated interior garnished with trompe l'œil paintings, original furnishings and ceramics. It's open from May to December, and 45-minute tours are conducted Tuesday to Sunday; admission fee.

Portland's busy wharves teem with fishing trawlers, cruise ships and ferries.

Local seafood, baked goods, cheeses, produce and specialty foods sold by the people who make, catch or grow them are colorfully displayed at the **Portland Public Market** ☎ (207) 228-2000, 25 Preble Street. An immense stone hearth is a gathering spot for lunchtime diners; upstairs there is plenty of seating with a pigeon's-eye view of the market proceedings; or there's a corner café serving soup, sandwiches and draft beer. Open year round; free parking. New York-based (but Maine-born) superchef Matthew Kenney's **Commissary** ☎ (207) 228-2057 rounds out the dining choices with upscale contemporary cuisine.

The **Portland Museum of Art** ☎ (207) 775-6148, 7 Congress Square, resembles a Roman amphitheater. Inside, beyond the double rotunda, is a fine collection of twentieth-century art interspersed with portal windows offering views on city street-life. The museum is strong on French Impressionist and post-impressionist painters such as Degas, Monet, Picasso and Renoir, as well as images of Maine and works by Maine artists. American master Winslow Homer, and Maine painters such as Marsden Hartley and Rockwell Kent are well represented. Open year-round Tuesday, Wednesday, Saturday and Sunday 10 AM to 5 PM, Thursday and Friday 10 AM to 9 PM. Tours are given at 2 PM and 6 PM each Thursday and Friday, also Mondays 10 AM to 5 PM Memorial Day to Columbus Day. There's a café on the lower level.

At the delightful **Children's Museum of Maine** ☎ (207) 828-1234, 142 Free Street (near the Portland Museum of Art), a whirlwind of make-believe gives children the chance to unwind. In the "Town," kids withdraw play money from an automated teller machine, from whence the little sprouts go to the grocery store where someone else's kid is operating a cash register. The big red fire truck is much loved with its flashing lights and long fire hose. In the Theater Space, children pull costumes from a box and put on an impromptu show. It's all so adorably Mr. Rogers. For older children, the museum offers a star lab and space shuttle, television studio, science exhibits and computer lab. Open Monday to Sunday from Memorial Day to Labor Day, Tuesday to Sunday the rest of the year.

SPORTS AND OUTDOOR ACTIVITIES

Spectator Sports

The **Portland Sea Dogs**, farm team for the Florida Marlins baseball club, play at Hadlock Field ☎ (207) 874-9300 TOLL-FREE (800) 936-3647, PO Box 636, Portland 04104, a small old-time stadium near downtown. Games tend to sell out a couple of weeks in advance, so call well ahead for tickets. The season runs from April to October.

Beaches

At Cape Elizabeth, **Crescent Beach State Park** offers ocean swimming, fishing, and a snack bar. A park entrance fee is charged. You can take the ferry to **Peaks Island Beach**, a former resort area with rides and theaters, now a tranquil swimming beach. In South Portland, there is sand and surf at **Willard Beach**.

Twelve miles (19 km) south of Portland is **Old Orchard Beach**, Maine's Coney Island. Because it is the first large saltwater beach south of Montreal, Old Orchard attracts large numbers of French Canadians. Many of the hotels and restaurants here employ bilingual staff to make these visitors feel at home. During the summer season, Old Orchard has many open-air concerts and special events.

Paddling

A good way to see Casco Bay is to get up an island kayaking expedition. **Maine Island Kayak Co.** ☎ (207) 766-2373 WEB SITE www.maineislandkayak.com, 70 Luther Street, Peaks Island 04108, arranges island-hopping trips, with half-day to 10-day trips throughout Maine, and provides rentals. The **L.L. Bean Outdoor Discovery School** TOLL-FREE (888) 552-3261 offers classes in paddling, cycling, outdoor skills and winter sports; call for a free course catalog.

Walking, Jogging, Bicycling and In-line Skating

Around town, there are wonderful walks along the **Eastern Promenade** with views of Casco Bay, and the **Western Promenade** with its Victorian-era residences. Part of a park system designed in 1905 by Frederick Law

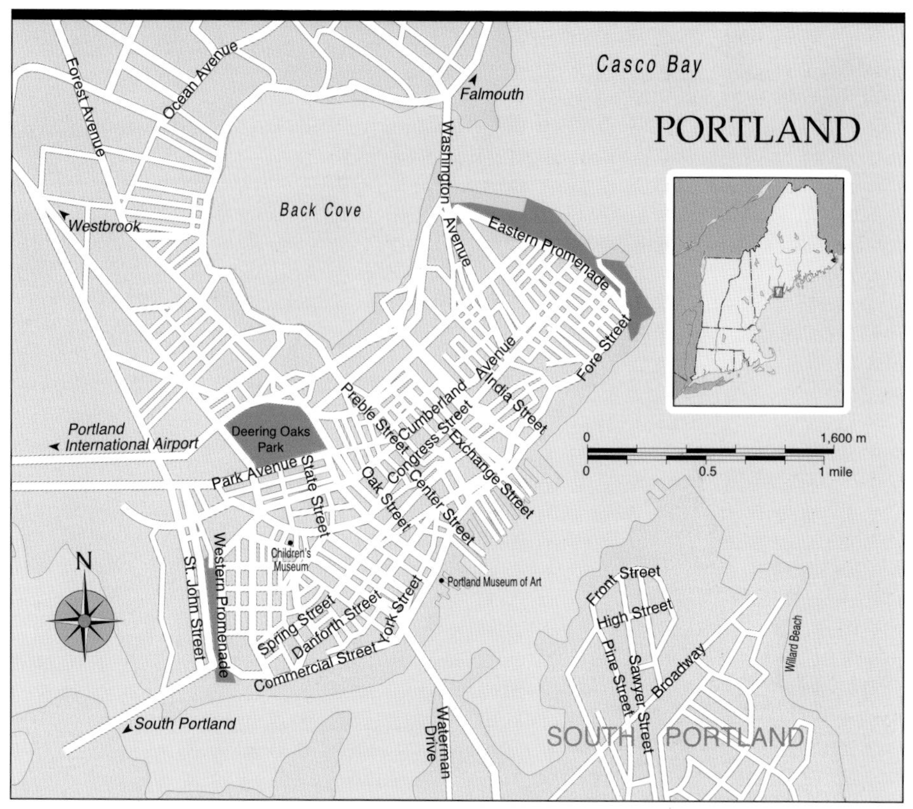

Olmsted's firm, the **Back Cove Recreation Path** is a 5.5-mile (8.8-km) easy paved loop around a saltwater cove north of the city center. Along the route, which parallels Baxter Boulevard, you can spot seabirds, watch windsurfers, and get a fine view of the Portland skyline. In Cape Elizabeth there's a walking path, with water and lighthouse views at **Two Lights State Park** and at **Fort Williams State Park**. See TOURS AND EXCURSIONS, below.

TOURS AND EXCURSIONS

Whether you're visiting Portland for an afternoon or a week, hop on the van with **Mainely Tours** ☎ (207) 774-0808, 5 ½ Moulton Street, for an expertly guided 90-minute tour of the city's neighborhoods and the Portland Head Light (see below) on an open-air trolley. The commentary is witty and enlightening, and the tour takes in sights you might otherwise miss, such as the 1807 Portland Observatory, one of the last "signalizing" towers in the country. You'll learn about cannonballs left over from the Revolutionary war, and local heroes from Longfellow to actor-filmmaker John Ford. The Portland driving tour picks up at major hotels and across from the visitor information center. Mainely Tours also offers a city tour combined with a harbor cruise.

Named by Captain John Smith, who believed he'd counted 365 of them, the **Calendar Islands** are reached via a short cruise on the **Casco Bay Lines** ☎ (207) 774-7871, 56 Commercial Street at the corner of Franklin Street. Options include a six-hour trip to Bailey's Island; a circumnavigation of the bay on the mail boat stopping at major islands such as Peaks and Chebeague; lobster-bake cruises, and sunset concert cruises. The classic trip, though, is a voyage to Great Diamond Island for lunch or cocktails at Diamond's Edge Restaurant ☎ (207) 766-5850.

Portland is a gateway to the Canadian province of Nova Scotia via the car and passenger ferry MF *Scotia Prince*, departing nightly from May through October. It's an 11-hour overnight voyage, which can include

Lincoln

dinner and gambling at the onboard casino (once you're in international waters). For reservations contact **Prince of Fundy Cruises** ☎ (207) 775-5616 TOLL-FREE (800) 341-7540, 468 Commercial Street (International Ferry Terminal), Portland 04101-4637.

South of the city in Cape Elizabeth is the **Portland Head Light** ☎ (207) 799-2661, 1000 Shore Road, in Fort Williams Park. Built in 1791 during the administration of George Washington, this lighthouse is the state's oldest, and one of the oldest in continuous use in the country. From the hurricane deck you can look out over Casco Bay's islands. Fort Williams Park is well worth exploring with its rolling green hills and seaside bluffs. There are several walking paths, picnic areas, and a small swimming beach for the hardy (or foolhardy). Open June through September, daily; open weekends only in May and November.

NIGHTLIFE AND THE ARTS

Check the free *Casco Bay Weekly* for current entertainment listings.

The acoustically dynamite **Merrill Auditorium** ☎ (207) 874-8200 EVENTS LINE, extension 305, 20 Myrtle Street (at City Hall), is an excellent place to see a show; world-class acts including the Vienna Boys Choir, the Alvin Ailey Dance Theater, and Greg Allman have performed here. The **Portland Symphony Orchestra** ☎ (207) 842-0800, PO Box 3573, Portland 04104, performs classics, pops and chamber concerts with renowned guest artists (conducted by Toshiyuki Shimada). In summers there are free open-air concerts in Congress Square.

For theater there is the **Portland Stage Company** ☎ (207) 774-0465, 25A Forest Avenue, with a fall-to-spring lineup of mainstream Broadway hits, classics, dramas, comedies and contemporary theater. Experimental plays, radical reinterpretations of classics, and new works are staged by **Mad Horse Theater Company** ☎ (207) 828-1270, 92 Oak Street.

Portland has quite a few good bars and clubs, though in the end, it's the small town atmosphere that wins out. They close at 1 AM. In any case, the main rock music venues are **Asylum** ☎ (207) 772-8274, 121 Center Street, The **Stone Coast Brewing Co.** ☎ (207) 773-2337, 14 York Street, which features local and regional rock bands, and **The Basement** ☎ (207) 775-6654, at the corner of Fore and Exchange streets (below Pizza Prima), hosts local legends of rock.

If you want to tip up a heady brew in good company, head for **Gritty McDuff's** ☎ (207) 772-2739, 396 Fore Street, or the **Shipyard Brewing Co.** ☎ (207) 761-0807, 86 Newbury Street, not far from the Old Port. The latter also offers free tours of the brew works daily from 3 PM and 5 PM.

SHOPPING

The Old Port's six blocks of galleries and shops offer such fineries as old nautical maps, local pottery and paintings, books, music and vintage clothing. Here are but a few:

Maine artisans show and sell their works at **Gallery 7** ☎ (207) 761-7007, 49 Exchange Street. **Exchange Street Gallery/R.N. Cohen Gallery** ☎ (207) 772-0633, 425 Fore Street, has prints of local landscapes from the Casco Bay Islands to the Portland Observatory.

OPPOSITE: Twelve miles (19 km) northwest of Portland, Sebago Lake is a natural spot for fishing swimming and boating. ABOVE: A city landmark, the 1807 Portland Observatory, is a "signalizing" tower formerly used to notify city merchants when a cargo ship was approaching the harbor.

Beautiful and unusual women's clothing, hats, wedding dresses, bags and jewelry are found at **Amaryllis** ((207) 772-4439, 41 Exchange Street, and antiques at **F.O. Bailey** ((207) 774-1479, 141 Middle Street. There are gourmet foods, including some Maine products such as blueberry jam, at **Stonewall Kitchen** ((207) 879-2409, 182 Middle Street; and Maine chocolates, jams and jellies at **Portland Wine and Cheese** ((207) 772-4647, 57 Exchange Street.

A short drive north of Portland is Freeport, home of the original L.L. Bean and L.L. Bean

Factory Store as well as dozens of other outlets and retailers. See SHOP TILL YOU DROP, page 47 in YOUR CHOICE.

WHERE TO STAY

Besides the obvious (but superbly situated) **Holiday Inn by the Bay** ((207) 775-2311 TOLL-FREE (800) 345-5050, 88 Spring Street, Portland 04101-3924, and the **Portland Regency** ((207) 774-4200 TOLL-FREE (800) 727-3436 FAX (207) 775-2150, 20 Milk Street, Portland 04101-5024, the city has some distinctive inns.

The Danforth ((207) 879-8755 TOLL-FREE (800) 991-6557 FAX (207) 879-8754 WEB SITE www.danforthmaine.com, 163 Danforth Street, Portland 04102 (mid-range to luxury), is a gorgeous three-story 1821 Victorian overlooking the harbor — climb to the cupola for a view of the water, or descend to the basement for a game of billiards. Guestrooms have working fireplaces and are elegantly decorated with meticulous attention to detail, such as bubble-glass doorknobs. There are cushioned window seats to take advantage of the views, sitting areas, and hearths in each room. You can enjoy a continental breakfast (included in rate) in the dining room, or ask for it to be brought to your room. The inn is a short walk from the Old Port and the Arts District.

Somewhat less pricey, the **Pomegranate Inn** ((207) 772-1006 TOLL-FREE (800) 356-0408, 49 Neal Street, Portland 04102 (mid-range to expensive), is a bed-and-breakfast inn situated in a Colonial Revival building. Featured in decorators' magazines as "a high-spirited house," the inn's common areas are a veritable gallery of art and antiques, while the eight guestrooms are festooned with wild flowers and are hand-painted by local artists.

Bargain hunters may want to consider the **Inn at Saint John** ((207) 773-6481, 939 Congress Street, Portland 04102-3031 (corner Saint John Street), in the western portion of the city, where some rooms rates fall into the high end of the budget bracket, the rest into the mid-range. The neighborhood is "in transition," but the price is right; the rate includes a continental breakfast.

A short distance out from the city center, **Andrews Lodging** ☎ (207) 797-9157 FAX (207) 797-9040 E-MAIL dandrew@maine.rr.com, 417 Auburn Street, Route 26, Portland 04103 (mid-range), offers a selection of smallish Victorian rooms and more spacious suites — five in all. Shared kitchen facilities and laundry make Andrews a good base for extended stays.

WHERE TO EAT

Located in a waterfront warehouse with harbor views, the **Fore Street Grill** ☎ (207) 775-2717, 288 Fore Street, attracts a cutting-edge crowd with its delicious food, lush displays of produce, open kitchen and wood-fired grill. It's a busy place, but Sam Hayward's food is so good you forget the din. Spit-roasted game meats are a specialty (expensive). The **Zephyr Grill** ☎ (207) 828-4033, at 653 Congress Street, serves a similar grilled-meats menu in a cozier, less-jammed setting (mid-range). Alternatively, opt for grilled fish at **Street & Company** ☎ (207) 775-0887, 33 Wharf Street, maybe the friendliest of the lot (mid-range to expensive).

A major stop on the tourist trail, **DiMillo's Floating Restaurant** ☎ (207) 772-2216, Long Wharf (mid-range), serves lobster and other sea fare amid a pleasant decor and water views aboard a large, docked cruise ship. Another Portland tradition, **Three Dollar Dewey's** ☎ (207) 772-3310, 241 Commercial Street (budget), taps Maine-brewed beers with heaping helpings of their famous chili.

You can join the locals at **Bintliff's American Café** ☎ (207) 774-0005, 98 Portland Street, High Street, which serves a fine fresh crab and scallop bisque and more ambitious fare such as grilled peach-glazed pork chops; or at the **Miss Portland Diner** ☎ (207) 773-3246, 49 Marginal Way, where meatloaf and mashed spuds make you dream of childhood (budget).

HOW TO GET THERE

Motorists coming from the south will take the Maine Turnpike (Interstate 95) to Exit 6A for downtown Portland. Portland is 166 miles (266 km) north of Boston, or about a two-hour drive.

The **Portland International Jetport** ☎ (207) 774-7301, at Exit 3 off of Interstate 95, is served by the following national and regional carriers: Business Express, Continental Airlines, Delta Airlines, Pine State Airlines TOLL-FREE (800) 353-6334, United Airlines, and US Airways (see GETTING THERE, page 341 in TRAVELERS' TIPS for other toll-free phone numbers).

MID COAST

The broad sandy beaches of the south give way at Mid Coast to a rocky, serrated shoreline and long gnarled peninsulas. It's a land of lighthouses and fishing villages, gorgeous bed-and-breakfast inns and lobster shacks — quintessentially Maine, in other words. Stretching from Brunswick to Belfast, this portion of the coast takes in the state's most renowned sights and sites: the Farnsworth Museum in Rockland, Pemaquid Lighthouse, the windjammers of Camden, Rockport and Rockland, and a host of homey

OPPOSITE, LEFT and RIGHT: Relaxing in the shade of Portland's tree-lined streets. ABOVE: Freeport's placid harbor belies the bustle of the downtown outlet malls.

ME 1562

harbors. Maine's Mid Coast is, in short, packed with scenery — but it's just as packed with tourist crowds; you may want to consider timing your visit to avoid the peak summer season.

BRUNSWICK

Brunswick, 26 miles (42 km) north of Portland, on Route 1, is known for its wide avenues, tall trees shading Federal-style mansions, and the Bowdoin College campus, alma mater of Henry Wadsworth Longfellow, Nathaniel Hawthorne and Franklin Pierce among other literary and political notables. Informational materials are available from the **Bath-Brunswick Region Chamber of Commerce** ☎ (207) 725-8797 or (207) 443-9751 FAX (207) 725-9787 or (207) 442-0808 E-MAIL chamber@midcoastmaine.com, 59 Pleasant Street, Brunswick 04011.

Brunswick's most important landmark, the pine-forested campus of **Bowdoin College** ☎ (207) 725-3000, was established in 1794 and is one of the country's top private colleges. The school's **Walker Art Museum** has a fine collection of paintings, including a Gilbert Stuart portrait of Thomas Jefferson. Another Bowdoin alumni, polar explorer Admiral Robert Peary, is honored at fascinating **Peary-MacMillan Arctic Museum** ☎ (207) 725-3416, Bowdoin College, Hubbard Hall (off College Street), which houses an incredible collection of artifacts, photographs and documents detailing Peary's North Pole expedition; open Tuesday to Sunday. Admission is free.

BATH

Ten miles (16 km) north of Brunswick (look for the sign for Historic Bath along Route 1), Bath is a shipbuilding center with a small waterfront area and a little downtown with a lost-in-the-1950s look, complete with candy-striped barbershop poles and a cast-iron clock keeping the citizenry on time.

Since 1889, the Bath Ironworks has made not only pleasure boats and freighters, but also destroyers, battleships and patrol boats; it remains one of the busiest boatyards in the nation for United States Navy ships. While national security interests keep the boatyard closed to visitors, Bath's shipbuilding legacy comes alive at the **Maine Maritime Museum** ☎ (207) 443-1316, 243 Washington Street, just off Route 1. Several buildings exhibit models, gadgets and other seafaring artifacts; a working apprentice boatyard demonstrates various stages of boat building. Tall ships regularly dock here for onboard tours, and there is a narrated boat ride up the Kennebec River.

WISCASSET

A surge of antique shops, country stores and craft shops along Route 1 is the prelude to Wiscasset, "the prettiest little village in Maine." This diminutive town rests alongside the wide basin of the Sheepscot River, dwarfed by the long span of the Route 1 bridge.

Wiscasset is a good place to stop for lunch or picnic supplies. **Red's Eats** ☎ (207) 882-6128, Main Street, is legendary — a tiny shack at the foot of the bridge where locals and tourists alike line up to get their fill of Red's lobster rolls and fried clams. The gourmet food shop **Treats** ☎ (207) 882-6192, Main Street, has an excellent wine selection as well as imported beer, fresh-baked breads and pastries and good strong coffee.

Wiscasset is about 160 miles (256 km) from Boston along Route 1.

THE BOOTHBAY PENINSULA

A watery region cut through with wetlands, inlets and rivers, the Boothbay Peninsula introduces itself with a drive through roller-coaster hills — passing through the town of Boothbay with its many graveyards — and ramshackle homesteads with names like Hardscrabble Farm. At the end of this rugged peninsula is Boothbay Harbor, situated between the Sheepscot and Damariscotta rivers.

Boothbay Harbor welcomes more than 60,000 visitors each summer. Though time-share condos abound, the town still clings to its past as a fishing village. Its streets are lined with small shops and seafood restaurants, and at nearby wharves, fishermen unload catches of fish and lobster. In warm weather, dozens of yachts fill the harbor,

A fishing shack at low tide, decked with found objects such as colorful buoys.

creating an unmatched spectacle of masts, sails, and colors. Special celebrations in the self-proclaimed "boating capital of New England" include **Windjammer Days** and **Friendship Sloop Days**, both held in June. Information on these and other events, as well as assistance with lodging, can be obtained from the **Boothbay Harbor Region Chamber of Commerce** ☎ (207) 633-2353 TOLL-FREE (800) 266-8422 E-MAIL seamaine @boothbayharbor.com, 192 Townsend Avenue, Boothbay Harbor 04538; you'll find their visitor center on the right on Route 27 shortly before entering the town center.

There are plenty of charter boats offering **harbor cruises** that include island clambakes, seal watching, lobster hauling, sunsets and more. Many excursion companies vie for your attention at the Boothbay Harbor wharf. Cap'n Fish Boat Trips ☎ (207) 633-3244, Pier 1, is one of them. You can cruise to Monhegan Island, sail a yacht or take a harbor tour with Balmy Days Cruises ☎ (207) 633-2284 TOLL-FREE (800) 298-2284, Commercial Street, Boothbay Harbor.

Over in smaller and quieter **East Boothbay**, you can put your kayak in the water at the town dock and paddle out to see the harbor seals. For a lovely drive take Route 96 to **Ocean Point**. As you descend the hill, there's a little gravel parking lot on the left. Park, walk, and smell the salt air.

Where to Stay and Eat

Some hotels in the Boothbay area are closed from late autumn to early spring. In the summer, demand is high so book early or call ahead. At the **Spruce Point Inn** ☎ (207) 633-4152 TOLL-FREE (800) 553-0289 FAX (207) 633-7138, PO Box 237, Grandview Avenue, Boothbay Harbor 04538, rates go from mid-range for rooms without sea view to luxury prices for rooms with a view. The inn also has 40 suites equipped Jacuzzi tubs, fireplaces and private patios. Room rates include breakfast and dinner, which can be enjoyed on the inn's new outdoor dining pavilion.

In East Boothbay, perched on a hillside overlooking Linekin Bay, **Five Gables Inn** ☎ (207) 633-4551 TOLL-FREE (800) 451-5048 E-MAIL info@fivegablesinn.com, PO Box 335, Murray Hill Road, East Boothbay 04544, is a the beautiful turn-of-the-century Victorian gothic with views of the harbor. Proprietors De and Mike Kennedy are transplanted southerners who've bloomed in this northern climate. De has decorated the rooms with a Maine theme using sailcloth for the bedspreads and furniture she has hand-painted. There are 15 rooms, some with fireplace, all but one with views of the bay and islands. The bountiful breakfast buffet, prepared by Mike, a Culinary Institute of America graduate, is outstanding. A broad verandah lined with comfy chairs is the perfect spot for breakfast or a lazy afternoon spent watching the lobster boats come and go.

The area has dozens of restaurants, but you'll need to make reservations well in advance for **Brown's Wharf Restaurant** ☎ (207) 633-5440, 105 Atlantic Avenue, which was Charles Kuralt's favorite Boothbay hangout. In the business for 50 years, they serve seafood dinners, including lobster fresh from local waters.

How to Get There

From Route 1 take Route 27 to the Boothbay Harbor region. To get to East Boothbay take Route 96; the junction is directly across from the Chamber of Commerce visitor center. Boothbay Harbor is 60 miles (just under 100 km) north of Portland, and 162 miles (260 km) from Boston.

PEMAQUID PENINSULA

At the head of the Pemaquid Peninsula, Damariscotta and Newcastle guard the gateway to the picturesque fishing village of New Harbor and Pemaquid Point, site of one of Maine's best-loved lighthouses. Informational materials on the region are available from the **Damariscotta Region Chamber of Commerce** ☎ (207) 563-8340, PO Box 13, Main Street, Damariscotta 04543.

Poised over a sea-sprayed bluff, the **Pemaquid Point Light** ☎ (207) 677-2494, built in 1827, might be the most painted and sketched lighthouse in the country. Photographers, too, love to capture the lighthouse's reflection in the nearby shallow pools left by the retreating surf. A small Fishermen's Museum in the lightkeeper's house tells the story of Maine lighthouses and the state's fishing industry. The Point, south of Damariscotta on Route 130, is also home to colonial **Pemaquid**. In 1965, amateur archaeologists uncovered here the foundations of seventeenth-century houses and other artifacts, which included a human skeleton outfitted in armor, believed to be a Viking. These discoveries are displayed at the tiny archaeological museum.

The much celebrated **Shaw's Lobster Pond** ((207) 677-2200, Route 32, New Harbor, is the biggest lobster-in-the-rough place on the peninsula. They also serve steaks.

MONHEGAN ISLAND

Nine miles (15 km) off the coast near Port Clyde, the cliffs of Monhegan rise out of the ocean: ledges of rock and forest less than two miles (three kilometers) long and one mile (one and a half kilometers) wide. Leif Ericsson is said to have walked Monhegan Island more than 1,000 years ago. English explorer John Cabot referred to it on his journeys. Its headlands were reputed to be hideaways for pirates, who plundered ships off the Maine coast. Beautiful scenery, art galleries, a quaint village, and whale- and seal-watching draw visitors to this island paradise. The ocean scenery and boulder-strewn coast are spectacular when viewed from atop **Lighthouse Hill**. Seventeen miles (27 km) of **hiking trails** traverse the 150-ft-tall (46-m) cliffs. The open meadows are blanketed with wildflowers and **Cathedral Woods** embraces stands of old-growth pines and firs.

None of the island's lodges are luxurious. The best is probably the **Island Inn** ((207) 596-0371 E-MAIL islandin@midcoast.com, Monhegan 04852 (mid-range to expensive), a three-story nineteenth-century building with a verandah looking out over the ferry landing. The 36 harbor- and meadow-view rooms have shared baths. The rate includes breakfast. Open late May to October. Day-trippers may want to dine or take out picnic sandwiches at the casually upscale **Barnacle**, under the same ownership as the inn.

Monhegan-Thomaston Boat Lines ((207) 372-8848, PO Box 238, Port Clyde 04855, serves Monhegan Island from Port Clyde (see also BOOTHBAY PENINSULA, page 315).

PENOBSCOT BAY

Penobscot Bay is Wyeth country — members of this family of painters continue to work and live here. It's also windjamming country, with dozens of yachting havens and ship building centers. It is a place where Yankee Maine meets yuppie New England, where Down East diners advertising "no ferns, no quiche" sit alongside upscale fishmongers pushing gourmet dinners cooked to order. Somehow all of this manages to coexist. Perhaps it's the presence of certain class-leveling institutions, such as the line of people waiting for lobster rolls outside the local clam shack on opening day.

ROCKLAND

The "Lobster Capital of the World," Rockland — on Route 1, 81 miles (130 km) north of Portland on the western edge of Penobscot Bay — is a modern-day seaport that also harbors an excellent art museum and perhaps the best cup of coffee in Maine (see WHERE TO STAY AND EAT, below). Its **Lobster Festival** is a three-day event held every August. Everything revolves around the catch — lobster boils, harvesting excursions, and even displays of lobster-trap building. For information on the festival as well as on year-round dining, attractions and lodging, contact the **Rockland-Thomaston Area Chamber of Commerce** ((207) 596-0376 TOLL-FREE (800) 562-2529, PO Box 508, Harbor Park, Rockland 04841, located at the Public Landing in Rockland.

At the **Farnsworth Art Museum** ((207) 596-6457, 352 Main Street, you can view works by three generations of Wyeths: N. C. Wyeth (1882–1945), Andrew Wyeth (1911–), and Jamie Wyeth (1946–). Featured as well are the works of masters such as the terracotta sculptures and paintings of Louise Nevelson (1899–1988), and the paintings of Winslow Homer and Rockwell Kent. The collection is especially noted for its coastal landscape oils and watercolors by artists who lived and worked on the Maine Coast. It's the only museum fully dedicated to telling Maine's role in the history of art. Behind the museum in a restored church building, the

Wyeth Center is a stunning space that stages special exhibitions focusing on the Wyeths. The complex is open daily year Memorial Day to Columbus Day 9 AM to 5 PM, the rest of year Tuesday to Saturday 10 AM to 5 PM, Sunday 1 PM to 5 PM; an admission fee is charged.

About 25 minutes south of Rockland is the village of Cushing looking very much like a Wyeth tableau. Here you'll find the **Olson House** ☎ (207) 354-0102, a nineteenth-century Maine saltwater farmhouse. The Olsons and the village itself were the subjects of many of Andrew Wyeth's paintings, including *Christina's World*. Tours are conducted from Memorial Day to Columbus Day. Pick up a map at the Farnsworth Museum in Rockland for directions to the house.

Maine State Ferry ☎ (207) 596-2202 offers **island excursions** from Rockland to North Haven, Matinicus, and Vinalhaven. The only original three-masted schooner in the famed Windjammer fleet, the ***Victory Chimes*** ☎ (207) 594-0755 TOLL-FREE (800) 745-5651 E-MAIL vchimes@sunline.net, PO Box 1401, Rockland 04841, sails out of Rockland Harbor (see CRUISE ON A WINDJAMMER, page 18 in TOP SPOTS).

Where to Stay and Eat

North and south of Rockland there are strings of the quaint motels, simple places in a gorgeous setting looking out over the Penobscot Bay. The **Trade Winds Motor Inn** ☎ (207) 596-6661 TOLL-FREE (800) 834-3130, 2 Park View Drive, Rockland 04841-3447, is a homey place on the water; rooms are comfortably arranged with balconies offering gorgeous views of the busy harbor. Look for the cast-iron lobster. The more upscale, **East Wind Inn** ☎ (207) 372-6366 TOLL-FREE (800) 241-8439, Mechanic Street, Tenants Harbor 04860, has 26 rooms in pleasant surroundings. A quiet fishing village, Tenants Harbor is part of the region celebrated in Sarah Orne Jewett's *The Country of Pointed Firs*. The inn is located about 15 minutes off of Route 1, and it is convenient to the Monhegan Island ferry landing. It is open from April to December (expensive).

For a hearty breakfast and lunch there is the **Second Read Bookstore** ☎ (207) 594-4123, 328 Main Street, Rockland, serving up delicious grilled panini sandwiches, flaky croissants and cappuccino.

Look for **Lighthouse Espresso Drive-Thru** ☎ (207) 596-5936, 739 Main Street, on the right-hand side of Route 1 North as you leave Rockland. This stubby replica lighthouse was the brainchild of a couple from Seattle who retired in Maine and couldn't find a good cup of coffee. Drive up and order a double cappuccino or whatever strikes your fancy. Your superb cup of coffee comes with a Tootsie Roll.

CAMDEN AND ROCKPORT

Camden, with its sparkling harbor, is a Maine classic. A yachting center and one of the loveliest towns in New England, it is also in its undemonstrative way an oasis of Down East

wealth and glamour. At any time of year, you can browse through the expensive shops that cater to Camden's decidedly upscale clientele. On the Public Landing at Camden, you'll find the busy **Camden-Rockport-Lincolnville Chamber of Commerce** ((207) 236-4404 FAX (207) 236-4315 WEB SITE www.visitcamden.com, PO Box 919, Camden 04843; or visit them at the Public Landing.

For a long view of Penobscot Bay, head to the hills — the 6,000-acre (2,430-hectare) **Camden Hills State Park**, two miles (just over three kilometers) north of Camden on Route 1. Hike up **Mount Battie** (800 ft or 244 m), or take the toll road, a short steep drive to a parking lot at the top. From a crenellated tower at the summit you can see the bay to the east as well as a corner of Megunticook Lake and surrounding mountains to the west.

As you drive south from Camden to Rockport along Chestnut Street look for Aldemere Farm, a private working dairy farm. You can stop along the roadside and see their rare breed of cow — with its distinctive black front and black hindquarters "belted" with a milky-white stripe in the middle.

Rockport is perched helter-skelter on a patch of hills overlooking a harbor with a lighthouse at the northern tip. This tiny fishing and shipbuilding village was made a Historic District in the 1970s, and lists more

Cruising on Penobscot Bay off the island of Isleboro.

than 120 registered buildings. Rockport is also an artist's center, home to several exhibition spaces including **Maine Coast Artists** ((207) 236-2875, whose gallery is situated in a renovated livery building. In the center of town, the **Maine Photographic Workshop** ((207) 236-8581, 2 Central Street, hosts photographers and lecturers from around the world. Look into their workshop gallery where they often mount exhibitions of visiting artists (see SPECIAL INTERESTS, page 56 in YOUR CHOICE). The restored **Town Hall/ Opera House**, on Central Street, is known for its superior acoustics and sponsors the summer Bay Chamber Concert series, theater, and other cultural events ((207) 236-2823 TOLL-FREE (888) 707-2770, PO Box 191, Camden 04843. At the **Artisans College** ((207) 236-6071, 9 Elm Street, visitors can observe classes in the traditional art of wooden boat construction.

The **Rockport Marine Park** is located south of the village on Pascal Avenue. Along with perusing the outdoor exhibit on the area's eighteenth- to nineteenth-century lime industry, you can say hello to the statue of André the harbor seal, of children's book fame. You'll also find a **visitor center** here at the waterfront with information on the immediate area as well as on other parts of the state.

In summer the harbor is filled with graceful yachts, sailboats with colorful canvases, and every other kind of floating vessel imaginable. Rockport's windjammer fleet offers three- to six-day island cruises from May to October. For a brochure on other cruise options, contact the **Maine Windjammer Association** TOLL-FREE (800) 807-9463 WEB SITE www.sailmainecoast.com, PO Box 317P, Augusta 04332. You can also get information on schooner cruises from the Camden-Lincolnville-Rockport Chamber of Commerce ((207) 236-4404. **Sightseeing cruises** and sailing trips on old schooners depart from the Town and Public landings (contact the chamber of commerce for information), offering tours of Penobscot Bay and views of Mounts Battie and Megunticook (see above).

In winter, bitter winds laden with moisture sweep in from Penobscot Bay, which means plenty of snow for the **Camden Snow Bowl** ((207) 236-3438, PO Box 1207, Camden

04843, which offers both alpine and cross-country runs. There are 10 trails, a 45-degree toboggan chute, snow-tubing, and ice skating on Hosmer Pond. Summer options including hiking and children's recreation. Open daily.

Camden is located on Route 1, about 200 miles (320 km) north of Boston and 85 miles (136 km) north of Portland. Rockport is about seven miles (11 km) south of Camden.

Where to Stay and Eat

Lodging along Penobscot Bay comes in all shapes and sizes. Built from the timbers of a Portland granary, the luxury **Samoset Resort** ((207) 594-2511 TOLL-FREE (800) 341-1650, 220 Warrenton Street, Rockport 04856, has 150 rooms and suites with views of the golf

course or bay. On a hillside overlooking the bay, **Camden Harbour Inn** ((207) 236-4200 TOLL-FREE (800) 236-4266, 83 Bayview Street, Camden 04843 (luxury) was built in 1874. In the early days guests arrived by steamship from Boston and Bangor. The steamships are gone but the inn still welcomes guests in quintessential New England style. Guestrooms are furnished with period antiques. It's located three blocks from the center of Camden.

At the **Best Western Camden River House** ((207) 236-0500 TOLL-FREE (800) 755-7483 FAX (207) 236-4711, 11 Tannery Lane, Camden 04843, the two-story lobby is a stab at glamour, but this hotel is otherwise predictable. The pricier rooms have queen-size beds and balconies. There is a small heated pool and sauna as well as a fitness room. The rate (mid-range to expensive) includes a continental breakfast.

Dinners at the **Whitehall Inn** ((207) 236-3391 TOLL-FREE (800) 789-6565 (expensive) are always memorable. **Frogwater Café** ((207) 236-8998, 31 Elm Street, may look like a cafeteria, but the food is top-notch. The owners are graduates of the New England Culinary Institute, and the inexpensive gourmet fare is served in a congenial setting. Open for lunch and dinner Thursday to Tuesday. **Moody's Diner** ((207) 832-7785, Route 1, Waldoboro, has banned smoking, making the pies taste all the better. Open daily 24 hours.

The view of Camden and its harbor from 800-ft (244-m) Mount Battie in Camden Hills State Park.

BELFAST AND SEARSPORT

A former fishing and trading center, Belfast is becoming something of a cultural center, with artists, writers, and craftspeople moving into the area. The **Belfast Area Chamber of Commerce** ☎ (207) 338-5900, PO Box 58, Belfast 04915, runs a walk-in information center at the waterfront.

The area's major attraction is found in nearby downtown Searsport. The **Penobscot Marine Museum** ☎ (207) 548-2529, on Church Street (off Route 1), contains one of New England's finest collections of furnishings, artifacts, ship models, paintings, and small craft. The compound of 13 old and new buildings presents the story of people and places whose nineteenth-century lives and fortunes rose and fell with the sea. It is open from Memorial Day to mid-October; an admission fee is charged.

Belfast is located on Route 1 about 20 miles (32 km) north of Camden and 103 miles (165 km) north of Portland. Searsport is six miles (just under 10 km) further north.

BLUE HILL AND CASTINE

The village of Blue Hill, with its historical buildings and its mountain backdrop, looks southeast to Mount Desert Island. There has long been a strong alternative presence here — it's not difficult to find the vegetarian café, the good bread bakery, and the laid-back coffee shop. And Blue Hill has a concentration of artisans and craftspeople perhaps unmatched in the United States. It's a quiet, off-the-beaten-track base for exploring Mount Desert Island as well as nearby Castine, to the west.

Home to the Maine Maritime Academy, Castine is a little jewel offering a busy waterfront, charming hostelries and boutiques, wooded trails and some grand Georgian and Federalist architecture. Pick up the Castine Merchants Association brochure at any of the businesses in town and follow the walking tour. The **Blue Hill Chamber of Commerce** ☎ (207) 374-3242 WEB SITE www.bluehillme.com, PO Box 520, Blue Hill 04614, provides informational materials on Castine and Blue Hill.

In Blue Hill, the **Kneisel Chamber Music School** presents concerts in July and August every Friday and Sunday afternoon in a wooded 150-seat amphitheater setting. Blue Hill has an excellent selection of galleries and studios. **Rackcliffe Pottery** ☎ (207) 374-2297 TOLL-FREE (888) 631-3321, Ellsworth (Route 172) north of town, makes functional pieces using local clay and glazes. **Mark Bell Pottery** ☎ (207) 374-5881 (from Blue Hill Center go one and a half miles or just under two and a half kilometers south on Route 15) produces delicate porcelain bowls, bottles and vases with richly colored glazes. **Handworks Gallery** ☎ (207) 374-5613, Main Street, offers a good representation of local artisan's works, with silk weaving, exquisite jewelry, and furniture. Expect to see some outstanding contemporary art at the **Leighton Gallery** ☎ (207) 374-5001, Parker Point Road; it's been called one of the best galleries on the East Coast.

The **Blue Hill Fair** ☎ (207) 374-3701, held each Labor Day weekend at the fairgrounds at the edge of town, epitomizes the traditional agricultural fair of New England, with farm exhibits, livestock shows, pig scamble, blueberry pie eating contest, fireworks, horse racing and a large midway.

Where to Stay and Eat

The Federal-style **Blue Hill Inn** ☎ (207) 374-2844 TOLL-FREE (800) 826-7415 FAX (207) 374-2829, Union Street, Blue Hill 04614 (mid-range to expensive), has 11 guestrooms with painted wood floors, fireplaces and towering four-poster beds piled high with down comforters. Some rooms have old-style claw-foot bathtubs, while others have modern bathrooms. Every room is a treasure trove of antiques. In a modern wing a spacious and sunny suite has everything you could need for a relaxed vacation, right down to a kitchen equipped with an electric wok and espresso machine. A delightful breakfast, included in the room rate, begins with fresh-squeezed orange juice followed by your choice of the chef's famous Greek omelet, Amaretto French toast, or blueberry pancakes.

Although the Blue Hill Inn no longer serves dinner, you can get a full helping of expert contemporary cuisine in a historic setting at **Arborvine**, Main Street (Tenney Hill). Set in an 1823 Cape entwined with Dutchman's Pipe, the restaurant has two cozy and romantic candlelit dining rooms in the front of the building and a larger common dining room. Drawing primarily on local products, the menu might include Damariscotta oysters on the half shell, sliced pork with roasted pears and an apple-brandy glaze, or roast duck with a blood orange glaze. The wine list is exceptional for the region, nicely balancing American and French wines with a small selection of outstanding New Zealand bottles to complement the fish dishes.

A couple of other places in the village offer good eating. **Firepond** ☎ (207) 374-9970, Main Street (upper-range) is a romantic spot, with its outdoor seating under a candlelit grape arbor; try the lobster with a three-cheese cream sauce. For lunch and tea (11 AM to 5 PM) there is **Jean Paul's Bistro** ☎ (207) 374-5852, Main Street, where you can sit on Adirondack chairs overlooking the bay. Open mid-June to Labor Day.

How to Get There

Blue Hill is located on Route 15/176. Those coming from Mount Desert Isle will take Route 172 from Ellsworth. From Bucksport take Route 15.

DEER ISLE AND STONINGTON

Deer Isle has been a retreat since the nineteenth century, when families arrived on steamers and stayed for the summer. You'll wish you could stay the summer — the island is beautiful and just far enough off the beaten path to have (thus far) escaped the crowding and commercialism of other Penobscot Bay spots. Rural, splendidly austere when the fog rolls in, Deer Isle has wonderful hiking paths, some 20 craft galleries, excellent accommodation and fine dining. Fishing is still the mainstay of the economy, and one of the island's major celebrations, is the annual **Fishermen's Day**, which takes place at the Stonington Fish Pier in early August, with Coast Guard demonstrations, wacky rowboat races, and more. The **Deer Isle-Stonington Chamber of Commerce** ☎ (207) 348-6124 E-MAIL deerisle@acadia.net, PO Box 459, Stonington 04681-0459, runs a visitor center, about a quarter mile (half a kilometer) after you cross the suspension bridge onto the island. The volunteer staff lives to serve you.

What to See and Do

As you tool around the island, you'll want to pass through **Deer Isle Village**. Built along a causeway, a narrow strip of land between wetlands, the village has a few galleries and the old brick-red shingled Pilgrims Inn (see below).

Down the road a piece is **Nervous Nellie's Jams and Jellies** ☎ (207) 348-6182 TOLL-FREE (800) 777-6845, 598 Sunshine Road, RR 1, Box 474A, Deer Isle 04627. Part jam kitchen, part open-air gallery, part playground and completely fun, Nervous Nellie's is a great place to take kids, but adults will love it just as much. In the summer you can watch the delicious sauces being cooked up in the jam kitchen. Along with the sweet stuff there are such condiments as hot tomato chutney and pepper jelly. The Mountainville Café is open May through October serving coffee, tea and scones topped with Nervous Nellie's products. Throughout the property are playful sculptures by Peter Beerits. These wood and found-object sculptures are set up in dioramas, some in the woods, others are in the fields. Open year-round. To get there, take Route 15 from Deer Isle Village to follow Sunshine Road east for about three miles (just under five kilometers).

Amongst the buoys and seashells, tourists browse through "oriental things" at Boothbay Harbor.

Haystack Mountain School of Crafts ☎ (207) 348-2306, PO Box 516, Stinson Neck Road, Deer Isle 04627, attracts professional craftspeople from around the world for workshops and residencies. Visitors can explore its intriguing "floating campus," built on piers and boardwalks over boreal woodland on a hillside overlooking Jericho Bay. Open from June to August. The school offers a tour for the public each Wednesday at 1 PM; a donation is requested.

Several nature preserves offer hiking opportunities. **Crockett Cove Woods** ☎ (207) 367-2674, is a 98-acre (39-hectare) reservation has four interlinked trails. A coastal "fog forest," lichens and moss grow thick here and you'll need rubber boots to keep your feet dry. Open daily sunrise to sunset year round. If you visit the island in July or August, don't miss the water lilies that blanket **Ames Pond**. To get there from Stonington take Indian Point Road east just under a mile (a bit over a kilometer) to the pond.

Kayaking trips are arranged and guided by **Granite Island Guide Service** ☎ (207) 348-2668, RR 1, Box 610A, Deer Isle 04627, who offer morning, afternoon, and sunset tours around the island and surrounded uninhabited islets. They also have an inn-to-inn kayaking tour in September.

Stonington is the island's commercial center, a fishing village loaded with charm and fascinating maritime activities. Schooners from the Penobscot Bay windjammer fleet anchor in Stonington Harbor throughout the summer. In the late fall, you can watch sea-urchin divers collecting their prickly catch. Trips to the outlying islands of Isle au Haut, Vinalhaven, and North Haven depart from Stonington Harbor.

Where to Stay and Eat

Though there are not vast numbers of accommodations on the island, what there is here is special. **Pilgrim's Inn** ☎ (207) 348-6615, Main Street, Deer Isle 04627 (mid-range), was built in 1793 and has been beautifully restored. This wood-frame building with broad fireplaces has rooms with private or shared bath. The room rate includes breakfast and dinner at the inn's acclaimed restaurant. Several cottages are also available year-round. An excellent value and one of my favorite Maine stays, **The Inn on the Harbor** ☎ (207) 367-2420 TOLL-FREE (800) 942-2420, Main Street, PO Box 69, Stonington 04681, has 13 perfect, sunny rooms, most of which have large windows with views over the harbor — where you can watch the schooners coming and going. The rate (mid-range) includes a continental breakfast and evening wine and sherry. It is open year-round.

On Isle au Haut, Acadia National Park's outermost island refuge, the **Keeper's House** ☎ (207) 367-2261, PO Box 26, Isle au Haut 04645, is a former lighthouse that has been transformed into a unique inn with four rooms in the keeper's house and one room in a former oil shed (luxury). Electricity is limited. Room rates include breakfast, box lunches for day hikes, and gourmet seafood and fowl dinners served by lantern and candles. Guests have use of the inn's bikes. Open mid-May through November.

On Little Deer Isle (between the mainland and Deer Isle), at **Eaton's Lobster Pool** ☎ (207) 348-2383, Blastow's Cove, hungry diners order crustaceans by the pound and enjoy a wonderful view of the cove and dramatic sunsets from the rustic dining room.

How to Get There

Motorists will take Route 1 to Route 175, which connects with Route 15 to Deer Isle. The Île au Haut Company ☎ (207) 367-6516, RR 1, Box 3636, Stonington 04681, runs *Miss Lizzie* from Stonington to Isle au Haut Monday to Saturday (except on post office holidays). The 90-minute cruise departs from Atlantic Avenue Dock in Stonington.

ACADIA NATIONAL PARK AND MOUNT DESERT ISLAND

Acadia is one of the nation's smallest and most distinctive national parks — and one of its most accessible. Miles of Park Service footpaths crisscross the island from beach to peak, through pine forest and meadow. Old carriage roads give bikers and equestrians the run of the interior. And an auto road lazily loops the park, making its spectacular scenery accessible even to whirlwind day-trippers (see EXPLORE ACADIA in TOP SPOTS, page 15).

Mount Desert (pronounced Des*ert*) was christened by French explorer Samuel de Champlain, who noticed the island's treeless mountain peaks and named it Île de Mont Desert. Had he inspected more closely, Champlain might have chosen a different name for this land of dense forests, ponds and bays.

The park, established in 1916, occupies most of Mount Desert Island, as well as parts of Isle au Haut to the south (see DEER ISLE AND STONINGTON, page 323) and the Schoodic Peninsula to the north. Much of the land comprising the park was donated by George B. Dorr and by John D. Rockefeller Jr., who also paid for construction of many of the park's roads. Today, almost three million people visit Acadia annually.

Travelers stretch their legs and take in the salt air along Acadia's Park Loop Road.

The weather is more moderate here along the coast than in interior Maine. This meeting ground of Arctic flora and Virginia mountain vegetation revels in mild summers and moderate winters.

GENERAL INFORMATION

The place to begin your tour of the park is at the **Visitor Center** ☎ (207) 288-3338, Hull's Cove, Route 3, Bar Harbor 04609. It is open mid-April to November. From November to April information is also available at **Acadia Park Headquarters**, Route 233, west of Bar Harbor. There is an entrance fee for the park.

There is a free **shuttle bus** between Bar Harbor's village green and Sand Beach in Acadia. It runs from late June through to Labor Day.

For visitor information on Bar Harbor itself, the **Bar Harbor Chamber of Commerce** ☎ (207) 288-5103 FAX (207) 288-2565, PO Box 158, 93 Cottage Street, Bar Harbor 04609, has prepared several free brochures and maps for vacation planning. Once in Bar Harbor, pay them a visit at their offices in the basement of Town Hall.

Even if you choose to stay in Bar Harbor, don't miss the island's small harbor towns, each with its distinct personality. For information on Seal Harbor, Mount Desert, Northeast Harbor, Otter Creek, and Somesville there is the **Mount Desert Chamber of Commerce** ☎ (207) 276-5040, PO Box 675, Northeast Harbor 04662, with a walk-in booth at the marina in Northeast Harbor. For information on Southwest Harbor, contact the **Southwest Harbor-Tremont Chamber of Commerce** ☎ (207) 244-9264 TOLL-FREE (800) 423-9264.

WHAT TO SEE AND DO

Acadia National Park

Park rangers can help in planning tours, including **naturalist-led hiking treks** or the self-guided 20-mile (32-km) **Park Loop Road**, enhanced by prerecorded cassette tapes (available for purchase) that describe points of interest, history, and geography.

When Mount Desert voted to allow cars on the island, John D. Rockefeller Jr. retaliated by building 57 miles (91 km) of **carriage roads** along which automobiles were forbidden. These graceful byways are perfect for exploring by mountain bike, on horseback or the old-fashioned way in horse and buggy. In winter, if the snow sticks, they're open for cross-country skiing. **Horse-drawn open carriage tours** leave from Wildwood Stables ☎ (207) 276-3622, a mile (just over one and a half kilometers) south of the Jordan Pond House, near Seal Harbor, on the Park Loop Road. There are six one- and two-hour trips schedule daily from mid-June to Columbus Day; a fare is charged.

The bare granite of **Cadillac Mountain** (1,530 ft or 466 m) crowns Mount Desert Island. From the summit there are unparalleled views of the ocean and rugged island interiors, including Mount Katahdin, Maine's highest peak. On a clear morning you can catch the country's first glimpse of the sun's rays, as this is the highest point on the east coast. The mountain was named after Antonine de Mothe Cadillac who took possession of the mountain in the 1600s under a land grant. A trail leads to the top; there is also an automobile road.

Bar Harbor

Most people use Bar Harbor as their base for exploring the national park. When they're not hiking, biking, or cross-country skiing in the park, there are plenty of distractions in town.

Bar Harbor once rivaled Newport, Rhode Island, for its wealth and extravagance. In the late nineteenth century the island attracted artists who came to paint its extraordinary beauty. They were soon followed by rich East Coast families, such as the Rockefellers and Vanderbilts, who built mansions and elegant summer cottages, transforming Mount Desert, and more specifically Bar Harbor, into their playground.

In 1947, a great fire burning out of control for nearly a month destroyed much of the island, including most of the mansions. They were replaced by more modest motels and hotels and the island opened up to accommodate tourists of all means. The few mansions that survived have been transformed into elegant inns.

A number of footpaths are accessible from downtown. The **shore path**, estab-

lished in 1880 by private landowners, starts at Bar Harbor Inn. It's best at sunrise. Bar Harbor has dramatic, 12-ft (three-and-a-half-meter) tides. At low tide a causeway connects the town with **Bar Island**. Locals will tell you that you must time your visit carefully, or you might be out on the island for longer than you intended. To get the pathway, from Main Street walk west on West Street to Bridge Street. You can also drive out on the causeway. But there's no reason to do this as long as you are able-bodied. Once on the island you can ramble along the paths or rest along the shore with its view of the town.

The **Abbe Museum** ☎ (207) 288-3519, has one of the largest collections of Native

American basketry and craftwork in the Northeast. The Abbe's collection also includes bone artifacts, quill baskets and birchbark canoes. The museum's new year-round location is at 26 Mount Desert Street in downtown Bar Harbor. There is also a seasonal (late May to late October) exhibition space, located two miles (three kilometers) south of Bar Harbor at Sieur de Monts Springs, where Route 3 meets the Park Loop Road. It is next to Wild Gardens of Acadia, which displays more than 300 species of local plants.

Aside from exploring the charming row of boutiques and galleries along the main drag, you should visit the town's two marvelous public gardens, the **Asticou** and **Thuya** gardens ☎ (207) 276-5130, on Route 3. The Asticou Garden is at its most brilliant when the azaleas flower in the spring with 50 or 60 varieties of the hearty bloom, as well as rhododendrons and laurel. Asticou is on Route 198 at the north end of Northeast Harbor. The Thuya Garden features perennial borders, sculpted shrubbery, and oriental touches, on a hillside north of the Asticou.

Outdoor dining at Bar Harbor.

Elsewhere on the Island

Though you say "Mount De*sert*" in Bar Harbor, it's "Mount *De*sert" in **Northeast Harbor**. Northeast's well-bred residents frown on mixing the English "mount" with the French pronunciation of "desert." Summer quarters for a who's who of literary, financial, and entertainment personalities (Margarite Yourcenar, David Rockefeller, Walter Cronkite, Martha Stewart, for example), Northeast is the most intact of the island's "golden age" colonies. From Northeast Harbor, *Sea Princess* Naturalist Cruises ☎ (207) 276-5352 WEB SITE www.barharborcruises.com, sail out to Cranberry Island up into the fiord, giving passengers a view of some multi-million-dollar residences.

The local chamber of commerce can provide additional information should you wish to visit these gardens.

Sometimes called "the quiet side" of Mount Desert Island, **Southwest Harbor** has real Down East flavor. Though it is becoming gentrified, Southwest has long been a factory town — there was a herring cannery there until the herring were fished out. Islanders can hardly believe that there are now bed and breakfasts popping up around Southwest's marina.

There are some worthwhile sights to take in in town, including the **Southwest Harbor Oceanarium** ☎ (207) 244-7330, at the tip of

Clark Point next to Beal's Lobster Pound. This small four-room building was once a fishing shack. Now it's a hands-on exhibit space featuring horseshoe crabs, sea cucumbers, giant sea stars, spiny sea urchins, and slimy-footed snails. Guided tours are offered. The **Wendell Gilley Museum** ☎ (207) 244-7555, Herrick Road (corner of Route 102), is devoted to the work of America's premier waterfowl carvers. There is an award-winning documentary video and demonstrations of the craft. Visitors can create their own winged creatures in the museum's Bird Shop. Open Tuesday through Sunday June through October, weekends May, November and December.

The old Underwood Sardine factory once employed half the residents of **Bass Harbor**. The factory closed about 20 years ago, but this little town still has the third-largest commercial fishing fleet in Maine. Bass has a rural feel, with houses set higgledy-piggledy on the hills over the harbor rather than forming the strict New England "Main Street." A cluster of seafood shacks is found where it should be: the dock. You can visit the **Bass Harbor Light** and take in the seafaring atmosphere there. Built in 1858, it is situated on the southernmost tip of the island. In those days, one in five Maine residents was a mariner. Looking out to sea from the lighthouse yard, you can see a group of islands that were inhabited by fishermen. These days, Swan's is the only one of the islands that has a year-round population.

SPORTS AND OUTDOOR ACTIVITIES

For park information, contact the Superintendent, Acadia National Park ☎ (207) 288-3338, PO Box 177, Bar Harbor 04609.

Beaches

A shimmering crescent backed by grassy dunes and tide pools, **Sand Beach** is the only sandy beach on this granite isle. You can swim here… if you have a strong constitution; even at the height of summer the water is an icy 50°F (10°C).

Bicycling and Horseback Riding

Winding through Acadia are 44 miles (70 km) of **carriage paths**, interlaced byways that are closed to motor vehicles. The scenery is unparalleled, with cliff views of the islands in Frenchman Bay, 17 unique granite bridges, miles of shoreline, fresh lakes, bald mountains, and forests of alternating conifer and hardwood. All of the paths are gravel-covered, but they vary from fine to rough; some require mountain bikes rather than racing-type bikes.

Trails

Nearly 200 miles (322 km) of footpaths and trails wind through Acadia, running the gamut from flat easy strolls to grueling vertical climbs. From the Jordan Pond parking area, one of the easier one-mile wooded loop trails can be topped off by a visit to **Jordan Pond House**, famous for its popovers. At

Sand Beach, **Great Head Trail** is a moderate 1.4-mile (2.2-km) path that leads off from the east side and runs around the high headland with marvelous views of the beach and sea. On the opposite end of the sand, the **Ocean Trail** is an easy four-mile (six-and-a-half kilometer) round-trip to Otter Point, passing along the way Thunder Hole where the surf creates a stupendous roar at high tide. A hike up the **Precipice Trail**, using ladders and handrails, is rewarded by a summit-top mountain vista. Open only in fall, once the peregrine falcons have completed their nesting season. **Beehive Trail** is another iron-rung ladder trail, this one climbing to 518-ft (155-m) with views of Frenchmans Bay and Beaver Pond. For more information on hiking and climbing in Acadia, see RECOMMENDED READING, page 353, for specialized guidebooks. Park Service budget cuts have closed some trails, so check with rangers for the latest details.

TOURS AND EXCURSIONS

There are whale-watching and puffin-sighting excursions with the **Bar Harbor Whalewatch Co.** ☏ (207) 288-2386, 39 Cottage Street; and **Acadian Whale Watcher** ☏ (207) 288-9794 TOLL-FREE (800) 421-3307, Bar Harbor Whale Museum, 52 West Street, Bar Harbor.

Guided bus tours with Oli's Trolley ☏ (207) 288-9899 motor through the park, stopping for picture snapping and ogling. You can also

Sunset on Mount Desert Island.

hop aboard one of Acadia Air's ☎ (207) 667-5534 **sightseeing planes** at the Bar Harbor Airport, in Trenton (along Route 3).

Bar Harbor is an embarkation point for ferry trips to **Nova Scotia** in neighboring Canada. There's an information center on Cottage Street, next to the Criterion Theater, where you can speak with a Tourism Nova Scotia representative, make reservations, and pick up Nova Scotia brochures. **Northumberland/Bay Ferries** TOLL-FREE (888) 249-7245, 121 Eden Street, Bar Harbor 04609, runs a high-speed catamaran that takes about two and a half hours to reach Yarmouth, Nova Scotia (from May to October).

WHERE TO STAY AND EAT

Hidden away from the bustle of Bar Harbor, the **Inn at Canoe Point** ☎ (207-288-9511 FAX (207) 288-2870 E-MAIL canoe.point@ juno.com, Route 3, Eden Street, PO Box 216, Bar Harbor 04644 (expensive to luxury), is a beautiful waterside inn on two acres (just under a hectare) hugging a quiet cove. There are five guestrooms; the rate includes breakfast.

A five-minute walk from the town center, **Mira Monte Inn** ☎ (207) 288-4263 TOLL-FREE (800) 553-5109 FAX (207) 288-3115 E-MAIL Marian@miramonte.com, 69 Mount Desert Street, Bar Harbor 04609 (expensive to luxury), started life as one of Bar Harbor's grand summer "cottages." Some of the inn's 16 cottages, suites and guestrooms have private garden entrances. They come well equipped with queen-size canopy beds and large modern bathrooms, and most have either a fireplace or a balcony. There is a fireplace in the library and parlor where guests gather for afternoon tea and sherry. Breakfast with a hot main course is served each morning in the dining room. Innkeeper Marion Burns has an encyclopedic knowledge of the area and many fascinating stories to tell as a lifelong resident of Bar Harbor. It's easy to see why she has been voted Maine's "Innkeeper of the Year."

Located in Parish Hall of Saint Savior's Church, **Hostelling International Bar Harbor** ☎ (207) 288-5587, 27 Kennebec Street, PO Box 32, Bar Harbor 04609, has 20 beds in two dormitory rooms. Open mid-June to Labor Day.

There's plenty of good eating in Bar Harbor, starting with **George's** ☎ (207) 288-4505, 7 Stephens Lane, tucked away in a landscaped garden just off Main Street, where white linens and candlelight set the tone. A meal here might begin with arugula salad with fresh figs, walnuts, and goat cheese in a balsamic vinaigrette. The house specialty is the lobster strudel — tender bits of lobster ragout wrapped in filo pastry. There is an expertly chosen wine list. Desserts are wonderful. If the chocolate pâté with champagne sauce is on the menu, don't hesitate for a moment.

The **Pier** ☎ (207) 288-2110, 55 West Street (expensive), is a seafood restaurant known more for the views than the quality of the food. Go before dark or there won't be any seeing with your seafood. For better cooking head to **Galyn's Galley** ☎ (207) 288-9706, 17 Main Street, which serves everything from haddock to shark. Have your lobster whole, with scallops, shrimp and mussels, with fettuccine or paired with prime rib. Noted for excellent service, it is well patronized by locals so you must make reservations.

Lompoc Café and Brew Pub ☎ (207) 288-9392, brews Bar Harbor Real Ales. Sample a few brews before you order — the ginger wheat beer is excellent; light-bodied with a fresh flavor. The menu lists Middle Eastern and Indonesian starters, as well as inventive pizzas (budget). There is also vegetarian lasagna, gorgeous salads and good homemade soups, such as curried lentil served with homemade French bread.

For lodging in Northeast Harbor, there is the gray-shingled 1883 **Asticou Inn** ☎ (207) 276-3344, PO Box 406, Northeast Harbor 04662, overlooking the yacht-filled harbor (expensive to luxury). Painted wood floors and floral French wallpaper decorate the rooms. Bathrooms are tiny, but do have tubs. Unfortunately the fireplaces are purely decorative. In back the lawn slopes down to a pool overlooking the harbor.

A laid-back seafood snack can be enjoyed at the **Docksider** ☎ (207) 276-3965, Sea Street, a white shack above the marina, where you can make a picnic on deck of their Maine lobster "live and boiled."

Southwest Harbor has several bed-and-breakfast inns, as well as the old **Claremont**

Hotel ✆ (207) 244-5036 TOLL-FREE (800) 244-5036, PO Box 137, Southwest Harbor 04679 — with its green rocking chairs and a lawn that rolls away to the edge of Somes Sound — built by a retired sea captain in 1884 who meant it to reflect the islands' rustic way of life (mid-range to expensive). Besides hotel rooms there are cottages and a guesthouse. The dining room overlooks the water. Open mid-June to mid-October. You may have to book at least a year in advance for a room in the peak months of July and August.

HOW TO GET THERE

Motorists coming from the south can either follow Coastal Route 1 or take the faster Maine Turnpike (Interstate 95) as far as Brunswick before joining Route 1. Add an hour to your driving time if you choose the "coastal route" — a misnomer as Route 1 runs well inland. To see Maine's knockout coast you must get off Route 1 and onto the byways. From Route 1 take Route 3 East to Ellsworth. Continue through Ellsworth on Route 3.

Colgan Air TOLL-FREE (800) 523-3273 serves the **Bar Harbor Airport** ✆ (207) 667-7329, Route 1, in Ellsworth.

WESTERN MOUNTAINS AND LAKES

I have in my possession a picture postcard of Mooselookmeguntic Lake taken from a place called "Height of Land" along Route 17 near Oquossoc. I'm not making that up. This blue lake is one of the many scenic bodies of water in Maine's western land-of-lakes. An area rich in opportunities for outdoor adventures, western Maine is sparsely populated, but easy accessible. Here you'll find Maine's best skiing, summer and fall hiking in the foothills of the White Mountains, as well as swimming, boating, and fishing in pristine waters.

BETHEL

Bethel was founded in 1774 as "Sudbury Canada" in honor of the original grantees from Sudbury, Massachusetts, who fought a campaign to conquer Canada in 1690. These days this pretty town of 2,500 inhabitants is more concerned with conquering the hearts of the tourists and sports enthusiasts drawn to the foothills of the White Mountains for the winter scenery and for cross-country and alpine skiing. The **Bethel Area Chamber of Commerce** ✆ (207) 824-2282, PO Box 1247, 8 Station Place, Bethel 04217-0439, is a valuable resource. Along with a wide range of services and informational materials, they run a **central reservation service** TOLL-FREE (800) 442-5826.

Most people come to Bethel for the slopes. **Sunday River** ✆ (207) 824-3000 TOLL-FREE (800) 543-2754, PO Box 450, Sunday River Road, Bethel 04217, is the second largest ski area in New England. A fast-food approach to the genre, this ski area is big and efficient, but lacking in character. Part of the vast American Ski Company chain, Sunday River prides itself on teaching beginners, offering a separate base lodge and a sequence of activities calculated to demystify the learning process and avoid the confusion that novices often encounter. The drawback is that there is no private instruction for beginners.

The **Nordic Center** ✆ (207) 824-6276 at the Bethel Inn & Country Club sells an all-day trail pass that includes use of their heated pool and sauna. Eighteen miles (30 km) of trails for novice to expert skiers wind through the golf course and spruce forests. You can rent gear, including snowshoes, at their Nordic shop, which also sells beautiful Norwegian sweaters. There is also **Carter's X-C Ski Center** ✆ (207) 539-4848, boasting 1,000 acres (400 hectares) of skiing terrain with views of the Androscoggin River and surrounding mountains.

One of the state's most scenic areas, **Grafton Notch State Park** ✆ (207) 824-2912, Route 26, Grafton Township (mailing address: HC 61, Box 330, Newry 04261), is a 3,000-acre (1,200-hectare) preserve of forest and waterfalls. The beautiful **Screw Auger Falls Gorge**, so-named because it resembles a corkscrew-like logging tool, is on the south side of the highway a mile (just over one and a half kilometers) into the park. This spectacular 23-ft-deep (seven-meter), 150-ft-long (45-m) gorge is less than 10 ft (three meters) wide at its narrowest point with smooth granite walls sculpted by glacial-melt water. The **Appalachian Trail** crosses through

Grafton Notch State Park. Contact the park headquarters for information.

Where to Stay and Eat

There is plenty of high-quality lodging in Bethel. Crowning Bethel Common, the bright yellow **Bethel Inn & Country Club** ((207) 824-2175 TOLL-FREE (800) 654-0125, PO Box 49, Bethel 04217 (mid-range to expensive), is a gracious old inn with 57 rooms and 40 modern townhouses. Rooms in the new wing are palatial, with gas fireplaces and queen beds. Rates include dinner in the inn's elegant restaurant, which serves New England fare. There is a golf course and a heated pool.

Also in the village, the **Victoria** ((207) 824-8060 TOLL-FREE (888) 774-1235, 32 Main Street, PO Box 249, Bethel 04217 (mid- to upper-range), is a fine old mansion with 15 rooms decorated with period antiques. The rate includes breakfast. The restaurant is the most romantic spot in town (expensive).

Situated in a 140-year-old farmhouse in a quiet corner near the village center, **Rivendell House** ((802) 824-0508, 16 Park Street, PO Box 74, Bethel 04217 (mid-range), is a bed and breakfast with two cheerful and attractive rooms. Proprietors Allen and Jacquelyn Cressy opened for business in 1998 and are bursting with enthusiasm for their house and the outdoor offerings of the area; expect the warmest of welcomes. Allen prepares a country breakfast each morning.

Telemark Inn Wilderness Ski Lodge ((207) 836-2703, RFD 2, PO Box 800, Bethel 04217 (mid-range to expensive), has basic lodging along with a world of outdoor activities at your doorstep, including cross-country skiing, snowshoeing and dog-sledding on 370 acres (148 hectares) of private forest. Backcountry skiers can access the Caribou/Speckled Wilderness Area from the inn's groomed trail system. In the summer there are canoe trips on the Androscoggin, wildlife excursions, hiking and mountain biking.

Sunday River (above) has several standard hotels as well as a "ski dorm" for budget lodging.

How to Get There

Bethel is located at the intersection of Routes 2 and 26. It is about 67 miles (107 km) northwest of Portland.

RANGELEY LAKES REGION

In summer and fall, the rugged Rangeley Lakes region is one of the prettiest sections of inland New England. The region's hundred or so lakes and ponds are surrounded by the thickly wooded Longfellow Mountains, including Saddleback Mountain where Saddleback Ski Area shares some gorgeous real estate with the Appalachian Trail. This is one of the most dramatic sections of the trail, offering views of Mount Washington in New Hampshire. In winter the region echoes with the chainsaw buzz of snowmobilers, who pour in on weekends to take advantage of the 150 miles (240 km) of trails — more than any other region in Maine — riding into the woods and from town to town, stopping

along the way for lunch, and socializing at places that cater to this fun-loving crowd.

Informational materials are available from **Rangeley Lakes Region Chamber of Commerce** ☎ (207) 864-5364 TOLL-FREE (800) 685-2537 FAX (207) 864-5366 E-MAIL mtlakes@rangeley.org, PO Box 317, Rangeley 04970. You'll find helpful staff at the information center located next to the town park on Main Street, in Rangeley.

The town of **Rangeley** on the northeast shore of Rangeley Lake is the hub for snowmobiling activity as well as for hunting, angling, and a wealth of other outdoor activities. It's an affable town with a compact business district and charming inns, and an excellent dining room at the Rangeley Inn. In March, mushers gather from far and wide for the **New England Sled Dog Races** in Rangeley; and in mid-January each year the **Snide** draws snowmobilers from throughout New England for racing events out on the frozen lake. Contact the local chamber of commerce (above) for information on these and other seasonal events.

You can rent snowmobiles and gear from **Rev-It-Up Sport Shop** ☎ (207) 864-2452, Route 4, Rangeley. Be sure to take all precautions and follow all safety rules, as this is, by nature, a dangerous sport. The chamber of commerce (above) has trail maps covering the region.

Since the mid-1800s, Rangeley has lured fishing enthusiasts who come for lakes filled

Sebago Lake is the southern complement to Maine's more remote northern Lakes Region.

with landlocked salmon and trout. Casting in streams can be rewarding here, too; you can learn the secrets of successful fly-fishing with **Rapid River Fly Fishing & Guide Service** ☎ (207) 392-3333 E-MAIL flyfishing fantasy@conknet.com. Sporting goods shops and outfitters supply fishing permits.

At **Saddleback Ski Area** ☎ (207) 864-5671, the summit rises to 4,116 ft (1,255 m), with a vertical drop of 1,826 ft (557 m). There are 40 runs, including some steep, mogul-filled slopes. This is a laid-back ski area and much less crowded than most other New England ski runs. Saddleback sponsors an annual contest in March — anyone who can ski Bronco from top to bottom without falling or stopping earns free ski passes.

Where to Stay and Eat

Accommodation in Rangeley is graciously provided by the **Rangeley Inn** ☎ (207) 864-3341 TOLL-FREE (800) 666-3687 FAX (207) 864-3634 E-MAIL rangeinn@rangeley.org, PO Box 160, 51 Main Street, Rangeley 04970-0160 (budget to mid-range), a turn-of-the-twentieth-century hunting lodge that hasn't changed much since its early days, except for the addition of modern comforts. Its lost-in-time ambiance begins at the front desk, where old room-service switchboards still hang on the walls. The 15 guestrooms in the old inn are loaded with character, while the newer motel rooms have extras such as wood-burning stoves and hot tubs. The motel and two cabins are on the shore of Haley Pond, a bird sanctuary. The Rangeley Inn has an excellent **dining room** serving continental fare with outdoor seating in summer. On the menu are salmon, filet mignon, and lamb roast — well prepared and nicely seasoned. An extensive wine list complements the meal. You can also dine in the informal pub with its center hearth and enjoy local brews from the tap.

For an inexpensive lunch, do as the locals and head for **People's Choice** ☎ (207) 864-5220, Main Street, for hot sandwiches such as chicken filet with honey mustard sauce or a classic tuna melt (budget).

How to Get There

Rangeley is about two and a half hours from Portland and four and a half from Boston. From the south, take Interstate 95 to the

Maine Turnpike to Exit 12 at Lewiston/Auburn. Follow Route 4 North through Farmington to Rangeley. Motorist coming from the west should follow Route 17, otherwise known as "**Moose Alley**." This Maine Scenic Highway is a beautiful drive that twists along the tree-lined Swift River as it tumbles over boulders and deep pools and crosses mountaintops offering vistas of the lake-dotted region.

CARRABASSETT VALLEY AND KINGFIELD

Surrounded by the Longfellow and Bigelow ranges, the beautiful town of Carrabassett Valley is famous for Sugarloaf/USA — Maine's top ski resort. A hiker's nirvana, the surrounding mountains boast 10 of Maine's

4,000-footers (1,200 m). A few miles further south along Route 27, Kingfield is the soul if not the heart of the region. Here on the edge of backcountry Maine, this surprisingly sophisticated little town has an excellent museum along with some fascinating and quirky old inns and excellent restaurants. **Sugarloaf Area Chamber of Commerce** WEB SITE www.sugarloafareachamber.com, PO Box 2151, RR 1, Kingfield 04947, has a drop-in information center along Route 16 between Sugarloaf/USA and Kingfield.

In Kingfield, don't miss the **Stanley Museum** ☎ (207) 265-2729, on School Street, where you'll learn about the Stanley family through artifacts, videos, and photographs. The Stanleys — twin brothers who hailed from Kingfield — invented a version of the photographic plate. They eventually sold out to George Eastman, using their earnings to begin a new enterprise, development of a steam-powered car, dubbed the Stanley Steamer. Three of the brothers' meticulously restored steam-powered cars are on display. There are also superb photographs of Maine life by the twins' elder sister Chansonetta Stanley Emmons. The museum's curator, Sue Davis, is not only a historian but a crack mechanic as well. Ask her anything. Open Tuesday to Sunday from May to October and from December to March; a small admission fee is charged.

Sugarloaf/USA ☎ (207) 237-2000 TOLL-FREE (800) 843-5623 E-MAIL info@sugarloaf.com,

Porker and piglets at the Fryeburg Fair which takes place in late September or early October each year.

RR 1, PO Box 5000, Carrabassett Valley 04947-9799, is Maine's premier ski resort and among the most popular in New England. It is a blend of old-time Yankee, deep-woods wilderness, relaxed hospitality, and superb skiing. A latticework of 126 trails and glades totaling more than 45 miles (72 km), and with a vertical drop of 2,820 ft (846 m), it offers something for every skier. Novice runs drop off the hills into the center of the ski village, which is filled with shops, restaurants, and watering holes. When the snow melts, mountain biking takes over (see SPORTING SPREE, page 32 in YOUR CHOICE).

At the base of the Sugarloaf/USA service road you can get a delightful taste of **dog sledding** through the Maine woods with White Howling Express. The outfit offers short trips with six to twelve affectionate white Samoyeds. For information and reservations, contact: Tim Diehl, T.A.D. Dog Sled Services ☎ (207) 246-4461 (evenings only), PO Box 147, Stratton 04982. The base is located on Route 27 in the Carrabassett Valley, 500 ft (150 m) (see GO FOR THE SNOW, page 20 in TOP SPOTS).

Where to Stay and Eat

You have to love a hotel that puts a rubber ducky in your bathtub. Nicknamed "the Ritz in the woods," **The Herbert** ☎ (207) 265-2000 TOLL-FREE (800) THE-HERB, Main Street, Kingfield 04947 (budget to expensive), is an offbeat, once grand, hotel. Rooms are spacious and comfortable. Breakfast (included) is congenial — toast a bagel, snag some juice from the refrigerator and settle down with the sociable breakfast crowd or take your booty to your room. Open year-round. It's located about 15 miles (24 km) from the slopes at Sugarloaf.

Three Stanley Avenue ☎ (207) 265-5541, PO Box 169, 3 Stanley Avenue, Kingfield 04947 (budget), is a pleasant bed-and-breakfast place in a beautiful Victorian. Next door and under the same ownership, **One Stanley Avenue** ☎ (207) 265-5541, 1 Stanley Avenue, Kingfield (mid-range) is open mid-December to mid-April. Don't miss a dinner here if you can help it. Start with smoked mussels and move on to a deliciously prepared main course such as roast duck with apricot sauce. Reservations are essential.

There are two hotels along with scores of condominium rentals at **Sugarloaf/USA** ☎ (207) 237-2000 TOLL-FREE (800) 843-5623 (for lodging on the mountain) or (800) 843-2732 (for lodging in the surrounding area) E-MAIL info@sugarloaf.com, and some 20 restaurants and bars.

How to Get There

Sugarloaf/USA is 113 miles (181 km) from Portland in the town of Carrabassett Valley; Kingfield is 15 miles (24 km) south of Sugarloaf on Route 27.

THE NORTH WOODS

A region of wilderness superlatives — Maine's North Woods boast the state's tallest peak, Mount Katahdin, and its roughest rivers, which boil and flume through granite canyons. This is prime fishing and paddling territory. **Moosehead**, the largest lake in Maine, lies about 90 miles (145 km) beyond Bangor. It covers more than 120 sq miles (310 sq km), with a shoreline of 420 miles (677 km). Much of the shore is accessible only by canoe or float plane, both of which are available for rent or charter at **Greenville** at the south end of the lake.

The region remains rich in wildlife, including, deer, bear and moose; the lake's waters abound with salmon and trout. Lodges and former hunting camps now emphasize animal-watching activities. The **Moosehead Lake Region Chamber of Commerce** ☎ (207) 695-2702 TOLL-FREE (888) 876-2778 WEB SITE www.mooseheadlake.org, PO Box 581, Main Street, Greenville 04441, claims no visitor will be disappointed with facilities in the area and provides free maps and brochures.

Northeast of Moosehead Lake is **Baxter State Park**. Percival Proctor Baxter, Governor of the State of Maine, was an early environmentalist. Knowing that civilization would one day overtake the wilderness, he dreamed of setting aside great tracts of land in central Maine as a nature preserve. Unable during his two terms as governor to persuade the legislature to support his intent, Baxter undertook nonetheless to make his dream a reality. A man of considerable wealth, he devoted his life to the purchase and consolidation of 200,000 acres (81,000 hectares) of wild land, which he then deeded to Maine as a state park on the condition that the land remain "forever wild."

Information can also be obtained from the **Katahdin Area Chamber of Commerce** ((207) 723-4443, 1029 Central Street, Millinocket 04462. For park information and camping reservations contact the reservations Clerk, **Baxter State Park Headquarters** ((207) 723-5140, 64 Balsam Drive, Millinocket 04462.

Baxter State Park is an area of dense forests, pristine streams, lakes and mountains, and it shelters abundant wildlife. Apart from a few narrow unpaved roads, access to its interior is chiefly by the 162-mile (261-km) system of hiking trails. Baxter is dominated by Mount Katahdin, at 5,271 ft (1,607 m) the highest peak in the state, second tallest in New England and one of the highest points east of the Rocky Mountains. One of the park's loveliest sights, Chimney Pond, is accessible by a three-hour moderate hike from the Chimney Pond parking lot. A campground at the pond (reservations are usually necessary in summer) offers grand views of Katahdin's sheer, massive granite walls towering straight up from the far side of the pond. Moose often linger on Sandy Stream Pond Trail. The Cathedral Trail demands serious rock-climbing techniques to reach the Katahdin summit. The northern portion of the Appalachian Trail leads to both Big and Little Niagara Falls. Baxter Peak is one of the four Katahdin summits, the others being Hamlin, Pamola (named after the Abenaki god) and South. The last two are connected by one of the park's most extraordinary geologic features: the Knife Edge, a razor-thin, serrated wall of granite 4,000 ft (1,219 m) high.

Performance art, Maine style: Wild Mountain Man and his résumé.

HOW TO GET THERE

Greenville is 158 miles (253 km) from Portland. Take the turnpike to Exit 39 (Newport) and head north on Routes 7/11 to Route 23 in Dexter. From here go north to Route 6/15 near Sangerville, following this route on to Greenville.

Baxter State Park is 86 miles (138 km) north of Bangor. To get there take Interstate 95 to Medway (Exit 56) and go west 11 miles (18 km) on Route 11/157 to the town of Millinocket, from where you head northwest through town and follow signs to the park.

Travelers' Tips

GETTING THERE

Most major international airlines provide service to Boston. Fares are sometimes cheaper, however, to Providence or New York.

Some North American carriers offer in-country flight coupons at substantial savings to foreign travelers. These programs change from year to year, so check with you travel agent when planning your trip.

Airline carriers serving Boston's Logan International Airport are as follows:

Aer Lingus TOLL-FREE (888) 474-7424
Air Canada TOLL-FREE (888) 247-2262
Air France TOLL-FREE (800) 237-2747
Air Jamaica TOLL-FREE (800) 523-3515
Air Nova TOLL-FREE (888) 247-2262
Air Tran TOLL-FREE (800) 247-8726
Alaska Air TOLL-FREE (800) 252-7522
Alitalia TOLL-FREE (800) 223-5730
American TOLL-FREE (800) 433-7300
American Eagle TOLL-FREE (800) 433-7300
America West TOLL-FREE (800) 235-9292
ATA TOLL-FREE (800) 225-2995
British Airways TOLL-FREE (800) 247-9297
Cape Air TOLL-FREE (800) 352-0714
Continental TOLL-FREE (800) 525-0280
Delta Air Lines TOLL-FREE (800) 221-1212
Frontier TOLL-FREE (800) 432-1359
Icelandair TOLL-FREE (800) 223-5500
KLM TOLL-FREE (800) 374-7747
Lufthansa TOLL-FREE (800) 645-3880
Midway Airlines TOLL-FREE (800) 446-4392
Midwest Express TOLL-FREE (800) 452-2022
Northwest TOLL-FREE (800) 225-2525
Qantas TOLL-FREE (800) 227-4500
Swiss TOLL-FREE (800) 221-4750
United/United Express TOLL-FREE (800) 241-6522
US Airways TOLL-FREE (800) 428-4322
Virgin Atlantic Airways TOLL-FREE (800) 862-8621

Airlines serving Warwick, Rhode Island's T.F. Green Airport are as follows:

Air Ontario TOLL-FREE (888) 247-2262
American/American Eagle TOLL-FREE (800) 433-7300
Cape Air TOLL-FREE (800) 352-0714
Continental/Continental Express TOLL-FREE (800) 525-0280
Delta Express TOLL-FREE (866) 235-9359
Northwest Airlines TOLL-FREE (800) 225-2525
Southwest Airlines TOLL-FREE (800) 435-9792
United/United Express TOLL-FREE (800) 241-6522
US Airways/US Airways Express TOLL-FREE (800) 428-4322

Amtrak, the only passenger rail in the United States, connects some major New England cities and offers frequent service to Boston from Montreal and New York, and northern service from Boston to Portland, Maine, with stops along the way. Amtrak is now operating Acela (pronounced "a-CELL-a"), its new **high-speed trains** serving the Northeast Corridor. Acela trains run between Boston, New York and Washington, DC, and will eventually cut travel time between Boston and New York from the current four hours to three hours. For up-to-date information on the high-speed rail, visit the Amtrak WEB SITE www.amtrak.com.

Other major routes are as follows:

The ***Lakeshore Limited*** connects Boston, Worcester, Springfield and Pittsfield with Chicago and points in between including Detroit, Buffalo and Albany, New York.

Boston, Providence and New Haven are the major New England stops on the ***Northeast Direct***, which runs south to Philadelphia, Baltimore, Washington, DC, and Norfolk, Virginia. The ***Twilight Shoreliner*** operates between Boston and Newport News, Virginia, with luxury sleeping cars.

The ***Vermonter*** has daily service between Washington, DC, and Saint Albans, Vermont, with stops in Connecticut, Massachusetts, and along the length of Vermont. The train has a car for stowing bikes, skis and snowboards. The ***Ethan Allen Express*** starts in New York City and runs daily to Rutland, Vermont, via New York State.

For prices and schedules, call Amtrak TOLL-FREE (800) 872-7245, or contact one of these international agents:

Australia: Asia Pacific ✆ (02) 9319-6624, 4 Davies Street, Surry Hills, Sydney; or Special Interest ✆ (03) 9877-3322, 96 Canterbury Road, Blackburn South, Melbourne.

France: Wingate Travel ✆ (01) 44 77 30 16, 19 bis rue du Mont-Thabor, Paris.

On the deck of the *Mayflower II:* This replica of the ship that brought the Pilgrims to Plymouth in 1620 was built in England in 1957 and sailed the Atlantic to dock at its present home in Plymouth Harbor.

Great Britain: Destination Marketing Limited ℂ (020) 7253-9009, Molasses House, Plantation Wharf, London; or Trailfinders Limited ℂ (020) 7937-5400, 215 Kensington High Street, London.
Italy: Tabb, S.R.L. ℂ (02) 657-1141, Piazza della Repubblica 28, Milano.
New Zealand: Walshes World ℂ (09) 379-3708, Ding Wall Building, 87 Queen Street, Auckland.
South Africa: World Travel Agency ℂ (011) 403-2638, 8th Floor, Eurite House, 20 De Kott Street, Braamfrontein, Johannesburg.

Spain: Expomundo ℂ 542-1348, Santa Cruz de Marcenado, 31, Oficina 10, Madrid.

Amtrak also connects New England cities to the Canadian national rail system **VIA Rail** TOLL-FREE (888) 842-7733 WEB SITE www.viarail.com.

Greyhound Bus Lines TOLL-FREE (800) 231-2222 WEB SITE www.greyhound.com, has such a huge route system that you should have no difficulty in getting to most points in New England from almost anywhere in the United States and Canada. It also has a complicated system of fares, discount fares, seasonal rates, unlimited-travel passes, and so on. Travel agents can help with such things (for more information, see GETTING AROUND, page 344).

ARRIVING

TRAVEL DOCUMENTS

When arriving in the United States, Canadian citizens who plan to stay fewer than 90 days need only show proof of identification and residence (a driver's license will do); a passport isn't necessary although it might be useful as identification for financial transactions.

A number of countries are participating in the visa waiver pilot program whereby citizens of participating countries can travel to the United States for 90 days or fewer without obtaining a visa. Check with your travel agent for the current rules and participating countries. Citizens of the European Union, Australia, New Zealand and Japan do not need visas for stays up to 90 days.

Visitors from other countries should contact the United States embassy or consulate in their country for the exact details for obtaining a visa.

CUSTOMS

United States customs allows you to bring in duty-free gifts valued up to $100. For more specific information, including shopping restrictions, contact your local American embassy or consulate branch. Carrying non-prescription narcotic drugs into the country may well result in a long prison sentence. When entering the United States, foreign visitors should allow a minimum of an hour to clear customs at Boston or New York. For European travelers, the close scrutiny of customs and immigration officers is sometimes shocking and annoying. During the peak summer season, foreign passport holders have had to wait up to two hours before even reaching passport control at New York's Kennedy International Airport. At Boston Logan this rarely happens.

EMBASSIES AND CONSULATES

Embassies are located in Washington, DC. To obtain a phone number, call directory assistance ℂ 411.

A few foriegn countries maintain consulates in Boston; these include the **Canadian Consulate** ☎ (617) 262-3760, 3 Copley Place, Suite 400, Boston, Massachusetts 02116; the **French Consulate** ☎ (617) 542-7374, 31 Saint James Avenue, Boston, Massachusetts 02116; the **Italian Consulate** ☎ (617) 542-0483, 100 Boylston Street, Boston, Massachusetts 02116; the **Spanish Consulate** ☎ (617) 536-2506, 545 Boylston Street, Boston, Massachusetts 02116; and the **Consulate of the United Kingdom** ☎ (617) 248-9555, 1 Memorial Drive, Cambridge, Massachusetts 02138.

TOURIST INFORMATION

Each of the six New England states has a bureau dedicated to dispensing information on subjects of interest to tourists. The GENERAL INFORMATION sections of the preceding chapters list the local agencies; here, then, are the state tourism offices:

Connecticut Office of Tourism, Department of Economic and Community Development ☎ (860) 270-8080 TOLL-FREE (800) 282-6863 WEB SITE www.tourism.state.ct.us, 505 Hudson Street, Hartford, Connecticut 06106.

Maine Office of Tourism ☎ (207) 287-5711 TOLL-FREE (888) 624-6345 (only for brochure request) WEB SITE www.visitmaine.com, 59 State House Station, Augusta, Maine 04333.

Massachusetts Office of Travel and Tourism ☎ (617) 973-8500 TOLL-FREE (800) 227-6277 WEB SITE www.mass-vacation.com, 10 Park Plaza, Suite 4510, Boston, Massachusetts 02116.

New Hampshire Office of Tourism and Travel Development ☎ (603) 271-2666 TOLL-FREE (800) 386-4664 (to request the free vacation kit only) WEB SITE www.visitnh.gov, PO Box 1856, Concord, New Hampshire 03302-1856.

Rhode Island Tourism Division ☎ (401) 222-2601 TOLL-FREE (800) 556-2484 WEB SITE www.ritourism.com, 7 Jackson Walkway, Providence, Rhode Island 02903.

Vermont Department of Tourism and Marketing ☎ (802) 828-3237 TOLL-FREE (800) 837-6668 WEB SITE www.travel-vermont.com, 6 Baldwin Street, Drawer 33, Montpelier, Vermont 05633-1301.

For one-stop shopping there is **Discover New England** ☎ (802) 253-2500 FAX (802) 253-9064 WEB SITE www.discovernewengland.org, 1250 Waterbury Road, PO Box 3809, Stowe, Vermont 05672, an official representative of the six New England state tourism

OPPOSITE: Flags on display at Massachusetts' State House. ABOVE: Hundred-year-old industrial architecture is refurbished as modern office space on Boston's waterfront.

bureaus. DNE provides free travel brochures, free travel planning assistance via their "e-concierge" program, and a database of travel resources.

GETTING AROUND

There is a host of **regional air carriers** that make the short hops from one New England airport to another. These carriers are noted under HOW TO GET THERE in the various destination sections.

The **bus** can get you about anywhere you want to go in New England, which is small, and bus travel can be an enjoyable as well as affordable way to go. Besides **Greyhound** TOLL-FREE (800) 231-2222 WEB SITE www.greyhound.com there are several regional companies that reach into the nooks and crannies that Greyhound misses:

Concord Trailways ☎ (603) 228-3300 or (617) 426-8080 FAX (603) 228-3524 TOLL-FREE (800) 639-3317, runs throughout New Hampshire with service to downtown Boston and Logan Airport.

Bonanza ☎ (401) 751-8800 or (617) 720-4110 TOLL-FREE (800) 451-3292 serves cities throughout Connecticut, Massachusetts, New York, Rhode Island and Vermont.

With service from Washington, DC, to New England and points in between, there is **Peter Pan Bus Lines Inc.** ☎ (413) 781-2900 TOLL-FREE (800) 343-9999 FAX (413) 731-9721. Locally, the company also serves many Massachusetts towns, southern New Hampshire, and selected cities in Connecticut.

PASSES

Greyhound issues a number of passes under the Ameripass program, offering unrestricted travel on Greyhound and its partners. The domestic **Ameripass** must be purchased in the United States (available at any Greyhound terminal). Prices range from $219 for seven days to $549 for 60 days, more in summer. Senior citizens and students receive a discount. Overseas visitors can purchase an international Ameripass with proof of residency in a foreign country (passport or visa). Prices range from $184 for seven days to $494 for 60 days. International passes for children (11 and under) are 20 to 40 percent lower. To request fare and schedule information from outside the United States, contact Greyhound via FAX (212) 967-2239 E-MAIL intlameripass@greyhound.com.

BY CAR

The United States highway system is sprawling and gasoline is cheap. But driving in Boston is a test of nerves and will, and driving on congested highways around all New England cities requires fast reflexes and, sometimes, the patience of Job.

Most airports, major hotels, or tourist centers have offices (or can provide information) for **car rentals**. To rent a car you must have a valid driver's license and a credit card (used for deposit), and be at least 25 years of age. Foreign drivers may need an international driver's license. Be sure to check out liability clauses in the rental agreement; they are not automatically included and your personal automobile insurance or credit card may cover none, part, or all of your liability risks. Check if your airline offers car rental packages with airfare. Car rental agencies include:
Hertz TOLL-FREE (800) 654-3131 TOLL-FREE IN CANADA (800) 263-0600 TOLL-FREE IN THE UNITED KINGDOM (0345) 555888;
Avis TOLL-FREE (800) 831-2847;
Alamo TOLL-FREE (877) 327-9633;
Budget TOLL-FREE (800) 527-7000 TOLL-FREE IN THE UNITED KINGDOM (0800) 181181;
Dollar/Europcar TOLL-FREE (800) 800-4000 TOLL-FREE IN THE UNITED KINGDOM (0990) 565656;
National TOLL-FREE (800) 227-7368.

Driving regulations will be familiar to anyone used to driving in Canada or continental Europe: You drive on the right and overtake on the left, vehicles approaching from the right have the right of way at intersections. All states except New Hampshire have made the use of seat belts compulsory. Driving under the influence of alcohol is punished with severe penalties and/or imprisonment.

The speed limit on highways is usually 65 mph (104 km/h), 50 mph (80 km/h) on smaller roads, and 25 mph (40 km/h) in towns. You must stop if you come upon a school bus with its red lights flashing. You may turn right at a red light (except when otherwise posted) if you stop first and make sure the way is clear.

Many 24-hour service stations flank the major highways, but those in towns tend to close around 9 PM (7 PM in small towns, and all day on Sundays). Gasoline (petrol) is sold by the gallon (one liter is about a quart; there are 3.8 liters in a gallon). Most stations take credit cards, and most are now self-service.

If you are involved an automobile accident, get to a telephone and dial the operator ("0"), who can connect you with the police and emergency services. Members of automobile clubs affiliated with the American Automobile Association (the Canadian Automobile Association and most European automobile clubs are) should bring their membership cards along with them, as they are entitled to membership benefits. For more information contact the **American Automobile Association** TOLL-FREE (800) 564-6222; **Canadian Automobile Association** ☎ (613) 226-7631, 1775 Courtwood Crescent, Ottawa, Ontario K2C 3J2; the **United Kingdom Automobile Association** ☎ (0990) 500600; or the **Royal Automobile Club** ☎ (0990) 722722 or (0345) 121345.

ACCOMMODATION

Wherever you go in New England, you will find accommodation to appeal to every taste and to suit every budget. If luxury and comfort are your priorities, there are deluxe hotels to rank with any in the world. If convenient locations while motoring are important, you will be pleased to know that there are motels in every price range sprinkled along the nation's main roads and highways. If you will be staying in one place for a longer period, particularly with children or in a group, you will get both privacy and savings (on food) in an efficiency apartment in one of New England's many condominium hotels.

If rustic charm is what you're looking for, there are delightful country inns throughout the region. A map of New England inns and a complete list of 380 member inns is available from the **New England Innkeepers Association** ☎ (603) 964-6698 FAX (603) 964-6792 E-MAIL neia@newenglandinns.com, PO Box 1089, North Hampton, New Hampshire 03862-1089. If conversation and "character" count, there is bound to be a **bed and breakfast** to fit the bill. Prices of these accommodations range from budget to deluxe. Many areas have bed-and-breakfast organizations; contact the local chambers of commerce or tourism organization listed under general information for information.

The following lodging chains have sites around New England: **Best Western** TOLL-FREE (800) 528-1234 WEB SITE www.bestwestern.com, **Comfort Inn** TOLL-FREE (800) 228-5150 WEB SITE www.comfortinn.com, **Days Inn** TOLL-FREE (800) 329-7466 WEB SITE www.daysinn.com, **EconoLodge** TOLL-FREE (800) 553-2666 WEB SITE www.econolodge.com, **Four Seasons** TOLL-FREE (800) 332-3442 WEB SITE www.fourseasons.com, **Hilton** TOLL-FREE (800) 445-8667 WEB SITE www.hilton.com, **Holiday Inn** TOLL-FREE (800) 465-4329 WEB SITE www.holidayinn.com, **Hyatt** TOLL-FREE (800) 233-1234 WEB SITE www.hyatt.com, **Marriott** TOLL-FREE (800) 228-9290 WEB SITE www.marriott.com, **Ramada** TOLL-FREE (800) 228-2828 WEB SITE www.ramada.com, **Sheraton** TOLL-FREE (800) 325-3535 WEB SITE www.sheraton.com, **Travelodge** TOLL-FREE (800) 578-7878 WEB SITE www.travelodge.com, and **Westin** TOLL-FREE (800) 262-9600 WEB SITE www.westin.com.

Boston's Red Line train trundles past a noonday gridlock, demonstrating the wisdom of using public transportation in this traffic-burdened city.

PRICES

Accommodation rates change often, so specific prices are not given in this guide. Rather, to give you an idea of the price tag, we have classified lodgings the following categories. Prices assume a double room, two-person occupancy in peak season:

- budget, less than (sometimes much less than) $100
- mid-range, $100 to $200
- expensive, $201 to $275
- luxury, more than $275 (sometimes much more)

Restaurant prices, ownership, chefs and specialties change rapidly, too. Do use the phone numbers provided in the text to avoid

disappointment. Price guidelines refer to the cost of a meal for one person including drinks and tip. They are as follows: budget, under $15; mid-range, $15 to $30; expensive, over $30.

TIPPING

Tips are not included on your tab unless you are dining with a large party. The standard tip is 15 to 20 percent. Don't hesitate to leave more if the service has been exceptional, but only leave less if your service expectations were not met.

You should also tip taxi drivers 15 percent of the fare, airport or hotel porters $1 to $1.50 per bag, and chambermaids $2 to $5 a day.

BASICS

TIME

New England is on Eastern Standard Time, which is five hours behind Greenwich Mean Time. So, for example, when it is noon in London it is 7 AM in Boston. Boston clocks are one hour ahead of Chicago, three hours ahead of California. New England clocks are six hours behind Western European, but there is a five-hour time differential between New England and Europe for a few weeks in October and April when the Europeans switch to Daylight Saving Time before the Americans.

ELECTRICITY

The electric current is 110–120 volts AC. Sockets take plugs with two flat prongs.

WEIGHTS AND MEASURES

The United States does not use the metric system. Conversions to and from United States standard measures are as follows:

inches to centimeters	multiply by 2.54
centimeters to inches	multiply by 0.39
feet to meters	multiply by 0.30
meters to feet	multiply by 3.28
yards to meters	multiply by 0.91
meters to yards	multiply by 1.09
miles to kilometers	multiply by 1.61
kilometers to miles	multiply by 0.62
km sq to miles sq	multiply by 0.38
acres to hectares	multiply by 0.40
hectares to acres	multiply by 2.47
ounces to grams	multiply by 28.35
grams to ounces	multiply by 0.035
pounds to kilograms	multiply by 0.45
kilograms to pounds	multiply by 2.21
gallons to liters	multiply by 3.79
liters to gallons	multiply by 0.26

CURRENCY

American coins are the penny, nickel, dime and quarter; the paper notes are of uniform size and color, however the new $20 bill features a larger portrait.

At press time the **exchange rate** for the US$1 with various foreign currencies was as follows:

US$1 = 0.99 EUR (euros)
US$1 = 0.63 GBP (United Kingdom pounds)
US$1 = 1.54 CAD (Canada dollars)
US$1 = 1.79 AUD (Australian dollars)

As in all countries with hard currencies, the banks offer the best exchange rates — much better than hotels, for example. Banking hours are Monday to Thursday from 10 AM to 4 PM, 10 AM to 6 PM on Friday. Trust companies and credit unions tend to have longer hours and may also be open on Saturday morning. Most major credit cards are accepted anywhere you are likely to go — including American Express, MasterCard, and Visa; consequently you are advised to carry a minimum of cash. If you prefer using non-plastic money, take it in the form of travelers' checks. They can be cashed everywhere, with proper identification (e.g. passport, driver's license), although the larger denominations will not always be welcome. Note, too, that traveler's checks should be treated as if they were cash; issuing companies are not required to replace lost or stolen checks if you have been careless with them.

In general, I would recommend floating through New England on a raft of plastic: your bank debit card. All New England financial institutions have automatic teller machines (ATMs), and you'll find ATMs located in large and small shopping centers, airports, train stations, and even many gas stations and corner stores. Before you leave home check with your bank to be certain your ATM card is on the Plus or Cirrus network; they can also provide you with a booklet listing networks worldwide on which your card will work. There may be a withdrawal fee of the equivalent of US$2. Your home bank computes the conversion rate.

There is a **currency exchange facility** in Terminal E at Logan International Airport that is open 24 hours a day. Major banks, as well as Thomas Cook and American Express, have currency exchange locations in downtown Boston. Outside of Boston exchange services in New England are limited.

HEALTH AND SAFETY

While health hazards are few and health care is excellent, it can be expensive to be sick or injured in New England. Overseas visitors should, therefore, arrange short-term medical coverage. An excellent medical emergency policy, which also includes personal travel insurance, is available from the **Europ Assistance Group** through its affiliates in a dozen or so countries, including: United Kingdom ☎ (1444) 411999 FAX (1444) 458173, Sussex House, Perrymount Road, Haywards Heath, West Sussex RH1 IDN, England; and

OPPOSITE: Mopeds for rent on Martha's Vineyard. ABOVE: "Under the boardwalk" at Old Orchard Beach, Maine.

France ☎ (01) 41858585 FAX (01) 41858305, 1 promenade de la Bonnette, 92230 Gennevilliers, France. **Wexas International** ☎ (020) 7589-3315 E-MAIL mship@wexas.com, 45–49 Brompton Road, Knightsbridge, London SW3 1DE, England, offers a similar policy, similarly priced.

Another wise precaution is to carry a card in your wallet giving your blood type and listing any allergies or chronic conditions (including the wearing of contact lenses) that might affect treatment in an emergency.

Beyond that, always carry insect repellent, because in summer northern New England has plenty of insects to repel, especially black flies and mosquitoes. A sunscreen lotion is also advisable.

Emergency services for fire, ambulance, and police are usually reached by dialing 911. For other types of emergencies, you should contact the operator by dialing zero "0."

No matter where you go in New England, you should take the same basic precautions that a sensible person would take anywhere: leave valuables in the hotel safe, lock your hotel room and car, do not leave valuable items visible in your car when unattended, do not carry all your cash and cards with you when you go out, do not go for late-night strolls through questionable areas. In short, exercise your common sense.

GAY AND LESBIAN TRAVELERS

Same gender couples will find travel more care free than in the past in New England. Vermont's civil union law, sanctioning non-traditional "marriages" has boosted that state's gay and lesbian tourism, and overt hostility toward same-gender couples has seriously declined. For current information on gay nightlife, businesses and services, especially in Boston, check out the G-Spot Guide to Gay Boston WEB SITE www.glee.vwh.net/gspot/boston/.

TRAVELERS WITH DISABILITIES

State and federal laws mandate wheelchair accessibility in most buildings open to the public, but access is sometimes hindered in historic buildings and small bed and breakfasts. Most hotels and restaurants, however, are very accessible. People with varying levels of mobility difficulties will find the database of **AccessAble Travel** WEB SITE www.access-able.com invaluable.

WHEN TO GO

The decision of when to go will depend on what you are going *for*, and by now you should have a good idea of what each region has to offer at what time of the year.

New England **summers** are glorious and comfortable, with lots of sun and gentle cooling breezes off the ocean, although hot and humid conditions are also common. Summer is the height of the tourist season, with most attractions open from late May to October. In early **fall** the leaves change to crimson, gold and orange. Days are warm and evenings cool. The countryside is at its best then. **Winters** can be bitterly cold, with snow and cutting winds. But such conditions rarely deter avid skiers. New England has more than 100 ski areas. It is neither the Alps nor the Rockies, but the slopes are good, the lift lines shorter, and the hospitality warm. **Spring** is often referred to as the mud season: lots of rain, with cool days and cooler nights. However, several airlines do offer special low fares during this traditional off-season period. Your reward is the freshness of spring with its new growth and blooming wild flowers and fruit trees. Average daily temperatures and average daily rainfall for six New England cities are as follows:

Boston, Massachusetts

January	28°F/-2.2°C	3.7 in/94.9 mm
April	46.8°F/8.2°C	3.6 in/92.7 mm
July	72.5°F/22.5°C	2.9 in/72.9 mm
October	52.7°F/11.5°C	3.4 in/86.6 mm

Burlington, Vermont

January	18.7°F/-7.4°C	1.8 in/46.4 mm
April	42.6°F/5.9°C	2.8 in/70.5 mm
July	69.8°F/21°C	3.6 in/90.2 mm
October	48.2°F/9°C	3 in/76.5 mm

Concord, New Hampshire

January	21°F/-6.1°C	2.7 in/69.7 mm
April	44.1°F/6.7°C	3 in/76.6 mm
July	69.6°F/20.9°C	3.1 in/79.8 mm
October	48.7°F/9.3°C	3.2 in/81.3 mm

Hartford, Connecticut

January	24.6°F/-4.1°C	3.3 in/82.8 mm
April	48.6°F/9.2°C	3.8 in/97.3 mm
July	73.6°F/23.1°C	3.4 in/86.1 mm
October	52.2°F/11.2°C	3.8 in/96 mm

Portland, Maine

January	20.8°F/-6.2°C	3.6 in/92.7 mm
April	43.2°F/6.2°C	4 in/101.8 mm
July	68.5°F/20.3°C	3 in/75.6 mm
October	48.4°F/9.1°C	3.7 in/94.4 mm

Providence, Rhode Island

January	28°F/-2.2°C	4 in/101.1 mm
April	47.3°F/8.5°C	4 in/102.1 mm
July	72.7°F/22.6°C	3 in/77.3 mm
October	53.6°F/12°C	3.6 in/92.5 mm

WHAT TO BRING

Be sure to take with you lists of the numbers of all travel documents, cards, and checks you will be carrying, along with any telephone numbers included on them. This will speed their replacement if lost. Also, take photocopies of your passport and any travel tickets: duplicates are issued more speedily if people can see a copy of the original. Always leave your inessential credit cards behind when you go on a trip, and of those you take with you carry only a couple in your wallet: any others should be tucked away in a safe place, as with your passport, driver's license, extra travelers' checks, etc.

As for clothing, New England styles tend to be casual, especially in Maine, Vermont and New Hampshire. However, when going out on the town in Boston, business wear is the standard. While season dictates other clothing needs, summer visitors should bring along a warm sweater or jacket in case of over-air-conditioned restaurants or cool evening temperatures. No matter the season, rain gear is essential. New England rain storms have a reputation for destroying flimsy umbrellas. If you want to stay dry, buy a sturdy one. You might also consider a waterproof raincoat, as the rain has a tendency to come at you from all sides, rendering that sturdy umbrella useless.

Second-hand clothing and bric-a-brac in rural northeast Connecticut.

PUBLIC HOLIDAYS

New Year's Day	January 1
Martin Luther King Day	January 15
Lincoln's Birthday	February 12
Washington's Birthday	February 22

Memorial Day	last Monday in May
Independence Day	July 4
Labor Day	1st Monday in September
Columbus Day	2nd Monday in October
Thanksgiving	4th Thursday in November
Christmas Day	25th December

During those holidays, federal, state and city offices close, as do, more importantly, the banks. In cities and towns, stores and many restaurants are closed on Sundays, but shopping malls are usually open seven days a week.

State holidays vary. For a calendar of state events, contact the state tourism agencies.

COMMUNICATION AND MEDIA

NEWSPAPERS

Pick up any local daily newspaper for the latest overview of local and national news. The *Boston Globe* is New England's regional paper of record. *USA Today*, a national daily, provides national news capsules. The *New York Times* is widely read in New England and available in major cities.

When in Boston and Cambridge, those aching for news from home can find comfort at the Harvard Square institution, **Out of Town News**. Look for the kiosk in the middle of the square. Out of Town has dailies from all over the world. They also sell a wide assortment of magazines and journals.

MAIL

Although main post offices in New England may open as early as 8 AM and close as late as 6 PM on weekdays, and some are open on Saturday mornings, you can avoid disappointment by going between 9 AM and 5 PM, Monday to Friday. Letters and postcards can be mailed at most hotels' front desks or at any blue United States Postal Service mailbox. At press time **postal rates** were 33¢ for a first-class letter and 20¢ for a postcard within the United States. International rates vary with destination, but are usually about twice the domestic tariff.

If sending mail to a United States address, be sure to include the **ZIP code**.

Following are **postal abbreviations** for the six New England States: Connecticut CT, Maine ME, Massachusetts MA, New Hampshire NH, Rhode Island RI, Vermont VT.

Most good hotels now have **fax** services and/or **Internet** connections available.

TELEPHONES

The American telephone system is efficient and economical. For **information** on local and long-distance telephone numbers dial 411. For calls requiring operator assistance — such as long-distance personal or collect calls, or for emergency calls — dial 0.

To place a **long-distance** call within the same area code, dial 1 + the number you are calling. To place a call outside your area code, dial 1 + area code + telephone number. For overseas calls, dial 011 + country code + city code + telephone number.

Calls placed in the evening or on the weekend are less expensive, although any call from a hotel will incur a (usually steep) surcharge. There are **public telephones** everywhere; they cost $.50 for a local call; prepaid phone cards are available in $10 and $20 amounts.

Throughout this book, when you see TOLL-FREE before a phone number it indicates that you can call that number free of charge in North America.

THE INTERNET

Just about everywhere you go in New England, you will find a bookstore, café or public library offering access to the Internet for a nominal fee (and sometimes for free). If you've signed up for one of the global **e-mail** accounts before leaving home (e.g., HotMail or Yahoo!, for example) then you are wired, too.

While some New England public libraries offer Internet access, availability varies because of computer station shortages and high demand. If the library lets you down, ask around for an Internet café.

The Internet is also becoming a powerful tool for researching and planning trips. Many, if not most, organizations, hotels and tour operators listed in this book have home pages on the web. Finding one of these home pages is a simple matter of logging on to your web browser (e.g., Netscape Navigator™ or Microsoft Internet Explorer™), locating the search function and typing in the name of the organization for which you are looking. You can also do keyword searches if you don't have a specific organization name in mind. Once on the web, your access to information is limited only by your ability to ask the right question.

Web sites are of varying quality. Some allow you to retrieve information, make contact via e-mail direct from the site, and even make a reservation. Others will have you pulling out your cyber hair.

The following sites are ones that I found useful in my research on this book. They offer pertinent information and essential services, as well as links to other home pages that will set you on your way into cyberspace.

RECOMMENDED WEB SITES

Accommodation

The Bed & Breakfast Channel www.bbchannel.com. A well-organized compendious listing of B&Bs all over the world. Includes ratings, recommendations and, for those who join the club, discounts.

Hostelling International — American Youth Hostels www.hiayh.org. One-stop shopping for hostel locations, membership information, reservations and publications. Also has travel news updates relevant to the budget traveler, tips on budget traveling, and workshop listings.

New England Innkeepers Association www.newenglandinns.com. A searchable database of member inns, on-line reservations for participating inns. Faster than the Bed & Breakfast Channel as its listings are limited to the region.

Travel Ideas and Resources

Airline Network www.airnet.co.uk. Cheap flights departing from the United Kingdom.

OPPOSITE: Students phone mom and dad in Harvard Square. ABOVE: Boston's Quincy Market draws shoppers, promenaders and diners to its mish mash of boutiques, entertainment, and eateries.

Unique in that it lists free stopovers ("optional gateways").
Atevo www.atevo.com. A comprehensive travel web site with all sorts of nooks and crannies to explore. It offers online reservations, but I found the engine lacking. It's best used as an online magazine and travel-idea generator.
Discover New England Online www.discovernewengland.com. The official umbrella site for the six New England state tourism agencies. Includes a searchable database, as well as a bulletin board and newsletter subscription. You can also order brochures on-line.
Excite Travel city.net. Type the name of the city and "go." Weather conditions, what to see and do, book lists and more.
Expedia.com www.expedia.com. The best choice for straightforward air-travel fare search and booking. Sign up for automatic updates on air routes of your choosing. When the rate drops by $50 or more, you'll be notified via e-mail.
Rec.Travel Library www.travel-library.com/north_america/index.html. A homespun site that has plenty of information, including personal advice and a list of answers to frequently asked questions about traveling in each of the six New England States. The site features useful links to many travel-related sites.
Visit New England www.visitnewengland.com. A compendious web site with information on every aspect of touring New England. Well organized. Easy to find information and not too sluggish. It's part of an umbrella site called Visit America.

Transportation
Amtrak www.amtrak.com. Very useful, with schedules, fares and on-line reservations.
Greyhound www.greyhound.com. Fares and schedules, discounts, pass information and a station locator.
Manchester Airport www.flymanchester.com.
Massport www.massport.com. Directions to Logan Airport, information about terminals, airlines serving Logan, and transportation options to and from the airport.
Massachusetts Bay Transportation Authority (MBTA) www.mbta.com. Order passes, browse and download schedules (in PDF format).
Prince of Fundy Cruises www.princeoffundy.com.
SmarTraveler www.smartravler.com. "Real-time" reports on Boston area traffic conditions, including Cape Cod. Also provides information on the MBTA.
Steamship Authority www.islandferry.com. Schedules, fares and vehicle reservations for the ferry trips to and between Woods Hole, Hyannis, Martha's Vineyard and Nantucket.

Outdoors
Appalachian Mountain Club www.outdoors.org. Lodging, adventures, guidebooks, information about conservation, trip planning and the free newsletter "Hut Flash."

Regional Visitors Information
Bar Harbor Chamber of Commerce www.acadia.net/bhcc
Berkshire Visitors Bureau www.berkshires.org
Block Island www.blockisland.com
Boston Convention and Visitors Bureau www.bostonusa.com
Cambridge (Massachusetts) Tourism www.cambridge-usa.org
Cape Cod Chamber of Commerce www.capecodchamber.org virtualcapecod.com/chambers
Kennebunk-Kennebunkport Chamber of Commerce www.kkcc.maine.org
Mount Washington Valley Chamber of Commerce www.mtwashingtonvalley.org
Mystic mysticmore.com
Nantucket Online www.nantucketonline.com. A well organized directory of essential addresses and phone numbers.
Portland Convention and Visitors Bureau www.visitportland.com
Providence www.providencecvb.com
Newport www.GoNewport.com
Stowe www.stowe.com

RECOMMENDED READING

To gain some insight into New England as it was eons before European contact, seek out two excellent books on the culture and history of original inhabitants: *The First*

Peoples of the Northeast, by Esther K. and John J.G. Braun (1994), and *Ninnuock (The People): The Algonkian People of New England*, by Steven F. Johnson (1995). Few volumes of popular history so well illuminate the birth of the American nation as David Hackett Fischer's *Paul Revere's Ride* (1994), which sketches the origins of the American Revolution in dramatic style and puts to rest some of the ill-informed myths about the roles played by various Boston patriots. The best examination of New England rural life in the early years of the country is Laurel Thatcher Ulrich's *A Midwife's Tale: The Life of Martha Ballard, Based on Her Diary, 1785–1812* (1991).

Although New England is one of the tamer parts of the United States, vast sectors of the region consist of back country and even true wilderness. Few books series are so crucial to responsible recreation in the wilds as the various guides published by the Appalachian Mountain Club (AMC). The AMC guides to sections of the Appalachian Trail are particularly helpful for hikers, offering both critical survival information and advice on side trails and detours. The guides have been issued for decades and are updated every two to three years to reflect current trail conditions. If your visits to the New England wilds will be somewhat tamer than backcountry hiking, you will still find the *National Audubon Society Field Guide to New England* by Peter Alden and Brian Cassie (1994) a useful and entertaining companion to identify local flora and fauna — all gloriously illustrated with color plates.

New England is particularly rich in literature. Two nineteenth-century classics are key to understanding the literary and philosophical underpinnings of the region: Herman Melville's *Moby-Dick* (1852) and Henry David Thoreau's *Walden, Life in the Woods* (1854). Their modern-day counterparts, one could argue, are John McPhee's *Survival of the Bark Canoe* (1982), a classic account of navigating the north woods by canoe, and *The Outermost House* by Henry Beston (1943), a philosophical naturalist's account of a year living isolated on the outer dunes of Cape Cod. Dealing with a similarly lost (or almost lost) world, June Sprigg's *Simple Gifts: Lessons in Living from a Shaker Village* (1998) recounts a summer the author spent living with the last seven surviving Shakers at Canterbury, New Hampshire. Sebastian Junger's *The Perfect Storm* (1997) remains the best accounting of New England fishing life. Anita Shreve's haunting *The Weight of Water* (1997) is a fictional retelling of the 1873 murders of two women on the Isles of Shoals. Many of Howard Frank Mosher's novels, notably *A Stranger in the Kingdom* (1995), are redolent with the touch and feel of Vermont's Northeast Kingdom. Carolyn Chute's *Beans of Egypt* (1985) is a hilarious take on the less picturesque side of life in Maine. Detective writer Robert B. Parker does a fine job sketching both the desirable and the seamier sides of Boston in his series of Spenser novels, including *Hugger Mugger* (2000). Don't forget the modern classics, including Jack Kerouac's *Maggie Cassidy* (1957), a tale of life in Lowell, Massachusetts.

Photography Credits

All photographs by Robert Holmes, with exception of the following:

Jane Booth Vollers: 22 *top and bottom*, 24, 27, 28, 29, 31, 33, 35, 36 *top and bottom*, 37, 38, 39, 40 *bottom*, 43, 51, 55, 58, 61, 65, 107, 108, 112, 116, 189, 201, 203, 205, 206, 246, 260, 285, 287, 303, 304, 319, 321, 333, 338, 347.

Ellis Klarenbeek: 5 *right*, 14, 72, 75, 80, 91, 93, 119, 153, 154, 244 *top and bottom*, 290, 298, 311, 312 *left*, 313, 252, 214, 215, 225, 339, 345.

Laura Purdom: cover and pages 47, 70, 127, 239, 241, 247, 275.

David Henry: pages 71, 79, 81, 87, 131, 141, 228, 343.

Marcia Schneldler: 25, 30, 325.

Preservation Society of Newport County: 23.

Stowe Mountain Resort/Chuck Washuck: 34.

Stowe Mountain Resort/Landwherle Studios: 21, 255.

Westin Hotel: 41.

Quick Reference A–Z Guide to Places and Topics

The symbols Ⓕ FAX, Ⓣ TOLL-FREE, Ⓔ E-MAIL, Ⓦ WEB-SITE refer to additional contact information found in the chapter listings.

The symbols Ⓕ FAX, Ⓣ TOLL-FREE, Ⓔ E-MAIL, Ⓦ WEB-SITE refer to additional contact information found in the chapter listings.

The symbols Ⓕ FAX, Ⓣ TOLL-FREE, Ⓔ E-MAIL, Ⓦ WEB-SITE refer to additional contact information found in the chapter listings.

N

The symbols Ⓕ FAX, Ⓣ TOLL-FREE, Ⓔ E-MAIL, Ⓦ WEB-SITE *refer to additional contact information found in the chapter listings*

NOTES